A DOCUMENTARY HISTORY OF U.S. FOREIGN RELATIONS THE MID-1890'S TO 1979

Selections from additions to Ruhl J. Bartlett's
The Record of American Diplomacy

Edited by
David F. Long
University of New Hampshire

University Press of America

Copyright © 1980 by

University Press of America, Inc.™

P.O. Box 19101, Washington, DC 20036

All rights reserved

Printed in the United States of America

ISBN: 0-8191-0866-9
Library of Congress Number: 79-5349

CONTENTS

A. **The Pacific, 1878-1893**
   1. Samoa and U.S., Treaty of 1878, 1
   2. Germany, Great Britain, and U.S., Samoan Treaty, 1889, 2
   3. Blaine to Comly on the U.S. in the Pacific, 1881, 3-4
   4. Stevens to Foster on Hawaii, 1892, 5
   5. Gresham to Cleveland on Hawaii, 1893, 6-7
   6. Cleveland's Hawaiian Dilemma, 1893, 8

B. **The British Guiana-Venezuelan Boundary Crisis, 1895-1896**
   7. Olney to Bayard on the Venezuelan Boundary Crisis, July 1895, 9-11
   8. Salisbury to Pauncefote on the Venezuelan Boundary Crisis, November 1895, 11-12
   9. Cleveland's Message to Congress, 17 December 1895, 12-13
   10. Salisbury to Pauncefote on the Venezuelan Boundary Settlement, 1896, 13-14
   11. Great Britain and Venezuela, Treaty of Boundary Settlement, 1896, 14

C. **Cuba, the Spanish-American War, and Imperialism, 1897-1900**
   12. Tetuán to de Lôme on Spain in Cuba, 1897, 15
   13. Day to Woodford on Spain in Cuba, March 1898, 16
   14. Woodford to President William McKinley on Spain in Cuba, 5 April 1898, 16-17
   15. McKinley's War Message, 11 April 1898, 17-18
   16. McKinley's Instructions to the Peace Commission, September 1898, 18-19
   17. Spain and U.S., Peace Treaty, December 1898, 19
   18. Beveridge on Imperialism, 1900, 20-21
   19. Platform of the U.S. Anti-Imperialist League, 1899, 21-22

D. **The Isthmian Canal and the T. Roosevelt Corollary, 1901-1905**
   20. Walker Commission's Canal Report, 1901, 23
   21. Great Britain and U.S., Second Hay-Pauncefote Treaty, 1901, 24
   22. Reyes to Hay on the U.S. in Panama, December 1903, 25
   23. Hay to Reyes on Panama, January 1904, 26-27
   24. Platt Amendment, 1901, 28
   25. T. Roosevelt's Corollary to the Monroe Doctrine, December 1904, 29
   26. Dawson to Hay on Santo Domingo, 1905, 30

E. **The Far East: China, 1882-1900**
   27. U.S. Chinese Exclusion Act, 1882, 31
   28. Denby to Sherman on the U.S. in China, 1898, 32
   29. Hay's "Open Door" Note, 1899, 33
   30. Reception of Hay's "Open Door" Note, 1899, 34
   31. Hay's Open Door Note, July 1900, 35

F. **The Far East: Japan, 1905-1913**
   32. Taft-Katsura Agreement, 1905, 35
   33. Root-Takahira Agreement, 1908, 36
   34. Lansing-Ishii Agreement, November 1917, 37
   35. Explanation of the Lansing-Ishii Agreement, November 1917, 38
   36. Gentlemen's Agreement and Japanese Exclusion, 1908-1924, 39-41
   37. Knox on the Neutralization of Manchuria, 1909, 42
   38. Banking Consortium, 1912, 43
   39. Wilson on the Banking Consortium, 1913, 44

G. **World War I Neutrality, 1914-1917**
   40. Lansing to Page on British Interference with American Trade, 1915, 45-47
   41. Phenix to Kellogg on British Interference with American Trade, 1914-1917, 47-48
   42. Bryan to Gerard on German U-boat Warfare, 1915, 49
   43. Bryan to Gerard, First *Lusitania* Note, May 1915, 50-51
   44. Lansing to Gerard, *Sussex* Note, May 1915, 51-52
   45. Wilson's Warning on the Danger of War, January 1916, 53-54
   46. Wilson's Terms of Peace, January 1917, 54-56
   47. Wilson's War Message, 2 April 1917, 56-57

H. **The Treaty of Versailles and the League of Nations, 1918-1920**
   48. Wilson's Fourteen Points, January 1918, 58
   49. League of Nations Covenant, Articles 10, 11, and 16, June 1919, 59
   50. Lodge Reservations to the Treaty of Versailles, November 1919, 60-61
   51. Harding and Pittman on the Lodge Reservations, November 1919, 61-63

52. Wilson, Harding, and Hoover on the League of Nations, 1919-1920, 63-65
53. Germany and U.S., Treaty of Peace, November 1921, 66

I. The Republican Postwar Settlement, 1921-1922

54. Washington Treaties, Naval Limitations Pact, 1922, 67
55. Washington Treaties, Nine-Power Pact, 1922, 68
56. Washington Treaties, Four-Power Pact, 1921, 69
57. Harding and Hughes on the Washington Treaties, 1922, 70

J. Interbellum Latin America, 1927-1936

58. Coolidge on U.S. Policy in Nicaragua, 1927, 71-72
59. Clark Memorandum to the Monroe Doctrine, 1928, 72-74
60. Stimson on Non-recognition in Latin America, 1931, 74-75
61. F.D. Roosevelt on the Good Neighbor Policy, 1936, 75
62. Buenos Aires Pact on Non-intervention, 1936, 76

K. Isolationism of the 1930s

63. Japan's Invasion of Manchuria, China's Appeal to U.S., 21 September 1931, 77
64. Japan's Invasion of Manchuria, Stimson to Japanese Ambassador Katsuji Debuchi, 22 September 1931, 77
65. Japan's Invasion of Manchuria, Stimson's Note to the League, 5 October 1931, 77-78
66. Japan's Invasion of Manchuria, U.S. Non-recognition Policy, 7 January 1932, 78
67. F.D. Roosevelt's Quarantine Speech, 5 October 1937, 78-79
68. First Neutrality Act, 21 August 1935, 80
69. Second Neutrality Act, 29 February 1936, 80-81
70. Third Neutrality Act, 1 May 1937, 81-82

L. U.S. Neutrality in World War II, 1939-1941

71. Fourth Neutrality Act, 4 November 1939, 83
72. Destroyer-Naval Bases Agreement, 1940, 83-84
73. Hull on the Far East, October 1940, 84-85
74. F.D. Roosevelt's Arsenal of Democracy Speech, 6 January 1941, 85-86
75. Lend-Lease Act, 11 March 1941, 86-87
76. Lindbergh on Isolationism, 23 April 1941, 87-89
77. F.D. Roosevelt on the Atlantic Charter, 21 August 1941, 90
78. Axis Pact, 27 September 1940, 91

79. Japanese Note to U.S., 20 November 1941, 91
80. U.S. Note to Japan, 26 November 1941, 92

M. <u>World War II Diplomacy, 1943-1945</u>

81. Cairo Conference, November 1943, 93
82. Teheran Conference, November-December 1943
83. Yalta (Crimea) Conference, 4-11 February 1945, 94-96
84. Potsdam Declaration on Japan, July 1945, 97
85. Potsdam (Berlin) Conference, 17 July-5 August 1945, 98-100
86. United Nations Charter, Preamble and Articles 1-7, 26 June 1945, 101

N. <u>U.S. and U.S.S.R., 1946-1972</u>

87. Baruch on Atomic Control, 14 June 1946, 102-104
88. Gromyko on Atomic Control, 5 March 1947, 104-106
89. Truman Doctrine, 12 March 1947, 106-108
90. Economic Cooperation Act, 3 April 1948, 109
91. North Atlantic Treaty (NATO), 4 April 1949, 110
92. Truman's "Point Four" Program, 5 June 1950, 111-112
93. United Nations on the Soviet Invasion of Hungary, 4 November 1956, 113
94. U.S. Rights in Berlin, 31 December 1958, 113-115
95. Eisenhower on the Summit Conference and the U-2 Incident, 25 March 1960, 115-117
96. Nuclear Test Ban Treaty, 5 August 1963, 117
* 97. Fulbright on U.S. Foreign Policy, 25 March 1964, 118-119
* 98. Cooper on the Soviet Invasion of Czechoslovakia, 20-21 August 1968, 120
* 99. U.S.-Soviet Strategic Arms Limitation Treaty (SALT I), 26 May 1972, 121

O. <u>U.S. and China, 1945-1978</u>

100. Truman on U.S. China Policy, 16 December 1945, 122-123
101. U.S. Trusteeship over the Japanese Mandated Islands, 2 April 1947, 123
102. Acheson on U.S. Policies in Asia, 12 January 1950, 123-125
103. Japan and U.S., Treaty of Peace, 8 September 1951, 125-126
104. Japan and U.S., Security Treaty, 8 September 1951, 126
105. U.N. Security Council on North Korea's Invasion of South Korea, 25 June 1950, 127
106. U.N. Security Council on North Korea's Invasion of South Korea, 27 June 1950, 127

* Selections not in Bartlett

    107. Truman on Taiwan (Republic of China), 27 June 1950, 127-128

    108. U.N. General Assembly on Communist China (People's Republic of China), 1 February 1951, 128

    109. Republican Senators on U.S. Far Eastern Policy, 17 August 1951, 128-129

    110. Korean Armistice Agreement, 27 June 1953, 129-130

    111. Wadsworth on China (People's Republic of China), 1 October 1960, 131-132

* 112. Katzenbach on China (People's Republic of China), 21 May 1968, 133

* 113. U.N. Recognition of the People's Republic of China, 22 September 1971, 134

* 114. Nixon's Visit to China, 21-28 February 1972, 134-135

* 115. U.S. Recognition of the People's Republic of China, 15 December 1978, 135

P. **U.S. and Southeast Asia, 1954-1973**

    116. Eisenhower on U.S. Indochinese Policy, 21 July 1954, 136

    117. Southeast Asia Collective Defense Treaty (SEATO), 8 September 1954, 136-137

    118. Taiwan (Republic of China) and U.S., Mutual Defense Treaty, 2 December 1954, 137-138

    119. Johnson on Aid to Vietnam, 31 December 1963, 138

* 120. Tonkin Gulf Resolution, 7 August 1964, 139

* 121. Johnson's Press Conference on the Tet Offensive in Vietnam, 2 February 1968, 139-140

* 122. Nixon's Speech on the U.S. Invasion of Cambodia, 30 April 1970, 140

* 123. Cease-fire in Vietnam, 23 January 1973, 141

* 124. Congress' "War Powers" Resolution, 4 October 1973, 142

* 125. Kissinger on the Fall of Vietnam, 29 April 1975, 143

Q. **U.S. and Latin America, 1960-1977**

    126. State Department on the Monroe Doctrine, 14 July 1960, 144

    127. Kennedy on the Latin American Alliance for Progress, 13 March 1961, 145-146

    128. Bay of Pigs Invasion of Cuba, April-May 1961, 146-147

    129. Rusk on Cuba, 2 February 1962, 147-148

    130. Cuban Missile Crisis, October-November 1962, 148-152

* 131. Johnson's Speech on the U.S. Invasion of the Dominican Republic, 2 May 1965, 153

* 132. U.S.-Panama Treaties, 7 September 1977, 154-155

* Selections not in Bartlett

R. **U.S. and the Middle East, 1950-1979**

    133. U.S., Great Britain, and France on Arab-Israeli Borders, 25 May 1950, 156

    134. Dulles on the Egyptian Aswan Dam Project, 2 April 1957, 156-157

    135. Dulles on the British-French-Israeli Invasion of Egypt, October-November 1956, 157-159

    136. Eisenhower Doctrine for the Middle East, 5 January 1957, 159-161

    137. Eisenhower on U.S. Invasion of Lebanon, 15 July 1958, 161-162

* 138. U.N. Security Council Resolution 242 on the Middle East, 22 November 1967, 163

* 139. Scali on the Middle Eastern Yom Kippur (Ramadan) War 6-25 October 1973, 164

* 140. Israeli-Egyptian Camp David Agreement, 17 September 1978, 165-166

* 141. Israeli-Egyptian Peace Treaty, 26 March 1979, 166-167

* 142. Ford-Shah Exchange of Toasts, 15 May 1975, 168

S. **U.S. and the Third World, 1960-1978**

    143. Lodge on the U.S. and South Africa, 1 April 1960, 169-170

    144. Herter on the U.N. in the Congo (Zaire), 21 July 1960, 170

    145. U.N. General Assembly on Colonial Independence, 14 December 1960, 171-172

* 146. Vance on U.S. Relations with Africa, 12 May 1968, 173-174

* Selections not in Bartlett

1. Samoa and U.S., Treaty of 1878

Signed 17 January 1878; ratifications exchanged 11 February 1878.

ARTICLE I. There shall be perpetual peace and friendship between the Government of the United States and the Government of the Samoan Islands.

Article II. Naval vessels of the United States shall have the privilege of entering and using the port of Pagopago, and establishing therein and on the shores thereof a station for coal and other naval supplies for their naval and commercial marine, and the Samoan Government will hereafter neither exercise nor authorize any jurisdiction within said port adverse to such rights of the United States or restrictive thereof. The same vessels shall also have the privilege of entering other ports of the Samoan Islands. The citizens of the United States shall likewise have free liberty to enter the same ports with their ships and cargoes of whatsoever kind, and to sell the same to any of the inhabitants of those islands, whether natives or foreigners, or to barter them for the products of the Islands. All such traffic in whatever articles of trade or barter shall be free, except that the trade in firearms and munitions of war in the Islands shall be subject to regulations by that government. . . .

Article V. If, unhappily, any differences should have arisen, or shall hereafter arise, between the Samoan Government and any other government in amity with the United States, the government of the latter will employ its good offices for the purpose of adjusting those differences upon a satisfactory and solid foundation. . . .

Article VII. The present treaty shall remain in force for ten years from its date. . . .

2. Germany, Great Britain, and U.S., Samoan Treaty, 1889

Signed at Berlin, 14 June 1889; ratifications exchanged 12 April 1890.

... *ARTICLE I.* It is declared that the Islands of Samoa are neutral territory in which the citizens and subjects of the Three Signatory Powers have equal rights of residence, trade and personal protection. The Three Powers recognize the independence of the Samoan Government and the free right of the natives to elect their Chief or King and choose their form of Government according to their own laws and customs. Neither of the Powers shall exercise any separate control over the Islands or the Government thereof. ...

Article III. Section 1. A Supreme Court shall be established in Samoa to consist of one Judge, who shall be styled Chief Justice of Samoa, and who shall appoint a Clerk and a Marshal of the Court; and record shall be kept of all orders and decisions made by the Court, or by the Chief Justice in the discharge of any duties imposed on him under this Act. The Clerk and Marshal shall be allowed reasonable fees to be regulated by order of the Court.

Section 2. With a view to secure judicial independence and the equal consideration of the rights of all parties, irrespective of nationality, it is agreed that the Chief Justice shall be named by the Three Signatory Powers in common accord; or, failing their agreement, he may be named by the King of Sweden and Norway. He shall be learned in law and equity, of mature years, and of good repute for his sense of honour, impartiality and justice. ...

Section 6. In case any question shall hereafter arise in Samoa respecting the rightful election or appointment of King or of any other Chief claiming authority over the Islands; or respecting the validity of the powers which the King or any Chief may claim in the exercise of his office, such question shall not lead to war but shall be presented for decision to the Chief Justice of Samoa, who shall decide it in writing, conformably to the provisions of this Act and to the laws and customs of Samoa not in conflict therewith; and the Signatory Governments will accept and abide by such decision.

Section 7. In case any difference shall arise between either of the Treaty Powers and Samoa which they shall fail to adjust by mutual accord, such difference shall not be held cause for war, but shall be referred for adjustment on the principles of justice and equity to the Chief Justice of Samoa, who shall make his decision thereon in writing.

Section 8. The Chief Justice may recommend to the Government of Samoa the passage of any law which he shall consider just and expedient for the prevention and punishment of crime and for the promotion of good order in Samoa outside the Municipal District and for the collection of taxes without the District.

Section 9. Upon the organization of the Supreme Court there shall be transferred to its exclusive jurisdiction

1. All civil suits concerning real property situated in Samoa and all rights affecting the same.

2. All civil suits of any kind between natives and foreigners or between foreigners of different nationalities.

3. All crimes and offences committed by natives against foreigners or committed by such foreigners as are not subject to any consular jurisdiction; subject however to the provisions of section 4 Article V defining the jurisdiction of the Municipal Magistrate of the District of Apia. ...

3. Blaine to Comly on the U.S. in the Pacific, 1881

Secretary of State James G. Blaine to James M. Comly, U.S. Minister in Hawaii.

Washington, December 1, 1881

... I HAVE HAD recent occasion to set forth the vitally integral importance of our Pacific possessions, in a circular letter addressed on the 24th of June last to our representatives in Europe, touching the necessary guarantees of the proposed Panama Canal as a purely American waterway to be treated as part of our own coast line. The extension of commercial empire westward from those states is no less vitally important to their development than is their communication with the Eastern coast by the Isthmian channel. And when we survey the stupendous progress made by the western coast during the thirty years of its national life as a part of our dominion, its enormous increase of population, its vast resources of agriculture and mines, and its boundless enterprise, it is not easy to set a limit to its commercial activity or foresee a check to its maritime supremacy in the waters of the Orient, so long as those waters afford, as now, a free and neutral scope for our peaceful trade.

In thirty years the United States has acquired a legitimately dominant influence in the North Pacific, which it can never consent to see decreased by the intrusion therein of any element of influence hostile to its own. The situation of the Hawaiian Islands, giving them the strategic control of the North Pacific, brings their possession within the range of questions of purely American policy, as much so as that of the Isthmus itself. Hence the necessity, as recognized in our existing treaty relations, of drawing the ties of intimate relationship between us and the Hawaiian Islands so as to make them practically a part of the American system without derogation of their absolute independence. The reciprocity treaty of 1875 has made of Hawaii the sugar-raising field of the Pacific slope and gives to our manufacturers therein the same freedom as in California and Oregon. . . .

The policy of this country with regard to the Pacific is the natural complement to its Atlantic policy. The history of our European relations for fifty years shows the jealous concern with which the United States has guarded its control of the coast from foreign interference, and this without extension of territorial possession beyond the main land. It has always been its aim to preserve the friendly neutrality of the adjacent states and insular possessions. Its attitude toward Cuba is in point. That rich island, the key to the Gulf of Mexico, and the field for our most extended trade in the Western Hemisphere is, though in the hands of Spain, a part of the American commercial system. Our relations, present and prospective, toward Cuba, have never been more ably set forth than in the remarkable note addressed by my predecessor, Mr. Secretary Everett, to the ministers of Great Britain and France in Washington, on the 1st of December, 1852, in rejection of the suggested tripartite alliance to forever determine the neutrality of the Spanish Antilles. In response to the proposal that the United States, Great Britain, and France, should severally and collectively agree to forbid the acquisition of control over Cuba, by any or all of them, Mr. Everett showed that, without forcing or even coveting possession of the island, its condition was essentially an American question; that the renunciation forever by this government of contingent interest therein would be far broader than the like renunciation by Great Britain or France; that if ever ceasing to be Spanish, Cuba must necessarily become American, and not fall under any other European domination, and that the ceaseless movement of segregation of American interests from European control and unification in a broader American sphere of independent life could not and should not be checked by any arbitrary agreement.

Nearly thirty years have demonstrated the wisdom of the attitude then maintained by Mr. Everett and have made indispensable its continuance and its extension to all parts of the American Atlantic system where a disturbance of the existing status might be attempted in the interest of foreign powers. The present attitude of this government toward any European project for the control of an isthmian route is but the logical sequence of the resistance made in 1852 to the attempted pressure of an active foreign influence in the West Indies.

Hawaii, although much farther from the Californian coast than is Cuba from the Floridian peninsula, holds in the western sea much the same position as Cuba in the Atlantic. It is the key to the maritime dominion of the Pacific states, as Cuba is the key to the Gulf trade. The material possession of Hawaii is not desired by the United States any more than was that of Cuba. But under no circumstances can the United States permit any change in the territorial control of either which would cut it adrift from the American system, whereto they both indispensably belong.

In this aspect of the question, it is readily seen with what concern this government must view any tendency toward introducing into Hawaii new social elements, destructive of its necessarily American character. The steady diminution of the native population of the islands, amounting to some ten per cent. between 1872 and 1878, and still continuing, is doubtless a cause of great alarm to the government of the kingdom, and it is no wonder that a solution should be sought with eagerness in any seemingly practicable quarter. The problem, however, is not to be met by a substitution of Mongolian supremacy for native control — as seems at first sight possible through the rapid increase in Chinese immigration to the islands. Neither is a wholesale introduction of the coolie element, professedly Anglo-Indian, likely to afford any more satisfactory outcome to the difficulty. The Hawaiian Islands cannot be joined to the Asiatic system. If they drift from their independent station it must be toward assimilation and identification with the American system, to which they belong by the operation of natural laws, and must belong by the operation of political necessity. . . .

In this line of action the United States does its simple duty both to Hawaii and itself; and it cannot permit such obvious neglect of national interest as would be involved by silent acquiescence in any movement looking to a lessening of those American ties and the substitution of alien and hostile interests. It firmly believes that the position of the Hawaiian Islands as the key to the dominion of the American Pacific demands their neutrality, to which end it will earnestly co-operate with the native government. And if, through any cause, the maintenance of such a position of neutrality should be found by Hawaii to be impracticable, this government would then unhesitatingly meet the altered situation by seeking an avowedly American solution for the grave issues presented. . . .

4. Stevens to Foster on Hawaii, 1892

John L. Stevens, U.S. Minister in Hawaii, to Secretary of State John W. Foster.

Honolulu, November 20, 1892

FIDELITY to the trust imposed on me by the President, the Department of State, and the Senate, requires that I should make a careful and full statement of the financial, agricultural, social, and political condition of these islands. An intelligent and impartial examination of the facts can hardly fail to lead to the conclusion that the relations and policy of the United States toward Hawaii will soon demand some change, if not the adoption of decisive measures, with the aim to secure American interests and future supremacy by encouraging Hawaiian development and aiding to promote responsible government in these islands. . . .

THE EXISTING BUSINESS STATUS

It is well to consider the existing state of things here resulting from the change in the United States sugar tariff. Only personal observation and a careful investigation of the facts can give an adequate idea of the severe blow sugar raised here has received. The production of sugar being the main business of the islands, the great reduction of the market price has effected powerfully the entire affairs and condition of the islands. I think it underestimating the truth to express the opinion that the loss to the owners of the sugar plantations and mills, etc., and the consequent depreciation of other property by the passage of the McKinley bill, wise and beneficial as that measure is proving to be for the vast interests of the United States, has not been less than $12,000,000, a large portion of this loss falling on Americans residing here and in California. Unless some positive measures of relief be granted, the depreciation of sugar property here will continue to go on. Wise, bold action of the United States will rescue the property holders from great loss, give the islands a government which will put an end to a worse than useless expenditure of a large proportion of the revenues of that country, using them for the building of roads and bridges, thus helping to develop the natural resources of the islands, aiding to diversify the industries, and to increase the number of the responsible citizens.

WHAT SHOULD BE DONE?

One of two courses seem to me absolutely necessary to be followed, either bold and vigorous measures for annexation or a "customs union," an ocean cable from the Californian coast to Honolulu, Pearl Harbor perpetually ceded to the United States, with an implied but not necessarily stipulated American protectorate over the islands. I believe the former to be the better, that which will prove much the more advantageous to the islands, and the cheapest and least embarrassing in the end for the United States. If it was wise for the United States, through Secretary Marcy, thirty-eight years ago, to offer to expend $100,000 to secure a treaty of annexation, it certainly can not be chimerical or unwise to expend $100,000 to secure annexation in the near future. To-day the United States has five times the wealth she possessed in 1854, and the reasons now existing for annexation are much stronger than they were then. I can not refrain from expressing the opinion with emphasis that the golden hour is near at hand. A perpetual customs union and the acquisition of Pearl Harbor, with an implied protectorate, must be regarded as the only allowable alternative. This would require the continual presence in the harbor of Honolulu of a United States vessel of war and the constant watchfulness of the United States minister while the present bungling, unsettled, and expensive political rule would go on, retarding the development of the islands, leaving at the end of twenty-five years more embarrassment to annexation than exists today, the property far less valuable, and the population less American than they would be if annexation were soon realized. . . .

To give Hawaii a highly favorable treaty while she remains outside the American Union would necessarily give the same advantages to hostile foreigners, those who would continue to antagonize our commercial and political interests here, as well as those of American blood and sympathies. It is a well authenticated fact that the American sentiment here in 1890, the last year of the great prosperity under the sugar provisions of the reciprocity treaty, was much less manifest than before the treaty had gone into effect, and less pronounced than when Secretary Marcy authorized the negotiation of the annexation treaty in 1854. It is equally true that the desire here at this time for annexation is much stronger than in 1889. Besides, so long as the islands retain their own independent government there remains the possibility that England or the Canadian Dominion might secure one of the Hawaiian harbors for a coaling station. Annexation excludes all dangers of this kind. . . .

5. Gresham to Cleveland on Hawaii, 1893

Secretary of State Walter Q. Gresham to President Grover Cleveland.

Washington, October 18, 1893

THE FULL and impartial reports submitted by the Hon. James H. Blount, your special commissioner to the Hawaiian Islands, established the following facts:

Queen Liliuokalani announced her intention on Saturday, January 14, 1893, to proclaim a new constitution, but the opposition of her ministers and others induced her to speedily change her purpose and make public announcement of that fact.

At a meeting in Honolulu, late on the afternoon of that day, a so-called committee of public safety, consisting of thirteen men, being all or nearly all who were present, was appointed "to consider the situation and devise ways and means for the maintenance of the public peace and the protection of life and property," and at a meeting of this committee on the 15th, or the forenoon of the 16th of January, it was resolved amongst other things that a provisional government be created "to exist until terms of union with the United States of America have been negotiated and agreed upon." At a mass meeting which assembled at 2 p.m. on the last-named day, the Queen and her supporters were condemned and denounced, and the committee was continued and all its acts approved.

Later the same afternoon the committee addressed a letter to John L. Stevens, the American minister at Honolulu, stating that the lives and property of the people were in peril and appealing to him and the United States forces at his command for assistance. This communication concluded "we are unable to protect ourselves without aid, and therefore hope for the protection of the United States forces." On receipt of this letter Mr. Stevens requested Capt. Wiltse, commander of the U.S.S. *Boston,* to land a force "for the protection of the United States legation, the United States consulate, and to secure the safety of American life and property." The well-armed troops, accompanied by two gatling guns, were promptly landed and marched through the quiet streets of Honolulu to a public hall, previously secured by Mr. Stevens for their accommodation. This hall was just across the street from the Government building, and in plain view of the Queen's palace. . . .

The station house was occupied by a well-armed force, under the command of a resolute capable, officer. The same afternoon the Queen, her ministers, representatives of the Provisional Government, and others held a conference at the palace. Refusing to recognize the new authority or surrender to it, she was informed that the Provisional Government had the support of the American minister, and, if necessary, would be maintained by the military force of the United States then present; that any demonstration on her part would precipitate a conflict with that force; that she could not, with hope of success, engage in war with the United States, and that resistance would result in a useless sacrifice of life. Mr. Damon, one of the chief leaders of the movement, and afterwards vice-president of the Provisional Government, informed the Queen that she could surrender under protest and her case would be considered later at Washington. . . .

In his dispatch to Mr. Foster of January 18, describing the so-called revolution, Mr. Stevens says:

The committee of public safety forthwith took possession of the Government building, archives, and treasury, and installed the Provisional Government at the head of the respective departments. This being an accomplished fact, I promptly recognized the Provisional Government as the *de facto* government of the Hawaiian Islands.

In Secretary Foster's communication of February 15 to the President, laying before him the treaty of annexation, with the view to obtaining the advice and consent of the Senate thereto, he says:

> At the time the Provisional Government took possession of the Government building no troops or officers of the United States were present or took any part whatever in the proceedings. No public recognition was accorded to the Provisional Government by the United States minister until after the Queen's abdication, and when they were in effective possession of the Government building, the archives, the treasury, the barracks, the police station, and all the potential machinery of the Government.

Similar language is found in an official letter addressed to Secretary Foster on February 3 by the special commissioners sent to Washington by the Provisional Government to negotiate a treaty of annexation.

These statements are utterly at variance with the evidence, documentary and oral, contained in Mr. Blount's reports. They are contradicted by declarations and letters of President Dole and other annexationists and by Mr. Stevens's own verbal admissions to Mr. Blount. . . .

The earnest appeals to the American minister for military protection by the officers of that Government, after it had been recognized, show the utter absurdity of the claim that it was established by a successful revolution of the people of the Islands. Those appeals were a confession by the men who made them of their weakness and timidity. Courageous men, conscious of their strength and the justice of their cause, do not thus act. It is not now claimed that a majority of the people, having the right to vote under the constitution of 1887, ever favored the existing authority or annexation to this or any other country. They earnestly desire that the government of their choice shall be restored and its independence respected.

Mr. Blount states that while at Honolulu he did not meet a single annexationist who expressed willingness to submit the question to a vote of the people, nor did he talk with one on that subject who did not insist that if the Islands were annexed suffrage should be so restricted as to give complete control to foreigners or whites. Representative annexationists have repeatedly made similar statements to the undersigned.

The Government of Hawaii surrendered its authority under a threat of war, until such time only as the Government of the United States, upon the facts being presented to it, should reinstate the constitutional sovereign, and the Provisional Government was created "to exist until terms of union with the United States of America have been negotiated and agreed upon." A careful consideration of the facts will, I think, convince you that the treaty which was withdrawn from the Senate for further consideration should not be resubmitted for its action thereon.

Should not the great wrong done to a feeble but independent State by an abuse of the authority of the United States be undone by restoring the legitimate government? Anything short of that will not, I respectfully submit, satisfy the demands of justice. . . .

6. Cleveland's Hawaiian Dilemma, 1893

President Cleveland to Congress, 18 December 1893.

IN MY RECENT annual message to the Congress I briefly referred to our relations with Hawaii and expressed the intention of transmitting further information on the subject when additional advices permitted.

Though I am not able now to report a definite change in the actual situation, I am convinced that the difficulties lately created both here and in Hawaii and now standing in the way of a solution through Executive action of the problem presented, render it proper, and expedient, that the matter should be referred to the broader authority and discretion of Congress, with a full explanation of the endeavor thus far made to deal with the emergency and a statement of the considerations which have governed my action.

I suppose that right and justice should determine the path to be followed in treating this subject. If national honesty is to be disregarded and a desire for territorial extension, or dissatisfaction with a form of government not own own, ought to regulate our conduct, I have entirely misapprehended the mission and character of our Government and the behavior which the conscience of our people demands of their public servants. . . .

As I apprehend the situation, we are brought face to face with the following conditions:

The lawful Government of Hawaii was overthrown without the drawing of a sword or the firing of a shot by a process every step of which, it may safely be asserted, is directly traceable to and dependent for its success upon the agency of the United States acting through its diplomatic and naval representatives.

But for the notorious predilections of the United States Minister for annexation, the Committee of Safety, which should be called the Committee of Annexation, would never have existed.

But for the landing of the United States forces upon false pretexts respecting the danger to life and property the committee would never have exposed themselves to the pains and penalties of treason by undertaking the subversion of the Queen's Government.

But for the presence of the United States forces in the immediate vicinity and in position to afford all needed protection and support the committee would not have proclaimed the provisional government from the steps of the Government building.

And finally, but for the lawless occupation of Honolulu under false pretexts by the United States forces, and but for Minister Stevens's recognition of the provisional government when the United States forces were its sole support and constituted its only military strength, the Queen and her Government would never have yielded to the provisional government, even for a time and for the sole purpose of submitting her case to the enlightened justice of the United States. . . .

I have not, however, overlooked an incident of this unfortunate affair which remains to be mentioned. The members of the provisional government and their supporters, though not entitled to extreme sympathy, have been led to their present predicament of revolt against the Government of the Queen by the indefensible encouragement and assistance of our diplomatic representative. This fact may entitle them to claim that in our effort to rectify the wrong committed some regard should be had for their safety. . . .

Actuated by these desires and purposes, and not unmindful of the inherent perplexities of the situation nor of the limitations upon my power, I instructed Minister Willis to advise the Queen and her supporters of my desire to aid in the restoration of the status existing before the lawless landing of the United States forces at Honolulu on the 16th of January last, if such restoration could be effected upon terms providing for clemency as well as justice to all parties concerned. The conditions suggested, as the instructions show, contemplate a general amnesty to those concerned in setting up the provisional government and a recognition of all its *bona fide* acts and obligations. In short, they require that the past should be buried, and that the restored Government should reassume its authority as if its continuity had not been interrupted. These conditions have not proved acceptable to the Queen, and though she has been informed that they will be insisted upon, and that, unless acceded to, the efforts of the President to aid in the restoration of her Government will cease, I have not thus far learned that she is willing to yield them her acquiescence. The check which my plans have thus encountered has prevented their presentation to the members of the provisional government, while unfortunate public misrepresentations of the situation and exaggerated statements of the sentiments of our people have obviously injured the prospects of successful Executive mediation. . . .

In commending this subject to the extended powers and wide discretion of the Congress, I desire to add the assurance that I shall be much gratified to coöperate in any legislative plan which may be devised for the solution of the problem before us which is consistent with American honor, integrity, and morality.

7. Olney to Bayard on the Venezuelan Boundary Crisis, July 1895

Secretary of State Richard Olney to Thomas F. Bayard, U.S. Ambassador in Great Britain.

Washington, July 20, 1895

I AM directed by the President to communicate to you his views upon a subject to which he has given much anxious thought and respecting which he has not reached a conclusion without a lively sense of its great importance as well as of the serious responsibility involved in any action now to be taken.

It is not proposed, and for present purposes is not necessary, to enter into any detailed account of the controversy between Great Britain and Venezuela respecting the western frontier of the colony of British Guiana. The dispute is of ancient date and began at least as early as the time when Great Britain acquired by the treaty with the Netherlands of 1814 "the establishments of Demerara, Essequibo, and Berbice.". . .

It does not seem to be asserted, for instance, that in 1814 the "establishments" then acquired by Great Britain had any clearly defined western limits which can now be identified and which are either the limits insisted upon today, or, being the original limits, have been the basis of legitimate territorial extensions. On the contrary, having the actual possession of a district called the Pomaron district, she apparently remained indifferent as to the exact area of the colony until 1840, when she commissioned an engineer, Sir Robert Schomburgk, to examine and lay down its boundaries. The result was the Schomburgk line which was fixed by metes and bounds, was delineated on maps, and was at first indicated on the face of the country itself by posts, monograms, and other like symbols. If it was expected that Venezuela would acquiesce in this line, the expectation was doomed to speedy disappointment. Venezuela at once protested and with such vigor and to such purpose that the line was explained to be only tentative — part of a general boundary scheme concerning Brazil and the Netherlands as well as Venezuela — and the monuments of the line set up by Schomburgk were removed by the express order of Lord Aberdeen. . . .

Several other features of the situation remain to be briefly noticed — the continuous growth of the undefined British claim, the fate of the various attempts at arbitration of the controversy, and the part in the matter heretofore taken by the United States. As already seen, the exploitation of the Schomburgk line in 1840 was at once followed by the protest of Venezuela and by proceedings on the part of Great Britain which could fairly be interpreted only as a disavowal of that line. Indeed — in addition to the facts already noticed — Lord Aberdeen himself in 1844 proposed a line beginning at the River Moroco, a distinct abandonment of the Schomburgk line. Notwithstanding this, however, every change in the British claim since that time has moved the frontier of British Guiana farther and farther to the westward of the line thus proposed. The Granville line of 1881 placed the starting point at a distance of twenty-nine miles from the Moroco in the direction of Punta Barima. The Rosebery line of 1886 placed it west of the Guiama River, and about that time, if the British authority known as the Statesman's Year Book is to be relied upon, the area of British Guiana was suddenly enlarged by some 33,000 square miles — being stated as 76,000 square miles in 1885 and 109,000 square miles in 1887. . . .

The important features of the existing situation, as shown by the foregoing recital, may be briefly stated.

1. The title to territory of indefinite but confessedly very large extent is in dispute between Great Britain on the one hand and the South American Republic of Venezuela on the other.

2. The disparity in the strength of the claimants is such that Venezuela can hope to establish her claim only through peaceful methods — through an agreement with her adversary either upon the subject itself or upon an arbitration.

3. The controversy, with varying claims on the part of Great Britain, has existed for more than half a century, during which period many earnest and persistent efforts of Venezuela to establish a boundary by agreement have proved unsuccessful.

4. The futility of the endeavor to obtain a conventional line being recognized, Venezuela for a quarter of a century has asked and striven for arbitration.

5. Great Britain, however, has always and continuously refused to arbitrate, except upon the condition of a renunciation of a large part of the Venezuelan claim and of a concession to herself of a large share of the territory in controversy.

6. By the frequent interposition of its good offices at the instance of Venezuela, by constantly urging and promoting the restoration of diplomatic relations between the two countries, by pressing for arbitration of the disputed boundary, by offering to act as arbitrator, by expressing its grave concern whenever new alleged instances of British aggression upon Venezuelan territory have been brought to its notice, the Government of the United States has made it clear to Great Britain and to the world that the controversy is one in which both its honor and its interests are involved and the continuance of which it can not regard with indifference. . . .

That America is in no part open to colonization, though the proposition was not universally admitted at the time of its first enunciation, has long been universally conceded. We are now concerned, therefore, only with that other practical application of the Monroe doctrine the disregard of which by an European power is to be deemed an act of unfriendliness towards the United States. The precise scope and limitations of this rule cannot be too clearly apprehended. It does not establish any general protectorate by the United States over other American states. It does not relieve any American state from its obligations as fixed by international law nor prevent any European power directly interested from enforcing such obligations or from inflicting merited punishment for the breach of them. It does not contemplate any interference in the internal affairs of any American state or in the relations between it and other American states. It does not justify any attempt on our part to change the established form of government of any American state or to prevent the people of such state from altering that form according to their own will and pleasure. The rule in question has but a single purpose and object. It is that no European power or combination of European powers shall forcibly deprive an American state of the right and power of self-government and of shaping for itself its own political fortunes and destinies. . . .

Is it true, then, that the safety and welfare of the United States are so concerned with the maintenance of the independence of every American state as against any European power as to justify and require the interposition of the United States whenever that independence is endangered? The question can be candidly answered in but one way. The states of America, South as well as North, by geographical proximity, by natural sympathy, by similarity of governmental constitutions, are friends and allies, commercially and politically, of the United States. To allow the subjugation of any of them by an European power is, of course, to completely reverse that situation and signifies the loss of all the advantages incident to their natural relations to us. But that is not all. The people of the United States have a vital interest in the cause of popular self-government. They have secured the right for themselves and their posterity at the cost of infinite blood and treasure. They have realized and exemplified its beneficent operation by a career unexampled in point of national greatness or individual felicity. They believe it to be for the healing of all nations, and that civilization must either advance or retrograde accordingly as its supremacy is extended or curtailed. Imbued with these sentiments, the people of the United States might not impossibly be wrought up to an active propaganda in favor of a cause so highly valued both for themselves and for mankind. But the age of the Crusades has passed, and they are content with such assertion and defense of the right of popular self-government as their own security and welfare demand. It is in that view more than in any other that they believe it not to be tolerated that the political control of an American state shall be forcibly assumed by an European power.

The mischiefs apprehended from such a source are none the less real because not immediately imminent in any specific case, and are none the less to be guarded against because the combination of circumstances that will bring them upon us cannot be predicted. The civilized states of Christendom deal with each other on substantially the same principles that regulate the conduct of individuals. The greater its enlightenment, the more surely every state perceives that its permanent interests require it to be governed by the immutable principles of right and justice. Each, nevertheless, is only too liable to succumb to the temptations offered by seeming special opportunities for its own aggrandizement, and each would rashly imperil its own safety were it not to remember that for the regard and respect of other states it must be largely dependent upon its own strength and power. Today the United States is practically sovereign on this continent, and its fiat is law upon the subjects to which it confines its interposition. Why? It is not because of the pure friendship or good will felt for it. It is not simply by reason of its high character as a civilized state, nor because wisdom and justice and equity are the invariable characteristics of the dealings of the United States. It is because, in addition to all other grounds, its infinite resources combined with its isolated position render it master of the situation and practically invulnerable as against any or all other powers.

All the advantages of this superiority are at once imperiled if the principle be admitted that European powers may convert American states into colonies or provinces of their own. The principle would be eagerly availed of, and every power doing so would immediately acquire a base of military operations against us. What one power was permitted to do could not be denied to another, and it is not inconceivable that the struggle now going on for the acquisition of Africa might be transferred to South America. If it were, the weaker countries would unquestionably be soon absorbed, while the ultimate result might be the partition of all South America between the various European powers. The disastrous consequences to the United States of such a condition of things are obvious. The loss of prestige, of authority, and of weight in the councils of the family of nations, would be among the least of them. Our only real rivals in peace as well as enemies in war would be found located at our very doors. Thus far in our history we have been spared the burdens and evils of immense standing armies and all the other accessories of huge warlike establishments, and the exemption has largely contributed to our national greatness and wealth as well as to the happiness of every citizen. But, with the powers of Europe permanently encamped on American soil, the ideal conditions we have thus far enjoyed can not be expected to continue. We too must be armed to the teeth, we too must convert the flower of our male population into soldiers and sailors, and by withdrawing them from the various pursuits of peaceful industry we too must practically annihilate a large share of the productive energy of the nation. . . .

Thus, as already intimated, the British demand that her right to a portion of the disputed territory shall be acknowledged before she will consent to an arbitration as to the rest seems to stand upon nothing but her own *ipse dixit*. She says to Venezuela, in substance: "You can get none of the debatable land by force, because you are not strong enough; you can get none by a treaty, because I will not agree; and you can take your chance of getting a portion by arbitration, only if you first agree to abandon to me such other portion as I may designate." It is not perceived how such an attitude can be defended nor how it is reconcilable with that love of justice and fair play so eminently characteristic of the English race. It in effect deprives Venezuela of her free agency and puts her under virtual duress. Territory acquired by reason of it will be as much wrested from her by the strong hand as if occupied by British troops or covered by British fleets. It seems therefore quite impossible that this position of Great Britain should be assented to by the United States, or that, if such position be adhered to with the result of enlarging the bounds of British Guiana, it should not be regarded as amounting, in substance, to an invasion and conquest of Venezuelan territory. . . .

8. Salisbury to Pauncefote on the Venezuelan Boundary Crisis, November 1895

Prime Minister Lord Salisbury to Sir Julian Pauncefote, British Ambassador in the U.S.

Foreign Office, [London] November 26, 1895

. . . THE CONTENTIONS set forth by Mr. Olney . . . are represented by him as being an application of the political maxims which are well known in American discussion under the name of the Monroe doctrine. As far as I am aware, this doctrine has never been before advanced on behalf of the United States in any written communication addressed to the Government of another nation; but it has been generally adopted and assumed as true by many eminent writers and politicians in the United States. It is said to have largely influenced the Government of that country in the conduct of its foreign affairs: though Mr. Clayton, who was Secretary of State under President Taylor, expressly stated that that Administration had in no way adopted it. But during the period that has elapsed since the Message of President Monroe was delivered in 1823, the doctrine has undergone a very notable development, and the aspect which it now presents in the hands of Mr. Olney differs widely from its character when it first issued from the pen of its author. The two propositions which in effect President Monroe laid down were, first, that America was no longer to be looked upon as a field for European colonization; and, secondly, that Europe must not attempt to extend its political system to America, or to control the political condition of any of the American communities who had recently declared their independence. . . .

The dangers which were apprehended by President Monroe have no relation to the state of things in which we live at the present day. There is no danger of any Holy Alliance imposing its system upon any portion of the American Continent, and there is no danger of any European State treating any part of the American Continent as a fit object for European colonization. It is intelligible that Mr. Olney should invoke, in defence of the views on which he is now insisting, an authority which enjoys so high a popularity with his own fellow-countrymen. But the circumstances with which President Monroe was dealing, and those to which the present American Government is addressing itself, have very few features in common. Great Britain is imposing no "system" upon Venezuela, and is not concerning herself in any way with the nature of the political institutions under which the Venezuelans may prefer to live. But the British Empire and the Republic of Venezuela are neighbors, and they have differed for some time past, and continue to differ, as to the line by which their dominions are separated. It is a controversy with which the United States have no apparent practical concern. It is difficult, indeed, to see how it can materially affect any State or community outside those primarily interested, except perhaps other parts of Her Majesty's dominions, such as Trinidad.

The disputed frontier of Venezuela has nothing to do with any of the questions dealt with by President Monroe. It is not a question of the colonization by a European Power of any portion of America. It is not a question of the imposition upon the communities of South America of any system of government devised in Europe. It is simply the determination of the frontier of a British possession which belonged to the Throne of England long before the Republic of Venezuela came into existence. But even if the interests of Venezuela were so far linked to those of the United States as to give to the latter a *locus standi* in this controversy, their Government apparently have not formed, and certainly do not express, any opinion upon the actual merits of the dispute. The Government of the United States do not say that Great Britain, or that Venezuela, is in the right in the matters that are in issue. But they lay down that the doctrine of President Monroe, when he opposed the imposition of European systems, or the renewal of European colonization, confers upon them the right of demanding that when a European Power has a frontier difference with a South American community, the European Power shall consent to refer that controversy to arbitration; and Mr. Olney states that unless Her Majesty's Government accede to this demand, it will "greatly embarrass the future relations between Great Britain and the United States...."

In the remarks which I have made, I have argued on the theory that the Monroe doctrine in itself is sound. I must not, however, be understood as expressing any acceptance of it on the part of Her Majesty's Government. It must always be mentioned with respect, on account of the distinguished statesman to whom it is due, and the great nation who have generally adopted it. But international law is founded on the general consent of nations; and no statesmen, however eminent, and no nation, however powerful, are competent to insert into the code of international law a novel principle which was never recognized before, and which has not since been accepted by the Government of any other country. The United States have a right, like any other nation, to interpose in any controversy by which their own interests are affected; and they are the judge whether those interests are touched, and in what measure they should be sustained. But their rights are in no way strengthened or extended by the fact that the controversy affects some territory which is called American. Mr. Olney quotes the case of the recent Chilean war, in which the United States declined to join with France and England in an effort to bring hostilities to a close, on account of the Monroe doctrine. The United States were entirely in their right in declining to join in an attempt at pacification if they thought fit; but Mr. Olney's principle that "American questions are for American decision," even if it receive any countenance from the language of President Monroe (which it does not), can not be sustained by any reasoning drawn from the law of nations....

9. Cleveland's Message to Congress, 17 December 1895

IN MY ANNUAL message addressed to the Congress on the third instant I called attention to the pending boundary controversy between Great Britain and the Republic of Venezuela and recited the substance of a representation made by this Government to Her Britannic Majesty's Government suggesting reasons why such dispute should be submitted to arbitration for settlement, and inquiring whether it would be so submitted....

If a European power, by an extension of its boundaries, takes possession of the territory of one of our neighboring Republics against its will and in derogation of its rights, it is difficult to see why to that extent such European power does not thereby attempt to extend its system of government to that portion of this continent which is thus taken. This is the precise action which President Monroe declared to be "dangerous to our peace and safety," and it can make no difference whether the European system is extended by an advance of frontier or otherwise.

It is also suggested in the British reply that we should not seek to apply the Monroe doctrine to the pending dispute because it does not embody any principle of international law which "is founded on the general consent of nations," and that "no statesman, however eminent, and no nation, however powerful, are competent to insert into the code of international law a novel principle which was never recognized before, and which has not since been accepted by the Government of any other country."

Practically the principle for which we contend has peculiar if not exclusive relation to the United States. It may not have been admitted in so many words to the code of international law, but since in international councils every nation is entitled to the rights belonging to it, if the enforcement of the Monroe doctrine is something we may justly claim it has its place in the code of international law as certainly and as securely as if it were specifically mentioned, and where the United States is a suitor before the high tribunal that administers international law the question to be determined is whether or not we present claims which the justice of that code of law can find to be right and valid....

In the belief that the doctrine for which we contend was clear and definite, that it was founded upon substantial considerations and involved our safety and welfare, that it was fully applicable to our present conditions and to the state of the world's progress and that it was directly related to the pending controversy and without any conviction as to the final merits of the dispute, but anxious to learn in a satisfactory and conclusive manner whether Great Britain sought, under a claim of boundary, to extend her possessions on this continent without right, or whether she merely sought possession of territory fairly included within her lines of ownership, this Government proposed to the Government of Great Britain a resort to arbitration as the proper means of settling the question to the end that a vexatious boundary dispute between the two contestants might be determined and our exact standing and relation in respect to the controversy might be made clear.

It will be seen from the correspondence herewith submitted that this proposition has been declined by the British Government, upon grounds which in the circumstances seem to me to be far from satisfactory. It is deeply disappointing that such an appeal actuated by the most friendly feelings towards both nations directly concerned, addressed to the sense of justice and to the magnanimity of one of the great powers of the world and touching its relations to one comparatively weak and small, should have produced no better results. . . .

Assuming, however, that the attitude of Venezuela will remain unchanged, the dispute has reached such a stage as to make it now incumbent upon the United States to take measures to determine with sufficient certainty for its justification what is the true divisional line between the Republic of Venezuela and British Guiana. The inquiry to that end should of course be conducted carefully and judicially and due weight should be given to all available evidence records and facts in support of the claims of both parties.

In order that such an examination should be prosecuted in a thorough and satisfactory manner I suggest that the Congress make an adequate appropriation for the expenses of a Commission, to be appointed by the Executive, who shall make the necessary investigation and report upon the matter with the least possible delay. When such report is made and accepted it will in my opinion be the duty of the United States to resist by every means in its power as a willful aggression upon its rights and interests the appropriation by Great Britain of any lands or the exercise of governmental jurisdiction over any territory which after investigation we have determined of right belongs to Venezuela.

In making these recommendations I am fully alive to the responsibility incurred, and keenly realize all the consequences that may follow.

I am nevertheless firm in my conviction that while it is a grievous thing to contemplate the two great English-speaking peoples of the world as being otherwise than friendly competitors in the onward march of civilization, and strenuous and worthy rivals in all the arts of peace, there is no calamity which a great nation can invite which equals that which follows a supine submission to wrong and injustice and the consequent loss of national self respect and honor beneath which are shielded and defended a people's safety and greatness.

10. Salisbury to Pauncefote on the Venezuelan Boundary Settlement, 1896

Foreign Office, [London] *May 22, 1896*

I SENT YOU in a dispatch under date of the 18th instant some observations upon Mr. Olney's communication to you with regard to the subject of general arbitration.

As it is possible, however, that we shall not see our way to surmount the difficulties which still separate the views of the two Governments in regard to the larger and more general question, I propose in this dispatch to convey to you proposals for the settlement of the Venezuelan dispute, which I should be glad if you would submit to the Government of the United States, acting as the friend of Venezuela in this matter. From the first our objection has been to subject to the decision of an arbiter, who, in the last resort, must, of necessity, be a foreigner, the rights of British colonists who have settled in the territory which they had every ground for believing to be British, and whose careers would be broken, and their fortunes possibly ruined, by a decision that the territory on which they have settled was subject to the Venezuelan Republic. At the same time we are very conscious that the dispute between ourselves and the Republic of Venezuela affects a very large portion of land which is not under settlement, and which could be disposed of without any injustice to any portion of the colonial population. We are very willing that the territory which is comprised within this definition should be subjected to the results of an arbitration, even though some portion of it should be found to fall within the Schomburgk line. With that end in view, we propose the following basis of settlement of the Venezuelan boundary dispute:

A commission to be created by agreement between Great Britain and the United States, consisting of four members, namely, two British subjects and two citizens of the United States; the above commission to investigate and to report upon the facts which affect the rights of the United Netherlands and of Spain, respectively, at the date of the acquisition of British Guiana by Great Britain.

This commission will only examine into questions of fact, without reference to the inferences that may be founded on them; but the finding of a majority of the commission upon those questions shall be binding upon both Governments.

Upon the report of the above commission being issued, the two Governments of Great Britain and Venezuela, respectively, shall endeavor to agree to a boundary line upon the basis of such report. Failing agreement, the report, and every other matter concerning this controversy on which either Government desire to insist, shall be submitted to a tribunal of three, one nominated by Great Britain, the other by Venezuela, and the third by the two so nominated; which tribunal shall fix the boundary line upon the basis of such report, and the line so fixed shall be binding upon Great Britain and Venezuela. Provided, always, that in fixing such line the tribunal shall not have power to include as the territory of Venezuela any territory which was bona fide occupied by subjects of Great Britain on the 1st of January, 1887, or as the territory of Great Britain any territory bona fide occupied by Venezuelans at the same date.

In respect to any territory with which, by this provision, the tribunal is precluded from dealing, the tribunal may submit to the two Powers any recommendations which seem to it calculated to satisfy the equitable rights of the parties, and the two Powers will take such recommendations into their consideration.

It will be evident from this proposal that we are prepared to accept the finding of a commission voting as three to one upon all the facts which are involved in the question of Dutch and Spanish rights at the time of the cession of Guiana to Great Britain. We are also prepared to accept the decision of an arbitral tribunal with regard to the ownership of all portions of the disputed territory which are not under settlement by British subjects or Venezuelan citizens. If the decision of the commission shall affect any territory which is so settled, it will be in the power of either Government to decline to accept the decision so arrived at, so far as it affects the territory alleged to be settled. But I need not point out to you that even upon that question, although the decision of the arbitral tribunal will not have a final effect, it will, unless it be manifestly unfair, offer a presumption, against which the protesting Government will practically find it difficult to contend.

11. Great Britain and Venezuela,
Treaty of Boundary Settlement, 1896

As agreed upon by Great Britain and
U.S.

[*November 12, 1896*]

I. AN ARBITRAL tribunal shall be immediately appointed to determine the boundary line between the colony of British Guiana and the Republic of Venezuela.

II. The tribunal shall consist of two members nominated by the judges of the Supreme Court of the United States and two members nominated by the judges of the British supreme court of justice and of a fifth juror selected by the four persons so nominated, or, in the event of their failure to agree within three months from the time of their nomination, selected by His Majesty the King of Sweden and Norway.

The person so selected shall be president of the tribunal.

The persons nominated by the judges of the Supreme Court of the United States and of the British supreme court of justice, respectively, may be judges of either of said courts.

III. The tribunal shall investigate and ascertain the extent of the territories belonging to or that might lawfully be claimed by the United Netherlands or by the Kingdom of Spain, respectively, at the time of the acquisition by Great Britain of the colony of British Guiana — and shall determine the boundary line between the colony of British Guiana and the Republic of Venezuela.

IV. In deciding the matters submitted the arbitrators shall ascertain all the facts which they deem necessary to a decision of the controversy and shall be governed by the following rules, which are agreed upon by the high contracting parties as rules to be taken as applicable to the case, and by such principles of international law not inconsistent therewith as the arbitrators shall determine to be applicable to the case.

Rules

(a) Adverse holding or prescription during a period of fifty years shall make a good title. The arbitrators may deem exclusive political control of a district, as well as actual settlement thereof, sufficient to constitute adverse holding or to make title by prescription.

(b) The arbitrators may recognize and give effect to rights and claims resting on any other ground whatever, valid according to international law, and on any principles of international law which the arbitrators may deem to be applicable to the case and which are not in contravention of the foregoing rule.

(c) In determining the boundary line, if territory of one party be found by the tribunal to have been at the date of this treaty in the occupation of the subjects or citizens of the other party, such effect shall be given to such occupation as reason, justice, the principles of international law, and the equities of the case shall, in the opinion of the tribunal, require.

12. Tetuán to de Lôme on Spain in Cuba, 1897

Duke de Tetuán, Spanish Foreign Minister to Dupuy de Lôme, Spanish Minister in U.S.

August 4, 1897

... ALL CIVILIZED countries which, like Spain at present, have found themselves under the harsh necessity of resorting to arms to crush rebellions, not always so evidently unjustifiable as that of Cuba, proceed and have proceeded in the same manner. In the United States itself, during the war of secession, recourse was had to concentrations of peaceable inhabitants, to seizures and confiscation of property, to the destruction of all agricultural and industrial property, particularly of cotton and tobacco, without the safeguard of their foreign flags, in the case of the important factories of Roswell, for instance, sufficing to save them; to the burning of entire cities; to the ruin and devastation of immense and most fertile regions — in short, to the destruction of all the property of the adversary, to the abolition of constitutional rights by the total suspension of the writ of habeas corpus, and to the development of a military and dictatorial system which, in the states opposed to the Union, lasted many years after the termination of the bloody contest. . . .

The invincible General Sherman explained on various occasions the supreme justice of these acts, and in perusing his memoirs and the official reports which he addressed to the directing council of war at Washington are found remarkable statements as to the severity with which it is necessary to proceed against the enemy to make the operations of the military forces efficient and successful. "War is war," said this able general, "and the tremendous responsibility for civil wars rests upon their authors and upon those who are their direct or indirect instruments. . . ."

Moreover, we must bear in mind that this system of the total destruction of Cuban property has always been advocated by the filibustering junta at New York, composed, in great part, of naturalized North Americans, and that this very junta has issued the most cruel orders; so that, by a most amazing coincidence, the authors of the admittedly abominable devastation which, according to the secretary of state, has so greatly aroused the sympathies of the North American people, are citizens of the Union and organizations working without hinderance in its bosom. . . .

13. Day to Woodford on Spain in Cuba, March 1898

Secretary of State William R. Day to Stewart L. Woodford, U.S. Minister in Spain.

Washington, March 26, 1898

THE PRESIDENT'S desire is for peace. He can not look upon the suffering and starvation in Cuba save with horror. The concentration of men, women, and children in the fortified towns and permitting them to starve is unbearable to a Christian nation geographically so close as ours to Cuba. All this has shocked and inflamed the American mind, as it has the civilized world, where its extent and character are known. It was represented to him in November that the Blanco government would at once release the suffering and so modify the Weyler order as to permit those who were able to return to their homes and till the fields from which they had been driven. There has been no relief to the starving except such as the American people have supplied. The reconcentration order has not been practically superseded. There is no hope of peace through Spanish arms. The Spanish Government seems unable to conquer the insurgents. More than half of the island is under control of the insurgents; for more than three years our people have been patient and forbearing; we have patrolled our coast with zeal and at great expense, and have successfully prevented the landing of any armed force on the island. The war has disturbed the peace and tranquillity of our people. We do not want the island. The President has evidenced in every way his desire to preserve and continue friendly relations with Spain. He has kept every international obligation with fidelity. He wants an honorable peace. He has repeatedly urged the Government of Spain to secure such a peace. She still has the opportunity to do it, and the President appeals to her from every consideration of justice and humanity to do it. Will she? Peace is the desired end.

For your own guidance, the President suggests that if Spain will revoke the reconcentration order and maintain the people until they can support themselves and offer to the Cubans full self-government, with reasonable indemnity, the President will gladly assist in its consummation. If Spain should invite the United States to mediate for peace and the insurgents would make like request, the President might undertake such office of friendship.

[*Mr. Day to Mr. Woodford*] [7]

Washington, March 27, 1898

... SEE IF the following can be done:

First. Armistice until October 1. Negotiations meantime looking for peace between Spain and insurgents through friendly offices of President United States.

Second. Immediate revocation of reconcentrado order so as to permit people to return to their farms, and the needy to be relieved with provisions and supplies from United States cooperating with authorities so as to afford full relief.

Add, if possible:

Third. If terms of peace not satisfactorily settled by October 1, President of the United States to be final arbiter between Spain and insurgents.

If Spain agrees, President will use friendly offices to get insurgents to accept plan. Prompt action desirable.

14. Woodford to President William McKinley on Spain in Cuba, 5 April 1898.

Madrid, April 5, 1898

SHOULD the Queen proclaim the following before 12 o'clock noon of Wednesday, April 6, will you sustain the Queen, and can you prevent hostile action by Congress?

At the request of the Holy Father, in this Passion Week and in the name of Christ, I proclaim immediate and unconditional suspension of hostilities in the island of Cuba.

This suspension is to become immediately effective so soon as accepted by the insurgents in that island, and is to continue for the space of six months, to the 5th day of October, eighteen ninety-eight.

I do this to give time for passions to cease, and in the sincere hope and belief that during this suspension permanent and honorable peace may be obtained between the insular government of Cuba and those of my subjects in that island who are now in rebellion against the authority of Spain.

I pray the blessing of Heaven upon this Truce of God, which I now declare in His name and with the sanction of the Holy Father of all Christendom.

April 5, 1898

Please read this in the light of all my previous telegrams and letters. I believe that this means peace, which the sober judgment of our people will approve long before next November, and which must be approved at the bar of final history.

I permit the papal nuncio to read this telegram, upon my own responsibility and without committing you in any manner. I dare not reject this last chance for peace. I will show your reply to the Queen in person, and I believe that you will approve this last conscientious effort for peace.

15. McKinley's War Message, 11 April 1898

President McKinley to Congress.

OBEDIENT to that precept of the Constitution which commands the President to give from time to time to the Congress information of the state of the Union and to recommend to their consideration such measures as he shall judge necessary and expedient, it becomes my duty now to address your body with regard to the grave crisis that has arisen in the relations of the United States to Spain by reason of the warfare that for more than three years has raged in the neighboring island of Cuba. . . .

Since the present revolution began, in February, 1895, this country has seen the fertile domain at our threshold ravaged by fire and sword in the course of a struggle unequaled in the history of the island and rarely paralleled as to the numbers of the combatants and the bitterness of the contest by any revolution of modern times where a dependent people striving to be free have been opposed by the power of the sovereign state. . . .

The war in Cuba is of such a nature that short of subjugation or extermination a final military victory for either side seems impracticable. The alternative lies in the physical exhaustion of the one or the other party, or perhaps of both — a condition which in effect ended the ten years' war by the truce of Zanjon. The prospect of such a protraction and conclusion of the present strife is a contingency hardly to be contemplated with equanimity by the civilized world, and least of all by the United States, affected and injured as we are, deeply and intimately, by its very existence.

Realizing this, it appeared to be my duty, in a spirit of true friendliness, no less to Spain than to the Cubans who have so much to lose by the prolongation of the struggle, to seek to bring about an immediate termination of the war. To this end I submitted, on the 27th ultimo, as a result of much representation and correspondence, through the United States minister at Madrid, propositions to the Spanish Government looking to an armistice until October 1 for the negotiation of peace with the good offices of the President.

In addition, I asked the immediate revocation of the order of reconcentration, so as to permit the people to return to their farms and the needy to be relieved with provisions and supplies from the United States, cooperating with the Spanish authorities, so as to afford full relief.

The reply of the Spanish cabinet was received on the night of the 31st ultimo. It offered, as the means to bring about peace in Cuba, to confide the preparation thereof to the insular parliament, inasmuch as the concurrence of that body would be necessary to reach a final result, it being, however, understood that the powers reserved by the constitution to the central Government are not lessened or diminished. As the Cuban parliament does not meet until the 4th of May next, the Spanish Government would not object, for its part, to accept at once a suspension of hostilities if asked for by the insurgents from the general in chief, to whom it would pertain, in such case, to determine the duration and conditions of the armistice. . . .

The forcible intervention of the United States as a neutral to stop the war, according to the large dictates of humanity and following many historical precedents where neighboring States have interfered to check the hopeless sacrifices of life by internecine conflicts beyond their borders, is justifiable on rational grounds. It involves, however, hostile constraint upon both the parties to the contest as well to enforce a truce as to guide the eventual settlement.

The grounds for such intervention may be briefly summarized as follows:

First. In the cause of humanity and to put an end to the barbarities, bloodshed, starvation, and horrible miseries now existing there, and which the parties to the conflict are either unable or unwilling to stop or mitigate. It is no answer to say this is all in another country, belonging to another nation, and is therefore none of our business. It is specially our duty, for it is right at our door.

Second. We owe it to our citizens in Cuba to afford them that protection and indemnity for life and property which no government there can or will afford, and to that end to terminate the conditions that deprive them of legal protection.

Third. The right to intervene may be justified by the very serious injury to the commerce, trade, and business of our people, and by the wanton destruction of property and devastation of the island.

Fourth, and which is of the utmost importance. The present condition of affairs in Cuba is a constant menace to our peace, and entails upon this Government an enormous expense. With such a conflict waged for years in an island so near us and with which our people have such trade and business relations; when the lives and liberty of our citizens are in constant danger and their property destroyed and themselves ruined; where our trading vessels are liable to seizure and are seized at our very door by war ships of a foreign nation, the expeditions of filibustering that we are powerless to prevent altogether, and the irritating questions and entanglements thus arising — all these and others that I need not mention, with the resulting strained relations, are a constant menace to our peace, and compel us to keep on a semi-war footing with a nation with which we are at peace. . . .

The long trial has proved that the object for which Spain has waged the war can not be attained. The fire of insurrection may flame or may smolder with varying seasons, but it has not been and it is plain that it can not be extinguished by present methods. The only hope of relief and repose from a condition which can no longer be endured is the enforced pacification of Cuba. In the name of humanity, in the name of civilization, in behalf of endangered American interests which give us the right and the duty to speak and to act, the war in Cuba must stop.

In view of these facts and of these considerations, I ask the Congress to authorize and empower the President to take measures to secure a full and final termination of hostilities between the Government of Spain and the people of Cuba, and to secure in the island the establishment of a stable government, capable of maintaining order and observing its international obligations, insuring peace and tranquillity and the security of its citizens as well as our own, and to use the military and naval forces of the United States as may be necessary for these purposes. . . .

The issue is now with the Congress. It is a solemn responsibility. I have exhausted every effort to relieve the intolerable condition of affairs which is at our doors. Prepared to execute every obligation imposed upon me by the Constitution and the law, I await your action.

Yesterday, and since the preparation of the foregoing message, official information was received by me that the latest decree of the Queen Regent of Spain directs General Blanco, in order to prepare and facilitate peace, to proclaim a suspension of hostilities, the duration and details of which have not yet been communicated to me.

This fact with every other pertinent consideration will, I am sure, have your just and careful attention in the solemn deliberations upon which you are about to enter. If this measure attains a successful result, then our aspirations as a Christian, peace-loving people will be realized. If it fails, it will be only another justification for our contemplated action.

16. McKinley's Instructions to the Peace Commission, September 1898

Washington, September 16, 1898

BY A PROTOCOL signed at Washington August 12, 1898, a copy of which is herewith inclosed, it was agreed that the United States and Spain would each appoint not more than five commissioners to treat of peace, and that the Commissioners so appointed should meet a Paris not later than October 1, 1898. . . .

By these instructions you will observe that the evacuation of Cuba, Porto Rico, and other Spanish Islands in the West Indies is treated as a military operation, and will, when carried into effect, leave the evacuated places in the military occupation of the United States. . . .

It will be proper to confirm these transactions by appropriate clauses in the treaty of peace.

Similar clauses will be inserted in respect to the island ceded to the United States in the Ladrones. This Government has selected the Island of Guam, and you are instructed to embody in the treaty of peace a proper stipulation of cession. . . .

In the correspondence leading up to the signature of that instrument you will observe that this Government waived, for the time being, the requirement of a pecuniary indemnity from Spain. This concession was made in the hope that Spain would thereby be enabled promptly to accept our terms. But if the Spanish Commissioners should, contrary to our just expectations, put forward and insist upon a claim for compensation for public property, you are instructed to put forward as a counterclaim a demand for an indemnity for the cost of the war. . . .

It is my earnest wish that the United States in making peace should follow the same high rule of conduct which guided it in facing war. It should be as scrupulous and magnanimous in the concluding settlement as it was just and humane in its original action. The luster and the moral strength attaching to a cause which can be confidently rested upon the considerate judgment of the world should not under any illusion of the hour be dimmed by ulterior designs which might tempt us into excessive demands or into an adventurous departure on untried paths. It is believed that the true glory and the enduring interests of the country will most surely be served if an unselfish duty conscientiously accepted and a signal triumph honorably achieved shall be crowned by such an example of moderation, restraint, and reason in victory as best comports with the traditions and character of our enlightened Republic.

Our aim in the adjustment of peace should be directed to lasting results and to the achievement of the common good under the demands of civilization, rather than to ambitious designs. The terms of the protocol were framed upon this consideration. The abandonment of the Western Hemisphere by Spain was an imperative necessity. In presenting that requirement, we only fulfilled a duty universally acknowledged. It involves no ungenerous reference to our recent foe, but simply a recognition of the plain teachings of history, to say that it was not compatible with the assurance of permanent peace on and near our own territory that the Spanish flag should remain on this side of the sea. This lesson of events and of reason left no alternative as to Cuba, Porto Rico, and the other islands belonging to Spain in this hemisphere.

The Philippines stand upon a different basis. It is none the less true, however, that, without any original thought of complete or even partial acquisition, the presence and success of our arms at Manila imposes upon us obligations which we can not disregard. The march of events rules and overrules human action. Avowing unreservedly the purpose which has animated all our effort, and still solicitous to adhere to it, we can not be unmindful that, without any desire or design on our part, the war has brought us new duties and responsibilities which we must meet and discharge as becomes a great nation on whose growth and career from the beginning the Ruler of Nations has plainly written the high command and pledge of civilization.

Incidental to our tenure in the Philippines is the commercial opportunity to which American statesmanship can not be indifferent. It is just to use every legitimate means for the enlargement of American trade; but we seek no advantages in the Orient which are not common to all. Asking only the open door for ourselves, we are ready to accord the open door to others. The commercial opportunity which is naturally and inevitable associated with this new opening depends less on large territorial possession than upon an adequate commercial basis and upon broad and equal privileges. . . .

In view of what has been stated, the United States can not accept less than the cession in full right and sovereignty of the island of Luzon. It is desirable, however, that the United States shall acquire the right of entry for vessels and merchandise belonging to citizens of the United States into such ports of the Philippines as are not ceded to the United States upon terms of equal favor with Spanish ships and merchandise, both in relation to port and customs charges and rates of trade and commerce, together with other rights of protection and trade accorded to citizens of one country within the territory of another. You are therefore instructed to demand such concession, agreeing on your part that Spain shall have similar rights as to her subjects and vessels in the ports of any territory in the Philippines ceded to the United States. . . .

17. Spain and U.S., Peace Treaty, December 1898

Signed at Paris 10 December 1898; ratifications exchanged 11 April 1899.

. . . *ARTICLE I.* Spain relinquishes all claim of sovereignty over and title to Cuba.

And as the island is, upon its evacuation by Spain, to be occupied by the United States, the United States will, so long as such occupation shall last, assume and discharge the obligations that may under international law result from the fact of its occupation, for the protection of life and property.

Article II. Spain cedes to the United States the island of Porto Rico and other islands now under Spanish sovereignty in the West Indies, and the island of Guam in the Marianas or Ladrones.

Article III. Spain cedes to the United States the archipelago known as the Philippine Islands. . . .

The United States will pay to Spain the sum of twenty million dollars ($20,000,000) within three months after the exchange of the ratifications of the present treaty.

Article IV. The United States will, for the term of ten years from the date of the exchange of the ratifications of the present treaty, admit Spanish ships and merchandise to the ports of the Philippine Islands on the same terms as ships and merchandise of the United States.

Article V. The United States will, upon the signature of the present treaty, send back to Spain, at its own cost, the Spanish soldiers taken as prisoners of war on the capture of Manila by the American forces. The arms of the soldiers in question shall be restored to them.

Spain will, upon the exchange of the ratifications of the present treaty, proceed to evacuate the Philippines, as well as the island of Guam, on terms similar to those agreed upon by the Commissioners appointed to arrange for the evacuation of Porto Rico and other islands in the West Indies, under the Protocol of August 12, 1898, which is to continue in force till its provisions are completely executed. . . .

Article X. The inhabitants of the territories over which Spain relinquishes or cedes her sovereignty shall be secured in the free exercise of their religion. . . .

18. Beveridge on Imperialism, 1900

Speech of Indiana Senator Albert J. Beveridge in the Senate, 9 January 1900.

MR. PRESIDENT, I address the Senate at this time because Senators and Members of the House on both sides have asked that I give to Congress and the country my observations in the Philippines and the far East, and the conclusions which those observations compel; . . .

Mr. President, the times call for candor. The Philippines are ours forever, "territory belonging to the United States," as the Constitution calls them. And just beyond the Philippines are China's illimitable markets. We will not retreat from either. We will not repudiate our duty in the archipelago. We will not abandon our opportunity in the Orient. We will not renounce our part in the mission of our race, trustee, under God, of the civilization of the world. And we will move forward to our work, not howling out regrets like slaves whipped to their burdens, but with gratitude for a task worthy of our strength, and thanksgiving to Almighty God that He has marked us as His chosen people, henceforth to lead in the regeneration of the world.

This island empire is the last land left in all the oceans. If it should prove a mistake to abandon it, the blunder once made would be irretrievable. If it proves a mistake to hold it, the error can be corrected when we will. Every other progressive nation stands ready to relieve us.

But to hold it will be no mistake. Our largest trade henceforth must be with Asia. The Pacific is our ocean. More and more Europe will manufacture the most it needs, secure from its colonies the most it consumes. Where shall we turn for consumers of our surplus? Geography answers the question. China is our natural customer. She is nearer to us than to England, Germany, or Russia, the commercial powers of the present and the future. They have moved nearer to China by securing permanent bases on her borders. The Philippines give us a base at the door of all the East.

Lines of navigation from our ports to the Orient and Australia; from the Isthmian Canal to Asia; from all Oriental ports to Australia, converge at the Philippines. They are a self-supporting, dividend-paying fleet, permanently anchored at a spot selected by the strategy of Providence, commanding the Pacific. And the Pacific is the ocean of the commerce of the future. Most future wars will be conflicts for commerce. The power that rules the Pacific, therefore, is the power that rules the world. And, with the Philippines, that power is and will forever be the American Republic. . . .

Nothing is so natural as trade with one's neighbors. The Philippines make us the nearest neighbors of all the East. Nothing is more natural than to trade with those you know. This is the philosophy of all advertising. The Philippines bring us permanently face to face with the most sought-for customers of the world. National prestige, national propinquity, these and commercial activity are the elements of commercial success. The Philippines give the first; the character of the American people supply the last. It is a providential conjunction of all the elements of trade, of duty, and of power. If we are willing to go to war rather than let England have a few feet of frozen Alaska, which affords no market and commands none, what should we not do rather than let England, Germany, Russia, or Japan have all the Philippines? And no man on the spot can fail to see that this would be their fate if we retired. . . .

Here, then, Senators, is the situation. Two years ago there was no land in all the world which we could occupy for any purpose. Our commerce was daily turning toward the Orient, and geography and trade developments made necessary our commercial empire over the Pacific. And in that ocean we had no commercial, naval, or military base. To-day we have one of the three great ocean possessions of the globe, located at the most commanding commercial, naval, and military points in the eastern seas, within hail of India, shoulder to shoulder with China, richer in its own resources than any equal body of land on the entire globe, and peopled by a race which civilization demands shall be improved. Shall we abandon it? That man little knows the common people of the Republic, little understands the instincts of our race, who thinks we will not hold it fast and hold it forever, administering just government by simplest methods. We may trick up devices to shift our burden and lessen our opportunity; they will avail us nothing but delay. We may tangle conditions by applying academic arrangements of self-government to a crude situation; their failure will drive us to our duty in the end. . . .

But, Senators, it would be better to abandon this combined garden and Gibraltar of the Pacific, and count our blood and treasure already spent a profitable loss, than to apply any academic arrangement of self-government to these children. They are not capable of self-government. How could they be? They are not of a self-governing race. They are Orientals, Malays, instructed by Spaniards in the latter's worst estate.

They know nothing of practical government except as they have witnessed the weak, corrupt, cruel, and capricious rule of Spain. What magic will anyone employ to dissolve in their minds and characters those impressions of governors and governed which three centuries of misrule has created? What alchemy will change the oriental quality of their blood and set the self-governing currents of the American pouring through their Malay veins? How shall they, in the twinkling of an eye, be exalted to the heights of self-governing peoples which required a thousand years for us to reach, Anglo-Saxon though we are? . . .

Mr. President, self-government and internal development have been the dominant notes of our first century; administration and the development of other lands will be the dominant notes of our second century. And administration is as high and holy a function as self-government, just as the care of a trust estate is as sacred an obligation as the management of our own concerns. Cain was the first to violate the divine law of human society which makes of us our brother's keeper. And administration of good government is the first lesson in self-government, that exalted estate toward which all civilization tends. . . .

The Declaration of Independence does not forbid us to do our part in the regeneration of the world. If it did, the Declaration would be wrong, just as the Articles of Confederation, drafted by the very same men who signed the Declaration, was found to be wrong. The Declaration has no application to the present situation. It was written by self-governing men for self-governing men. . . .

Senators in opposition are estopped from denying our constitutional power to govern the Philippines as circumstances may demand, for such power is admitted in the case of Florida, Louisiana, Alaska. How, then, is it denied in the Philippines? Is there a geographical interpretation to the Constitution? Do degrees of longitude fix constitutional limitations? Does a thousand miles of ocean diminish constitutional power more than a thousand miles of land? . . .

No; the oceans are not limitations of the power which the Constitution expressly gives Congress to govern all territory the nation may acquire. The Constitution declares that "Congress shall have power to dispose of and make all needful rules and regulations respecting the territory belonging to the United States." Not the Northwest Territory only; not Louisiana or Florida only; not territory on this continent only, but any territory anywhere belonging to the nation. The founders of the nation were not provincial. Theirs was the geography of the world. They were soldiers as well as landsmen, and they knew that where our ships should go our flag might follow. They had the logic of progress, and they knew that the Republic they were planting must, in obedience to the laws of our expanding race, necessarily develop into the greater Republic which the world beholds to-day, and into the still mightier Republic which the world will finally acknowledge as the arbiter, under God, of the destinies of mankind. And so our fathers wrote into the Constitution these words of growth, of expansion, of empire, if you will, unlimited by geography or climate or by anything but the vitality and possibilities of the American people: "Congress shall have power to dispose of and make all needful rules and regulations respecting the territory belonging to the United States. . . ."

Mr. President, this question is deeper than any question of party politics; deeper than any question of the isolated policy of our country even; deeper even than any question of constitutional power. It is elemental. It is racial. God has not been preparing the English-speaking and Teutonic peoples for a thousand years for nothing but vain and idle self-contemplation and self-admiration. No! He has made us the master organizers of the world to establish system where chaos reigns. He has given us the spirit of progress to overwhelm the forces of reaction throughout the earth. He has made us adepts in government that we may administer government among savage and senile peoples. Were it not for such a force as this the world would relapse into barbarism and night. And of all our race He has marked the American people as His chosen nation to finally lead in the regeneration of the world. This is the divine mission of America, and it holds for us all the profit, all the glory, all the happiness possible to man. We are trustees of the world's progress, guardians of its righteous peace. The judgment of the Master is upon us: "Ye have been faithful over a few things; I will make you ruler over many things."

What shall history say of us? Shall it say that we renounced that holy trust, left the savage to his base condition, the wilderness to the reign of waste, deserted duty, abandoned glory, forget our sordid profit even, because we feared our strength and read the charter of our powers with the doubter's eye and the quibbler's mind? Shall it say that, called by events to captain and command the proudest, ablest, purest race of history in history's noblest work, we declined that great commission? Our fathers would not have had it so. No! They founded no paralytic government, incapable of the simplest acts of administration. They planted no sluggard people, passive while the world's work calls them. They established no reactionary nation. They unfurled no retreating flag. . . .

Blind indeed is he who sees not the hand of God in events so vast, so harmonious, so benign. Reactionary indeed is the mind that perceives not that this vital people is the strongest of the saving forces of the world; that our place, therefore, is at the head of the constructing and redeeming nations of the earth; and that to stand aside while events march on is a surrender of our interests, a betrayal of our duty as blind as it is base. Craven indeed is the heart that fears to perform a work so golden and so noble; that dares not win a glory so immortal. . . .

Mr. President and Senators, adopt the resolution offered, that peace may quickly come and that we may begin our saving, regenerating, and uplifting work. . . . Reject it, and the world, history, and the American people will know where to forever fix the awful responsibility for the consequences that will surely follow such failure to do our manifest duty. How dare we delay when our soldiers' blood is flowing? [Applause in the galleries]. . . .

19. Platform of the U.S. Anti-Imperialist League, 1899

Adopted at Chicago, 18 October 1899.

WE HOLD that the policy known as imperialism is hostile to liberty and tends toward militarism, an evil from which it has been our glory to be free. We regret that it has become necessary in the land of Washington and

Lincoln to reaffirm that all men, of whatever race or color, are entitled to life, liberty, and the pursuit of happiness. We maintain that governments derive their just powers from the consent of the governed. We insist that the subjugation of any people is "criminal aggression" and open disloyalty to the distinctive principles of our government.

We earnestly condemn the policy of the present National Administration in the Philippines. It seeks to extinguish the spirit of 1776 in those islands. We deplore the sacrifice of our soldiers and sailors, whose bravery deserves admiration even in an unjust war. We denounce the slaughter of the Filipinos as a needless horror. We protest against the extension of American sovereignty by Spanish methods.

We demand the immediate cessation of the war against liberty, begun by Spain and continued by us. We urge that Congress be promptly convened to announce to the Filipinos our purpose to concede to them the independence for which they have so long fought and which of right is theirs.

The United States have always protested against the doctrine of international law which permits the subjugation of the weak by the strong. A self-governing state cannot accept sovereignty over an unwilling people. The United States cannot act upon the ancient heresy that might makes right.

Imperialists assume that with the destruction of self-government in the Philippines by American hands, all opposition here will cease. This is a grievous error. Much as we abhor the war of "criminal aggression" in the Philippines, greatly as we regret the blood of the Filipinos is on American hands, we more deeply resent the betrayal of American institutions at home. The real firing line is not in the suburbs of Manila. The foe is of our own household. The attempt of 1861 was to divide the country. That of 1899 is to destroy its fundamental principles and noblest ideals.

Whether the ruthless slaughter of the Filipinos shall end next month or next year is but an incident in a contest that must go on until the Declaration of Independence and the Constitution of the United States are rescued from the hands of their betrayers. Those who dispute about standards of value while the Republic is undermined will be listened to as little as those who would wrangle about the small economies of the household while the house is on fire. The training of a great people for a century, the aspiration for liberty of a vast immigration are forces that will hurl aside those who in the delirium of conquest seek to destroy the character of our institutions.

We deny that the obligation of all citizens to support their Government in times of grave National peril applies to the present situation. If an Administration may with impunity ignore the issues upon which it was chosen, deliberately create a condition of war anywhere on the face of the globe, debauch the civil service for spoils to promote the adventure, organize a truth-suppressing censorship and demand of all citizens a suspension of judgment and their unanimous support while it chooses to continue the fighting, representative government itself is imperiled.

We propose to contribute to the defeat of any person or party that stands for the forcible subjugation of any people. We shall oppose for reelection all who in the White House or in Congress betray American liberty in pursuit of un-American gains. We still hope that both of our great political parties will support and defend the Declaration of Independence in the closing campaign of the century.

We hold, with Abraham Lincoln, that "no man is good enough to govern another man without that man's consent. When the white man governs himself, that is self-government, but when he governs himself and also governs another man, that is more than self-government — that is despotism." "Our reliance is in the love of liberty which God has planted in us. Our defense is in the spirit which prizes liberty as the heritage of all men in all lands. Those who deny freedom to others deserve it not for themselves, and under a just God cannot long retain it."

We cordially invite the cooperation of all men and women who remain loyal to the Declaration of Independence and the Constitution of the United States.

20. Walker Commission's Canal Report, 1901

Conclusions

THE INVESTIGATIONS of this Commission have shown that the selection of "the most feasible and practicable route" for an isthmian canal must be made between the Nicaragua and Panama locations. Furthermore, the complete problem involves both the sea-level plan of canal and that with locks. The Panama route alone is feasible for a sea-level canal, although both are entirely practicable and feasible for a canal with locks. The time required to complete a sea-level canal on the Panama route, probably more than twice that needed to build a canal with locks, excludes it from favorable consideration aside from other serious features of its construction. It is the conclusion of this Commission, therefore, that a plan of canal with locks should be adopted. . . .

The existence of a harbor at each terminus of the Panama route, and a line of railroad across the isthmus, will make it practicable to commence work there, after the concessions are acquired, as soon as the necessary plant can be collected and put in place, and the working force organized. This period of preparation is estimated at one year. In Nicaragua this period is estimated at two years, so as to include also the construction of working harbors and terminal and railroad facilities.

The work of excavation on the Nicaragua route is distributed; it is heaviest near Conchuda, at Tamborcito, and in the divide west of the lake. On the Panama route it is largely concentrated in the Culebra and Emperador cuts, which are practically one. As a rule distributed work affords a greater number of available points of attack, contributing to a quicker completion; but in either of these cases such difficulties as may exist can be successfully met with suitable organization and efficient appliances. . . .

Except for the items of risks and delays, the time required to pass through the canals need be taken into account only as an element in the time required by vessels to make their voyages between terminal ports. Compared on this basis, the Nicaragua route is the more advantageous for all transisthmian commerce except that originating or ending on the west coast of South America. For the commerce in which the United States is most interested, that between our Pacific ports and Atlantic ports, European and American, the Nicaragua route is shorter by about one day. The same advantage exists between our Atlantic ports and the Orient. For our Gulf ports the advantage of the Nicaragua route is nearly two days. For commerce between North Atlantic ports and the west coast of South America the Panama route is shorter by about two days. Between Gulf ports and the west coast of South America the saving is about one day. . . .

The Nicaragua route lies in a region of sparse population and not in a pathway of much trade or movement of people; conditions productive of much sickness do not exist. On the other hand, a considerable population has long existed on the Panama route and it lies on a pathway of comparatively large trade along which currents of moving people from infected places sometimes converge, thus creating conditions favorable to epidemics. Existing conditions indicate hygienic advantages for the Nicaragua route, although it is probable that no less effective sanitary measures must be taken during construction in the one case than in the other. . . .

The Republics of Nicaragua and Costa Rica are untrammeled by any existing concessions or treaty obligations and are free to grant to the United States the rights necessary for the attainment of these ends; and in December, 1900, demonstrated their willingness to have their territory so occupied by the United States by executing protocols by which it was agreed that they would enter into negotiations to settle in detail the plan and agreements necessary to accomplish the construction and provide for the ownership of the proposed canal whenever the President of the United States is authorized by law to acquire the necessary control and authority.

The Government of Colombia, on the contrary, in whose territory the Panama route lies, has granted concessions which belong to or are controlled by the New Panama Canal Company and have many years to run. These concessions, limited in time and defective in other ways, would not be adequate authority for the purposes of the United States, but while they exist Colombia is not free to treat with this Government. If the Panama route is selected these concessions must be removed in order that the two Republics may enter into a treaty to enable the United States to acquire the control upon the isthmus that will be necessary and to fix the consideration. . . .

After considering all the facts developed by the investigations made by the Commission and the actual situation as it now stands, and having in view the terms offered by the new Panama Canal Company, this Commission is of the opinion that "the most practicable and feasible route" for an isthmian canal, to be "under the control, management, and ownership of the United States," is that known as the Nicaragua route.

J. G. Walker,
Rear-Admiral, United States Navy

21. Great Britain and U.S., Second Hay-Pauncefote Treaty, 1901

Signed at Washington, 18 November 1901; ratifications exchanged 21 February 1902.

... ARTICLE I. The High Contracting Parties agree that the present Treaty shall supersede the afore-mentioned Convention of the 19th April, 1850.

Article II. It is agreed that the canal may be constructed under the auspices of the Government of the United States, either directly at its own cost, or by gift or loan of money to individuals or Corporations, or through subscription to or purchase of stock or shares, and that, subject to the provisions of the present Treaty, the said Government shall have and enjoy all the rights incident to such construction, as well as the exclusive right of providing for the regulation and management of the canal.

Article III. The United States adopts, as the basis of the neutralization of such ship canal, the following Rules, substantially as embodied in the Convention of Constantinople, signed the 28th October, 1888, for the free navigation of the Suez Canal, that is to say:

1. The canal shall be free and open to the vessels of commerce and of war of all nations observing these Rules, on terms of entire equality, so that there shall be no discrimination against any such nation, or its citizens or subjects, in respect of the conditions or charges of traffic, or otherwise. Such conditions and charges of traffic shall be just and equitable.

2. The canal shall never be blockaded, nor shall any right of war be exercised nor any act of hostility be committed within it. The United States, however, shall be at liberty to maintain such military police along the canal as may be necessary to protect it against lawlessness and disorder.

3. Vessels of war of a belligerent shall not revictual nor take any stores in the canal except so far as may be strictly necessary; and the transit of such vessels through the canal shall be effected with the least possible delay in accordance with the Regulations in force, and with only such intermission as may result from the necessities of the service.

Prizes shall be in all respects subject to the same Rules as vessels of war of the belligerents.

4. No belligerent shall embark or disembark troops, munitions of war, or warlike materials in the canal, except in case of accidental hindrance of the transit, and in such case the transit shall be resumed with all possible dispatch.

5. The provisions of this Article shall apply to waters adjacent to the canal, within 3 marine miles of either end. Vessels of war of a belligerent shall not remain in such waters longer than twenty-four hours at any one time, except in case of distress, and in such case shall depart as soon as possible; but a vessel of war of one belligerent shall not depart within twenty-four hours from the departure of a vessel of war of the other belligerent.

6. The plant, establishments, buildings, and all works necessary to the construction, maintenance, and operation of the canal shall be deemed to be part thereof, for the purposes of this Treaty, and in time of war, as in time of peace, shall enjoy complete immunity from attack or injury by belligerents, and from acts calculated to impair their usefulness as part of the canal. ...

22. Reyes to Hay on the U.S. in Panama, December 1903

Rafael Reyes, Colombian Minister in U.S., to Secretary of State John Hay.

Legation of Colombia, Washington, December 23, 1903

THE GOVERNMENT and people of Colombia consider themselves aggrieved by that of the United States in that they are convinced that the course followed by its administration, in relation to the events that have developed and recently been accomplished at Panama, have worked deep injury to their interests. . . .

It is proper to observe that under our constitution the Congress is the principal guardian, defender, and interpreter of our laws. And it can not be denied by anyone, I take it, that the Hay-Herran convention provides for the execution of public works on a vast scale and for the occupancy in perpetuity of a portion of the territory of Colombia, the occupant being not a juridical person whose acts were to be governed by the civil law and the Colombian code, but rather a sovereign political entity, all of which would have given occasion for frequent conflicts, since there would have been a coexistence in Panama of two public powers, the one national, the other foreign.

Hence the earnest efforts evinced by the Senate in ascertaining whether the American Government would agree to accept certain amendments tending especially to avoid as far as practicable any restriction in the treaty of the jurisdiction of the nation within its own territory. There is abundant evidence of the efforts of the Senate in that direction, and I firmly believe that it would have approved the convention with amendments that would probably have been acceptable to the United States had not the American minister at Bogotá repeatedly declared in the most positive manner that his Government would reject any amendment that might be offered. . . .

All governments being, as is well known, bound to respect the rights born of the independence and sovereignty of nations, the premature recognition by the United States of the province of Panama, rising in arms to detach itself from the country of which it is a part, while it is a matter of public knowledge that the mother country commands sufficient forces to subdue it, constitutes, according to the most ancient and modern authorities on international law, not only a grave offense to Colombia, but also a formal attack upon her wealth.

For, as the territory forms the most important part of the national wealth, its dismemberment impairs the revenues applied to the discharge of corporate obligations among which are foreign debts and those enterprises entailed on the insurgent province, from which Colombia derives a considerable income.

If there be an end and eternal and immutable principles in right, that right of Colombia has been injured by the United States by an incredible transgression of the limits set by equity and justice. . . .

It will be well to say that before the news was divulged that a revolution was about to break out on the Isthmus, American cruisers which reached their destination precisely on the eve of the movement were plowing the waters of the Atlantic and Pacific Oceans. Cablegrams that are given public circulation in an official document show that two days before the movement the Secretary of the Navy issued orders to those cruisers not to permit the landing of troops of the Government of Colombia on Panama's territory.

A military officer of the Government of the United States stopped the railway from carrying to Panama, as it was under obligations to do, a battalion that had just arrived at Colon from Bogotá at the very time when its arrival in that city would have impeded or suppressed any revolutionary attempt. A few days thereafter, when my Government intrusted me with the duty of leading the army that was to embark at Puerto Colombia to go and restore order on the Isthmus, being unacquainted except in an imperfect manner with the attitude assumed by the American war ships, I had the honor to address a note on the subject to Vice Admiral Coghlan, and in his reply, which was not delayed, he tells me that—

his present orders are to prevent the landing of soldiers with hostile intent within the boundary of the State of Panama. . . .

In the note of Mr. Seward, Secretary of State, to Mr. Adams, United States minister, in 1861, this doctrine is found:

We freely admit that a nation may, and even ought, to recognize a new State which has absolutely and beyond question effected its independence, and permanently established its sovereignty; and that a recognition in such a case affords no just cause of offense to the government of the country from which the new State has so detached itself. On the other hand, we insist that a nation that recognizes a revolutionary State, with a view to aid its effecting its sovereignty and independence, commits a great wrong against the nation whose integrity is thus invaded, and makes itself responsible for a just and ample redress. (Foreign Relations, 1861, pp. 76–7.)

damages, until the said party considering itself offended shall have laid before the other a statement of such injuries or damages, verified by competent proofs, demanding justice and satisfaction, and the same shall have been denied, in violation of the laws and of international right.

Since the aforesaid treaty is the law which governs between the two countries, and now that the weakness and ruin of my country, after three years of civil war scarcely at an end, and in which her bravest sons were lost by thousands, place her in the unhappy position of asking justice of the Government of your excellency, I propose that the claims which I make in the present note on account of the violation of the aforesaid treaty, and all other claims which may hereafter be made in connection with the events of Panama, be submitted to the Arbitration Tribunal of The Hague. . . .

23. Hay to Reyes on Panama, January 1904

Washington, January 5, 1904

THE GOVERNMENT of the United States has carefully considered the grave complaints so ably set forth in the "statement of grievances" presented on behalf of the Government and people of Colombia, with your note of the 23d ultimo. . . .

On June 28, 1902, the President of the United States gave his approval to the act now commonly referred to as the Spooner Act, to provide for the construction of the interoceanic canal. Following the report of the Isthmian Canal Commission, which confirmed the opinion expressed by the Colombian Government, it embodied the formal decision of the United States in favor of the Panama route. It accordingly authorized the President to acquire, at a cost not exceeding $40,000,000, "the rights, privileges, franchises, concessions," and other property of the New Panama Canal Company, including its interest in the Panama Railroad Company, and to obtain from Colombia on such terms as he might deem reasonable perpetual control for the purposes of the canal of a strip of land not less than six miles wide, such control to include jurisdiction to make and, through such tribunals as might be agreed on, to enforce such police and sanitary rules and regulations as should be necessary to the preservation of order and of the public health.

The act also provided, in a clause to which your statement adverts, that, in case the President should "be unable to obtain for the United States a satisfactory title to the property of the New Panama Canal Company and the control of the necessary territory of the Republic of Colombia," together with the "rights" mentioned in connection therewith, "within a reasonable time and upon reasonable terms," he should turn to Nicaragua. But this provision, while it indicated that the construction of the canal was not wholly to depend upon the success or failure to make reasonable terms with Colombia and the canal company, by no means implied that the question of routes was a matter of indifference.

In the nature of things it could not be so. Not only was the work to endure for all time, but its prompt construction was felt to be of vast importance; and it could not be a matter of less concern to the United States than to Colombia that this Government might possibly be forced to adopt a route which would, as the Colombian minister had observed —

be longer, more expensive, both in construction and maintenance, and less adapted to the commerce of the world than the short and half-finished canal available at Panama. . . .

After the Spooner Act was approved, negotiations were duly initiated by Colombia. They resulted on January 22, 1903, in the conclusion of the Hay-Herran convention. By this convention every reasonable desire of the Colombian Government was believed to be gratified. . . .

Some time after the convention was signed the Government of the United States learned, to its utter surprise, that the Government of Colombia was taking with the canal company the position that a further permission, in addition to that contained in the convention, was necessary to the transfer of its concessions and those of the Panama Railroad Company, respectively, to the United States, and that, as a preliminary to this permission, the companies must enter into agreements with Colombia for the cancellation of all her obligations to either of them under the concession. This proceeding seemed all the more singular in the light of the negotiations between the two Governments. The terms in which the convention authorized the New Panama Canal Company to sell and transfer its "rights, privileges, properties, and concessions" to the United States were the same as those embodied in the original draft of a treaty presented to this Government by the Colombian minister on March 31, 1902.

No change in this particular was ever suggested by Colombia, in all the discussions that followed, until November 11, 1902. On that day the Colombian minister presented a memorandum in which it was proposed that the authorization should be so modified that "the permission accorded by Colombia to the canal and the railroad companies to transfer their rights to the United States" should "be regulated by a previous special arrangement entered into by Colombia." To this proposal this department answered that "the United States considers this suggestion wholly inadmissible." The proposition was then abandoned by Colombia, and the convention was nearly three months later signed without any modification of the absolute authorization to sell. . . .

The explanations put forward in Colombia's "statement of grievances" merely repeat the pleas devised at the Colombian capital. The sudden discovery that the terms of the convention, as proposed and signed by the Colombian Government, involved a violation of the Colombian constitution, because it required a cession to the United States of the "sovereignty" which is expressly recognized and confirmed, could be received by this Government only with the utmost surprise. Nevertheless, the Colombian Senate unanimously rejected the convention.

This fact was communicated to the department by Doctor Herran on the 22d of August last, by means of a copy of a cablegram from his Government. In that telegram the "impairment" of Colombian "sovereignty" was mentioned as one of the "reasons advanced in debate" for the Senate's action; but joined with it there was another reason, with which the department had long been familiar, namely, the "absence" of a "previous agreement" of the companies with the Colombian Government for the transfer of their privileges. To these reasons there was added a reference to the representations made by Mr. Beaupré; but it was said to be "probable" that the Colombian Congress would "provide bases" for "reopening negotiations. . . ."

Advices came to this Government, not only through the press but also through its own officials, of the existence of dangerous conditions on the Isthmus, as well as in the adjacent States whose interests were menaced. Disorders in that quarter were not new. In the summer of 1902, as well as in that of 1901, this Government had been obliged by its forces to maintain order on the transit route, and it took steps, as it had done on previous occasions, to perform a similar duty should the necessity arise. The form the trouble might take could not be foreseen, but it was important to guard against any destructive effects.

The reasonableness of these precautions soon became evident. The people of Panama rose against an act of the Government at Bogotá that threatened their most vital interests with destruction and the interests of the whole world with grave injury. The movement assumed the form of a declaration of independence. The avowed object of this momentous step was to secure the construction of the interoceanic canal. It was inspired by the desire of the people at once to safeguard their own interests and at the same time to assure the dedication of the Isthmus to the use for which Providence seemed to have designed it. . . .

By the declaration of independence of the Republic of Panama a new situation was created. On the one hand stood the Government of Colombia invoking in the name of the treaty of 1846 the aid of this Government in its efforts to suppress the revolution; on the other hand stood the Republic of Panama that had come into being in order that the great design of that treaty might not be forever frustrated, but might be fulfilled. The Isthmus was threatened with desolation by another civil war, nor were the rights and interests of the United States alone at stake, the interests of the whole civilized world were involved. The Republic of Panama stood for those interests; the Government of Colombia opposed them. Compelled to choose between these two alternatives, the Government of the United States, in no wise responsible for the situation that had arisen, did not hesitate. It recognized the independence of the Republic of Panama, and upon its judgment and action in the emergency the powers of the world have set the seal of their approval.

In recognizing the independence of the Republic of Panama the United States necessarily assumed toward that Republic the obligations of the treaty of 1846. Intended, as the treaty was, to assure the protection of the sovereign of the Isthmus, whether the government of that sovereign ruled from Bogotá or from Panama, the Republic of Panama, as the successor in sovereignty of Colombia, became entitled to the rights and subject to the obligations of the treaty. . . .

Under all the circumstances the department is unable to regard the complaints of Colombia against this Government, set forth in the "Statement of grievances," as having any valid foundation. The responsibility lies at Colombia's own door rather than at that of the United States. This Government, however, recognizes the fact that Colombia has, as she affirms, suffered an appreciable loss. This Government has no desire to increase or accentuate her misfortunes, but is willing to do all that lies in its power to ameliorate her lot. The Government of the United States, in common with the whole civilized world, shares in a sentiment of sorrow over the unfortunate conditions which have long existed in the Republic of Colombia by reason of the factional and fratricidal wars which have desolated her fields, ruined her industries, and impoverished her people.

Entertaining these feelings, the Government of the United States would gladly exercise its good offices with the Republic of Panama, with a view to bring about some arrangement on a fair and equitable basis. For the acceptance of your proposal of a resort to The Hague tribunal, this Government perceives no occasion. . . .

24. Platt Amendment, 1901

Provisions concerning Cuba added to the U.S. Army Appropriations Bill, 2 March 1901.

... PROVIDED FURTHER, That in fulfillment of the declaration contained in the joint resolution approved April twentieth, eighteen hundred and ninety-eight, entitled, "For the recognition of the independence of the people of Cuba, demanding that the Government of Spain relinquish its authority and government in the island of Cuba, and to withdraw its land and naval forces from Cuba and Cuban waters, and directing the President of the United States to use the land and naval forces of the United States to carry these resolutions into effect," the President is hereby authorized to "leave the government and control of the island of Cuba to its people" so soon as a government shall have been established in said island under a constitution which, either as a part thereof or in an ordinance appended thereto, shall define the future relations of the United States with Cuba, substantially as follows:

I. That the government of Cuba shall never enter into any treaty or other compact with any foreign power or powers which will impair or tend to impair the independence of Cuba, nor in any manner authorize or permit any foreign power or powers to obtain by colonization or for military or naval purposes or otherwise, lodgment in or control over any portion of said island.

II. That said government shall not assume or contract any public debt, to pay the interest upon which, and to make reasonable sinking fund provision for the ultimate discharge of which, the ordinary revenues of the island, after defraying the current expenses of government shall be inadequate.

III. That the government of Cuba consents that the United States may exercise the right to intervene for the preservation of Cuban independence, the maintenance of a government adequate for the protection of life, property, and individual liberty, and for discharging the obligations with respect to Cuba imposed by the treaty of Paris on the United States, now to be assumed and undertaken by the government of Cuba.

IV. That all Acts of the United States in Cuba during its military occupancy thereof are ratified and validated, and all lawful rights acquired thereunder shall be maintained and protected.

V. That the government of Cuba will execute, and as far as necessary extend, the plans already devised or other plans to be mutually agreed upon, for the sanitation of the cities of the island, to the end that a recurrence of epidemic and infectious diseases may be prevented, thereby assuring protection to the people and commerce of Cuba, as well as to the commerce of the southern ports of the United States and the people residing therein.

VI. That the Isle of Pines shall be omitted from the proposed constitutional boundaries of Cuba, the title thereto being left to future adjustment by treaty.

VII. That to enable the United States to maintain the independence of Cuba, and to protect the people thereof, as well as for its own defense, the government of Cuba will sell or lease to the United States lands necessary for coaling or naval stations at certain specified points, to be agreed upon with the President of the United States.

VIII. That by way of further assurance the government of Cuba will embody the foregoing provisions in a permanent treaty with the United States.

25. T. Roosevelt's Corollary to the Monroe Doctrine, December 1904

President Roosevelt's Annual Message to Congress, 6 December 1904.

... IT IS NOT TRUE that the United States feels any land hunger or entertains any projects as regards the other nations of the Western Hemisphere save such as are for their welfare. All that this country desires is to see the neighboring countries stable, orderly, and prosperous. Any country whose people conduct themselves well can count upon our hearty friendship. If a nation shows that it knows how to act with reasonable efficiency and decency in social and political matters, if it keeps order and pays its obligations, it need fear no interference from the United States. Chronic wrongdoing, or an impotence which results in a general loosening of the ties of civilized society, may in America, as elsewhere, ultimately require intervention by some civilized nation, and in the Western Hemisphere the adherence of the United States to the Monroe Doctrine may force the United States, however reluctantly, in flagrant cases of such wrongdoing or impotence, to the exercise of an international police power. If every country washed by the Caribbean Sea would show the progress in stable and just civilization which with the aid of the Platt amendment Cuba has shown since our troops left the island, and which so many of the republics in both Americas are constantly and brilliantly showing, all question of interference by this Nation with their affairs would be at an end. Our interests and those of our southern neighbors are in reality identical. They have great natural riches, and if within their borders the reign of law and justice obtains, prosperity is sure to come to them. While they thus obey the primary laws of civilized society they may rest assured that they will be treated by us in a spirit of cordial and helpful sympathy. We would interfere with them only in the last resort, and then only if it became evident that their inability or unwillingness to do justice at home and abroad had violated the rights of the United States or had invited foreign aggression to the detriment of the entire body of American nations. It is a mere truism to say that every nation, whether in America or anywhere else, which desires to maintain its freedom, its independence, must ultimately realize that the right of such independence can not be separated from the responsibility of making good use of it. ...

26. Dawson to Hay on Santo Domingo, 1905

U.S. diplomat Thomas C. Dawson to Secretary of State John Hay.

Santo Domingo, January 2, 1905

I HAVE the honor to confirm your telegram, as follows:

Washington, December 30, 1904

Confidential. You will sound the President of Santo Domingo, discreetly but earnestly and in a perfectly friendly spirit, touching the disquieting situation which is developing owing to the pressure of other governments having arbitral awards in their favor and who regard our award as conflicting with their rights. Already one European Government strongly intimates that it may resort to occupation of some Dominican customs ports to secure its own payment. There appears to be a concert among them. You will ascertain whether the Government of Santo Domingo would be disposed to request the United States to take charge of the collection of duties and effect an equitable distribution of the assigned quotas among the Dominican Government and the several claimants. We have grounds to think that such arrangement would satisfy the other powers, besides serving as a practical guaranty of the peace of Santo Domingo from external influence or internal disturbance.

and to say that I immediately called upon President Morales.

We entered upon a full and friendly discussion of the international relations and internal politics of this country as affected by its financial obligations, in the course of which I did not disguise from him my conviction that the European creditors would wait no longer for their money. He frankly answered that such was his own conviction and that he was daily expecting a European demand, backed by a war vessel, and a demand from me for the four northern ports under the Improvement award. He clearly realizes that the European creditors will accept no guaranty he can offer, and each would insist on having the full annual amount provided for its own protocol, leaving him nothing, or next to nothing, to run the administration. He said that personally he had long been of the opinion that the best solution was for the United States to take charge of the collection of the revenues, guaranteeing to the Dominican Government enough to live on and arranging with the creditors.

I asked him if he was prepared to make, in the name of his government, a request that my government undertake this task. He answered that he was almost ready; that the opposition to American intervention within his cabinet and among his prominent supporters had much diminished in the last two weeks; Minister Velasquez had despaired of carrying out his own plan; the arrangement at Monte Christi was not working well; it had been proposed in the last cabinet meeting to ask the United States to take charge of that port.

I told him I could not recommend such a proposition to my government; that if we were forced to ask for more ports under the award it would be for Sanchez and Samana, as well as Monte Christi; that I appreciated how great were the political difficulties he was struggling against — difficulties which arose from the deeply grounded prejudice against any sort of American intervention existing among some of his supporters — but that it was for him and not me to say if he had succeeded in removing that prejudice, or if the time had come for him to act in spite of it.

He then asked me to make a written proposition, stating the proportion or amount that I would recommend to be allowed for administrative expenses of the Dominican Government. I begged him to excuse me from doing so, and suggested that the first step had better be a proposition from the Dominican Government, embodying the principle of American collection on a basis that seemed to him just and practicable. He agreed, and said that his own idea was 40 per cent for the creditors and 60 per cent to the Dominican Government.

I expressed some doubts as to whether my government could reach an arrangement with the creditors if limited to such a sum, but agreed to submit it as a tentative proposition as soon as his doubts as to the attitude of his anti-American supporters should be cleared up. Thereupon he asked me to talk with Joubert and Velasquez, with a view to emphasizing the impression already made by the former on the latter's mind. The President said that if Velasquez could be brought to agree, Vasquez and Caceres would follow. Joubert had already half convinced him that the American Government had no selfish or ulterior views in this matter, and an interview with me would tend to convince him further that an American intervention in the custom-houses would be conducted in a manner that would offend Dominican pride as little as possible and not destroy the prerogatives of the office of minister of finance.

Accordingly, in the last three days, I have had several interviews with the President, Joubert, Velasquez, and Sanchez, and this morning I felt justified in sending you the telegram which I hereby confirm:

Santo Domingo, January 2, 1905

Dominican President disposed to request United States take charge of collections all customs on the following conditions: Distribute 40 per cent annual receipts among all creditors — remaining 60 to the Dominican Government.

In the course of these interviews I have been obliged to reject several suggestions which seemed to be inadmissible. The first was that I should commit myself personally in favor of the proposed division of the revenues — 40 per cent and 60 per cent. I remain free to suggest, either personally or officially, if I should be so instructed, either a different percentage or minimum sums for creditors and government, respectively, with a percentage division of the excess. . . .

27. U.S. Chinese Exclusion Act, 1882

Act of Congress, 6 May 1882.

BE IT enacted by the Senate and House of Representatives of the United States of America in Congress assembled, That from and after the expiration of ninety days next after the passage of this act, and until the expiration of ten years next after the passage of this act, the coming of Chinese laborers to the United States be, and the same is hereby, suspended; and during such suspension it shall not be lawful for any Chinese laborer to come, or, having so come after the expiration of said ninety days, to remain within the United States.

Sec. 2. That the master of any vessel who shall knowingly bring within the United States on such vessel, and land or permit to be landed, any Chinese laborer, from any foreign port or place, shall be deemed guilty of a misdemeanor, and on conviction thereof shall be punished by a fine of not more than five hundred dollars for each and every such Chinese laborer so brought, and may be also imprisoned for a term not exceeding one year.

Sec. 3. That the two foregoing sections shall not apply to Chinese laborers who were in the United States on the seventeenth day of November, eighteen hundred and eighty, or who shall have come into the same before the expiration of ninety days next after the passage of this act. . . .

Sec. 13. That this act shall not apply to diplomatic and other officers of the Chinese Government traveling upon the business of that government, whose credentials shall be taken as equivalent to the certificate in this act mentioned, and shall exempt them and their body and household servants from the provisions of this act as to other Chinese persons.

Sec. 14. That hereafter no State court or court of the United States shall admit Chinese to citizenship; and all laws in conflict with this act are hereby repealed.

Sec. 15. That the words "Chinese laborers," wherever used in this act, shall be construed to mean both skilled and unskilled laborers and Chinese employed in mining.

28. Denby to Sherman on the U.S. in China, 1898

Charles Denby, U.S. Minister in China, to Secretary of State John Sherman.

January 31, 1898

... IN THE MIDST of these events it may not be improper to consider our own position regarding China. I am very thoroughly aware that since Washington's Farewell Address was uttered we have been, what may be called, innately conservative on the question of interfering in the affairs of foreign powers. He would be a bold man who in the United States would advocate political entanglement in the affairs of Europe, Asia, or Africa. That our abnegation tends to weaken our influence and to make us a quantité négligeable is undoubtedly true, but it has its compensations in the enforcement of the Monroe Doctrine.

Still, while preserving all the sanctity of the "Farewell Address," it is worth enquiring whether there is not some middle ground on which we may stand with advantage. We have fifteen hundred missionaries here. Should China be partitioned among the European powers it is quite certain that the work of these missionaries would be impeded. From any country under Russian control they would be excluded. In any country under French control they would be impeded and embarrassed. These missionaries are entitled to our protection just the same as mercantile people are.

Partition would tend to destroy our markets. The Pacific Ocean is destined to bear on its bosom a larger commerce than the Atlantic. As the countries in the Far East and Australia develop their resources the commerce of the United States with them will assume proportions greater in their directness and scope, than our commerce with Europe.

In these countries we are destined to find our best customers for manufactured, as well as natural, and agricultural products.

Here are diverse and varied sources of interest in the Far East which directly touch us.

Having such interests in China, is it our duty to remain mute should her autonomy be attacked? Is it exactly right to announce, as was lately done in Reuter's telegrams, that we take no interest in territorial questions? We have a certain moral interest in the affairs of the world, and, in my opinion, that influence should be exacted in all cases in which our interests demand its exercise. We should urge on China the reform of all evils in her government which touch American interests, and the adoption of vigorous measures in the line of material progress. This policy will to her be the surest pathway to independence and prosperity. I have persistently urged this policy. We should not hesitate, also, I think, to announce our disapproval of acts of brazen wrong, and spoliation, perpetrated by other nations towards China, — should any such occur.

In this connection it may not be improper to cite the following extract from the first Article of the Treaty of 1858 between the United States and China: "And if any other nation should act unjustly or oppressively the United States will exert their good offices on being informed of the case, to bring about an amicable arrangement of the question thus showing their friendly feelings. . . ."

29. Hay's "Open Door" Note, 1899

Secretary of State John Hay to Andrew D. White, U.S. Ambassador in Germany.

Department of State, Washington, September 6, 1899

AT THE TIME when the Government of the United States was informed by that of Germany that it had leased from His Majesty the Emperor of China the port of Kiao-chao and the adjacent territory in the province of Shantung, assurances were given to the ambassador of the United States at Berlin by the Imperial German minister for foreign affairs that the rights and privileges insured by treaties with China to citizens of the United States would not thereby suffer or be in anywise impaired within the area over which Germany had thus obtained control.

More recently, however, the British Government recognized by a formal agreement with Germany the exclusive right of the latter country to enjoy in said leased area and the contiguous "sphere of influence or interest" certain privileges, more especially those relating to railroads and mining enterprises; but as the exact nature and extent of the rights thus recognized have not been clearly defined, it is possible that serious conflicts of interest may at any time arise not only between British and German subjects within said area, but that the interests of our citizens may also be jeopardized thereby.

Earnestly desirous to remove any cause of irritation and to insure at the same time to the commerce of all nations in China the undoubted benefits which should accrue from a formal recognition by the various powers claiming "spheres of interest" that they shall enjoy perfect equality of treatment for their commerce and navigation within such "spheres," the Government of the United States would be pleased to see His German Majesty's Government give formal assurances, and lend its cooperation in securing like assurances from the other interested powers, that each, within its respective sphere of whatever influence —

First. Will in no way interfere with any treaty port or any vested interest within any so-called "sphere of interest" or leased territory it may have in China.

Second. That the Chinese treaty tariff of the time being shall apply to all merchandise landed or shipped to all such ports as are within said "sphere of interest" (unless they be "free ports"), no matter to what nationality it may belong, and that duties so leviable shall be collected by the Chinese Government.

Third. That it will levy no higher harbor dues on vessels of another nationality frequenting any port in such "sphere" than shall be levied on vessels of its own nationality, and no higher railroad charges over lines built, controlled, or operated within its "sphere" on merchandise belonging to citizens or subjects of other nationalities transported through such "sphere" than shall be levied on similar merchandise belonging to its own nationals transported over equal distances.

The liberal policy pursued by His Imperial German Majesty in declaring Kiao-chao a free port and in aiding the Chinese Government in the establishment there of a customhouse are so clearly in line with the proposition which this Government is anxious to see recognized that it entertains the strongest hope that Germany will give its acceptance and hearty support.

The recent ukase of His Majesty the Emperor of Russia declaring the port of Ta-lien-wan open during the whole of the lease under which it is held from China to the merchant ships of all nations, coupled with the categorical assurances made to this Government by His Imperial Majesty's representative at this captial at the time and since repeated to me by the present Russian ambassador, seem to insure the support of the Emperor to the proposed measure. Our ambassador at the Court of St. Petersburg has in consequence, been instructed to submit it to the Russian Government and to request their early consideration of it. A copy of my instruction on the subject to Mr. Tower is herewith inclosed for your confidential information.

The commercial interests of Great Britain and Japan will be so clearly served by the desired declaration of intentions, and the views of the Governments of these countries as to the desirability of the adoption of measures insuring the benefits of equality of treatment of all foreign trade throughout China are so similar to those entertained by the United States, that their acceptance of the propositions herein outlined and their cooperation in advocating their adoption by the other powers can be confidently expected. I inclose herewith copy of the instruction which I have sent to Mr. Choate on the subject.

In view of the present favorable conditions, you are instructed to submit the above considerations to His Imperial German Majesty's Minister for Foreign Affairs, and to request his early consideration of the subject.

30. Reception of Hay's "Open Door" Note, 1899

[*Lord Salisbury to J. H. Choate*]

London, November 30, 1899

WITH REFERENCE to my note of September 29 last, I have the honor to state that I have carefully considered, in communication with my colleagues, the proposal contained in your excellency's note of September 22 that a declaration should be made by foreign powers claiming "spheres of interest" in China as to their intentions in regard to the treatment of foreign trade and interest therein.

I have much pleasure in informing your excellency that Her Majesty's Government will be prepared to make a declaration in the sense desired by your Government in regard to the leased territory of Weihai-Wei and all territory in China which may hereafter be acquired by Great Britain by lease or otherwise, and all spheres of interest now held or that may hereafter be held by her in China, provided that a similar declaration is made by other powers concerned.

[*Count Mouravieff to Charlemagne Tower*]

Ministry of Foreign Affairs, December 18–30, 1899

I HAD the honor to receive your excellency's note dated the 8th–20th of September last, relating to the principles which the Government of the United States would like to see adopted in commercial matters by the powers which have interests in China.

In so far as the territory leased by China to Russia is concerned, the Imperial Government has already demonstrated its firm intention to follow the policy of "the open door" by creating Dalny (Ta-lien-wan) a free port; and if at some future time that port, although remaining free itself, should be separated by a customs limit from other portions of the territory in question, the customs duties would be levied, in the zone subject to the tariff, upon all foreign merchandise without distinction as to nationality.

As to the ports now opened or hereafter to be opened to foreign commerce by the Chinese Government, and which lie beyond the territory leased to Russia, the settlement of the question of customs duties belongs to China herself, and the Imperial Government has no intention whatever of claiming any privileges for its own subjects to the exclusion of other foreigners. It is to be understood, however, that this assurance of the Imperial Government is given upon condition that a similar declaration shall be made by other powers having interests in China. . . .

[*Viscount Aoki to A. E. Buck*]

Department of Foreign Affairs, Tokio, the 26th day, the 12th month of the 3d year of Meiji.
(December 26, 1899)

I HAVE the honor to acknowledge the receipt of the note No. 176 of the 20th instant, in which, pursuing the instructions of the United States Government, your excellency was so good as to communicate to the Imperial Government the representations of the United States as presented in notes to Russia, Germany, and Great Britain on the subject of commercial interests of the United States in China.

I have the happy duty of assuring your excellency that the Imperial Government will have no hesitation to give their assent to so just and fair a proposal of the United States, provided that all the other powers concerned shall accept the same.

[*Count von Bülow to Andrew D. White*]

Foreign Office, Berlin, February 19, 1900

YOUR EXCELLENCY informed me, in a memorandum presented on the 24th of last month, that the Government of the United States of America had received satisfactory written replies from all the powers to which an inquiry had been addressed similar to that contained in your excellency's note of September 26 last, in regard to the policy of the open door in China. While referring to this, your excellency thereupon expressed the wish that the Imperial Government would now also give its answer in writing.

Gladly complying with this wish, I have the honor to inform your excellency, repeating the statements already made verbally, as follows: As recognized by the Government of the United States of America, according to your excellency's note referred to above, the Imperial Government has, from the beginning, not only asserted, but also practically carried out to the fullest extent, in its Chinese possessions, absolute equality of treatment of all nations with regard to trade, navigation, and commerce. The Imperial Government entertains no thought of departing in the future from this principle, which at once excludes any prejudicial or disadvantageous commercial treatment of the citizens of the United States of America, so long as it is not forced to do so, on account of considerations of reciprocity, by a divergence from it by other governments. If, therefore, the other powers interested in the industrial development of the Chinese Empire are willing to recognize the same principles, this can only be desired by the Imperial Government, which in this case upon being requested will gladly be ready to participate with the United States of America and the other powers in an agreement made upon these lines, by which the same rights are reciprocally secured.

31. Hay's Open Door Note, July 1900

Circular telegram sent to the nations active in China.

Washington, July 3, 1900

IN THIS critical posture of affairs in China it is deemed appropriate to define the attitude of the United States as far as present circumstances permit this to be done. We adhere to the policy initiated by us in 1857 of peace with the Chinese nation, of furtherance of lawful commerce, and of protection of lives and property of our citizens by all means guaranteed under extraterritorial treaty rights and by the law of nations. If wrong be done to our citizens we propose to hold the responsible authors to the uttermost accountability. We regard the condition at Pekin as one of virtual anarchy, whereby power and responsibility are practically devolved upon the local provincial authorities. So long as they are not in overt collusion with rebellion and use their power to protect foreign life and property, we regard them as representing the Chinese people, with whom we seek to remain in peace and friendship. The purpose of the President is, as it has been heretofore, to act concurrently with the other powers; first, in opening up communication with Pekin and rescuing the American officials, missionaries, and other Americans who are in danger; secondly, in affording all possible protection everywhere in China to American life and property; thirdly, in guarding and protecting all legitimate American interests; and fourthly, in aiding to prevent a spread of the disorders to the other provinces of the Empire and a recurrence of such disasters. It is of course too early to forecast the means of attaining this last result; but the policy of the Government of the United States is to seek a solution which may bring about permanent safety and peace to China, preserve Chinese territorial and administrative entity, protect all rights guaranteed to friendly powers by treaty and international law, and safeguard for the world the principle of equal and impartial trade with all parts of the Chinese Empire. . . .

32. Taft-Katsura Agreement, 1905

William H. Taft, U.S. Secretary of War, and Count Taro Katsura, Prime Minister of Japan.

. . . COUNT KATSURA and Secretary Taft had a long and confidential conversation on the morning of July 27. . . .

First, in speaking of some pro-Russians in America who would have the public believe that the victory of Japan would be a certain prelude to her aggression in the direction of the Philippine Islands, Secretary Taft observed that Japan's only interest in the Philippines would be, in his opinion, to have these islands governed by a strong and friendly nation like the United States, . . . Count Katsura confirmed in the strongest terms the correctness of his views on the point and positively stated that Japan does not harbor any aggressive designs whatever on the Philippines. . . .

Second, Count Katsura observed that the maintenance of general peace in the extreme East forms the fundamental principle of Japan's international policy. Such being the case, . . . the best, and in fact the only, means for accomplishing the above object would be to form good understanding between the three governments of Japan, the United States and Great Britain. . . .

Third, in regard to the Korean question Count Katsura observed that Korea being the direct cause of our war with Russia, it is a matter of absolute importance to Japan that a complete solution of the peninsula question should be made as the logical consequence of the war. If left to herself after the war, Korea will certainly draw back to her habit of improvidently entering into any agreements or treaties with other powers, thus resuscitating the same international complications as existed before the war. In view of the foregoing circumstances, Japan feels absolutely constrained to take some definite step with a view to precluding the possibility of Korea falling back into her former condition and of placing us again under the necessity of entering upon another foreign war. Secretary Taft fully admitted the justness of the Count's observations and remarked to the effect that, in his personal opinion, the establishment by Japanese troops of a suzerainty over Korea to the extent of requiring that Korea enter into no foreign treaties without the consent of Japan was the logical result of the present war and would directly contribute to permanent peace in the East. His judgment was that President Roosevelt would concur in his views in this regard, although he had no authority to give assurance of this. . . .

33. Root-Takahira Agreement, 1908

Secretary of State Elihu Root and K. Takahira, Japanese Ambassador in U.S.

Imperial Japanese Embassy, Washington, November 30, 1908

THE EXCHANGE of views between us, which has taken place at the several interviews which I have recently had the honor of holding with you, has shown that Japan and the United States holding important outlying insular possessions in the region of the Pacific Ocean, the Governments of the two countries are animated by a common aim, policy, and intention in that region.

Believing that a frank avowal of that aim, policy, and intention would not only tend to strengthen the relations of friendship and good neighborhood, which have immemorially existed between Japan and the United States, but would materially contribute to the preservation of the general peace, the Imperial Government have authorized me to present to you an outline of their understanding of that common aim, policy and intention:

1. It is the wish of the two Governments to encourage the free and peaceful development of their commerce on the Pacific Ocean.

2. The policy of both Governments, uninfluenced by any aggressive tendencies, is directed to the maintenance of the existing status quo in the region above mentioned and to the defense of the principle of equal opportunity for commerce and industry in China.

3. They are accordingly firmly resolved reciprocally to respect the territorial possessions belonging to each other in said region.

4. They are also determined to preserve the common interest of all powers in China by supporting by all pacific means at their disposal the independence and integrity of China and the principle of equal opportunity for commerce and industry of all nations in that Empire.

5. Should any event occur threatening the status quo as above described or the principle of equal opportunity as above defined, it remains for the two Governments to communicate with each other in order to arrive at an understanding as to what measures they may consider it useful to take.

If the foregoing outline accords with the view of the Government of the United States, I shall be gratified to receive your confirmation. . . .

34. Lansing-Ishii Agreement, November 1917

Secretary of State Robert Lansing and Japanese diplomat Viscount Kikujiro Ishii.

Department of State, Washington, November 2, 1917

I HAVE the honor to communicate herein my understanding of the agreement reached by us in our recent conversations touching the questions of mutual interest to our Governments relating to the Republic of China.

In order to silence mischievous reports that have from time to time been circulated, it is believed by us that a public announcement once more of the desires and intentions shared by our two Governments with regard to China is advisable.

The Governments of the United States and Japan recognize that territorial propinquity creates special relations between countries, and consequently the Government of the United States recognizes that Japan has special interests in China, particularly in the part to which her possessions are contiguous.

The territorial sovereignty of China, nevertheless, remains unimpaired, and the Government of the United States has every confidence in the repeated assurances of the Imperial Japanese Government that while geographical position gives Japan such special interests they have no desire to discriminate against the trade of other nations or to disregard the commercial rights heretofore granted by China in treaties with other powers.

The Governments of the United States and Japan deny that they have any purpose to infringe in any way the independence or territorial integrity of China, and they declare, furthermore, that they always adhere to the principle of the so-called "open door" or equal opportunity for commerce and industry in China.

Moreover, they mutually declare that they are opposed to the acquisition by any government of any special rights or privileges that would affect the independence or territorial integrity of China, or that would deny to the subjects or citizens of any country the full enjoyment of equal opportunity in the commerce and industry of China.

I shall be glad to have Your Excellency confirm this understanding of the agreement reached by us.

Protocol to Accompany the Lansing-Ishii Agreement [13]

In the course of the conversations between the Japanese Special Ambassador and the Secretary of State of the United States which have led to the exchange of notes between them dated this day, declaring the policy of the two Governments with regard to China, the question of embodying the following clause in such declaration came up for discussion: "they (the governments of Japan and the United States) will not take advantage of the present conditions to seek special rights or privileges in China which would abridge the rights of the subjects or citizens of other friendly states."

Upon careful examination of the question, it was agreed that the clause above quoted being superfluous in the relations of the two Governments and liable to create erroneous impression in the minds of the public, should be eliminated from the declaration.

It was, however, well understood that the principle enunciated in the clause which was thus suppressed was in perfect accord with the declared policy of the two Governments in regard to China.

35. Explanation of the Lansing-Ishii Agreement, November 1917

SIMULTANEOUSLY with the note of November 8, 1917, by which it communicated to the Wai Chiao Pu the text of this exchange of notes, the American Legation in Peking, conveyed under the instructions of its government, to the Chinese Minister for Foreign Affairs the following communication:

"The visit of the Imperial Japanese Mission to the United States afforded an opportunity for free and friendly discussion of interests of the United States and Japan in the Orient by openly proclaiming that the policy of Japan as regards China is not one of aggression and by declaring that there is no intention to take advantage commercially or indirectly of the special relations to China created by geographical position. The representatives of Japan have cleared the diplomatic atmosphere of the suspicions which had been so carefully spread by German propaganda.

"The Governments of the United States and Japan again declare their adherence to the Open Door Policy and recommit themselves, as far as these two Governments are concerned, to the maintenance of equal opportunity for the full enjoyment by the subjects or citizens of any country in the commerce and industry of China. Japanese commercial and industrial enterprises in China manifestly have, on account of the geographical relation of the two countries, a certain advantage over similar enterprises on the part of the citizens or subjects of any other country.

"The Governments of the United States and Japan have taken advantage of a favorable opportunity to make an exchange of expressions with respect to their relations with China. This understanding is formally set forth in the Notes exchanged and now transmitted. The statements in the Notes require no explanation. They not only contain a reaffirmation of the Open Door Policy but introduce a principle of non-interference with the sovereignty and territorial integrity of China which, generally applied, is essential to perpetual international peace, as has been so clearly declared by President Wilson."

On November 9, 1917, the Wai Chiao Pu replied to the following effect:

"The Government of the United States and the Government of Japan have recently, in order to silence mischievous reports, effected an exchange of notes at Washington concerning their desires and intentions with regard to China. A copy of the said notes have been communicated to the Chinese Government by the Japanese Minister at Peking, and the Chinese Government, in order to avoid misunderstanding, hastens to make the following declaration so as to make known the view of the Government:

"The principle adopted by the Chinese Government toward the friendly nations has always been one of justice and equality, and consequently the rights enjoyed by the friendly nations derived from the treaties have been consistently respected, and so even with the special relations between countries created by the fact of territorial contiguity but only in so far as they have already been provided for in her existing treaties. Hereafter the Chinese Government will still adhere to the principle hitherto adopted and hereby it is again declared that the Chinese Government will not allow herself to be bound by any agreement entered into by other nations."

36. Gentlemen's Agreement and Japanese Exclusion, 1908-1924

Department of State to House of Representatives, 8 February 1924.

... IT IS HARDLY necessary for me to say that I am in favor of suitable restrictions upon immigration. The questions which especially concern the Department of State in relation to the international effects of the proposed measure are these: (1) The question of treaty obligations; (2) the provision excluding Japanese; (3) the establishment of the quotas upon the basis of the census of 1890. ...

Article 1 of the treaty between the United States and Japan, concluded in 1911, provides:

The citizens or subjects of each of the high contracting parties shall have liberty to enter, travel, and reside in the territories of the other to carry on trade, wholesale and retail, to own or lease and occupy houses, manufactories, warehouses and shops, to employ agents of their choice, to lease land for residential and commercial purposes, and generally to do anything incident to or necessary for trade upon the same terms as native citizens or subjects, submitting themselves to the laws and regulations there established. ...

In my opinion the restrictions of the proposed measure, in view of their application under the definition of "immigrant," are in conflict with treaty provisions. ... Accordingly, I take the liberty of suggesting that there be included in section 3 of the proposed measure an additional exception to read as follows: "an alien entitled to enter the United States under the provisions of a treaty. ..."

Section 12 (b) provides as follows:

No alien ineligible to citizenship shall be admitted to the United States unless such alien (1) is admissible as a nonquota immigrant under the provisions of subdivisions (b), (d), or (g) of section 4; or (2) is the wife or unmarried child under eighteen years of age of an immigrant admissible under such subdivision (d), and is accompanying or following to join him; or (3) is not an immigrant as defined in sections 3. ...

It is apparent that Section 12, sub-division (b) taken in connection with Sections 3 and 4 of the proposed measure, operates to exclude Japanese. This is inconsistent with the provision of the treaty of 1911 abovementioned, and with respect to those defined as immigrants who do not come within the treaty, it establishes a statutory exclusion.

So far as the latter class is concerned, the question presented is one of policy. There can be no question that such a statutory exclusion will be deeply resented by the Japanese people. It would be idle to insist that the provision is not aimed at the Japanese, for the proposed measure (Sec. 25) continues in force the existing legislation regulating Chinese immigration and the barred-zone provisions of our immigration laws which prohibit immigration from certain other portions of Asia. The practical effect of Section 12 (b) is to single out Japanese immigrants for exclusion. The Japanese are a sensitive people, and unquestionably would regard such a legislative enactment as fixing a stigma upon them. I regret to be compelled to say that I believe such legislative action would largely undo the work of the Washington Conference on Limitation of Armament, which so greatly improved our relations with Japan. The manifestation of American interest and generosity in providing relief to the sufferers from the recent earthquake disaster in Japan would not avail to diminish the resentment which would follow the enactment of such a measure, as this enactment would be regarded as an insult not to be palliated by any act of charity. It is useless to argue whether or not such a feeling would be justified; it is quite sufficient to say that it would exist. It has already been manifested in the discussions in Japan with respect to the pendency of this measure, and no amount of argument can avail to remove it.

The question is thus presented whether it is worth while thus to affront a friendly nation with whom we have established most cordial relations and what gain there would be from such action. Permit me to suggest that the legislation would seem to be quite unnecessary even for the purpose for which it is devised. It is to be noted that if the provision of sub-division (b) of Section 12 were eliminated and the quota provided in Section 10 of the proposed measure were to be applied to Japan, there would be a total of only 246 Japanese immigrants entitled to enter under the quota as thus determined. That is to say, this would be the number equal to two per cent. of the number of residents in the United States as determined by the census of 1890 plus 200. There would remain, of course, the non-quota immigrants, but if it could possibly be regarded that the provisions of Section 4 would unduly enlarge the number admitted, these provisions could be modified without involving a statutory discrimination aimed at the Japanese. We now have an understanding with the Japanese Government whereby Japan undertakes to prevent the immigration of laborers from Japan to the United States except the parents, wives, and children of those already resident here. Furthermore, the Japanese Government, incidentally to this undertaking, now regulates immigration to territory contiguous to the United States with the object of preventing the departure from Japan of persons who are likely to obtain surreptitious entry into this country.

If the provision of Section 12 (b) were to be deleted and the provision in regard to certificates for immigrants to this country were to become applicable to Japan, we should with the present understanding with the Japanese Government be in a position to obtain active cooperation by the Japanese authorities in the granting of passports and immigration certificates. We could in addition be assured that the Japanese Government would give its assistance in scrutinizing and regulating immigration from Japan to American territory contiguous to the United States. It is believed that such an arrangement involving a double control over the Japanese quota of less than 250 a year would accomplish a much more effective regulation of unassimilable and undesirable classes of Japanese immigrants than it would be practicable for us, with our long land frontier lines on both north and south, to accomplish by attempting to establish a general bar against Japanese subjects to the loss of cooperation with the Japanese Government in controlling the movement of their people to the United States and adjacent territories.

I am unable to perceive that the exclusion provision is necessary and I must strongly urge upon you the advisability, in the interest of our international relations, of eliminating it. The Japanese Government has already brought the matter to the attention of the Department of State and there is the deepest interest in the attitude of Congress with respect to this subject. . . .

[*Japanese Opposition to the Selective Immigration Act*] [17]

IN VIEW of certain statements in the report of the House Committee on Immigration — "Report No. 350, March 24, 1924" — regarding the so-called "Gentlemen's Agreement," some of which appear to be misleading, I may be allowed to state to you the purpose and substance of that agreement as it is understood and performed by my Government, which understanding and practice are, I believe, in accord with those of your Government on this subject.

The Gentlemen's Agreement is an understanding with the United States Government by which the Japanese Government voluntarily undertook to adopt and enforce certain administrative measures designed to check the emigration to the United States of Japanese laborers. . . .

One object of the Gentlemen's Agreement is, as is pointed out above, to stop the emigration to the United States of all Japanese laborers other than those excepted in the Agreement, which is embodied in a series of long and detailed correspondence between the two Governments, publication of which is not believed to serve any good purpose, but the essential terms and practice of which may be summed up as follows:

(1) The Japanese Government will not issue passports good for the Continental United States to laborers, skilled or unskilled, except those previously domiciled in the United States, or parents, wives, or children under twenty years of age of such persons. The form of the passport is so designed as to omit no safeguard against forgery, and its issuance is governed by various rules of detail in order to prevent fraud.

The Japanese Government accepted the definition of "laborer" as given in the United States Executive Order of April 8, 1907.

(2) Passports are to be issued by a limited number of specially authorized officials only, under close supervision of the Foreign Office, which has the supreme control of the matter and is equipped with the necessary staff for the administration of it. . . .

(3) Issuance of passports to so-called "picture brides" has been stopped by the Japanese Government since March 1, 1920, although it had not been prohibited under the terms of the Gentlemen's Agreement.

(4) Monthly statistics covering incoming and outgoing Japanese are exchanged between the American and Japanese Governments.

(5) Although the Gentlemen's Agreement is not applicable to the Hawaiian Islands, measures restricting issuance of passports for the Islands are being enforced in substantially the same manner as those for the Continental United States.

(6) The Japanese Government are further exercising strict control over emigration of Japanese laborers to foreign territories contiguous to the United States in order to prevent their surreptitious entry into the United States.

A more condensed substance of these terms is published in the Annual Report of the United States Commissioner-General of Immigration for 1908, 1909 and 1910 on pages 125–6, 121, and 124–5, respectively.

As I stated above, the Japanese Government have been most faithfully observing the Gentlemen's Agreement in every detail of its terms, which fact is, I believe, well known to the United States Government. I may be permitted, in this connection, to call your attention to the official figures published in the Annual Reports of the United States Commissioner-General of Immigration, showing the increase or decrease of Japanese population in the Continental United States by immigration and emigration. According to these reports in the years 1908–1923 the total numbers of Japanese admitted to and departed from the Continental United States were respectively 120,317 and 111,636. In other words the excess of those admitted over those departed was in fifteen years only 8,681, that is to say, the annual average of 578. . . .

Further, if I may speak frankly, at the risk of repeating what, under instructions from my Government, I have represented to you on former occasions, the mere fact that a certain clause, obviously aimed against Japanese as a nation, is introduced in the proposed immigration bill, in apparent disregard of the most sincere and friendly endeavors on the part of the Japanese Government to meet the needs and wishes of the American Government and people, is mortifying enough to the Government and people of Japan. . . .

To Japan the question is not one of expediency, but of principle. To her the mere fact that a few hundreds or thousands of her nationals will or will not be admitted into the domains of other countries is immaterial, so long as no question of national susceptibilities is involved. The important question is whether Japan as a nation is or is not entitled to the proper respect and consideration of other nations. In other words the Japanese Government ask of the United States Government simply that proper consideration ordinarily given by one nation to the self respect of another, which after all forms the basis of amicable international intercourse throughout the civilized world. . . .

It is indeed difficult to believe that it can be the intention of the people of your great country, who always stand for high principles of justice and fair-play in the intercourse of nations, to resort — in order to secure the annual exclusion of 146 Japanese — to a measure which would not only seriously offend the just pride of a friendly nation, that has been always earnest and diligent in its efforts to preserve the friendship of your people, but would also seem to involve the question of the good faith and therefore of the honor of their Government, or at least of its executive branch.

Relying upon the confidence you have been good enough to show me at all times, I have stated or rather repeated all this to you very candidly and in a most friendly spirit, for I realize, as I believe you do, the grave consequences which the enactment of the measure retaining that particular provision would inevitably bring upon the otherwise happy and mutually advantageous relations between our two countries.

[An Explanation to Japan] [18]

THE AMBASSADOR called at the Secretary's request.

The Secretary said that he desired to speak of the Immigration Bill which had been passed by both Houses of Congress and was now before the President. The Secretary called attention to the efforts which he had made and which the President had made to secure the elimination or modification of the provision relating to the exclusion of aliens ineligible for citizenship. The Secretary said that despite these efforts the overwhelming opinion of Congress was in favor of the retention of the provision. This was not due to a lack of friendship on the part of the American people toward the Japanese people. That friendship and cordial interest had been abundantly demonstrated. It was due to the strong sentiment in Congress that the question of immigration should not be dealt with by international agreements or understandings but by legislation enacted by Congress. Congress was intent upon asserting its prerogative in this matter and had rejected all overtures of the President and the Secretary for securing opportunity for mutually satisfactory agreements by which the question of admission could be dealt with.

The Secretary said that he wished to call the attention of the Ambassador to the exact situation with which the President was now confronted. The exclusion provision was not before him as a separate matter. If it were, the President would unhesitatingly disapprove it. But this exclusion provision was part of a comprehensive immigration bill. While the Secretary believed that there was strong sentiment throughout the country supporting the position taken by the President and the Secretary as to the exclusion provision, it was also true that there was a very strong sentiment demanding general legislation in restriction of immigration. The Bill was a comprehensive measure dealing in great detail with this subject and providing the necessary administrative machinery. It was necessary that legislation should be passed of this sort before the expiration of the present law on June 30th. It was necessary that such legislation should be passed well in advance of that date so that instructions could be given to consuls. If the President disapproved this measure there would be great confusion and the most serious difficulties might result. On the other hand, the sentiment in Congress was so strong, as the Ambassador had observed from the votes already taken, that there was very little doubt but that if the bill were vetoed, it would be passed over the veto, and no good would have resulted but there would be considerable bitterness and probably acrimonious debate. The President felt in view of all these considerations that he could not properly disapprove the Bill. But he desired that the Japanese Government should know that his approval of the Bill did not imply any change in his sentiment with regard to this provision or any lack of cordial feeling toward Japan. The President had fully endorsed the position the Secretary had taken. . . .

The Ambassador expressed his appreciation of what the Secretary had said. He said that he could understand the Secretary's view and that he would try to make it clear to his Government, but that while the Foreign Office might appreciate the difficulties of the situation, he was quite sure that the Japanese people would not understand it and would be greatly disappointed. . . .

37. Knox on the Neutralization of Manchuria, 1909

Secretary of State Philander C. Knox to Whitelaw Reid, U.S. Ambassador in Great Britain.

Washington, D. C. November 6, 1909

NOW THAT there has been signed and ratified by an unpublished imperial decree an agreement by which the American and British interests are to cooperate in the financing and construction of the Chinchow-Tsitsihar-Aigun Railroad, the Government of the United States is prepared cordially to cooperate with His Britannic Majesty's Government in diplomatically supporting and facilitating this enterprise, so important alike to the progress and to the commercial development of China. The Government of the United States would be disposed to favor ultimate participation to a proper extent on the part of other interested powers whose inclusion might be agreeable to China and which are known to support the principle of equality of commercial opportunity and the maintenance of the integrity of the Chinese Empire. However, before the further elaboration of the actual arrangement, the Government of the United States asks His Britannic Majesty's Government to give their consideration to the following alternative and more comprehensive projects: First, perhaps the most effective way to preserve the undisturbed enjoyment by China of all political rights in Manchuria and to promote the development of those Provinces under a practical application of the policy of the open door and equal commercial opportunity would be to bring the Manchurian highways, the railroads, under an economic, scientific, and impartial administration by some plan vesting in China the ownership of the railroads through funds furnished for that purpose by the interested powers willing to participate. . . . The Government of the United States has some reason to hope that such a plan might meet favorable consideration on the part of Russia and has reason to believe that American financial participation would be forthcoming. Second, should this suggestion not be found feasible in its entirety, then the desired end would be approximated, if not attained, by Great Britain and the United States diplomatically supporting the Chinchow-Aigun arrangement and inviting the interested powers friendly to complete commercial neutralization of Manchuria to participate in the financing and construction of that line and of such additional lines as future commercial development may demand, and at the same time to supply funds for the purchase by China of such of the existing lines as might be offered for inclusion in this system. The Government of the United States hopes that the principle involved in the foregoing suggestions may commend itself to His Britannic Majesty's Government. . . .

38. Banking Consortium, 1912

Paris, June 18, 1912

AN AGREEMENT made the 18th day of June 1912 between the Hong Kong & Shanghai Banking Corporation having its office at 31 Lombard Street in the city of London (hereinafter called "the Hong Kong Bank") of the first part The Deutsch-Asiatische Bank having its office at 31 Unter den Linden Berlin (hereinafter called "the German Bank") of the second part The Banque de l'Indo-Chine having its office at 15 bis Rue Lafitte Paris (hereinafter called "the French Bank") of the third part MESSRS. J. P. MORGAN & CO., Messrs. Kuhn, Loeb & Co., The First National Bank and the National City Bank all of New York (hereinafter called "the American Group") acting as to the United Kingdom by Messrs. Morgan, Grenfell & Co. of 22 Old Broad Street in the city of London as to Germany by Messrs. M. M. Warburg & Co. of Hamburg and as to France by Messrs. Morgan, Harjes & Co. of Paris and Messrs. M. M. Warburg & Co. (all hereinafter collectively called "the American Agents") of the fourth part The Russo-Asiatic Bank having its office at 62 Nevsky Prospect St. Petersburg in Russia (hereinafter called "the Russian Bank") of the fifth part and The Yokohama Specie Bank Limited having its office at Yokohama Japan (hereinafter called "the Japanese Bank") of the sixth part. . . .

2. This agreement relates to the Reorganization Loan [£60,000,000] and to the future business hereinafter in this clause mentioned and is made on the principle of complete equality in every respect between the parties hereto and each of the parties hereto shall take an equal share in all operations and jointly sign all contracts and shall bear in equal shares all charges in connection with any business (except stamp duties and any charges of and in connection with the realization by each of the parties hereto in their respective markets of its share in the operations) and each of the parties hereto shall conclude all contracts with equal rights and obligations as between themselves and each party shall have the same rights privileges prerogatives advantages responsibilities and obligations of every sort and kind. The said preliminary advances shall acccordingly be borne by each of the parties hereto in equal shares and any sums which may have already been paid by the first four parties hereto in respect of preliminary advances or otherwise in connection with the said Reorganization Loan shall as soon as may be after the execution hereof be adjusted on the above-mentioned basis of equality. Until the Reorganization Loan shall have been issued or until a majority of the parties hereto shall have decided not to proceed further with the issue thereof or until a period of five years from the date hereof shall have elapsed whichever event shall first happen each of the parties hereto will offer to the other parties hereto an equal participation with itself in any loan or advance business into which it may after the date of this agreement enter with the Chinese Government with any of the provinces forming part of China with Chinese Government departments or with companies having Chinese Government or Provincial Government guarantees it being understood that there are excepted from this provision (1) current banking business as well as small financial operations coming within the scope of the same and (2) loans or advances to companies having Chinese Government or Provincial Government guarantees provided that such loans or advances do not involve an issue during the currency of this agreement to the public of bonds or other securities. Should one or more of the parties hereto decline a participation in any such future loan or advance business as aforesaid or in the Reorganization Loan or any part thereof the party or parties accepting a participation therein shall be free to undertake the same but shall issue on its or their markets only. Where one or more of the parties who have accepted a participation in any such future loan or advance business notifies the other parties who have also accepted a participation of its intention not to issue its or their participation the party or parties to whom such notice shall be addressed will issue the participation of the party or parties giving such notice upon the same terms and conditions *mutatis mutandis* as are hereinafter contained with regard to the Residuary Participation in the Reorganization Loan.

39. Wilson on the Banking Consortium, 1913

Public Statement of President Woodrow Wilson.

March 18, 1913

"WE ARE informed that at the request of the last Administration a certain group of American bankers undertook to participate in the loan now desired by the Government of China (approximately one hundred twenty-five million dollars). Our Government wished American bankers to participate along with the bankers of other nations, because it desired that the good-will of the United States towards China should be exhibited in this practical way, that American capital should have access to that great country, and that the United States should be in a position to share with the other powers any political responsibilities that might be associated with the development of the foreign relations of China in connection with her industrial and commercial enterprises. The present Administration has been asked by this group of bankers whether it would also request them to participate in the loan. The representatives of the bankers through whom the Administration was approached declared that they would continue to seek their share of the loan under the proposed agreements only if expressly requested to do so by the Government. The Administration has declined to make such request, because it did not approve the conditions of the loan or the implications of responsibility on its own part which it was plainly told would be involved in the request.

"The conditions of the loan seem to us to touch very nearly the administrative independence of China itself, and this Administration does not feel that it ought, even by implication, to be a party to those conditions. The responsibility on its part which would be implied in requesting the bankers to undertake the loan might conceivably go the length in some unhappy contingency of forcible interference in the financial, and even the political, affairs of that great Oriental State, just now awakening to a consciousness of its power and of its obligations to its people. The conditions include not only the pledging of particular taxes, some of them antiquated and burdensome, to secure the loan but also the administration of those taxes by foreign agents. The responsibility on the part of our Government implied in the encouragement of a loan thus secured and administered is plain enough and is obnoxious to the principles upon which the Government of our people rests.

"The Government of the United States is not only willing, but earnestly desirous, of aiding the great Chinese people in every way that is consistent with their untrammeled development and its own immemorial principles. The awakening of the people of China to a consciousness of their responsibilities under free government is the most significant, if not the most momentous, event of our generation. With this movement and aspiration the American people are in profound sympathy. They certainly wish to participate and participate very generously in the opening to the Chinese and to the use of the world the almost untouched and perhaps unrivaled resources of China.

"The Government of the United States is earnestly desirous of promoting the most extended and intimate trade relationship between this country and the Chinese Republic. The present Administration will urge and support the legislative measures necessary to give American merchants, manufacturers, contractors, and engineers the banking and other financial facilities which they now lack and without which they are at a serious disadvantage as compared with their industrial and commercial rivals. This is its duty. This is the main material interest of its citizens in the development of China. Our interests are those of the Open Door — a door of friendship and mutual advantage. This is the only door we care to enter."

40. Lansing to Page on British Interference with American Trade, 1915

Secretary of State Lansing to Walter H. Page, U.S. Ambassador in Great Britain.

Washington, October 21, 1915

I DESIRE that you present a note to Sir Edward Grey in the sense of the following:

1. The Government of the United States has given careful consideration to your excellency's notes of January 7, February 10, June 22, July 23, July 31 (2), August 13, and to a *note verbale* of the British Embassy of August 6, relating to restrictions upon American commerce by certain measures adopted by the British Government during the present war. This Government has delayed answering the earlier of these notes in the hope that the . . . "measures taken by the Allied Governments," would in practice not unjustifiably infringe upon the neutral rights of American citizens engaged in trade and commerce. It is, therefore, a matter of regret that this hope has not been realized, but that, on the contrary, interferences with American ships and cargoes destined in good faith to neutral ports and lawfully entitled to proceed have become increasingly vexatious, causing American shipowners and American merchants to complain to this Government of the failure to take steps to prevent an exercise of belligerent power in contravention of their just rights. As the measures complained of proceed directly from orders issued by the British Government, are executed by British authorities, and arouse a reasonable apprehension that, if not resisted, they may be carried to an extent even more injurious to American interests, this Government directs the attention of His Majesty's Government to the following considerations. . . .

3. *First*. The detentions of American vessels and cargoes which have taken place since the opening of hostilities have, it is presumed, been pursuant to the enforcement of the orders in council, which were issued on August 20 and October 29, 1914, and March 11, 1915, and relate to contraband traffic and to the interception of trade to and from Germany and Austria-Hungary. In practice, these detentions have not been uniformly based on proofs obtained at the time of seizure, but many vessels have been detained while search was made for evidence of the contraband character of cargoes or of an intention to evade the non-intercourse measures of Great Britain. The question, consequently, has been one of evidence to support a belief of — in many cases, a bare suspicion of — enemy destination, or occasionally of enemy origin of the goods involved. Whether this evidence should be obtained by search at sea before vessels or cargo is taken into port, and what the character of the evidence should be, which is necessary to justify the detention, are the points to which I direct your excellency's attention.

4. In regard to search at sea, an examination of the instructions issued to naval commanders of the United States, Great Britain, Russia, Japan, Spain, Germany, and France from 1888 to the beginning of the present war shows that search in port was not contemplated by the Government of any of these countries. . . .

7. The British contention that "modern conditions" justify bringing vessels into port for search is based upon the size and seaworthiness of modern carriers of commerce and the difficulty of uncovering the real transaction in the intricate trade operations of the present day. It is believed that commercial transactions of the present time, hampered as they are by censorship of telegraph and postal communications on the part of belligerents, are essentially no more complex and disguised than in the wars of recent years, during which the practice of obtaining evidence in port to determine whether a vessel should be held for prize proceedings was not adopted. The effect of the size and seaworthiness of merchant vessels upon their search at sea has been submitted to a board of naval experts, which reports that:

At no period has it been considered necessary to remove every package of a ship's cargo to establish the character and nature of her trade or the service on which she is bound, nor is such removal necessary. . . .

8. Turning to the character and sufficiency of the evidence of the contraband nature of shipments to warrant the detention of a suspected vessel or cargo for prize proceedings, it will be recalled that when a vessel is brought in for adjudication, courts of prize have heretofore been bound by well-established and long-settled practice to consider at the first hearing only the ship's papers and documents, and the goods found on board, together with the written replies of the officers and seamen to standing interrogatories taken under oath, alone and separately, as soon as possible and without communication with or instruction by counsel, in order to avoid possibility of corruption and fraud.

9. Additional evidence was not allowed to be introduced except upon an order of the court for "further proof," and then only after the cause had been fully heard upon the facts already in evidence or when this evidence furnished a ground for prosecuting the inquiry further. This was the practice of the United States courts during the War of 1812, the American Civil War, and the Spanish-American War, as is evidenced by the reported decisions of those courts, and has been the practice of the British prize courts for over a century. This practice has been changed by the British prize court rules adopted for the present war by the order in council of August 5. Under these new rules there is no longer a "first hearing" on the evidence derived from the ship, and the prize court is no longer precluded from receiving extrinsic evidence for which a suggestion has not been laid in the preparatory evidence. The result is, as pointed out above, that innocent vessels or cargoes are now seized and detained on mere suspicion while efforts are made to obtain evidence from extraneous sources to justify the detention and the commencement of prize proceedings. The effect of this

new procedure is to subject traders to risk of loss, delay, and expense, so great and so burdensome as practically to destroy much of the export trade of the United States to neutral countries of Europe....

14. When goods are clearly intended to become incorporated in the mass of merchandise for sale in a neutral country, it is an unwarranted and inquisitorial proceeding to detain shipments for examination as to whether those goods are ultimately destined for the enemy's country or use. Whatever may be the conjectural conclusions to be drawn from trade statistics, which, when stated by value, are of uncertain evidence as to quantity, the United States maintains the right to sell goods into the general stock of a neutral country, and denounces as illegal and unjustifiable any attempt of a belligerent to interfere with that right on the ground that it suspects that the previous supply of such goods in the neutral country, which the imports renew or replace, has been sold to an enemy. That is a matter with which the neutral vendor has no concern and which can in no way affect his rights of trade. Moreover, even if goods listed as conditional contraband are destined to an enemy country through a neutral country, that fact is not in itself sufficient to justify their seizure.

15. In view of these considerations, the United States, reiterating its position in this matter, has no other course but to contest seizures of vessels at sea upon conjectural suspicion and the practice of bringing them into port for the purpose, by search or otherwise, of obtaining evidence, for the purpose of justifying prize proceedings, of the carriage of contraband or of breaches of the order in council of March 11. Relying upon the regard of the British Government for the principles of justice so frequently and uniformly manifested prior to the present war, this Government anticipates that the British Government will instruct their officers to refrain from these vexatious and illegal practices.

16. *Secondly.* The Government of the United States further desires to direct particular attention to the so-called "blockade" measures imposed by the order in council of March 11. The British note of July 23, 1915, appears to confirm the intention indicated in the note of March 15, 1915, to establish a blockade so extensive as to prohibit trade with Germany or Austria-Hungary, even through the ports of neutral countries adjacent to them. Great Britain, however, admits that it should not, and gives assurances that it will not, interfere with trade with the countries contiguous to the territories of the enemies of Great Britain. Nevertheless, after over six months' application of the "blockade" order, the experience of American citizens has convinced the Government of the United States that Great Britain has been unsuccessful in her efforts to distinguish between enemy and neutral trade. Arrangements have been made to create in these neutral countries special consignees, or consignment corporations, with power to refuse shipments and to determine when the state of the country's resources requires the importation of new commodities. American commercial interests are hampered by the intricacies of these arrangements, and many American citizens justly complain that their *bona-fide* trade with neutral countries is greatly reduced as a consequence, while others assert that their neutral trade, which amounted annually to a large sum, has been entirely interrupted....

19. The Declaration of Paris in 1856, which has been universally recognized as correctly stating the rule of international law as to blockade, expressly declares that "blockades, in order to be binding, must be effective; that is to say, maintained by force sufficient really to prevent access to the coast of the enemy." The effectiveness of a blockade is manifestly a question of a fact. It is common knowledge that the German coasts are open to trade with the Scandinavian countries and that German naval vessels cruise both in the North Sea and the Baltic and seize and bring into German ports neutral vessels bound for Scandinavian and Danish ports. Furthermore, from the recent placing of cotton on the British list of contraband of war, it appears that the British Government have themselves been forced to the conclusion that the blockade is ineffective to prevent shipments of cotton from reaching their enemies, or else that they are doubtful as to the legality of the form of blockade which they have sought to maintain....

21. Finally, there is no better settled principle of the law of nations than that which forbids the blockade of neutral ports in time of war. The Declaration of London, though not regarded as binding upon the signatories because not ratified by them, has been expressly adopted by the British Government without modification as to blockade in the British order in council of October 29, 1914. Article 18 of the Declaration declares specifically that "the blockading forces must not bar access to neutral ports or coasts." This is, in the opinion of this Government, a correct statement of the universally accepted law as it exists to-day and as it existed prior to the Declaration of London....

32. Before closing this note, in which frequent reference is made to contraband traffic and contraband articles, it is necessary, in order to avoid possible misconstruction, that it should be clearly understood by His Majesty's Government that there is no intention in this discussion to commit the Government of the United States to a policy of waiving any objections which it may entertain as to the propriety and right of the British Government to include in their list of contraband of war certain articles which have been so included. The United States Government reserves the right to make this matter the subject of a communication to His Majesty's Government at a later day.

33. I believe it has been conclusively shown that the methods sought to be employed by Great Britain to obtain and use evidence of enemy destination of cargoes bound for neutral ports, and to impose a contraband character upon such cargoes, are without justification; that the blockade, upon which such methods are partly founded, is ineffective, illegal, and indefensible; that the judicial procedure offered as a means of reparation for an international injury is inherently defective for the purpose; and that in many cases jurisdiction is asserted in violation of the law of nations.

The United States, therefore, can not submit to the curtailment of its neutral rights by these measures, which are admittedly retaliatory, and therefore illegal, in conception and in nature, and intended to punish the enemies of Great Britain for alleged illegalities on their part. The United States might not be in a position to object to them if its interests and the interests of all neutrals were unaffected by them, but, being affected, it can not with complacence suffer further subordination of its rights and interests to the plea that the exceptional geographic position of the enemies of Great Britain require or justify oppressive and illegal practices. . . .

41. Phenix to Kellogg on British Interference with American Trade, 1914–1917

Assistant Secretary of State Spencer Phenix to Secretary of State Frank B. Kellogg, 9 November 1926.

. . . ON JANUARY 28, 1921, the Senate adopted a resolution (No. 438) requesting the President, if not incompatible with the public interest, "to inform the Senate whether any, and if any, what measures have been taken relating to claims and complaints of citizens of the United States against the British Government growing out of restraints on American commerce, and the alleged unlawful seizure and sale of American ships and cargoes by British authorities during the late war. . . .

On April 29, 1926, the Department of State was informed that the British Government was prepared to enter at once upon a preliminary examination of the papers bearing on the claims in question pursuant to the procedure suggested in its *aide memoire* of April, and that J. Joyce Broderick, Esquire, Commercial Counselor of the British Embassy, had been instructed to undertake this examination for the British Government in conjunction with a representative of the Department of State. The British Government's acceptance in principle of the plan outlined by the Department's *aide memoire* of April 7, 1926, marked the first real progress toward a solution of this problem.

In the meantime, the Department of State had undertaken a thorough re-examination of the papers in its claims files. This examination indicated that the volume of correspondence was so great that it would be most confusing were an effort made to deal with it in its existing form. Accordingly a staff of assistant solicitors was instructed to go through all the files and summarize in brief memoranda the significant facts in each individual case. This work required several months time and resulted in the preparation of about 2200 separate memoranda, or synopses, many of which covered more than one complaint since frequently a single complainant would be interested in several different ships or consignments. . . .

The duty of representing the Department of State in the joint informal conferences with Mr. Broderick was assigned to me, and, in the light of the facts disclosed by my examination of such memoranda as had then been prepared, I was authorized provisionally to withdraw from consideration during our conferences all cases falling within the following categories, and to state that they would not be presented by the Department if a satisfactory general agreement were reached by the two Governments:

1. Cases involving an actual loss of $500 or less.
2. Cases arising from the inclusion of names in the so-called "black lists" unless special grounds for espousal exist.
3. Cases involving alleged wrongful detention, expulsion or mistreatment of American citizens unless there is clearly evidence of injustice resulting in substantial loss or injury, or of needlessly harsh or arbitrary action.
4. Cases involving claims for purely speculative profits.
5. Cases involving losses due to British export or import or bunker restrictions or maximum price orders unless there has been discrimination against the American interests involved.
6. Cases where without unreasonable delay or expense the subject matter has been released to the interested party in good condition, or its fair cash value paid over to him. . . .

The work of summarizing the cases in the claims file and of preparing memoranda was completed in July, and as soon as these memoranda had been arranged alphabetically and numbered serially, Mr. Broderick and I made a rapid review of them all for the purpose of applying the six rules above mentioned wherever the facts justified. We found that nearly 50 per cent of the cases presented in the summaries could be eliminated by the application of these rules or for equally valid reasons. The remaining 50 per cent consisted principally of cases where the Department's information was inadequate to permit the application of any recognized rules, and it was with respect to this residue that the examination of the records in London was undertaken. . . .

My examination of the British records was completed during the third week of October and Mr. Broderick and I then went over a second time the entire lot of cases for the purpose of reconsidering them in the light of the additional information obtained in London, and of applying the rules of provisional exclusion to which reference has already been made. During this review of the cases the number of the applicable rule was entered by me on the original summary, and when that work was completed I prepared a list of all of the 2658 cases showing with respect to each the rule of exclusion, if any, which had been applied. . . .

It will be noted . . . that of the 2658 cases which have been the subject of my inquiries, 2501 are susceptible of elimination by the application of the above mentioned rules. This leaves a residue of 157 cases for further consideration, included in which are 62 concerning which information has not yet been obtained from the British authorities. . . .

As indicated above, I am of the opinion that 83 of the 95 cases which have been reserved for the Department's further consideration can properly be eliminated for the reasons stated. The remaining 12 cases include 11 which seem to me to possess conspicuous merit. . . .

I should not close this report without recording the fact that I was accorded the most whole-hearted and cordial cooperation by all officials of the British Government with whom I came into contact during my mission. . . . As pointed out, however, in the report which I submitted to Mr. Olds in London last September, there seem to be two fundamental considerations in the minds of the British authorities. The first is that the British Government will not admit that the legality of any of its acts in blockading Germany is open to question by the Government of the United States, and the second is that in view of the political dangers inherent in this entire problem, any settlement requiring an appropriation of funds by Parliament to pay "blockade" claims as such, would, as a matter of practical politics, be impossible. It seems to be generally felt that any British Government which requested an appropriation for this purpose would fall, as would any Government which admitted that the legality of the British Navy's operations during the war was open to question. In these circumstances it seems certain that any proposal by the Government of the United States for the settlement of the claims question which does not take full account of these two elements of the situation will be foredoomed to failure. On the other hand it seems to me that the British Government will accept a formula which does not raise the question of the validity of the blockade, and which permits the settlement of meritorious claims, either through a lump sum adjustment, or through a balancing of accounts between the two Governments.

There is one further aspect of the matter to which the Department should give attention and that is the position of the United States as a belligerent in the next war. We are one of the principal naval forces of the world and should we be involved in another war it would be to our interest to have our naval forces free to operate in any way which would render them most effective against the enemy. We shall undoubtedly find it necessary to restrict neutral maritime commerce with our enemy, and I think it can safely be said that our efforts in that direction might be wholly ineffectual if we limited ourselves to visit and search on the high seas. We shall unquestionably want to pursue very much the same procedure as that followed by the British. In these circumstances we should take no general position in our present discussions which might later hamper our freedom of action in case of emergency.

42. Bryan to Gerard on German U-boat Warfare, 1915

Secretary of State William J. Bryan to James W. Gerard, U.S. Ambassador in Germany.

Washington, February 10, 1915

PLEASE ADDRESS a note immediately to the Imperial German Government to the following effect:

The Government of the United States, having had its attention directed to the proclamation of the German Admiralty issued on the 4th of February, that the waters surrounding Great Britain and Ireland, including the whole of the English Channel, are to be considered as comprised within the seat of war; . . . and that neutral vessels expose themselves to danger within this zone of war because, . . . it may not be possible always to exempt neutral vessels from attacks intended to strike enemy ships, feels it to be its duty to call the attention of the Imperial German Government, . . . to the very serious possibilities of the course of action apparently contemplated under that proclamation.

The Government of the United States views those possibilities with such grave concern that it feels it to be its privilege, and indeed its duty in the circumstances, to request the Imperial German Government to consider before action is taken the critical situation in respect of the relations between this country and Germany which might arise were the German naval forces, in carrying out the policy foreshadowed in the Admiralty's proclamation, to destroy any merchant vessel of the United States or cause the death of American citizens.

It is of course not necessary to remind the German Government that the sole right of a belligerent in dealing with neutral vessels on the high seas is limited to visit and search, unless a blockade is proclaimed and effectively maintained, which this Government does not understand to be proposed in this case. To declare or exercise a right to attack and destroy any vessel entering a prescribed area of the high seas without first certainly determining its belligerent nationality and the contraband character of its cargo would be an act so unprecedented in naval warfare that this Government is reluctant to believe that the Imperial Government of Germany in this case contemplates it as possible. The suspicion that enemy ships are using neutral flags improperly can create no just presumption that all ships traversing a prescribed area are subject to the same suspicion. It is to determine exactly such questions that this Government understands the right of visit and search to have been recognized. . . .

If the commanders of German vessels of war should act upon the presumption that the flag of the United States was not being used in good faith and should destroy on the high seas an American vessel or the lives of American citizens, it would be difficult for the Government of the United States to view the act in any other light than as an indefensible violation of neutral rights which it would be very hard indeed to reconcile with the friendly relations now so happily subsisting between the two governments.

If such a deplorable situation should arise, the Imperial German Government can readily appreciate that the Government of the United States would be constrained to hold the Imperial German Government to a strict accountability for such acts of their naval authorities and to take any steps it might be necessary to take to safeguard American lives and property and to secure to American citizens the full enjoyment of their acknowledged rights on the high seas. . . .

43. Bryan to Gerard, First Lusitania Note, May 1915

William J. Bryan to James W. Gerard.

Washington, May 13, 1915

PLEASE CALL on the Minister of Foreign Affairs and, after reading to him this communication, leave him with a copy.

In view of the recent acts of the German authorities in violation of American rights on the high seas which culminated in the torpedoing and sinking of the British steamship *Lusitania* on May 7th, 1915, by which over 100 American citizens lost their lives, it is clearly wise and desirable that the Government of the United States and the Imperial German Government should come to a clear and full understanding as to the grave situation which has resulted.

The sinking of the British passenger steamer *Falaba* by a German submarine on March 28, through which Leon C. Thrasher, an American citizen, was drowned; the attack on April 28 on the American vessel *Cushing* by a German aeroplane; the torpedoing on May 1 of the American vessel *Gulflight* by a German submarine, as a result of which two or more American citizens met their death; and, finally, the torpedoing and sinking of the steamship *Lusitania*, constitute a series of events which the Government of the United States has observed with growing concern, distress, and amazement. . . .

The Government of the United States has been apprised that the Imperial German Government considered themselves to be obliged by the extraordinary circumstances of the present war and the measures adopted by their adversaries in seeking to cut Germany off from all commerce, to adopt methods of retaliation which go much beyond the ordinary methods of warfare at sea, in the proclamation of a war zone from which they have warned neutral ships to keep away. This Government has already taken occasion to inform the Imperial German Government that it cannot admit the adoption of such measures or such a warning of danger to operate as in any degree an abbreviation of the rights of American shipmasters or of American citizens bound on lawful errands as passengers on merchant ships of belligerent nationality; and that it must hold the Imperial German Government to a strict accountability for any infringement of those rights, intentional or incidental. It does not understand the Imperial German Government to question those rights. It assumes, on the contrary, that the Imperial Government accept, as of course, the rule that the lives of non-combatants, whether they be of neutral citizenship or citizens of one of the nations at war, can not lawfully or rightfully be put in jeopardy by the capture or destruction of an unarmed merchantman, and recognize also, as all other nations do, the obligation to take the usual precaution of visit and search to ascertain whether a suspected merchantman is in fact of belligerent nationality or is in fact carrying contraband of war under a neutral flag.

The Government of the United States, therefore, desires to call the attention of the Imperial German Government with the utmost earnestness to the fact that the objection to their present method of attack against the trade of their enemies lies in the practical impossibility of employing submarines in the destruction of commerce without disregarding those rules of fairness, reason, justice, and humanity, which all modern opinion regards as imperative. It is practically impossible for the officers of a submarine to visit a merchantman at sea and examine her papers and cargo. It is practically impossible for them to make a prize of her; and, if they can not put a prize crew on board of her, they can not sink her without leaving her crew and all on board of her to the mercy of the sea in her small boats. These facts it is understood the Imperial German Government frankly admit. We are informed that, in the instances of which we have spoken, time enough for even that poor measure of safety was not given, and in at least two of the cases cited, not so much as a warning was received. Manifestly submaries can not be used against merchantmen, as the last few weeks have shown, without an inevitable violation of many sacred principles of justice and humanity.

American citizens act within their indisputable rights in taking their ships and in traveling wherever their legitimate business calls them upon the high seas, and exercise those rights in what should be the well-justified confidence that their lives will not be endangered by acts done in clear violation of universally acknowledged international obligations, and certainly in the confidence that their own Government will sustain them in the exercise of their rights. . . .

Long acquainted as this Government has been with the character of the Imperial German Government and with the high principles of equity by which they have in the past been actuated and guided, the Government of the United States can not believe that the commanders of the vessels which committed these acts of lawlessness did so except under a misapprehension of the orders issued by the Imperial German naval authorities. It takes it for granted that, at least within the practical possibilities of every such case, the commanders even of submarines were expected to do nothing that would involve the lives of non-combatants or the safety of neutral ships, even at the cost of failing of their object of capture or destruction. It confidently expects, therefore, that the Imperial German Government will disavow the acts of which the Government of the United States complains, that they will make reparation so far as reparation is possible for injuries which are without measure, and that they will take immediate steps to prevent the recurrence of anything so obviously subversive of the principles of warfare for which the Imperial German Government have in the past so wisely and so firmly contended.

The Government and people of the United States look to the Imperial German Government for just, prompt, and enlightened action in this vital matter with the greater confidence because the United States and Germany are bound together not only by special ties of friendship but also by the explicit stipulations of the treaty of 1828 between the United States and the Kingdom of Prussia.

Expressions of regret and offers of reparation in case of the destruction of neutral ships sunk by mistake, while they may satisfy international obligations, if no loss of life results, can not justify or excuse a practice, the natural and necessary effect of which is to subject neutral nations and neutral persons to new and immeasurable risks.

The Imperial German Government will not expect the Government of the United States to omit any word or any act necessary to the performance of its sacred duty of maintaining the rights of the United States and its citizens and of safeguarding their free exercise and enjoyment.

Secretary of State Robert Lansing to James W. Gerard.

Washington, April 18, 1916

YOU ARE instructed to deliver to the Secretary of Foreign Affairs a communication reading as follows:

I did not fail to transmit immediately, by telegraph, to my Government your excellency's note of the 10th instant in regard to certain attacks by German submarines, and particularly in regard to the disastrous explosion which, on March 24, last wrecked the French S. S. *Sussex* in the English Channel. I have now the honor to deliver, under instructions from my Government, the following reply to your excellency:

Information now in the possession of the Government of the United States fully established the facts in the case of the *Sussex*, and the inferences which my Government has drawn from that information it regards as confirmed by the circumstances set forth in your excellency's note of the 10th instant. On the 24th of March 1916, at about 2.50 o'clock in the afternoon, the unarmed steamer *Sussex*, with 325 or more passengers on board, among whom were a number of American citizens, was torpedoed while crossing from Folkstone to Dieppe. The *Sussex* had never been armed; was a vessel known to be habitually used only for the conveyance of passengers across the English Channel; and was not following the route taken by troopships or supply ships. About 80 of her passengers, non-combatants of all ages and sexes, including citizens of the United States, were killed or injured. . . .

The Government of the United States, after having given careful consideration to the note of the Imperial Government of the 10th of April, regrets to state that the impression made upon it by the statements and proposals contained in that note is that the Imperial Government has failed to appreciate the gravity of the situation which has resulted, not alone from the attack on the *Sussex*, but from the whole method and character of submarine warfare as disclosed by the unrestrained practice of the commanders of German undersea craft during the past twelvemonth and more in the indiscriminate destruction of merchant vessels of all sorts, nationalities, and destinations. If the sinking of the *Sussex* had been an isolated case, the Government of the United States might find it possible to hope that the officer who was responsible for that act had wilfully violated his orders or had been criminally negligent in taking none of the precautions they prescribed, and that the ends of justice might be satisfied by imposing upon him an adequate punishment, coupled with a formal disavowal of the act and payment of a suitable indemnity by the Imperial Government. But, though the attack upon the *Sussex* was manifestly indefensible and caused a loss of life so tragical as to make it stand forth as one of the most terrible examples of the inhumanity of submarine warfare as the commanders of German vessels are conducting it, it unhappily does not stand alone.

On the contrary, the Government of the United States is forced by recent events to conclude that it is only one instance, even though one of the most extreme and most distressing instances, of the deliberate method and spirit of indiscriminate destruction of merchant vessels of all sorts, nationalities, and destinations which have become more and more unmistakable as the activity of German undersea vessels of war has in recent months been quickened and extended.

The Imperial Government will recall that when, in February 1915, it announced its intention of treating the waters surrounding Great Britain and Ireland as embraced within the seat of war and of destroying all merchant ships owned by its enemies that might be found within that zone of danger, and warned all vessels, neutral as well as belligerent, to keep out of the waters thus proscribed or to enter them at their peril, the Government of the United States earnestly protested. . . .

The Imperial Government, notwithstanding, persisted in carrying out the policy announced, expressing the hope that the dangers involved, at any rate to neutral vessels, would be reduced to a minimum by the instructions which it had issued to the commanders of its submarines, and assuring the Government of the United States that it would take every possible precaution both to respect the rights of neutrals and to safeguard the lives of non-combatants.

In pursuance of this policy of submarine warfare against the commerce of its adversaries, thus announced and thus entered upon in despite of the solemn protest of the Government of the United States, the commanders of the Imperial Government's undersea vessels have carried on practices of such ruthless destruction which have made it more and more evident as the months have gone by that the Imperial Government has found it impracticable to put any such restraints upon them as it had hoped and promised to put. . . .

The Government of the United States has been very patient. At every stage of this distressing experience of tragedy after tragedy it has sought to be governed by the most thoughtful consideration of the extraordinary circumstances of an unprecedented war and to be guided by sentiments of very genuine friendship for the people and Government of Germany. It has accepted the successive explanations and assurances of the Imperial Government as, of course, given in entire sincerity and good faith, and has hoped, even against hope, that it would prove to be possible for the Imperial Government so to order and control the acts of its naval commanders as to square its policy with the recognized principles of humanity as embodied in the law of nations. It has made every allowance for unprecedented conditions and has been willing to wait until the facts became unmistakable and were susceptible of only one interpretation.

It now owes it to a just regard for its own rights to say to the Imperial Government that that time has come. It has become painfully evident to it that the position which it took at the very outset is inevitable, namely, the use of submarines for the destruction of an enemy's commerce is, of necessity, because of the very character of the vessels employed and the very methods of attack which their employment of course involves, utterly incompatible with the principles of humanity, the long-established and incontrovertible rights of neutrals, and the sacred immunities of non-combatants.

If it is still the purpose of the Imperial Government to prosecute relentless and indiscriminate warfare against vessels of commerce by the use of submarines without regard to what the Government of the United States must consider the sacred and indisputable rules of international law and the universally recognized dictates of humanity, the Government of the United States is at last forced to the conclusion that there is but one course it can pursue. Unless the Imperial Government should now immediately declare and effect an abandonment of its present methods of submarine warfare against passenger and freight-carrying vessels, the Government of the United States can have no choice but to sever diplomatic relations with the German Empire altogether. This action the Government of the United States contemplates with the greatest reluctance but feels constrained to take in behalf of humanity and the rights of neutral nations.

45. Wilson's Warning on the Danger of War, January 1916

Speech at Pittsburgh, 29 January 1916.

IN ORDINARY circumstances it has not been necessary for America to think of force, because everybody knows that there is latent in her as much force as resides anywhere in the world. This great body of 100,000,000 people has an average of intelligence and resourcefulness probably unprecedented in the history of the world. Nobody doubts that, given time enough, we can assert any amount of force that may be necessary; but when the world is on fire how much time can you afford to take to be ready? When you know that there are combustible materials in the life of the world and in your own national life, and that the sky is full of floating sparks from a great conflagration, are you going to sit down and say it will be time when the fire begins to do something about it? I do not believe that the fire is going to begin, but I would be surer of it if we were ready for the fire. And I want to come as your responsible servant and tell you this, that we do not control the fire. We are under the influences of it, but we are not at the sources of it. We are where it at any time may affect us, and yet we can not govern its spread and progress. If it once touches us, it may touch the very sources of our life, for it may touch the very things we stand for, and we might for a little while be unable successfully to vindicate and defend them. I am not come here to tell you of any immediate threat of a definite danger, because by very great patience, by making our position perfectly clear, and then steadfastly maintaining the same attitude throughout great controversies, we have so far held difficulty at arm's length; but I want you to realize the task you have imposed upon your Government.

There are two things which practically everybody who comes to the Executive Office in Washington tells me. They tell me, "The people are counting upon you to keep us out of this war." And in the next breath what do they tell, "The people are equally counting upon you to maintain the honor of the United States." Have you reflected that a time might come when I could not do both? And have you made yourselves ready to stand behind your Government for the maintenance of the honor of your country, as well as for the maintenance of the peace of the country? If I am to maintain the honor of the United States and it should be necessary to exert the force of the United States in order to do it, have you made the force ready? You know that you have not, and the very fact that the force is not ready may make the task you have set for me all the more delicate and all the more difficult. I have come away from Washington to remind you of your part in this great business. There is no part that belongs to me that I wish to shirk, but I wish you to bear the part that belongs to you. I want every man and woman of you to stand behind me in pressing a reasonable plan for national defense. . . .[15]

America is not afraid of anybody. I know that I express your feeling and the feeling of all our fellow citizens when I say that the only thing I am afraid of is not being ready to perform my duty. I am afraid of the danger of shame; I am afraid of the danger of inadequacy; I am afraid of the danger of not being able to express the great character of this country with tremendous might and effectiveness whenever we are called upon to act in the field of the world's affairs.

For it is character we are going to express, not power merely. The United States is not in love with the aggressive use of power. It despises the aggressive use of power. There is not a foot of territory belonging to any other Nation which this Nation covets or desires. There is not a privilege which we ourselves enjoy that we would dream of denying any other nation in the world. If there is one thing that the American people love and believe in more than another it is peace and all the handsome things that belong to peace. I hope that you will bear me out in saying that I have proved that I am a partisan of peace. I would be ashamed to be belligerent and impatient when the fortunes of my whole country and the happiness of all my fellow countrymen were involved. But I know that peace is not always within the choice of the Nation, and I want to remind you, and remind you very solemnly, of the double obligation you have laid upon me. I know you have laid it upon me because I am constantly reminded of it in conversation, by letter, in editorial, by means of every voice that comes to me out of the body of the Nation. You have laid upon me this double obligation: "We are relying upon you, Mr. President, to keep us out of this war, but we are relying upon you, Mr. President, to keep the honor of the Nation unstained."

Do you not see that a time may come when it is impossible to do both of these things? Do you not see that if I am to guard the honor of the Nation, I am not protecting it against itself, for we are not going to do anything to stain the honor of our own country. I am protecting it against things that I cannot control, the action of others. And where the action of others may bring us I cannot foretell. You may count upon my heart and resolution to keep you out of the war, but you must be ready if it is necessary that I should maintain your honor. That is the only thing a real man loves about himself. Some men who are not real men love other things about themselves, but the real man believes that his honor is dearer than his life; and a nation is merely all of us put together, and the Nation's honor is dearer than the Nation's comfort and the Nation's peace and the Nation's life itself. So that we must know what we have thrown into the balance; we must know the infinite issues which are impending every day of the year, and when we go to bed at night and when we rise in the morning, and at every interval of the rush of business, we must remind ourselves that we are part of a great body politic in which are vested some of the highest hopes of the human race. . . .[16]

I dare say you realize, therefore, the solemnity of the feeling with which I come to audiences of my fellow citizens at this time. I can not indulge the reckless pleasure of expressing my own private opinions and prejudices. I speak as the trustee of the Nation, called upon to speak its sober judgments and not its individual opinions; and it is with the feeling of this responsibility upon me that I have come to you to-night and have approached the other audiences that I have had the privilege of addressing upon this journey. Do you realize the peculiar difficulty of the situation in which your Executive is placed? You have laid upon me, not by implication, but explicitly — it has come to me by means of every voice that has been vocal in the Nation — you have laid upon me the double obligation of maintaining the honor of the United States and of maintaining the peace of the United States. Is it not conceivable that the two might become incompatible? Is it not conceivable that, however great our passion for peace, we would have to subordinate it to our passion for what is right? Is it not possible that in maintaining the integrity of the character of the United States it may become necessary to see that no man does that integrity too great violence?

It is a very terrible thing, ladies and gentlemen, to have the honor of the United States intrusted to your keeping. It is a great honor, that honor of the United States! In it runs the blood of generations of men who have built up ideals and institutions on this side of the water intended to regenerate mankind, and any man who does violence to right, any nation that does violence to the principles of just international understandings, is doing violence to the ideals of the United States. We observe the technical limits; we assert these rights only when our own citizens are directly affected, but you know that our feeling is just the same whether the rights of those individual citizens are affected or not, and that we feel all the concern of those who have built up things so great that they dare not let them be torn down or touched with profane hands.

Look at the task that is assigned to the United States, to assert the principles of law in a world in which the principles of law have broken down — not the technical principles of law, but the essential principles of right dealing and humanity as between nation and nation. Law is a very complicated term. It includes a great many things that do not engage our affections, but at the basis of the things that we are now dealing with lie the deepest affections of the human heart, the love of life, the love of righteousness, the love of fair dealing, the love of those things that are just and of good report. The things that are rooted in our very spirit are the stuff of the law that I am talking about now. . . .[17]

46. Wilson's Terms of Peace, January 1917

Speech to Senate, 22 January 1917.

ON THE eighteenth of December last I addressed an identic note to the governments of the nations now at war requesting them to state, more definitely than they had yet been stated by either group of belligerents, the terms upon which they would deem it possible to make peace. I spoke on behalf of humanity and of the rights of all neutral nations like our own, many of whose most vital interests the war puts in constant jeopardy. The Central Powers united in a reply which stated merely that they were ready to meet their antagonists in conference to discuss terms of peace. The Entente Powers have replied much more definitely and have stated, in general terms, indeed, but with sufficient definiteness to imply details, the arrangements, guarantees, and acts of reparation which they deem to be the indispensable conditions of a satisfactory settlement. We are that much nearer a definite discussion of the peace which shall end the present war. We are that much nearer the discussion of the international concert which must thereafter hold the world at peace. In every discussion of the peace that must end this war it is taken for granted that that peace must be followed by some definite concert of power which will make it virtually impossible that any such catastrophe should ever overwhelm us again. Every lover of mankind, every sane and thoughtful man, must take that for granted.

I have sought this opportunity to address you because I thought that I owed it to you, as the counsel associated with me in the final determination of our international obligations, to disclose to you without reserve the thought and purpose that have been taking form in my mind in regard to the duty of our Government in the days to come when it will be necessary to lay afresh and upon a new plan the foundations of peace among the nations.

It is inconceivable that the people of the United States should play no part in that great enterprise. To take part in such a service will be the opportunity for which they have sought to prepare themselves by the very principles and purposes of their polity and the approved practices of their Government ever since the days when they set up a new nation in the high and honourable hope that it might in all that it was and did show mankind the way to liberty. They cannot in honour withhold the service to which they are now about to be challenged. They do not wish to withhold it. But they owe it to themselves and to the other nations of the world to state the conditions under which they will feel free to render it.

That service is nothing less than this, to add their authority and their power to the authority and force of other nations to guarantee peace and justice throughout the world. Such a settlement cannot now be long postponed. It is right that before it comes this Government should frankly formulate the conditions upon which it would feel justified in asking our people to approve its formal and solemn adherence to a League for Peace. I am here to attempt to state those conditions. . . .

I do not mean to say that any American government would throw any obstacle in the way of any terms of peace the governments now at war might agree upon, or seek to upset them when made, whatever they might be. I only take it for granted that mere terms of peace between the belligerents will not satisfy even the belligerents themselves. Mere agreements may not make peace secure. It will be absolutely necessary that a force be created as a guarantor of the permanency of the settlement so much greater than the force of any nation now engaged or any alliance hitherto formed or projected that no nation, no probable combination of nations could face or withstand it. If the peace presently to be made is to endure, it must be a peace made secure by the organized major force of mankind. . . .

The equality of nations upon which peace must be founded if it is to last must be an equality of rights; the guarantees exchanged must neither recognize nor imply a difference between big nations and small, between those that are powerful and those that are weak. Right must be based upon the common strength, not upon the individual strength, of the nations upon whose concert peace will depend. Equality of territory or of resources there of course cannot be; nor any other sort of equality not gained in the ordinary peaceful and legitimate development of the peoples themselves. But no one asks or expects anything more than an equality of rights. Mankind is looking now for freedom of life, not for equipoises of power.

And there is a deeper thing involved than even equality of right among organized nations. No peace can last, or ought to last, which does not recognize and accept the principle that governments derive all their just powers from the consent of the governed, and that no right anywhere exists to hand peoples about from sovereignty to sovereignty as if they were property. . . .

So far as practicable, moreover, every great people now struggling towards a full development of its resources and of its powers should be assured a direct outlet to the great highways of the sea. Where this cannot be done by the cession of territory, it can no doubt be done by the neutralization of direct rights of way under the general guarantee which will assure the peace itself. With a right comity of arrangement no nation need be shut away from free access to the open paths of the world's commerce.

And the paths of the sea must alike in law and in fact be free. The freedom of the seas in the *sine qua non* of peace, equality, and cooperation. No doubt a somewhat radical reconsideration of many of the rules of international practice hitherto thought to be established may be necessary in order to make the seas indeed free and common in practically all circumstances for the use of mankind, but the motive for such changes is convincing and compelling. There can be no trust or intimacy between the peoples of the world without them. The free, constant, unthreatened intercourse of nations is an essential part of the process of peace and of development. It need not be difficult either to define or to secure the freedom of the seas if the governments of the world sincerely desire to come to an agreement concerning it.

It is a problem closely connected with the limitation of naval armaments and the cooperation of the navies of the world in keeping the seas at once free and safe. And the question of limiting naval armaments opens the wider and perhaps more difficult question of the limitation of armies and of all programs of military preparation. Difficult and delicate as these questions are, they must be faced with the utmost candour and decided in a spirit of real accommodation if peace is to come with healing in its wings, and come to stay. Peace cannot be had without concession and sacrifice. There can be no sense of safety and equality among the nations if great preponderating armaments are henceforth to continue here and there to be built up and maintained. The statesmen of the world must plan for peace and nations must adjust and accommodate their policy to it as they have planned for war and made ready for pitiless contest and rivalry. The question of armaments, whether on land or sea, is the most immediately and intensely practical question connected with the future fortunes of nations and of mankind. . . .

And in holding out the expectation that the people and Government of the United States will join the other civilized nations of the world in guaranteeing the permanence of peace upon such terms as I have named I speak with the greater boldness and confidence because it is clear to every man who can think that there is in this promise no breach in either our traditions or our policy as a nation, but a fulfilment, rather, of all that we have professed or striven for.

I am proposing, as it were, that the nations should with one accord adopt the doctrine of President Monroe as the doctrine of the world: that no nation should seek to extend its polity over any other nation or people, but that every people should be left free to determine its own polity, its own way of development, unhindered, unthreatened, unafraid, the little along with the great and powerful.

I am proposing that all nations henceforth avoid entangling alliances which would draw them into competitions of power, catch them in a net of intrigue and selfish rivalry, and disturb their own affairs with influences intruded from without. There is no entangling alliance in a concert of power. When all unite to act in the same sense and with the same purpose all act in the common interest and are free to live their own lives under a common protection.

I am proposing government by the consent of the governed; that freedom of the seas which in international conference after conference representatives of the United States have urged with the eloquence of those who are the convinced disciples of liberty; and that moderation of armaments which makes of armies and navies a power for order merely, not an instrument of aggression or of selfish violence.

These are American principles, American policies. We could stand for no others. And they are also the principles and policies of forward-looking men and women everywhere, of every modern nation, of every enlightened community. They are the principles of mankind and must prevail.

47. Wilson's War Message, 2 April 1917

Speech to Joint Session of Congress.

... ON THE THIRD of February last I officially laid before you the extraordinary announcement of the Imperial German Government that on and after the first day of February it was its purpose to put aside all restraints of law or of humanity and use its submarines to sink every vessel that sought to approach either the ports of Great Britain and Ireland or the western coasts of Europe or any of the ports controlled by the enemies of Germany within the Mediterranean. That had seemed to be the object of the German submarine warfare earlier in the war, but since April of last year the Imperial Government had somewhat restrained the commanders of its undersea craft in conformity with its promise then given to us that passenger boats should not be sunk and that due warning would be given to all other vessels which its submarines might seek to destroy, when no resistance was offered or escape attempted, and care taken that their crews were given at least a fair chance to save their lives in their open boats. The precautions taken were meager and haphazard enough, as was proved in distress instance after instance in the progress of the cruel and unmanly business, but a certain degree of restraint was observed. The new policy has swept every restriction aside. Vessels of every kind, whatever their flag, their character, their cargo, their destination, their errand, have been ruthlessly sent to the bottom without warning and without thought of help or mercy for those on board, the vessels of friendly neutrals along with those of belligerents. Even hospital ships and ships carrying relief to the sorely bereaved and stricken people of Belgium, though the latter were provided with safe conduct through the proscribed areas by the German Government itself and were distinguished by unmistakable marks of identity, have been sunk with the same reckless lack of compassion or of principle. ...

I am not now thinking of the loss of property involved, immense and serious as that is, but only of the wanton and wholesale destruction of the lives of non-combatants, men, women, and children, engaged in pursuits which have always, even in the darkest periods of modern history, been deemed innocent and legitimate. Property can be paid for; the lives of peaceful and innocent people cannot be. The present German submarine warfare against commerce is a warfare against mankind.

It is a war against all nations. American ships have been sunk, American lives taken, in ways which it has stirred us very deeply to learn of, but the ships and people of other neutral and friendly nations have been sunk and overwhelmed in the waters in the same way. There has been no discrimination. The challenge is to all mankind. Each nation must decide for itself how it will meet it. The choice we make for ourselves must be made with a moderation of counsel and a temperateness of judgment befitting our character and our motives as a nation. We must put excited feeling away. Our motive will not be revenge or the victorious assertion of the physical might of the nation, but only the vindication of right, of human right, of which we are only a single champion. . . .

There is one choice we cannot make, we are incapable of making: we will not choose the path of submission and suffer the most sacred rights of our Nation and our people to be ignored or violated. The wrongs against which we now array ourselves are no common wrongs; they cut to the very roots of human life.

With a profound sense of the solemn and even tragical character of the step I am taking and of the grave responsibilities which it involves, but in unhesitating obedience to what I deem my constitutional duty, I advise that the Congress declare the recent course of the Imperial German Government to be in fact nothing less than war against the government and people of the United States; that it formally accept the status of belligerent which has thus been thrust upon it; and that it take immediate steps not only to put the country in a more thorough state of defense but also to exert all its power and employ all its resources to bring the Government of the German Empire to terms and end the war. . . .

While we do these things, these deeply momentous things, let us be very clear, and make very clear to all the world what our motives and our objects are. My own thought has not been driven from its habitual and normal course by the unhappy events of the last two months, and I do not believe that the thought of the Nation has been altered or clouded by them. I have exactly the same things in mind now that I had in mind when I addressed the Senate on the twenty-second of January last; the same that I had in mind when I addressed the Congress on the third of February and on the twenty-sixth of February. Our object now, as then, is to vindicate the principles of peace and justice in the life of the world as against selfish and autocratic power and to set up amongst the really free and self-governed peoples of the world such a concert of purpose and of action as will henceforth insure the observance of those principles. Neutrality is no longer feasible or desirable where the peace of the world is involved and the freedom of its peoples, and the menace to that peace and fredom lies in the existence of autocratic governments backed by organized force which is controlled wholly by their will, not by the will of their people. We have seen the last of neutrality in such circumstances. We are at the beginning of an age in which it will be insisted that the same standards of conduct and of responsibility for wrong done shall be observed among nations and their governments that are observed among the individual citizens of civilized states.

We have no quarrel with the German people. We have no feeling towards them but one of sympathy and friendship. It was not upon their impulse that their government acted in entering this war. It was not with their previous knowledge or approval. It was a war determined upon as wars used to be determined upon in the old, unhappy days when peoples were nowhere consulted by their rulers and wars were provoked and waged in the interest of dynasties or of little groups of ambitious men who were accustomed to use their fellow men as pawns and tools. Self-governed nations do not fill their neighbor states with spies or set the course of intrigue to bring about some critical posture of affairs which will give them an opportunity to strike and make conquest. Such designs can be successfully worked out only under cover and where no one has the right to ask questions. Cunningly contrived plans of deception or aggression, carried, it may be, from generation to generation, can be worked out and kept from the light only within the privacy of courts or behind the carefully guarded confidences of a narrow and privileged class. They are happily impossible where public opinion commands and insists upon full information concerning all the nation's affairs. . . .

It is a distressing and oppressive duty, Gentlemen of the Congress, which I have performed in thus addressing you. There are, it may be, many months of fiery trial and sacrifice ahead of us. It is a fearful thing to lead this great peaceful people into war, into the most terrible and disastrous of all wars, civilization itself seeming to be in the balance. But the right is more precious than peace, and we shall fight for the things which we have always carried nearest our hearts, — for democracy, for the right of those who submit to authority to have a voice in their own Governments, for the rights and liberties of small nations, for a universal dominion of right by such a concert of free peoples as shall bring peace and safety to all nations and make the world itself at last free. To such a task we can dedicate our lives and our fortunes, everything that we are and everything that we have, with the pride of those who know that the day has come when America is privileged to spend her blood and her might for the principles that gave her birth and happiness and the peace which she has treasured. God helping her, she can do no other.

48. Wilson's Fourteen Points, January 1918

Speech to Joint Session of Congress, 8 January 1918.

... WE ENTERED this war because violations of right had occurred which touched us to the quick and made the life of our people impossible unless they were corrected and the world secured once for all against their recurrence. What we demand in this war, therefore, is nothing peculiar to ourselves. It is that the world be made fit and safe to live in; and particularly that it be made safe for every peace-loving nation which, like our own, wishes to live its own life, determine its own institutions, be assured of justice and fair dealing by the other peoples of the world as against force and selfish aggression. All the peoples of the world are in effect partners in this interest, and for our own part we see very clearly that unless justice be done to others it will not be done to us. The programme of the world's peace, therefore, is our programme; and that programme, the only possible programme, as we see it, is this:

I. Open covenants of peace, openly arrived at, after which there shall be no private international understandings of any kind but diplomacy shall proceed always frankly and in the public view.

II. Absolute freedom of navigation upon the seas, outside territorial waters, alike in peace and in war, except as the seas may be closed in whole or in part by international action for the enforcement of international covenants.

III. The removal, so far as possible, of all economic barriers and the establishment of an equality of trade conditions among all the nations consenting to the peace and associating themselves for its maintenance.

IV. Adequate guarantees given and taken that national armaments will be reduced to the lowest point consistent with domestic safety.

V. A free, open-minded, and absolutely impartial adjustment of all colonial claims, based upon a strict observance of the principle that in determining all such questions of sovereignty the interests of the populations concerned must have equal weight with the equitable claims of the government whose title is to be determined.

VI. The evacuation of all Russian territory and such a settlement of all questions affecting Russia as will secure the best and freest co-operation of the other nations of the world in obtaining for her an unhampered and unembarrassed opportunity for the independent determination of her own political development and national policy and assure her of a sincere welcome into the society of free nations under institutions of her own choosing; and, more than a welcome, assistance also of every kind that she may need and may herself desire. The treatment accorded Russia by her sister nations in the months to come will be the acid test of their good will, of their comprehension of her needs as distinguished from their own interests, and of their intelligent and unselfish sympathy.

VII. Belgium, the whole world will agree, must be evacuated and restored, without any attempt to limit the sovereignty which she enjoys in common with all other free nations. No other single act will serve as this will serve to restore confidence among the nations in the laws which they have themselves set and determined for the government of their relations with one another. Without this healing act the whole structure and validity of international law is forever impaired.

VIII. All French territory should be freed and the invaded portions restored, and the wrong done to France by Prussia in 1871 in the matter of Alsace-Lorraine, which has unsettled the peace of the world for nearly fifty years, should be righted, in order that peace may once more be made secure in the interest of all.

IX. A readjustment of the frontiers of Italy should be effected along clearly recognizable lines of nationality.

X. The peoples of Austria-Hungary, whose place among the nations we wish to see safeguarded and assured, should be accorded the freest opportunity of autonomous development.

XI. Rumania, Serbia, and Montenegro should be evacuated; occupied territories restored; Serbia accorded free and secure access to the sea; and the relations of the several Balkan states to one another determined by friendly counsel along historically established lines of allegiance and nationality; and international guarantees of the political and economic independence and territorial integrity of the several Balkan states should be entered into.

XII. The Turkish portions of the present Ottoman Empire should be assured a secure sovereignty, but the other nationalities which are now under Turkish rule should be assured an undoubted security of life and an absolutely unmolested opportunity of autonomous development, and the Dardanelles should be permanently opened as a free passage to the ships and commerce of all nations under international guarantees.

XIII. An independent Polish state should be erected which should include the territories inhabited by indisputably Polish populations, which should be assured a free and secure access to the sea, and whose political and economic independence and territorial integrity should be guaranteed by international covenant.

XIV. A general association of nations must be formed under specific covenants for the purpose of affording mutual guarantees of political independence and territorial integrity to great and small states alike.

In regard to these essential rectifications of wrong and assertions of right we feel ourselves to be intimate partners of all the governments and peoples associated together against the Imperialists. We cannot be separated in interest or divided in purpose. We stand together until the end. ...

49. League of Nations Covenant,
Articles 10, 11, and 16, June 1919

From the Treaty of Versailles between the Allied and Associated Powers and Germany. Signed 28 June 1918.

THE HIGH Contracting Parties,
In order to promote international co-operation and to achieve international peace and security
 by the acceptance of obligations not to resort to war,
 by the prescription of open, just and honourable relations between nations,
 by the firm establishment of the understandings of international law as the actual rule of conduct among Governments, and
 by the maintenance of justice and a scrupulous respect for all treaty obligations in the dealings of organized peoples with one another,
Agree to this Covenant of the League of Nations.

Article 1. The original Members of the League of Nations shall be those of the Signatories which are named in the Annex to this Covenant and also such of those other States named in the Annex as shall accede without reservation to this Covenant. Such accession shall be effected by a Declaration deposited with the Secretariat within two months of the coming into force of the Covenant. Notice thereof shall be sent to all other Members of the League.

Any fully self-governing State, Dominion or Colony not named in the Annex may become a Member of the League if its admission is agreed to by two-thirds of the Assembly, provided that it shall give effective guarantees of its sincere intention to observe its international obligations, and shall accept such regulations as may be prescribed by the League in regard to its military, naval and air forces and armaments.

Any Member of the League may, after two years' notice of its intention to do so, withdraw from the League, provided that all its international obligations and all its obligations under this Covenant shall have been fulfilled at the time of its withdrawal.

Article 10. The Members of the League undertake to respect and preserve as against external aggression the territorial integrity and existing political independence of all Members of the League. In case of any such aggression or in case of any threat or danger of such aggression the Council shall advise upon the means by which this obligation shall be fulfilled.

Article 11. Any war or threat of war, whether immediately affecting any of the Members of the League or not, is hereby declared a matter of concern to the whole League, and the League shall take any action that may be deemed wise and effectual to safeguard the peace of nations. In case any such emergency should arise the Secretary General shall on the request of any Member of the League forthwith summon a meeting of the Council.

It is also declared to be the friendly right of each Member of the League to bring to the attention of the Assembly or of the Council any circumstance whatever affecting international relations which threatens to disturb international peace or the good understanding between nations upon which peace depends.

Article 16. Should any Member of the League resort to war in disregard of its covenants under Articles 12, 13 or 15, it shall *ipso facto* be deemed to have committed an act of war against all other Members of the League, which hereby undertake immediately to subject it to the severance of all trade or financial relations, the prohibition of all intercourse between their nationals and the nationals of the covenant-breaking State, and the prevention of all financial, commercial or personal intercourse between the nationals of the covenant-breaking State and the nationals of any other State, whether a Member of the League or not.

It shall be the duty of the Council in such case to recommend to the several Governments concerned what effective military, naval or air force the Members of the League shall severally contribute to the armed forces to be used to protect the covenants of the League.

The Members of the League agree, further, that they will mutually support one another in the financial and economic measures which are taken under this Article, in order to minimise the loss and inconvenience resulting from the above measures, and that they will mutually support one another in resisting any special measures aimed at one of their number by the covenant-breaking State, and that they will take the necessary steps to afford passage through their territory to the forces of any of the Members of the League which are co-operating to protect the covenants of the League.

Any Member of the League which has violated any covenant of the League may be declared to be no longer a Member of the League by a vote of the Council concurred in by the Representatives of all the other Members of the League represented thereon.

50. Lodge Reservations to the Treaty of Versailles, November 1919

Massachusetts Senator Henry Cabot Lodge for the Committee on Foreign Relations, 6 November 1919.

RESOLVED (*two-thirds of the Senators present concurring therein*), That the Senate advise and consent to the ratification of the treaty of peace with Germany concluded at Versailles on the 28th day of June, 1919, subject to the following reservations and understandings, which are hereby made a part and condition of this resolution of ratification, which ratification is not to take effect or bind the United States until the said reservations and understandings adopted by the Senate have been accepted by an exchange of notes as a part and a condition of this resolution of ratification by at least three of the four principal allied and associated powers, to wit, Great Britain, France, Italy, and Japan:

1. The United States so understands and construes article 1 that in case of notice of withdrawal from the league of nations, as provided in said article, the United States shall be the sole judge as to whether all its international obligations and all its obligations under the said covenant have been fulfilled, and notice of withdrawal by the United States may be given by a concurrent resolution of the Congress of the United States.

2. The United States assumes no obligation to preserve the territorial integrity or political independence of any other country or to interfere in controversies between nations — whether members of the league or not — under the provisions of article 10, or to employ the military or naval forces of the United States under any article of the treaty for any purpose, unless in any particular case the Congress, which, under the Constitution, has the sole power to declare war or authorize the employment of the military or naval forces of the United States, shall by act or joint resolution so provide.

3. No mandate shall be accepted by the United States under article 22, part 1, or any other provision of the treaty of peace with Germany, except by action of the Congress of the United States.

4. The United States reserves to itself exclusively the right to decide what questions are within its domestic jurisdiction and declares that all domestic and political questions relating wholly or in part to its internal affairs, including immigration, labor, coastwise traffic, the tariff, commerce, the suppression of traffic in women and children, and in opium and other dangerous drugs, and all other domestic questions, are solely within the jurisdiction of the United States and are not under this treaty to be submitted in any way either to arbitration or to the consideration of the council or of the assembly of the league of nations, or any agency thereof, or to the decision or recommendation of any other power.

5. The United States will not submit to arbitration or to inquiry by the assembly or by the council of the league of nations, provided for in said treaty of peace, any questions which in the judgment of the United States depend upon or relate to its long-established policy, commonly known as the Monroe doctrine; said doctrine is to be interpreted by the United States alone and is hereby declared to be wholly outside the jurisdiction of said league of nations and entirely unaffected by any provision contained in the said treaty of peace with Germany.

6. The United States withholds its assent to articles 156, 157, and 158, and reserves full liberty of action with respect to any controversy which may arise under said articles between the Republic of China and the Empire of Japan.

7. The Congress of the United States will provide by law for the appointment of the representatives of the United States in the assembly and the council of the league of nations, and may in its discretion provide for the participation of the United States in any commission, committee, tribunal, court, council, or conference, or in the selection of any members thereof and for the appointment of members of said commissions, committees, tribunals, courts, councils, or conferences, or any other representatives under the treaty of peace, or in carrying out its provisions, and until such participation and appointment have been so provided for and the powers and duties of such representatives have been defined by law, no person shall represent the United States under either said league of nations

or the treaty of peace with Germany or be authorized to perform any act for or on behalf of the United States thereunder, and no citizen of the United States shall be selected or appointed as a member of said commissions, committees, tribunals, courts, councils, or conferences except with the approval of the Senate of the United States.

8. The United States understands that the reparation commission will regulate or interfere with exports from the United States to Germany, or from Germany to the United States, only when the United States by act or joint resolution of Congress approves such regulation or interference.

9. The United States shall not be obligated to contribute to any expenses of the league of nations, or of the secretariat, or of any commission, or committee, or conference, or other agency, organized under the league of nations or under the treaty or for the purpose of carrying out the treaty provisions, unless and until an appropriation of funds available for such expenses shall have been made by the Congress of the United States.

10. If the United States shall at any time adopt any plan for the limitation of armaments proposed by the council of the league of nations under the provisions of article 8, it reserves the right to increase such armaments without the consent of the council whenever the United States is threatened with invasion or engaged in war.

11. The United States reserves the right to permit, in its discretion, the nationals of a covenant-breaking State, as defined in article 16 of the covenant of the league of nations, residing within the United States or in countries other than that violating said article 16, to continue their commercial, financial, and personal relations with the nationals of the United States.

12. Nothing in articles 296, 297, or in any of the annexes thereto or in any other article, section, or annex of the treaty of peace with Germany shall, as against citizens of the United States, be taken to mean any confirmation, ratification, or approval of any act otherwise illegal or in contravention of the rights of citizens of the United States.

13. The United States withholds its assent to Part XIII (articles 387 to 427, inclusive) unless Congress by act or joint resolution shall hereafter make provision for representation in the organization established by said Part XIII, and in such event the participation of the United States will be governed and conditioned by the provisions of such act or joint resolution.

14. The United States assumes no obligation to be bound by any election, decision, report, or finding of the council or assembly in which any member of the league and its self-governing dominions, colonies, or parts of empire, in the aggregate have cast more than one vote, and assumes no obligation to be bound by any decision, report, or finding of the council or assembly arising out of any dispute between the United States and any member of the league if such member, or any self-governing dominion, colony, empire, or part of empire united with it politically has voted.

51. Harding and Pittman on the Lodge Reservations, November 1919.

Speeches of Senators Warren G. Harding of Ohio and Key Pittman of Nevada, 19 November 1919.

... I HAVE NOT liked this treaty; I think, as originally negotiated, it is the colossal blunder of all time; but, recognizing the aspirations of our own people and the people of the world to do something toward international cooperation for the promotion and preservation of peace and a more intimate and better understanding between nations, I have wished to make it possible to accept this covenant. I could, however, no more vote to ratify this treaty without reservations which make sure America's independence of action, which make sure the preservation of American traditions, which make sure and certain our freedom in choosing our course of action, than I could participate in a knowing betrayal of this Republic. . . .

We are content to give you your league of nations, doubtful as we are about the wisdom of the great experiment. . . .

If this ratification is made with the reservations which have been adopted, there remains the skeleton of a league on which the United States can, if it deems it prudent, proceed in deliberation and calm reflection toward the building of an international relationship which shall be effective in the future.

The trouble with the whole league covenant is that it was hastily negotiated to be made the foundation of a treaty of peace, when there ought to have been a treaty of peace negotiated with a league of nations created in the deliberate aftermath.

Under these circumstances, recognizing conditions, without discussing the partisan phase of it or any political advantage, we have this arrangement, and we must meet it as it exists; and those on the majority side, those against it irreconcilably, and those for the league want these reservations to go to the nations of the Old World to assert and make certain America's freedom of action in the future, and leave a semblance of a league on which to build. . . .

I know, Mr. President, that in this covenant we have originally bartered American independence in order to create a league. We have traded away America's freedom of action in order to establish a supergovernment of the world, and it was never intended to be any less. I speak for one who is old-fashioned enough to believe that the Government of the United States of America is good enough for me. In speaking my reverence for the Government of the United States of America, Senators, I want the preservation of those coordinate branches of government which were conceived and instituted by the fathers; and if there is nothing else significant in the action of this day, you can tell to the people of the United States of America and to the world that the Senate of the United States has once more reasserted its authority, and representative government abides. . . .

Pittman [Against the "Lodge" Reservations][14]

MR. PRESIDENT, while I have always believed that the treaty, particularly that part embracing the covenant of the league, carried with it practically all of the interpretations that were offered by the group referred to by the Senator from Ohio as the mild reservationists, I have never brought myself to the point where I would oppose this treaty, if there were reasonable reservations incorporated in the resolution of ratification. The only question that appeals to my mind to-night is this: Are there reservations included in the resolution of ratification that will not be accepted by those Governments that must accept those reservations to make our participation under the treaty legal?

The Senator from North Dakota [Mr. McCumber] has stated on the floor that in his opinion Great Britain, France, and Italy can not in honor accept the committee reservation with regard to Shantung. Are there other Senators on that side who agree with the Senator from North Dakota? If so, then those Senators can not sincerely vote for this resolution of ratification, if they are in favor of the ratification of the treaty. Surely they do not desire to consummate an act that, while it will not kill the treaty to-night, will result in the death of the treaty two months or three months hence. . . .

But what happened? Why was the Shantung provision put into the resolution? Because a majority of the Republican members of the Foreign Relations Committee, that framed these reservations, were and are now against the treaty. They have always been against the treaty from beginning to end, and they had the power in the committee to frame reservations that in their belief would kill it. They were not able upon the floor of the United States Senate, on a straight vote, to kill the league of nations and the treaty, but they hoped to kill it by subterfuge and they forced these reservations upon the Senate.

On the other side you cast to-night 13 votes against the resolution of ratification. You who on the Republican side favor the treaty have barely more than one-third of the Members of the Senate. You have never had a majority on the other side in favor of this treaty. We have more Members on this side in favor of this treaty; and yet you Republicans on the other side who favor this treaty, who do not constitute as many as we Democrats on this side who favor this treaty, will not stand by us in any amendment or any change that we offer to any one of these abominable reservations that were written by the "treaty killers" on the other side. . . .

All the way through, from the very beginning to the end, there were offered on the other side by the Senator from North Dakota [Mr. McCumber], or there were offered on this side by the Senator from Nebraska [Mr. Hitchcock] or other Democratic Senators, substitute reservations, for practically every reservation offered by the majority, and in nearly every case those reservations which were offered as substitutes were the reservations that had been prepared by the so-called mild reservationists on the Republican side, and yet the Democrats are said not to have offered any opportunity for compromise. The Democrats voted for them in every case, while the Republicans voted against them in every case.

I contend now, and the *Record* will disclose, that every reservation contained in the Republican resolution of ratification was dictated and framed by the identical men who voted to-night to kill the treaty. There was not a case but what, if those men had not voted against the substitutes for the Republican reservations, the substitutes would have carried. . . .

When you unmask all of the hypocrisy surrounding this whole transaction, when you see the leaders of the great Republican Party, representing the people of this country, pretending that they are doing everything in God's world to ratify a treaty, and at the same time you see them call to their aid to prepare the reservations the men who are killing the treaty, and you see them acting with them for the purpose of defeating amendments of Senators like the Senator from North Dakota [Mr. McCumber], who they admit are honestly for the treaty, their interest and sincerity and consistency at least are open to suspicion on the part of the people of the country.

But they say that we have offered no compromise. I say to you that we have offered compromises on the floor of the Senate which even the Senator from North Dakota would admit would have been accepted two months ago. Why will they not be accepted to-day? Conditions have not changed in the world. The reservations are just the same. The reasons they will not be accepted to-day, and he will admit it, are purely political reasons, and nothing else on earth. Then if he will not accept them on the ground of political reasons he need not appeal to us on the high ground that they are trying to ratify a treaty with those countries for the sake of humanity throughout the world. . . .

I simply want to say this in conclusion, because my time is nearly up, that if Senators on the other side who favor the treaty — and I do not know how many of you there are, and I doubt if there are very many of you — if those of you there who are honest and sincere, if those of you there who hold your country above your party, are willing to join us on this side, I feel assured we can get you enough votes to ratify this treaty with reservations that you yourselves would have accepted two months ago.

If you had adopted the amendment of the Senator from North Dakota with regard to the preamble, if you had adopted his suggestions with regard to article 1, if you had adopted his reservation with regard to the Monroe doctrine, if you had adopted his first suggestion with regard to Shantung, which I offered as a substitute, although there is very little left of the original covenant, and while we are simply standing in the league as advisors, and while we have thrown off the burden of responsibility, there would be something left that possibly when we come into our own senses we could later rectify.

It would be the foundation upon which Republicans and Democrats later on could build a better edifice than the Republican Party have left. Change it in those particulars and I will vote for your reservations, and I will vote for your resolution of ratification, bad and insignificant and destructive as it is.

On the other hand, if you do not cut out of the resolution of ratification those reservations that you know will destroy the treaty, if you persist in that fraud upon the American people and that fraud upon the world, then I tell you there are enough fearless Democrats on this side of the Chamber to prevent its ratification until the American people understand. We may adopt the policy of isolation, and profit; we may decide to remain in an existence of selfishness, greed, and war, but we will not stand for national cowardice, pretense, and dishonesty. . . .

52. Wilson, Harding, and Hoover on the League of Nations, 1919-1920

Speeches of Wilson, Harding, and Food Administrator Herbert C. Hoover.

. . . YOU HAVE heard a great deal about Article X of the Covenant of the League of Nations. Article X speaks the conscience of the world. Article X is the article which goes to the heart of this whole bad business, for that article says that the members of this League (that is intended to be all the great nations of the world) engage to respect and to preserve against all external aggression the territorial integrity and political independence of the nations concerned. That promise is necessary in order to prevent this sort of war from recurring, and we are absolutely discredited if we fought this war and then neglect the essential safeguard against it. You have heard it said, my fellow citizens, that we are robbed of some degree of our sovereign, independent choice by articles of that sort. Every man who makes a choice to respect the rights of his neighbors deprives himself of absolute sovereignty, but he does it by promising never to do wrong, and I cannot for one see anything that robs me of any inherent right that I ought to retain when I promise that I will do right, when I promise that I will respect the thing which, being disregarded and violated, brought on a war in which millions of men lost their lives, in which the civilization of mankind was in the balance, in which there was the most outrageous exhibition ever witnessed in the history of mankind of the rapacity and disregard for right of a great armed people.

We engage in the first sentence of Article X to respect and preserve from external aggression the territorial integrity and the existing political independence not only of the other member States, but of all States, and if any member of the League of Nations disregards that promise, then what happens? The council of the League advises what should be done to enforce the respect for that Covenant on the part of the nation attempting to violate it, and there is no compulsion upon us to take that advice except the compulsion of our good conscience and judgment. It is perfectly evident that if, in the judgment of the people of the United States the council adjudged wrong and that this was not a case for the use of force, there would be no necessity on the part of the Congress of the United States to vote the use of force. But there could be no advice of the council on any such subject without a unanimous vote, and the unanimous vote includes our own, and if we accepted the advice we would be accepting our own advice. For I need not tell you that the representatives of the Government of the United States would not vote without instructions from their Government at home, and that what we united in advising we could be certain that the American people would desire to do. There is in that Covenant not only not a surrender of the independent judgment of the Government of the United States, but an expression of it, because that independent judgment would have to join with the judgment of the rest.

But when is that judgment going to be expressed, my fellow citizens? Only after it is evident that every other resource has failed, and I want to call your attention to the central machinery of the League of Nations. If any member of that League, or any nation not a member, refuses to submit the question at issue either to arbitration or to discussion by the council, there ensues automatically by the engagements of this Covenant an absolute economic boycott. There will be no trade with that nation by any member of the League. There will be no interchange of communication by post or telegraph. There will be no travel to or from that nation. Its borders will be closed. No citizen of any other State will be allowed to enter it, and no one of its citizens will be allowed to leave it. It will be hermetically sealed by the united action of the most powerful nations in the world. And if this economic boycott bears with unequal weight, the members of the League agree to support one another and to relieve one another in any exceptional disadvantages that may arise out of it.

I want you to realize that this war was won not only by the armies of the world. It was won by economic means as well. Without the economic means the war would have been much longer continued. What happened was that Germany was shut off from the economic resources of the rest of the globe and she could not stand it. A nation that is boycotted is a nation that is in sight of surrender. Apply this economic, peaceful, silent, deadly remedy and there will be no need for force. It is a terrible remedy. It does not cost a life outside the nation boycotted, but it brings a pressure upon that nation which, in my judgment, no modern nation could resist. . . .

I was pointing out, my fellow citizens, this forenoon, that this Covenant is part of a great document. I wish I had brought a copy with me to show you its bulk. It is an enormous volume, and most of the things you hear talked about in that treaty are not the essential things. This is the first treaty in the history of civilization in which great powers have associated themselves together in order to protect the weak. I need not tell you that I speak with knowledge in this matter, knowledge of the purpose of the men with whom the American delegates were associated at the peace table. They came there, every one that I consulted with, with the same idea, that wars had arisen in the past because the strong took advantage of the weak, and that the only way to stop wars was to bind ourselves together to protect the weak; that the example of this war was the example which gave us the finger to point the way of escape: That as Austria and Germany had tried to put upon Serbia, so we must see to it that Serbia and the Slavic peoples associated with her, and the peoples of Rumania, and the people of Bohemia, and the peoples of Hungary and Austria for that matter, should feel assured in the future that the strength of the great powers was behind their liberty and their independence and was not intended to be used, and never should be used for aggression against them.

So when you read the Covenant, read the treaty with it. I have no doubt that in this audience there are many men which come from that ancient stock of Poland, for example, men in whose blood there is the warmth of old affections connected with that betrayed and ruined country, men whose memories run back to intolerable wrongs suffered by those they love in that country, and I call them to witness that Poland never could have won unity and independence for herself, and those gentlemen sitting at Paris presented Poland with a unity which she could not have won and an independence which she cannot defend unless the world guarantees it to her. There is one of the most noble chapters in the history of the world, that this war was concluded in order to remedy the wrongs which had bitten so deep into the experience of the weaker peoples of that great continent. The object of the war was to see to it that there was no more of that sort of wrong done. Now, when you have that picture in your mind, that this treaty was meant to protect those who could not protect themselves, turn the picture and look at it this way:

Those very weak nations are situated through the very tract of country — between Germany and Persia — which Germany had meant to conquer and dominate, and if the nations of the world do not maintain their concert to sustain the independence and freedom of those peoples, Germany will yet have her will upon them, and we shall witness the very interesting spectacle of having spent millions upon millions of American treasure and, what is much more precious, hundreds of thousands of American lives, to do a futile thing, to do a thing which we will then leave to be undone at the leisure of those who are masters of intrigue, at the leisure of those who are masters in combining wrong influences to overcome right influences, of those who are the masters of the very things that we hate and mean always to fight. For, my fellow citizens, if Germany should ever attempt that again, whether we are in the League of Nations or not, we will join to prevent it. We do not stand off and see murder done. We do not profess to be the champions of liberty and then consent to see liberty destroyed. We are not the friends and advocates of free government and then willing to stand by and see free government die before our eyes. If a power such as Germany was, but thank God no longer is, were to do this thing upon the fields of Europe, then America would have to look to it that she did not do it also upon the fields of the Western Hemisphere, and we should at last be face to face with a power which at the outset we could have crushed, and which now it is within our choice to keep within the harness of civilization. . . .

I want to call your attention, if you will turn to it when you go home, to Article XI, following Article X, of the Covenant of the League of Nations. That article, let me say, is the favorite article in the treaty, so far as I am concerned. It says that every matter which is likely to affect the peace of the world is everybody's business; that it shall be the friendly right of any nation to call attention in the League to anything that is likely to affect the peace of the world or the good understanding between nations, upon which the peace of the world depends, whether that matter immediately concerns the nation drawing attention to it or not. In other words, at present we have to mind our own business. Under the Covenant of the League of Nations we can mind other peoples' business, and anything that affects the peace of the world, whether we are parties to it or not, can by our delegates be brought to the attention of mankind. We can force a nation on the other side of the globe to bring to that bar of mankind any wrong that is afoot in that part of the world which is likely to affect good understanding between nations, and we can oblige them to show cause why it should not be remedied. There is not an oppressed people in the world which cannot henceforth get a hearing at that forum, and you know, my fellow citizens, what a hearing will mean if the cause of those people is just. The one thing that those who are doing injustice have most reason to dread is publicity and discussion, because if you are challenged to give a reason why you are doing a wrong thing it has to be an exceedingly good reason, and if you give a bad reason you confess judgment and the opinion of mankind goes against you. . . .[15]

The solemn thing about Article X is the first sentence, not the second sentence. The first sentence says that we will respect and preserve against external aggression the territorial integrity and existing political independence of other nations; and let me stop a moment on the words "external aggression." Why were they put in? Because every man who sat at that board held that the right of revolution was sacred and must not be interfered with. Any kind of a row can happen inside and it is nobody's right to interfere. The only thing that there is any right to object to or interfere with is external aggression, by some outside power undertaking to take a piece of territory or to interfere with the internal political arrangements of the country which is suffering from the aggression; because territorial integrity does not mean that you cannot invade another country; it means that you cannot invade it and stay there. I have not impaired the territorial integrity of your back yard if I walk into it, but I very much impair it if I insist upon staying there and will not get out, and the impairment of integrity contemplated in this article is the kind of impairment as the seizure of territory, as an attempt at annexation, as an attempt at continuing domination either of the territory itself or of the methods of government inside that territory.

When you read Article X, therefore, you will see that it is nothing but the inevitable, logical center of the whole system of the Covenant of the League of Nations, and I stand for it absolutely. If it should ever in any important respect be impaired, I would feel like asking the Secretary of War to get the boys who went across the water to fight together on some field where I could go and see them, and I would stand up before them and say, "Boys, I told you before you went across the seas that this was a war against wars, and I did my best to fulfill the promise, but I am obliged to come to you in mortification and shame and say I have not been able to fulfill the promise. You are betrayed. You fought for something that you did not get." And the glory of the Armies and the Navies of the United States is gone like a dream in the night, and there ensues upon it, in the suitable darkness of the night, the nightmare of dread which lay upon the nations before this war came; and there will come sometime, in the vengeful Providence of God, another struggle in which, not a few hundred thousand fine men from America will have to die, but as many millions as are necessary to accomplish the final freedom of the peoples of the world. . . .[16]

[Senator Harding's Position on the League]

. . . THE ISSUE, which our opponents are endeavoring to bring, is singularly simple and direct. The issue . . . does not present to the American people the question whether they shall favor some form of association among the nations for the purpose of preserving international peace, but whether they favor the particular League proposed by President Wilson.

The (Democratic) Platform, to be sure, approaches its endorsement with winding words . . . but it does, nevertheless, endorse the League as it stands. . . . It goes no further than to suggest that reservations will not be opposed which make clearer or more specific the obligations of the United States and the League.

But there is no need of reservations of this character. The obligations are clear enough and specific enough. I oppose the League not because I fail to understand . . . "what we are being let in for," but because I believe I understand precisely what we are being let in for.

I do not want to clarify these obligations; I want to turn my back on them. It is not interpretation but rejection, that I am seeking. My position is that the present league strikes a deadly blow at our constitutional integrity and surrenders to a dangerous extent our independence of action. . . .

The issue therefore is clear. I understand the position of the Democratic candidate and he understands mine. . . . It is that he favors going into the Paris League and I favor staying out. . . .

As soon as possible after my election I shall advise with the best minds in the United States. . . . I shall do this to the end that we shall have an association of nations for the promotion of international peace, but one which shall so definitely safeguard our sovereignty and recognise our ultimate and unmortgaged freedom of action . . . that it will have back of it the united support of the American people. . . .[17]

[Herbert Hoover on the League Issue]

. . . INASMUCH as forty nations, comprising three-quarters of the people of the globe have embraced the "League of Nations" as a term expressing certain ideas, I prefer that term, but I care little for terminology. . . . The essential thing is that the Republican Party has pledged itself by its platform, by the actions of its majority in the Senate, by the repeated statements of Senator Harding, that they undertake the fundamental mission to put into living being the principle of an organized association of nations for the preservation of peace. The carrying out of this promise is the test of the entire sincerity, integrity, and statesmanship of the Republican Party. . . .

If there be persons supporting the Republican Party today on the belief or hope that this party is the avenue to destruction of this great principle, that the party will not with sincerity and statesmanship carry out their pledges to bring it into effect, then they are counting on the insincerity and infidelity of the Republican Party and its nominee for the Presidency. . . .[18]

53. Germany and U.S., Treaty of Peace, November 1921

Signed at Berlin 25 August 1921; ratifications exchanged 11 November 1921.

... ARTICLE I. Germany undertakes to accord to the United States, and the United States shall have and enjoy, all the rights, privileges, indemnities, reparations or advantages specified in the aforesaid Joint Resolution of the Congress of the United States of July 2, 1921, including all the rights and advantages stipulated for the benefit of the United States in the Treaty of Versailles which the United States shall fully enjoy notwithstanding the fact that such Treaty has not been ratified by the United States.

Article II. With a view to defining more particularly the obligations of Germany under the foregoing Article with respect to certain provisions in the Treaty of Versailles, it is understood and agreed between the High Contracting Parties:

(1) That the rights and advantages stipulated in that Treaty for the benefit of the United States, which it is intended the United States shall have and enjoy, are those defined in Section I, of Part IV, and Parts V, VI, VIII, IX, X, XI, XII, XIV, and XV.

The United States in availing itself of the rights and advantages stipulated in the provisions of that Treaty mentioned in this paragraph will do so in a manner consistent with the rights accorded to Germany under such provisions.

(2) That the United States shall not be bound by the provisions of Part I of that Treaty, nor by any provisions of that Treaty including those mentioned in Paragraph (1) of this Article, which relate to the Covenant of the League of Nations, nor shall the United States be bound by any action taken by the League of Nations, or by the Council or by the Assembly thereof, unless the United States shall expressly give its assent to such action.

(3) That the United States assumes no obligations under or with respect to the provisions of Part II, Part III, Sections 2 to 8 inclusive of Part IV, and Part XIII of that Treaty.

(4) That, while the United States is privileged to participate in the Reparation Commission, according to the terms of Part VIII of that Treaty, and in any other Commission established under the Treaty or under any agreement supplemental thereto, the United States is not bound to participate in any such commission unless it shall elect to do so. . . .[20]

54. Washington Treaties, Naval Limitations Pact, 1922
Signed by U.S., Great Britain, Japan, France, and Italy, 6 February 1922.

... ARTICLE III. Subject to the provisions of Article II, the Contracting Powers shall abandon their respective capital ship building programs, and no new capital ships shall be constructed or acquired by any of the Contracting Powers except replacement tonnage which may be constructed or acquired as specified in Chapter II, Part 3. . . .

Article IV. The total capital ship replacement tonnage of each of the Contracting Powers shall not exceed in standard displacement, for the United States, 525,000 tons (533,400 metric tons); for the British Empire 525,000 tons (533,400 metric tons); for France 175,000 tons (177,800 metric tons); for Italy 175,000 tons (177,800 metric tons); for Japan 315,000 tons (320,040 metric tons).

Article V. No capital ship exceeding 35,000 tons (35,560 metric tons) standard displacement shall be acquired by, or constructed by, for, or within the jurisdiction of, any of the Contracting Powers.

Article VI. No capital ship of any of the Contracting Powers shall carry a gun with a calibre in excess of 16 inches (406 millimetres).

Article VII. The total tonnage for aircraft carriers of each of the Contracting Powers shall not exceed in standard displacement, for the United States 135,000 tons (137,160 metric tons); for the British Empire 135,000 tons (137,160 metric tons); for France 60,000 tons (60,960 metric tons); for Italy 60,000 tons (60,960 metric tons); for Japan 81,000 tons (82,296 metric tons). . . .

Article XI. No vessel of war exceeding 10,000 tons (10,160 metric tons) standard displacement, other than a capital ship or aircraft carrier, shall be acquired by, or constructed by, for, or within the jurisdiction of, any of the Contracting Powers. Vessels not specifically built as fighting ships nor taken in time of peace under government control for fighting purposes, which are employed on fleet duties or as troop transports or in some other way for the purpose of assisting in the prosecution of hostilities otherwise than as fighting ships, shall not be within the limitations of this Article. . . .

Article IX. The United States, the British Empire and Japan agree that the status quo at the time of the signing of the present Treaty, with regard to fortifications and naval bases, shall be maintained in their respective territories and possessions specified hereunder:

(1) The insular possessions which the United States now holds or may hereafter acquire in the Pacific Ocean, except (a) those adjacent to the coast of the United States, Alaska and the Panama Canal Zone, not including the Aleutian Islands, and (b) the Hawaiian Islands;

(2) Hongkong and the insular possessions which the British Empire now holds or may hereafter acquire in the Pacific Ocean, east of the meridian of 110° east longitude, except (a) those adjacent to the coast of Canada, (b) the Commonwealth of Australia and its Territories, and (c) New Zealand;

(3) The following insular territories and possessions of Japan in the Pacific Ocean, to wit: the Kurile Islands, the Bonin Islands, Anami-Oshima, the Loochoo Islands, Formosa and the Pescadores, and any insular territories or possessions in the Pacific Ocean which Japan may hereafter acquire.

The maintenance of the status quo under the foregoing provisions implies that no new fortifications or naval bases shall be established in the territories and possessions specified that no measures shall be taken to increase the existing naval facilities for the repair and maintenance of naval forces, and that no increase shall be made in the coast defenses of the territories and possessions above specified. This restriction, however, does not preclude such repair and replacement of worn-out weapons and equipment as is customary in naval and military establishments in time of peace. . . .[3]

55. Washington Treaties, Nine-Power Pact, 1922

Signed by U.S., British Empire, Japan, China, France, Italy, Belgium, the Netherlands, and Portugal, 6 February 1922.

... *Article I.* The Contracting Powers, other than China, agree:

(1) To respect the sovereignty, the independence, and the territorial and administrative integrity of China;

(2) To provide the fullest and most unembarrassed opportunity to China to develop and maintain for herself an effective and stable government;

(3) To use their influence for the purpose of effectually establishing and maintaining the principle of equal opportunity for the commerce and industry of all nations throughout the territory of China;

(4) To refrain from taking advantage of conditions in China in order to seek special rights or privileges which would abridge the rights of subjects or citizens of friendly States, and from countenancing action inimical to the security of such States.

Article II. The Contracting Powers agree not to enter into any treaty, agreement, arrangement or understanding, either with one another, or, individually or collectively, with any Power or Powers, which would infringe or impair the principles stated in Article I.

Article III. With a view to applying more effectually the principles of the Open Door or equality of opportunity in China for the trade and industry of all nations, the Contracting Powers, other than China, agree that they will not seek, nor support their respective nationals in seeking —

(a) any arrangement which might purport to establish in favor of their interests any general superiority of rights with respect to commercial or economic development in any designated region of China;

(b) any such monopoly or preference as would deprive the nationals of any other Power of the right of undertaking any legitimate trade or industry in China, or of participating with the Chinese Government, or with any local authority, in any category of public enterprise, or which by reason of its scope, duration or geographical extent is calculated to frustrate the practical application of the principle of equal opportunity.

It is understood that the foregoing stipulations of this Article are not to be so construed as to prohibit the acquisition of such properties or rights as may be necessary to the conduct of a particular commercial, industrial or financial undertaking or to the encouragement of invention and research.

China undertakes to be guided by the principles stated in the foregoing stipulations of this Article in dealing with applications for economic rights and privileges from Governments and nationals of all foreign countries, whether parties to the present Treaty or not.

Article IV. The Contracting Powers agree not to support any agreements by their respective nationals with each other designed to create Spheres of Influence or to provide for the enjoyment of mutually exclusive opportunities in designated parts of Chinese territory.

Article V. China agrees that, throughout the whole of the railways in China, she will not exercise or permit unfair discrimination of any kind. In particular there shall be no discrimination whatever, direct or indirect, in respect of charges or of facilities on the ground of the nationality of passengers or the countries from which or to which they are proceeding, or the origin or ownership of goods or the country from which or to which they are consigned, or the nationality or ownership of the ship or other means of conveying such passengers or goods before or after their transport on the Chinese Railways.

The Contracting Powers, other than China, assume a corresponding obligation in respect of any of the aforesaid railways over which they or their nationals are in a position to exercise any control in virtue of any concession, special agreement or otherwise.

Article VI. The Contracting Powers, other than China, agree fully to respect China's rights as a neutral in time of war to which China is not a party; and China declares that when she is a neutral she will observe the obligations of neutrality.

Article VII. The Contracting Powers agree that, whenever a situation arises which in the opinion of any one of them involves the application of the stipulations of the present Treaty, and renders desirable discussion of such application, there shall be full and frank communication between the Contracting Powers concerned. . . .[5]

56. Washington Treaties, Four-Power Pact, 1921
Signed by U.S., British Empire, Japan, and France, 13 December 1921.

... I. The High Contracting Parties agree as between themselves to respect their rights in relation to their insular possessions and insular dominions in the region of the Pacific Ocean.

If there should develop between any of the High Contracting Parties a controversy arising out of any Pacific question and involving their said rights which is not satisfactorily settled by diplomacy and is likely to affect the harmonious accord now happily subsisting between them, they shall invite the other High Contracting Parties to a joint conference to which the whole subject will be referred for consideration and adjustment.

II. If the said rights are threatened by the aggressive action of any other Power, the High Contracting Parties shall communicate with one another fully and frankly in order to arrive at an understanding as to the most efficient measures to be taken, jointly or separately, to meet the exigencies of the particular situation.

III. This Treaty shall remain in force for 10 years from the time it shall take effect, and after the expiration of said period it shall continue to be in force subject to the right of any of the High Contracting Parties to terminate it upon 12 months' notice.

IV. This Treaty shall be ratified as soon as possible in accordance with the constitutional methods of the High Contracting Parties and shall take effect on the deposit of ratifications, which shall take place at Washington, and thereupon the agreement between Great Britain and Japan, which was concluded at London on July 13, 1911, shall terminate. The Government of the United States will transmit to all the signatory Powers a certified copy of the *proces-verbal* of the deposit of ratifications. . . .[6]

57. Harding and Hughes on the Washington Treaties, 1922

Speeches of President Warren G. Harding, 10 February 1922; and Secretary of State Charles Evans Hughes, 1 February 1922.

I AM NOT unmindful, nor was the conference, of the sentiment in this Chamber against Old World entanglements. Those who made the treaties have left no doubt about their true import. Every expression in the conference has emphasized the purpose to be served and the obligations assumed. Therefore, I can bring you every assurance that nothing in any of these treaties commits the United States, or any other power, to any kind of an alliance, entanglement, or involvement. It does not require us or any power to surrender a worth-while tradition. . . .

The world has been hungering for a better relationship for centuries since it has attained its larger consciousness. The conception of the League of Nations was a response to a manifest world hunger. Whatever its fate, whether it achieves the great things hoped for, or comes to supersedure, or to failure, the American unwillingness to be a part of it has been expressed. That unwillingness has been kept in mind, and the treaties submitted to-day have no semblance or relationship save as the wish to promote peace has been the common inspiration.

The four-power treaty contains no war commitment. It covenants the respect of each nation's rights in relation to its insular possessions. In case of controversy between the covenanting powers it is agreed to confer and seek adjustment, and if said rights are threatened by the aggressive action of any outside power, these friendly powers, respecting one another, are to communicate, perhaps confer, in order to understand what action may be taken, jointly or separately, to meet a menacing situation. There is no commitment to armed force, no alliance, no written or moral obligation to join in defence, no expressed or implied commitment to arrive at any agreement except in accordance with our constitutional methods. It is easy to believe, however, that such a conference of the four powers is a moral warning that an aggressive nation, giving affront to the four great powers ready to focus world opinion on a given controversy, would be embarking on a hazardous enterprise.

Frankly, Senators, if nations may not safely agree to respect each other's rights, and may not agree to confer if one to the compact threatens trespass, or may not agree to advise if one party to the pact is threatened by an outside power, then all concerted efforts to tranquilize the world and stabilize peace must be flung to the winds. Either these treaties must have your cordial sanction, or every proclaimed desire to promote peace and prevent war becomes a hollow mockery. . . .[7]

Hughes

. . . I now have the honor to report on behalf of the committee of the Conference which has been dealing with the subject of armament, that the proposals of the American Government in relation to the limitation of naval armament have been considered and an agreement has been reached which is embodied in a treaty now presented for your adoption. . . .

May I say . . . that with respect to capital ships . . . the integrity of the plan proposed on behalf of the American Government has been maintained, and the spirit, in which that proposal was made, and in which it was received, has dominated the entire negotiations and brought them to a very successful conclusion. . . .

May I say . . . that no more extraordinary or significant treaty has ever been made. It is extraordinary because we no longer merely talk of the desirability of diminishing the burdens of naval armaments, but we actually limit them. It is extraordinary because this limitation is effected in that field in which nations have been most jealous of their power, and in which they have hitherto been disposed to resent any interference with their power.

I shall not enlarge upon the significance of the engagement. Of course, it is obvious that it means an enormous saving of money and the lifting of a very heavy and unnecessary burden from the peoples of the countries who unite in this agreement.

This treaty ends, absolutely ends, the race in competition in naval armament. At the same time it leaves the relative security of the great naval powers unimpaired.

The significance of the treaty is far more than that. In this treaty we are talking of arms in the language of peace. The best thing about the engagement is the spirit which has been manifested throughout our negotiations and to which is due our ability to reach this fortunate conclusion.

58. Coolidge on U.S. Policy in Nicaragua, 1927

Speech of President Calvin Coolidge to Congress, 10 January 1927.

TO THE CONGRESS of the United States:

While conditions in Nicaragua and the action of this Government pertaining thereto have in general been made public, I think the time has arrived for me officially to inform the Congress more in detail of the events leading up to the present disturbances and conditions which seriously threaten American lives and property, endanger the stability of all Central America, and put in jeopardy the rights granted by Nicaragua to the United States for the construction of a canal. It is well known that in 1912 the United States intervened in Nicaragua with a large force and put down a revolution, and that from that time to 1925 a legation guard of American marines was, with the consent of the Nicaraguan Government, kept in Managua to protect American lives and property. In 1923 representatives of the five Central American countries, namely, Costa Rica, Guatemala, Honduras, Nicaragua, and Salvador, at the invitation of the United States, met in Washington and entered into a series of treaties. These treaties dealt with limitation of armament, a Central American tribunal for arbitration, and the general subject of peace and amity. The treaty last referred to specifically provides in Article II that the Governments of the contracting parties will not recognize any other government which may come into power in any of the five Republics through a coup d'état, or revolution, and disqualifies the leaders of such coup d'état, or revolution, from assuming the presidency or vice presidency. . . .

The United States was not a party to this treaty, but it was made in Washington under the auspices of the Secretary of State, and this Government has felt a moral obligation to apply its principles in order to encourage the Central American States in their efforts to prevent revolution and disorder. . . .

The Nicaraguan constitution provides in article 106 that in the absence of the President and Vice President the Congress shall designate one of its members to complete the unexpired term of President. As President Solorzano had resigned and was then residing in California, and as the Vice President, Doctor Sacasa, was in Guatemala, having been out of the country since November, 1925, the action of Congress in designating Señor Diaz was perfectly legal and in accordance with the constitution. Therefore the United States Government on November 17 extended recognition to Señor Diaz. . . .

Immediately following the inauguration of President Diaz and frequently since that date he has appealed to the United States for support, has informed this Government of the aid which Mexico is giving to the revolutionists, and has stated that he is unable solely because of the aid given by Mexico to the revolutionists to protect the lives and property of American citizens and other foreigners. When negotiations leading up to the Corinto conference began, I immediately placed an embargo on the shipment of arms and ammunition to Nicaragua. The Department of State notified the other Central American States, to wit, Costa Rica, Honduras, Salvador, and Guatemala, and they assured the department they would cooperate in this measure. So far as known, they have done so. The State Department also notified the Mexican Government of this embargo and informally suggested to that government like action. The Mexican Government did not adopt the suggestion to put on an embargo, but informed the American ambassador at Mexico City that in the absence of manufacturing plants in Mexico for the making of arms and ammunition the matter had little practical importance.

As a matter of fact, I have the most conclusive evidence that arms and munitions in large quantities have been on several occasions since August, 1926, shipped to the revolutionists in Nicaragua. Boats carrying these munitions have been fitted out in Mexican ports, and some of the munitions bear evidence of having belonged to the Mexican Government. It also appears that the ships were fitted out with the full knowledge of and, in some cases, with the encouragement of Mexican officials and were in one instance, at least, commanded by a Mexican naval reserve officer. At the end of November, after spending some time in Mexico City, Doctor Sacasa went back to Nicaragua, landing at Puerto Cabezas, near Bragmans Bluff. He immediately placed himself at the head of the insurrection and declared himself President of Nicaragua. He has never been recognized by any of the Central American Republics nor by any other government, with the exception of Mexico, which recognized him immediately. As arms and munitions in large quanties were reaching the revolutionists, I deemed it unfair to prevent the recognized government from purchasing arms abroad, and, accordingly, the Secretary of State has notified the Diaz Government that licenses would be issued for the export of arms and munitions purchased in this country. It would be thoroughly inconsistent for this country not to support the government recognized by it while the revolutionists were receiving arms and munitions from abroad.

During the last two months the Government of the United States has received repeated requests from various American citizens, both directly and through our consuls and legation, for the protection of their lives and property. The Government of the United States has also received requests from the British chargé at Managua and from the Italian ambassador at Washington for the protection of their respective nationals. Pursuant to such requests, Admiral Latimer, in charge of the special service squadron, has not only maintained the neutral zone at Bluefields under the agreement of both parties but has landed forces at Puerto Cabezas and Rio Grande, and established neutral zones at these points where considerable numbers of Americans live and are engaged in carrying on various industries. He has also been authorized to establish such other neutral zones as are necessary for the purposes above mentioned.

For many years numerous Americans have been living in Nicaragua, developing its industries and carrying on business. At the present time there are large investments in lumbering, mining, coffee growing, banana culture, shipping, and also in general mercantile and other collateral business. All these people and these industries have been encouraged by the Nicaraguan Government. That Government has at all times owed them protection, but the United States has occasionally been obliged to send naval forces for their proper protection. In the present crisis such forces are requested by the Nicaraguan Government, which protests to the United States its inability to protect these interests and states that any measures which the United States deems appropriate for their protection will be satisfactory to the Nicaraguan Government.

In addition to these industries now in existence, the Government of Nicaragua, by a treaty entered into on the 5th day of August, 1914, granted in perpetuity to the United States the exclusive proprietary rights necessary and convenient for the construction, operation, and maintenance of an oceanic canal. . . .

There is no question that if the revolution continues American investments and business interests in Nicaragua will be very seriously affected, if not destroyed. The currency, which is now at par, will be inflated. American as well as foreign bond holders will undoubtedly look to the United States for the protection of their interests. . . .

Manifestly the relation of this Government to the Nicaraguan situation, and its policy in the existing emergency, are determined by the facts which I have described. The proprietary rights of the United States in the Nicaraguan canal route, with the necessary implications growing out of it affecting the Panama Canal, together with the obligations flowing from the investments of all classes of our citizens in Nicaragua, place us in a position of peculiar responsibility. I am sure it is not the desire of the United States to intervene in the internal affairs of Nicaragua or of any other Central American Republic. Nevertheless it must be said that we have a very definite and special interest in the maintenance of order and good government in Nicaragua at the present time, and that the stability, prosperity, and independence of all Central American countries can never be a matter of indifference to us. The United States can not, therefore, fail to view with deep concern any serious threat to stability and constitutional government in Nicaragua tending toward anarchy and jeopardizing American interests, especially if such state of affairs is contributed to or brought about by outside influences or by any foreign power. It has always been and remains the policy of the United States in such circumstances to take the steps that may be necessary for the preservation and protection of the lives, the property, and the interests of its citizens and of this Government itself. In this respect I propose to follow the path of my predecessors.

Consequently, I have deemed it my duty to use the powers committed to me to insure the adequate protection of all American interests in Nicaragua, whether they be endangered by internal strife or by outside interference in the affairs of that Republic.

59. Clark Memorandum on the Monroe Doctrine, 1928

Under Secretary of State J. Reuben Clark, 1928; published 1930.

Washington, D. C., December 17, 1928

HEREWITH I transmit a Memorandum on the Monroe Doctrine, prepared by your direction, given a little over two months ago. . . .

It is of first importance to have in mind that Monroe's declaration in its terms, relates solely to the relationships between European states on the one side, and, on the other side, the American continents, the Western Hemisphere, and the Latin American Governments which on December 2, 1823, had declared and maintained their independence which we had acknowledged. . . .

In the normal case, the Latin American state against which aggression was aimed by a European power, would be the beneficiary of the Doctrine not its victim. This has been the history of its application. The Doctrine makes the United States a guarantor, in effect, of the independence of Latin American states, though without the obligations of a guarantor to those states, for the United States itself determines by its sovereign will when, where, and concerning what aggressions it will invoke the Doctrine, and by what measures, if any, it will apply a sanction. In none of these things has any other state any voice whatever.

Furthermore while the Monroe Doctrine as declared, has no relation in its terms to an aggression by any other state than a European state, yet the principle "self-preservation" which underlies the Doctrine — which principle, as we shall see, is as fully operative without the Doctrine as with it — would apply to any non-American state in whatever quarter of the globe it lay, or even to an American state, if the aggressions of such state against other Latin American states were "dangerous to our peace and safety," or were a "manifestation of an unfriendly disposition towards the United States," or were "endangering our peace and happiness"; that is, if such aggressions challenged our existence. . . .

In this view, the Monroe Doctrine as such might be wiped out and the United States would lose nothing of its broad, international right; it would still possess, in common with every other member of the family of nations, the internationally recognized right of self-preservation, and this right would fully attach to the matters specified by the Doctrine if and whenever they threatened our existence, just as the right would attach in relation to any other act carrying a like menace. . . .

It is evident from the foregoing that the Monroe Doctrine is not an equivalent for "self-preservation"; and therefore the Monroe Doctrine need not, indeed should not, be invoked in order to cover situations challenging our self-preservation but not within the terms defined by Monroe's declaration. These other situations may be handled, and more wisely so, as matters affecting the national security and self-preservation of the United States as a great power. . . .

The statement of the Doctrine itself that "with the existing colonies or dependencies of any European power we have not interfered and shall not interfere," has been more than once reiterated.

It has also been announced that the Monroe Doctrine is not a pledge by the United States to other American states requiring the United States to protect such states, at their behest, against real or fancied wrongs inflicted by European powers, nor does it create an obligation running from the United States to any American state to intervene for its protection. . . .

The so-called "Roosevelt corollary" was to the effect, as generally understood, that in case of financial or other difficulties in weak Latin American countries, the United States should attempt an adjustment thereof lest European Governments should intervene, and intervening should occupy territory — an act which would be contrary to the principles of the Monroe Doctrine. This view seems to have had its inception in some observations of President Buchanan in his message to Congress of December 3, 1860, and was somewhat amplified by Lord Salisbury in his note to Mr. Olney of November 6, 1895, regarding the Venezuelan boundary dispute.

As has already been indicated above, it is not believed that this corollary is justified by the terms of the Monroe Doctrine, however much it may be justified by the application of the doctrine of self-preservation.

These various expressions and statements, as made in connection with the situations which gave rise to them, detract not a little from the scope popularly attached to the Monroe Doctrine, and they relieve that Doctrine of many of the criticisms which have been aimed against it.

Finally, it should not be overlooked that the United States declined the overtures of Great Britain in 1823 to make a joint declaration regarding the principles covered by the Monroe Doctrine, or to enter into a conventional arrangement regarding them. Instead this Government determined to make the declaration of high national policy on its own responsibility and in its own behalf. The Doctrine is thus purely unilateral. The United States determines when and if the principles of the Doctrine are violated, and when and if violation is threatened. We alone determine what measures if any, shall be taken to vindicate the principles of the Doctrine, and we of necessity determine when the principles have been vindicated. No other power of the world has any relationship to, or voice in, the implementing of the principles which the Doctrine contains. It is our Doctrine, to be by us invoked and sustained, held in abeyance, or abandoned as our high international policy or vital national interests shall seem to us, and to us alone, to demand.

It may, in conclusion, be repeated: The Doctrine does not concern itself with purely inter-American relations; it has nothing to do with the relationship between the United States and other American nations, except where other American nations shall become involved with European governments in arrangements which threaten the security of the United States, and even in such cases, the Doctrine runs against the European country, not the American nation, and the United States would primarily deal thereunder with the European country and not with the American nation concerned. The Doctrine states a case of the United States *vs.* Europe, and not of the United States *vs.* Latin America. Furthermore, the fact should never be lost to view that in applying this Doctrine during the period of one hundred years since it was announced, our Government has over and over again driven it in as a shield between Europe and the Americas to protect Latin America from the political and territorial thrusts of Europe; and this was done at times when the American nations were weak and struggling for the establishment of stable, permanent governments; when the political morality of Europe sanctioned, indeed encouraged, the acquisition of territory by force; and when many of the great powers of Europe looked with eager, covetous eyes to the rich, undeveloped areas of the American hemisphere. Nor should another equally vital fact be lost sight of, that the United States has only been able to give this protection against designing European powers because of its known willingness and determination, if and whenever necessary, to expend its treasure and to sacrifice American life to maintain the principles of the Doctrine. So far as Latin America is concerned, the Doctrine is now, and always has been, not an instrument of violence and oppression, but an unbought, freely bestowed, and wholly effective guaranty of their freedom, independence, and territorial integrity against the imperialistic designs of Europe.

60. Stimson on Non-recognition in Latin America, 1931

Speech of Secretary of State Henry L. Stimson, 6 February 1931.

... THE PRACTICE of this country as to the recognition of new governments has been substantially uniform from the days of the administration of Secretary of State Jefferson in 1792 to the days of Secretary of State Bryan in 1913. ...

The particular considerations upon which our action was regularly based were well stated by Mr. Adee, long the trusted Assistant Secretary of State of this Government, as follows:

Ever since the American Revolution entrance upon diplomatic intercourse with foreign states has been *de facto*, dependent upon the existence of three conditions of fact: the control of the administrative machinery of the state; the general acquiescence of its people; and the ability and willingness of their government to discharge international and conventional obligations. The form of government has not been a conditional factor in such recognition; in other words, the *de jure* element of legitimacy of title has been left aside. (*Foreign Relations of the United States, 1913*, p. 100.)

With the advent of President Wilson's administration this policy of over a century was radically departed from in respect to the Republic of Mexico, and, by a public declaration on March 11, 1913, it was announced that —

Cooperation (with our sister republics of Central and South America) is possible only when supported at every turn by the orderly processes of just government based upon law, not upon arbitrary or irregular force. We hold, as I am sure that all thoughtful leaders of republican government everywhere hold, that just government rests always upon the consent of the governed, and that there can be no freedom without order based upon law and upon the public conscience and approval. We shall look to make these principles the basis of mutual intercourse, respect, and helpfulness between our sister republics and ourselves. (*Foreign Relations of the United States,* 1913, p. 7.)

Mr. Wilson's government sought to put this new policy into effect in respect to the recognition of the then Government of Mexico held by President Victoriano Huerta. Although Huerta's government was in *de facto* possession, Mr. Wilson refused to recognize it, and he sought through the influence and pressure of his great office to force it from power. Armed conflict followed with the forces of Mexico, and disturbed relations between us and that republic lasted until a comparatively few years ago. . . .

The present administration has refused to follow the policy of Mr. Wilson and has followed consistently the former practice of this Government since the days of Jefferson. As soon as it was reported to us, through our diplomatic representatives, that the new governments in Bolivia, Peru, Argentina, Brazil, and Panama were in control of the administrative machinery of the state, with the apparent general acquiescence of their people, and that they were willing and apparently able to discharge their international and conventional obligations, they were recognized by our Government. And, in view of the economic depression, with the consequent need for prompt measures of financial stabilization, we did this with as little delay as possible in order to give those sorely pressed countries the quickest possible opportunities for recovering their economic poise.

Such has been our policy in all cases where international practice was not affected or controlled by preëxisting treaty. In the five republics of Central America, Guatemala, Honduras, Salvador, Nicaragua, and Costa Rica, however, we have found an entirely different situation existing from that normally presented under international law and practice. . . . In 1907 a period of strife, involving four of the five republics, had lasted almost without interruption for several years. In that year, on the joint suggestion and mediation of the Governments of the United States and Mexico, the five republics met for the purpose of considering methods intended to mitigate and, if possible, terminate the intolerable situation. By one of the conventions which they then adopted, the five republics agreed with one another as follows:

The Governments of the high contracting parties shall not recognize any other government which may come into power in any of the five republics as a consequence of a *coup d'état*, or of a revolution against the recognized government, so long as the freely elected representatives of the people thereof, have not constitutionally reorganized the country.

Sixteen years later, in 1923, the same five republics, evidently satisfied with the principle they had thus adopted and desiring to reinforce it and prevent any future evasions of that principle, met again, reenacted the same covenant, and further promised each other that even after a revolutionary government had been constitutionally reorganized by the representatives of the people, they would not recognize it if its president should have been a leader in the preceding revolution or related to such a leader by blood or marriage, or if he should have been a cabinet officer or held some high military command during the accomplishment of the revolution. Some four months thereafter, our own Government, on the invitation of these republics, who had conducted their meeting in Washington, announced, through Secretary Hughes, that the United States would in its future dealings with those republics follow out the same principle which they had thus established in their treaty. Since that time we have consistently adhered to this policy in respect to those five republics. . . .

61. F.D. Roosevelt on the Good Neighbor Policy, 1936

Speech of President Franklin D. Roosevelt, 14 August 1936.

. . . LONG BEFORE I returned to Washington as President of the United States, I had made up my mind that, pending what might be called a more opportune moment on other continents, the United States could best serve the cause of peaceful humanity by setting an example. That was why on the 4th of March, 1933, I made the following declaration:

In the field of world policy I would dedicate this nation to the policy of the good neighbor — the neighbor who resolutely respects himself and because he does so, respects the rights of others — the neighbor who respects his obligations and respects the sanctity of his agreements in and with a world of neighbors.

This declaration represents my purpose; but it represents more than a purpose, for it stands for a practice. To a measurable degree it has succeeded; the whole world now knows that the United States cherishes no predatory ambitions. We are strong; but less powerful nations know that they need not fear our strength. We seek no conquest; we stand for peace.

In the whole of the Western Hemisphere our good neighbor policy has produced results that are especially heartening.

The noblest monument to peace and to neighborly economic and social friendship in all the world is not a monument in bronze or stone but the boundary which unites the United States and Canada — 3,000 miles of friendship with no barbed wire, no gun or soldier, and no passport on the whole frontier.

Mutual trust made that frontier — to extend the same sort of mutual trust throughout the Americas was our aim.

The American republics to the south of us have been ready always to cooperate with the United States on a basis of equality and mutual respect, but before we inaugurated the good neighbor policy there was among them resentment and fear, because certain administrations in Washington had slighted their national pride and their sovereign rights.

In pursuance of the good neighbor policy, and because in my younger days I had learned many lessons in the hard school of experience, I stated that the United States was opposed definitely to armed intervention.

We have negotiated a Pan-American convention embodying the principle of non-intervention. We have abandoned the Platt amendment which gave us the right to intervene in the internal affairs of the Republic of Cuba. We have withdrawn American marines from Haiti. We have signed a new treaty which places our relations with Panama on a mutually satisfactory basis. We have undertaken a series of trade agreements with other American countries to our mutual commercial profit. At the request of two neighboring republics, I hope to give assistance in the final settlement of the last serious boundary dispute between any of the American nations.

Throughout the Americas the spirit of the good neighbor is a practical and living fact. The twenty-one American republics are not only living together in friendship and in peace; they are united in the determination so to remain. . . .

Of all the nations of the world today we are in many ways most singularly blessed. Our closest neighbors are good neighbors. If there are remoter nations that wish us not good but ill, they know that we are strong; they know that we can and will defend ourselves and defend our neighborhood.

We seek to dominate no other nation. We ask no territorial expansion. We oppose imperialism. We desire reduction in world armaments.

We believe in democracy; we believe in freedom; we believe in peace. We offer to every nation of the world the handclasp of the good neighbor. Let those who wish our friendship look us in the eye and take our hand.

62. Buenos Aires Pact on Non-Intervention, 1936

Signed 23 December 1936, proclaimed 16 September 1937.

... *ARTICLE 1.* The High Contracting Parties declare inadmissible the intervention of any one of them, directly or indirectly, and for whatever reason, in the internal or external affairs of any other of the Parties.

The violation of the provisions of this Article shall give rise to mutual consultation, with the object of exchanging views and seeking methods of peaceful adjustment.

Article 2. It is agreed that every question concerning the interpretation of the present Additional Protocol, which it has not been possible to settle through diplomatic channels, shall be submitted to the procedure of conciliation provided for in the agreements in force, or to arbitration, or to judicial settlement. ...

63. Japan's Invasion of Manchuria, China's Appeal to U.S., 21 September 1931

... JAPANESE troops near Shenyang (Mukden), without the slightest provocation, opened an attack on the Chinese barracks on September 18, at 10 p.m., and continued bombarding the Chinese camps and arsenal, killing a large number of Chinese people in spite of the complete non-resistance of the Chinese troops. The whole city of Chenyang and its vicinity were occupied by Japanese troops by September 19, at 6.30 a.m. The occupation of Antung is already confirmed, and possibly other places also are now under Japanese military control.

As the United States, China, and Japan are all signatory powers of the Kellogg pact, and as the United States is the sponsor of the sacred engagements contained in this treaty, the American Government must be deeply interested in this case of unprovoked and unwarranted attack and subsequent occupation of Chinese cities by Japanese troops, which constitutes a deliberate violation of the pact. The Chinese Government urgently appeals to the American Government to take such steps as will insure the preservation of peace in the Far East, and the upholding of the principle of peaceful settlement of international disputes.

64. Japan's Invasion of Manchuria, Stimson to Japanese Ambassador Katsuji Debuchi, 22 September 1931

Without going into the background, either as to the immediate provocation or remote causes or motivation, it appears that there has developed within the past four days a situation in Manchuria which I find surprising and view with concern. Japanese military forces, with some opposition at some points by Chinese military forces, have occupied the principal strategic points in south Manchuria, including the principal administrative center, together with some at least of the public utilities. It appears that the highest Chinese authority ordered the Chinese military not to resist, and that, when news of the situation reached Tokyo, but after most of the acts of occupation had been consummated, the Japanese Government ordered cessation of military activities on the part of the Japanese forces. Nevertheless, it appears some military movements have been continuously and are even now in process. The actual situation is that an arm of the Japanese Government is in complete control of south Manchuria.

The League of Nations has given evidence of its concern. The Chinese Government has in various ways invoked action on the part of foreign governments, citing its reliance upon treaty obligations and inviting special reference to the Kellogg pact.

This situation is of concern, morally, legally, and politically to a considerable number of nations. It is not exclusively a matter of concern to Japan and China. It brings into question at once the meaning of certain provisions of agreements, such as the nine powers treaty of February 6, 1922, and the Kellogg-Briand pact.

The American Government is confident that it has not been the intention of the Japanese Government to create or to be a party to the creation of a situation which brings the applicability of treaty provisions into consideration. The American Government does not wish to be hasty in formulating its conclusions or in taking a position. However, the American Government feels that a very unfortunate situation exists, which no doubt is embarrassing to the Japanese Government. It would seem that the responsibility for determining the course of events with regard to the liquidating of this situation rests largely upon Japan, for the simple reason that Japanese armed forces have seized and are exercising de facto control in south Manchuria.

It is alleged by the Chinese, and the allegation has the support of circumstantial evidence, that lines of communication outward from Manchuria have been cut or interfered with. If this is true, it is unfortunate.

It is the hope of the American Government that the orders which it understands have been given both by the Japanese and the Chinese Governments to their military forces to refrain from hostilities and further movements will be respected and that there will be no further application of force. It is also the hope of the American Government that the Japanese and the Chinese Governments will find it possible speedily to demonstrate to the world that neither has any intention to take advantage, in furtherance of its own peculiar interests, of the situation which has been brought about in connection with and in consequence of this use of force.

What has occurred has already shaken the confidence of the public with regard to the stability of conditions in Manchuria, and it is believed that the crystallizing of a situation suggesting the necessity for an indefinite continuance of military occupation would further undermine that confidence.

65. Japan's Invasion of Manchuria, Stimson's Note to the League, 5 October 1931

I believe that our cooperation in the future handling of this difficult matter should proceed along the course which has been followed ever since the first outbreak of the trouble fortunately found the Assembly, and Council of the League of Nations in session. The council has deliberated long and earnestly on this matter and the covenant of the League of Nations provides permanent and already tested machinery for handling such issues as between States members of the league. Both the Chinese and Japanese have presented and argued their cases before the council and the world has been informed through published accounts with regard to the proceedings there. The council has formulated conclusions and outlined a course of action to be followed by the disputants; and as the said disputants have made commitments to the council, it is most desirable that the league in no way relax its vigilance and in no way fail to assert all the pressure and authority within its competence toward regulating the action of China and Japan in the premises.

On its part the American Government acting independently through its diplomatic representatives will endeavor to reinforce what the league does and will make clear that it has a keen interest in the matter and is not oblivious to the obligations which the disputants have assumed to their fellow signatories in the pact of Paris as well as in the nine-power pact should a time arise when it would seem advisable to bring forward those obligations. By this course we avoid any danger of embarrassing the league in the course to which it is now committed.

66. Japan's Invasion of Manchuria, U.S. Non-Recognition Policy, 7 January 1932

With the recent military operations about Chinchow, the last remaining administrative authority of the Government of the Chinese Republic in South Manchuria, as it existed prior to September 18, 1931, has been destroyed. The American Government continues confident that the work of the neutral commission recently authorized by the Council of the League of Nations will facilitate an ultimate solution of the difficulties now existing between China and Japan. But in view of the present situation and of its own rights and obligations therein, the American Government deems it to be its duty to notify both the Governments of the Chinese Republic and the Imperial Japanese Government that it can not admit the legality of any situation de facto nor does it intend to recognize any treaty or agreement entered into between those governments, or agents thereof, which may impair the treaty rights of the United States or its citizens in China, including those which relate to the sovereignty, the independence, or the territorial and administrative integrity of the Republic of China, or to the international policy relative to China, commonly known as the open-door policy; and that it does not intend to recognize any situation, treaty, or agreement which may be brought about by means contrary to the covenants and obligations of the pact of Paris of August 27, 1928, to which treaty both China and Japan, as well as the United States, are parties.

67. F.D. Roosevelt's Quarantine Speech, 5 October 1937

... THE POLITICAL situation in the world, which of late has been growing progressively worse, is such as to cause grave concern and anxiety to all the peoples and nations who wish to live in peace and amity with their neighbors.

Some 15 years ago the hopes of mankind for a continuing era of international peace were raised to great heights when more than 60 nations solemnly pledged themselves not to resort to arms in furtherance of their national aims and policies. The high aspirations expressed in the Briand-Kellogg Peace Pact and the hopes for peace thus raised have of late given away to a haunting fear of calamity. The present reign of terror and international lawlessness began a few years ago.

It began through unjustified interference in the internal affairs of other nations or the invasion of alien territory in violation of treaties and has now reached a stage where the very foundations of civilization are seriously threatened. The landmarks and traditions which have marked the progress of civilization toward a condition of law, order, and justice are being wiped away.

Without a declaration of war and without warning or justification of any kind, civilians, including women and children, are being ruthlessly murdered with bombs from the air. In times of so-called peace ships are being attacked and sunk by submarines without cause or notice. Nations are fomenting and taking sides in civil warfare in nations that have never done them any harm. Nations claiming freedom for themselves deny it to others.

Innocent peoples and nations are being cruelly sacrificed to a greed for power and supremacy which is devoid of all sense of justice and humane consideration.

To paraphrase a recent author, "perhaps we foresee a time when men, exultant in the technique of homicide, will rage so hotly over the world that every precious thing will be in danger, every book and picture and harmony, every treasure garnered through two millenniums, the small, the delicate, the defenseless — all will be lost or wrecked or utterly destroyed."

If those things come to pass in other parts of the world let no one imagine that America will escape, that it may expect mercy, that this Western Hemisphere will not be attacked, and that it will continue tranquilly and peacefully to carry on the ethics and the arts of civilization.

If those days come "there will be no safety by arms, no help from authority, no answer in science. The storm will rage till every flower of culture is trampled and all human beings are leveled in a vast chaos."

If those days are not to come to pass — if we are to have a world in which we can breathe freely and live in amity without fear — the peace-loving nations must make a concerted effort to uphold laws and principles on which alone peace can rest secure.

The peace-loving nations must make a concerted effort in opposition to those violations of treaties and those ignorings of humane instincts which today are creating a state of international anarchy and instability from which there is no escape through mere isolation or neutrality.

Those who cherish their freedom and recognize and respect the equal right of their neighbors to be free and live in peace, must work together for the triumph of law and moral principles in order that peace, justice, and confidence may prevail in the world. There must be a return to a belief in the pledged word, in the value of a signed treaty. There must be recognition of the fact that national morality is as vital as private morality. . . .

There is a solidarity and interdependence about the modern world, both technically and morally, which makes it impossible for any nation completely to isolate itself from economic and political upheavals in the rest of the world, especially when such upheavals appear to be spreading and not declining. There can be no stability or peace either within nations or between nations except under laws and moral standards adhered to by all. International anarchy destroys every foundation for peace. It jeopardizes either the immediate or the future security of every nation, large or small. It is, therefore, a matter of vital interest and concern to the people of the United States that the sanctity of international treaties and the maintenance of international morality be restored.

The overwhelming majority of the peoples and nations of the world today want to live in peace. They seek the removal of barriers against trade. They want to exert themselves in industry, in agriculture, and in business, that they may increase their wealth through the production of wealth-producing goods rather than striving to produce military planes and bombs and machine guns and cannon for the destruction of human lives and useful property.

In those nations of the world which seem to be piling armament on armament for purposes of aggression, and those other nations which fear acts of aggression against them and their security, a very high proportion of their national income is being spent directly for armaments. It runs from 30 to as high as 50 percent. . . .

The situation is definitely of universal concern. The questions involved relate not merely to violations of specific provisions of particular treaties; they are questions of war and of peace, of international law, and especially of principles of humanity. It is true that they involve definite violations of agreements, and especially of the Covenant of the League of Nations, the Briand-Kellogg Pact, and the Nine Power Treaty. But they also involve problems of world economy, world security, and world humanity.

It is true that the moral consciousness of the world must recognize the importance of removing injustices and well-founded grievances; but at the same time it must be aroused to the cardinal necessity of honoring sanctity of treaties, of respecting the rights and liberties of others, and of putting an end to acts of international aggression.

It seems to be unfortunately true that the epidemic of world lawlessness is spreading.

When an epidemic of physical disease starts to spread, the community approves and joins in a quarantine of the patients in order to protect the health of the community against the spread of the disease.

It is my determination to pursue a policy of peace and to adopt every practicable measure to avoid involvement in war. It ought to be inconceivable that in this modern era, and in the face of experience, any nation could be so foolish and ruthless as to run the risk of plunging the whole world into war by invading and violating in contravention of solemn treaties the territory of other nations that have done them no real harm and which are too weak to protect themselves adequately. Yet the peace of the world and the welfare and security of every nation is today being threatened by that very thing.

No nation which refuses to exercise forbearance and to respect the freedom and rights of others can long remain strong and retain the confidence and respect of other nations. No nation ever loses its dignity or good standing by conciliating its differences and by exercising great patience with and consideration for the rights of other nations.

68. First Neutrality Act, 21 August 1935

RESOLVED *by the Senate and House of Representatives of the United States of America in Congress assembled,* That upon the outbreak or during the progress of war between, or among, two or more foreign states, the President shall proclaim such fact, and it shall thereafter be unlawful to export arms, ammunition, or implements of war from any place in the United States, or possessions of the United States, to any port of such belligerent states, or to any neutral port for transshipment to, or for the use of, a belligerent country.

The President, by proclamation, shall definitely enumerate the arms, ammunition, or implements of war, the export of which is prohibited by this Act.

The President may, from time to time, by proclamation, extend such embargo upon the export of arms, ammunition, or implements of war to other states as and when they may become involved in such war. . . .

Except with respect to prosecutions committed or forfeitures incurred prior to March 1, 1936, this section and all proclamations issued thereunder shall not be effective after February 29, 1936. . . .

Within ninety days after the effective date of this Act, or upon first engaging in business, every person who engages in the business of manufacturing, exporting, or importing any of the arms, ammunition, and implements of war referred to in this Act, whether as an exporter, importer, manufacturer, or dealer, shall register with the Secretary of State his name, or business name, principal place of business, and places of business in the United States, and a list of the arms, ammunition, and implements of war which he manufactures, imports, or exports.

Every person required to register under this section shall notify the Secretary of State of any change in the arms, ammunition, and implements of war which he exports, imports, or manufactures; and upon such notification the Secretary of State shall issue to such person an amended certificate of registration, free of charge, which shall remain valid until the date of expiration of the original certificate. Every person required to register under the provisions of this section shall pay a registration fee of $500, and upon receipt of such fee the Secretary of State shall issue a registration certificate valid for five years, which shall be renewable for further periods of five years upon the payment of each renewal of a fee of $500.

It shall be unlawful for any person to export, or attempt to export, from the United States any of the arms, ammunition, or implements of war referred to in this Act to any other country or to import, or attempt to import, to the United States from any other country any of the arms, ammunition, or implements of war referred to in this Act without first having obtained a license therefor. . . .

Sec. 3. Whenever the President shall issue the proclamation provided for in section 1 of this Act, thereafter it shall be unlawful for any American vessel to carry any arms, ammunition, or implements of war to any port of the belligerent countries named in such proclamation as being at war, or to any neutral port for transshipment to, or for the use of, a belligerent country. . . .

Sec. 6. Whenever, during any war in which the United States is neutral, the President shall find that the maintenance of peace between the United States and foreign nations, or the protection of the lives of citizens of the United States, or the protection of the commercial interests of the United States and its citizens, or the security of the United States requires that the American citizens should refrain from traveling as passengers on the vessels of any belligerent nation, he shall so proclaim, and thereafter no citizen of the United States shall travel on any vessel of any belligerent nation except at his own risk, unless in accordance with such rules and regulations as the President shall prescribe. . . .

69. Second Neutrality Act, 29 February 1936

RESOLVED *by the Senate and House of Representatives of the United States of America in Congress assembled,* That section 1 of the joint resolution (Public Resolution Numbered 67, Seventy-fourth Congress) approved August 31, 1935, be, and the same hereby is, amended by striking out in the first section, on the second line, after the word "assembled" the following words: "That upon the outbreak or during the progress of war between", and inserting therefor the words: "Whenever the President shall find that there exists a state of war between"; and by striking out the word "may" after the word "President" and before the word "from" in the twelfth line, and inserting in lieu thereof the word "shall"; and by substituting for the last paragraph of said section the following paragraph: "except with respect to offenses committed, or forfeitures incurred prior to May 1, 1937, this section and all proclamations issued thereunder shall not be effective after May 1, 1937."

Sec. 2. There are hereby added to said joint resolution two new sections, to be known as section 1a and 1b, reading as follows:

Sec. 1a. Whenever the President shall have issued his proclamation as provided for in section 1 of this Act, it shall thereafter during the period of the war be unlawful for any person within the United States to purchase, sell, or exchange bonds, securities, or other obligations of the government of any belligerent country, or of any political subdivision thereof, or of any person acting for or on behalf of such government, issued after the date of such proclamation, or to make any loan or extend any credit to any such government or person: *Provided,* That if the President shall find that such action will serve to protect the commercial or other interests of the United States or its nationals, he may, in his discretion, and to such extent and under such regulation as he may prescribe, except from the operation of this section ordinary commercial credits and shorttime obligations in aid of legal transactions and of a character customarily used in normal peace-time commercial transactions. . . .

Sec. 1b. This Act shall not apply to an American republic or republics engaged in war against a non-American state or states, provided the American republic is not cooperating with a non-American state or states in such war.

70. Third Neutrality Act, 1 May 1937

SECTION 1. (a) Whenever the President shall find that there exists a state of war between, or among, two or more foreign states, the President shall proclaim such fact, and it shall thereafter be unlawful to export, or attempt to export, or cause to be exported, arms, ammunition, or implements of war from any place in the United States to any belligerent state named in such proclamation, or to any neutral state for transshipment to, or for the use of, any such belligerent state.

(b) The President shall, from time to time, by proclamation, extend such embargo upon the export of arms, ammunition, or implements of war to other states as and when they may become involved in such war.

(c) Whenever the President shall find that a state of civil strife exists in a foreign state and that such civil strife is of a magnitude or is being conducted under such conditions that the export of arms, ammunition, or implements of war from the United States to such foreign state would threaten or endanger the peace of the United States, the President shall proclaim such fact, and it shall thereafter be unlawful to export, or attempt to export, or cause to be exported, arms, ammunition, or implements of war from any place in the United States to such foreign state, or to any neutral state for transshipment to, or for the use of, such foreign state.

(d) The President shall, from time to time by proclamation, definitely enumerate the arms, ammunition, and implements of war, the export of which is prohibited by this section. The arms, ammunition, and implements of war so enumerated shall include those enumerated in the President's proclamation Numbered 2163, of April 10, 1936, but shall not include raw materials or any other articles or materials not of the same general character as those enumerated in the said proclamation, and in the Convention for the Supervision of the International Trade in Arms and Ammunition and in Implements of War, signed at Geneva June 17, 1925. . . .

Section 2. (a) Whenever the President shall have issued a proclamation under the authority of section 1 of this Act and he shall thereafter find that the placing of restrictions on the shipment of certain articles or materials in addition to arms, ammunition, and implements of war from the United States to belligerent states, or to a state wherein civil strife exists, is necessary to promote the security or preserve the peace of the United States or to protect the lives of citizens of the United States, he shall so proclaim, and it shall thereafter be unlawful, except under such limitations and exceptions as the President may prescribe as to lakes, rivers, and inland waters bordering on the United States, and as to transportation on or over lands bordering on the United States, for any American vessel to carry such articles or materials to any belligerent state, or to any state wherein civil strife exists, named in such proclamation issued under the authority of section 1 of this Act, or to any neutral state for transshipment to, or for the use of, any such belligerent state or any such state wherein civil strife exists. The President shall by proclamation from time to time definitely enumerate the articles and materials which it shall be unlawful for American vessels to so transport.

(b) Whenever the President shall have issued a proclamation under the authority of section 1 of this Act and he shall thereafter find that the placing of restrictions on the export of articles or materials from the United States to belligerent states, or to a state wherein civil strife exists, is necessary to promote the security or preserve the peace of the United States or to protect the lives or commerce of citizens of the United States, he shall so proclaim, and it shall thereafter be unlawful, except under such limitations and exceptions as the President may prescribe as to lakes, rivers, and inland waters bordering on the United States, and as to transportation on or over land bordering on the United States, to export or transport, or attempt to export or transport, or cause to be exported or transported, from the United States to any belligerent state, or to any state wherein civil strife exists, named in such proclamation issued under the authority of section 1 of this Act, or to any neutral state for transshipment to, or for the use of, any such belligerent state or any such state wherein civil strife exists, any articles or materials whatever until all right, title, and interest therein shall have been transferred to some foreign government, agency, institution, association, partnership, corporation, or national. . . .

Section 3. (a) Whenever the President shall have issued a proclamation under the authority of section 1 of this Act, it shall thereafter be unlawful for any person within the United States to purchase, sell, or exchange bonds, securities, or other obligations of the government of any belligerent state or of any state wherein civil strife exists, named in such proclamation, or of any political subdivision of any such state, or of any person acting for or on behalf of the government of any such state, or of any faction or asserted government within any such state wherein civil strife exists, or of any person acting for or on behalf of any faction or asserted government within any such state wherein civil strife exists, issued after the date of such proclamation, or to make any loan or extend any credit to any such government, political subdivision, faction, asserted government, or person, or to solicit or receive any contribution for any such government, political subdivision, faction, asserted government, or person: *Provided,* That if the President shall find that such action will serve to protect the commercial or other interests of the United States or its citizens, he may, in his discretion, and to such extent and under such regulations as he may prescribe, except from the operation of this section ordinary commercial credits and shorttime obligations in aid of legal transactions and of a character customarily used in normal peacetime commercial transactions. . . .

Section 4. This Act shall not apply to an American republic or republics engaged in war against a non-American state or states, provided the American republic is not cooperating with a non-American state or states in such war.

Section 5. (a) There is hereby established a National Munitions Control Board (hereinafter referred to as the "Board") to carry out the provisions of this Act. . . .

(d) It shall be unlawful for any person to export, or attempt to export, from the United States to any other state, any of the arms, ammunition, or implements of war referred to in this Act, or to import, or attempt to import, to the United States from any other state, any of the arms, ammuni-

tion, or implements of war referred to in this Act, without first having obtained a license therefor. . . .

Section 6. (a) Whenever the President shall have issued a proclamation under the authority of section 1 of this Act, it shall thereafter be unlawful, until such proclamation is revoked, for any American vessel to carry any arms, ammunition, or implements of war to any belligerent state, or to any state wherein civil strife exists, named in such proclamation, or to any neutral state for transshipment to, or for the use of, any such belligerent state or any such state wherein civil strife exists. . . .

Section 9. Whenever the President shall have issued a proclamation under the authority of section 1 of this Act it shall thereafter be unlawful for any citizen of the United States to travel on any vessel of the state or states named in such proclamation, except in accordance with such rules and regulations as the President shall prescribe. . . .

Section 10. Whenever the President shall have issued a proclamation under the authority of section 1, it shall thereafter be unlawful, until such proclamation is revoked, for any American vessel engaged in commerce with any belligerent state, or any state wherein civil strife exists, named in such proclamation, to be armed or to carry any armament, arms, ammunition, or implements of war, except small arms and ammunition therefor which the President may deem necessary and shall publicly designate for the preservation of discipline aboard such vessels. . . .

71. Fourth Neutrality Act, 4 November 1939

... RESOLVED *by the Senate and House of Representatives of the United States of America in Congress assembled,*

Section 1. (a) That whenever the President, or the Congress by concurrent resolution, shall find that there exists a state of war between foreign states, and that it is necessary to promote the security or preserve the peace of the United States or to protect the lives of citizens of the United States, the President shall issue a proclamation naming the states involved; and he shall, from time to time, by proclamation, name other states as and when they may become involved in the war. . . .

Section 2. (a) Whenever the President shall have issued a proclamation under the authority of section 1 (a) it shall thereafter be unlawful for any American vessel to carry any passengers or any articles or materials to any state named in such proclamation. . . .

(c) Whenever the President shall have issued a proclamation under the authority of section 1 (a) it shall thereafter be unlawful to export or transport, or attempt to export or transport, or cause to be exported or transported, from the United States to any state named in such proclamation, any articles or materials (except copy-righted articles or materials) until all right, title, and interest therein shall have been transferred to some foreign government, agency, institution, association, partnership, corporation, or national. . . .

Section 3. (a) Whenever the President shall have issued a proclamation under the authority of section 1 (a), and he shall thereafter find that the protection of citizens of the United States so requires, he shall, by proclamation, define combat areas, and thereafter it shall be unlawful, except under such rules and regulations as may be prescribed, for any citizen of the United States or any American vessel to proceed into or through any such combat area. The combat areas so defined may be made to apply to surface vessels or aircraft, or both. . . .

Section 5. (a) Whenever the President shall have issued a proclamation under the authority of section 1 (a) it shall thereafter be unlawful for any citizen of the United States to travel on any vessel of any state named in such proclamation, except in accordance with such rules and regulations as may be prescribed. . . .

Section 6. Whenever the President shall have issued a proclamation under the authority of section 1 (a), it shall thereafter be unlawful, until such proclamation is revoked, for any American vessel, engaged in commerce with any foreign state to be armed, except with small arms and ammunition therefor, which the President may deem necessary and shall publicly designate for the preservation of discipline aboard any such vessel.

under the authority of section 1 (a), it shall thereafter be unlawful for any person within the United States to purchase, sell, or exchange bonds, securities, or other obligations of the government of any state named in such proclamation, or of any political subdivision of any such state, or of any person acting for or on behalf of the government of any such state, or political subdivision thereof, issued after the date of such proclamation, or to make any loan or extend any credit (other than necessary credits accruing in connection with the transmission of telegraph, cable, wireless and telephone services) to any such government, political subdivision, or person. The provisions of this subsection shall also apply to the sale by any person within the United States to any person in a state named in any such proclamation of any articles or materials listed in a proclamation referred to in or issued under the authority of section 12 (i). . . .

Section 9. This joint resolution (except section 12) shall not apply to any American republic engaged in war against a non-American state or states, provided the American republic is not cooperating with a non-American state or states in such war. . . .

Section 12. (a) There is hereby established a National Munitions Control Board (hereinafter referred to as the "Board"). . . .

(b) Every person who engages in the business of manufacturing, exporting, or importing any arms, ammunition, or implements of war listed in a proclamation referred to in or issued under the authority of subsection (i) of this section, whether as an exporter, importer, manufacturer, or dealer, shall register with the Secretary of State his name, or business name, principal place of business, and places of business in the United States, and a list of the arms, ammunition, and implements of war which he manufactures, imports, or exports. . . .

(d) It shall be unlawful for any person to export, or attempt to export, from the United States to any other state, any arms, ammunition, or implements of war listed in a proclamation referred to in or issued under the authority of subsection (i) of this section, or to import, or attempt to import, to the United States from any other state, any of the arms, ammunition, or implements of war listed in any such proclamation, without first having submitted to the Secretary of State the name of the purchaser and the terms of sale and having obtained a license therefor. . . .

72. Destroyer–Naval Bases Agreement, 1940

F.D. Roosevelt Message, 3 September 1940.

I TRANSMIT herewith for the information of the Congress notes exchanged between the British Ambassador at Washington and the Secretary of State on September 2, 1940, under which this Government has acquired the right to lease naval and air bases in Newfoundland, and in the islands of Bermuda, the Bahamas, Jamaica, St. Lucia, Trinidad, and Antigua, and in British Guiana; also a copy of an opinion of the Attorney General dated August 27, 1940, regarding my authority to consummate this arrangement.

The right to bases in Newfoundland and Bermuda are gifts — generously given and gladly received. The other bases mentioned have been acquired in exchange for fifty of our over-age destroyers.

This is not inconsistent in any sense with our status of peace. Still less is it a threat against any nation. It is an epochal and far-reaching act of preparation for continental defense in the face of grave danger.

Preparation for defense is an inalienable prerogative of a sovereign state. Under present circumstances this exercise of sovereign right is essential to the maintenance of our peace and safety. This is the most important action in the reinforcement of our national defense that has been taken since the Louisiana Purchase. Then as now, considerations of safety from overseas attack were fundamental.

The value to the Western Hemisphere of these outposts of security is beyond calculation. Their need has long been recognized by our country, and especially by those primarily charged with the duty of charting and organizing our own naval and military defense. They are essential to the protection of the Panama Canal, Central America, the Northern portion of South America, The Antilles, Canada, Mexico, and our own Eastern and Gulf Seaboards. Their consequent importance in hemispheric defense is obvious. For these reasons I have taken advantage of the present opportunity to acquire them.

73. Hull on the Far East, October 1940

Memorandum of Secretary of State Cordell Hull, 8 October 1940.

THE JAPANESE Ambassador called at his request. He first expressed his regret at the unsatisfactory relations existing between our two countries at this time. . . .

The Ambassador then said that he was instructed by his Government to hand me a note dated October 7, 1940 . . . relative to our scrap iron and steel embargo which was recently proclaimed. . . .

I said that it was really amazing for the Government of Japan, which has been violating in the most aggravating manner valuable American rights and interests throughout most of China, and is doing so in many instances every day, to question the fullest privilege of this Government from every standpoint to impose the proposed scrap iron and steel embargo, and that to go still further and call it an unfriendly act was still more amazing in the light of the conduct of the Japanese Government in disregarding all law, treaty obligations and other rights and privileges and the safety of Americans while it proceeded at the same time to seize territory by force to an ever-increasing extent. I stated that of all the countries with which I have had to deal during the past eight years, the Government of Japan has the least occasion or excuse to accuse this Government of an unfriendly act. I concluded with the statement that apparently the theory of the Japanese Government is for all other nations to acquiesce cheerfully in all injuries inflicted upon their citizens by the Japanese policy of force and conquest, accompanied by every sort of violence, unless they are to run the risk of being guilty of an unfriendly act.

The Ambassador again said that he very much regretted the serious differences between our two countries, but that he naturally hoped that trouble may yet be avoided. He added that any Japanese or any American must know that strife between the two countries would be extremely tragic for both alike. To this I replied that, of course, it would be exceedingly unfortunate for such occurrence to take place, but I added that my Government has been patient, extremely patient, and that the Ambassador will bear witness to the long and earnest efforts that he and I have made, and that I have made prior to his coming here, to promote and preserve friendly and satisfactory relations with Japan. I went on to say that we have stood for law and order and treaty observance and justice along with genuine friendliness between our two countries; that it was clear now, however, that those who are dominating the external policies of Japan are, as we here have believed for some years, bent on the conquest by force of all worthwhile territory in the Pacific Ocean area without limit as to extent in the South and in southern continental areas of that part of the world, and that we and all other nations are expected, as stated, to sit perfectly quiet and be cheerful and agreeable, but static, while most of Asia is Manchuria-ized, which would render practically impossible all reasonable or satisfactory relations so far as other nations are concerned; and that corresponding lower levels of existence would be the ultimate lot of the people of most of Asia. The least objection to or taking of issue with Japan with respect to the foregoing matters would be called an unfriendly act, and, as Prime Minister Konoye said recently to the press, it would be the occasion for war so far as Japan was concerned. I added that, of course, if any one country is sufficiently desirous of trouble, it can always find any one of innumerable occasions to start such trouble. In brief, it is not left to the other country to participate in such decision.

The Ambassador undertook to repeat the old line of talk about how fair Japan proposed to be with respect to all rights and privileges of foreign nations within its conquered territory. He agreed that no purpose would be served now to go over the many conversations we have had with respect to these matters. I held up the succession of injuries to American rights and interests in China whenever he referred to the scrap iron embargo.

I reiterated the view that it was unheard of for one country engaged in aggression and seizure of another country, contrary to all law and treaty provisions, to turn to a third peacefully disposed nation and seriously insist that it would be guilty of an unfriendly act if it should not cheerfully provide some of the necessary implements of war to aid the aggressor nation in carrying out its policy of invasion. I made it clear that it is the view of this Government that two nations, one in Europe and one in Asia, are undertaking to subjugate both of their respective areas of the world, and to place them on an international order and on a social basis resembling that of 750 years ago. In the face of this world movement, extending itself from day to day, peaceful and interested nations are to be held up to denunciation and threats if they dare to engage in any lawful acts or utterances in opposition to such wide movements of world conquest.

The Ambassador had little to say. He said virtually nothing in attempted extenuation except that his Government would expect everybody to receive considerate and fair treatment throughout the conquered areas. He emphasized equal treatment, and I replied that when the best interests of other nations in peace and law and order were being destroyed, it was not a matter of any concern as to whether there was discrimination between the nations which were victims of such movements.

74. F.D. Roosevelt's Arsenal of Democracy Speech, 6 January 1941

I ADDRESS YOU, the Members of the Seventy-seventh Congress, at a moment unprecedented in the history of the Union. I use the word "unprecedented," because at no previous time has American security been as seriously threatened from without as it is today.

Our national policy is this:

First, by an impressive expression of the public will and without regard to partisanship, we are committed to all-inclusive national defense.

Second, by an impressive expression of the public will and without regard to partisanship, we are committed to full support of all those resolute peoples, everywhere, who are resisting aggression and are thereby keeping war away from our hemisphere. By this support, we express our determination that the democratic cause shall prevail; and we strengthen the defense and security of our own Nation.

Third, by an impressive expression of the public will and without regard to partisanship, we are committed to the proposition that principles of morality and considerations for our own security will never permit us to acquiesce in a peace dictated by aggressors and sponsored by appeasers. We know that enduring peace cannot be bought at the cost of other people's freedom.

In the recent national election there was no substantial difference between the two great parties in respect to that national policy. No issue was fought out on this line before the American electorate. Today, it is abundantly evident that American citizens everywhere are demanding and supporting speedy and complete action in recognition of obvious danger.

Therefore, the immediate need is a swift and driving increase in our armament production.

To change a whole nation from a basis of peacetime production of implements of peace to a basis of wartime production of implements of war is no small task. And the greatest difficulty comes at the beginning of the program, when new tools and plant facilities and new assembly lines and shipways must first be constructed before the actual matériel begins to flow steadily and speedily from them.

The Congress, of course, must rightly keep itself informed at all times of the progress of the program. However, there is certain information, as the Congress itself will readily recognize, which, in the interests of our own security and those of the nations we are supporting, must of needs be kept in confidence.

New circumstances are constantly begetting new needs for our safety. I shall ask this Congress for greatly increased new appropriations and authorizations to carry on what we have begun.

I also ask this Congress for authority and for funds sufficient to manufacture additional munitions and war supplies of many kinds, to be turned over to those nations which are now in actual war with aggressor nations.

Our most useful and immediate role is to act as an arsenal for them as well as for ourselves. They do not need man power. They do need billions of dollars worth of the weapons of defense.

The time is near when they will not be able to pay for them in ready cash. We cannot, and will not, tell them they must surrender, merely because of present inability to pay for the weapons which we know they must have.

I do not recommend that we make them a loan of dollars with which to pay for these weapons — a loan to be repaid in dollars.

I recommend that we make it possible for those nations to continue to obtain war materials in the United States, fitting their orders into our own program. Nearly all of their matériel would, if the time ever came, be useful for our own defense.

Taking counsel of expert military and naval authorities, considering what is best for our own security, we are free to decide how much should be kept here and how much should be sent abroad to our friends who by their determined and heroic resistance are giving us time in which to make ready our own defense.

For what we send abroad, we shall be repaid, within a reasonable time following the close of hostilities, in similar materials, or, at our option, in other goods of many kinds which they can produce and which we need.

Let us say to the democracies: "We Americans are vitally concerned in your defense of freedom. We are putting forth our energies, our resources, and our organizing powers to give you the strength to regain and maintain a free world. We shall send you, in ever-increasing numbers, ships, planes, tanks, guns. This is our purpose and our pledge."

In fulfillment of this purpose we will not be intimidated by the threats of dictators that they will regard as a breach of international law and as an act of war our aid to the democracies which dare to resist their aggression. Such aid is not an act of war, even if a dictator should unilaterally proclaim it so to be.

When the dictators are ready to make war upon us, they will not wait for an act of war on our part. They did not wait for Norway or Belgium or the Netherlands to commit an act of war.

Their only interest is in a new one-way international law, which lacks mutuality in its observance, and, therefore, becomes an instrument of oppression.

The happiness of future generations of Americans may well depend upon how effective and how immediate we can make our aid felt. No one can tell the exact character of the emergency situations that we may be called upon to meet. The Nation's hands must not be tied when the Nation's life is in danger.

We must all prepare to make the sacrifices that the emergency — as serious as war itself — demands. Whatever stands in the way of speed and efficiency in defense preparations must give way to the national need.

A free nation has the right to expect full cooperation from all groups. A free nation has the right to look to the leaders of business, of labor, and of agriculture to take the lead in stimulating effort, not among other groups but within their own groups.

I have called for personal sacrifice. I am assured of the willingness of almost all Americans to respond to that call.

A part of the sacrifice means the payment of more money in taxes. In my Budget message I recommend that a greater portion of this great defense program be paid for from taxation than we are paying today. No person should try, or be allowed, to get rich out of this program; and the principle of tax payments in accordance with ability to pay should be constantly before our eyes to guide our legislation.

If the Congress maintains these principles, the voters, putting patriotism ahead of pocketbooks, will give you their applause.

In the future days, which we seek to make secure, we look forward to a world founded upon four essential human freedoms.

The first is freedom of speech and expression — everywhere in the world.

The second is freedom of every person to worship God in his own way — everywhere in the world.

The third is freedom from want — which, translated into world terms, means economic understandings which will secure to every nation a healthy peacetime life for its inhabitants — everywhere in the world.

The fourth is freedom from fear — which, translated into world terms, means a world-wide reduction of armaments to such a point and in such a thorough fashion that no nation will be in a position to commit an act of physical aggression against any neighbor — anywhere in the world.

That is no vision of a distant millennium. It is a definite basis for a kind of world attainable in our own time and generation. That kind of world is the very antithesis of the so-called new order of tyranny which the dictators seek to create with the crash of a bomb.

To that new order we oppose the greater conception — the moral order. A good society is able to face schemes of world domination and foreign revolutions alike without fear.

Since the beginning of our American history we have been engaged in change — in a perpetual peaceful revolution — a revolution which goes on steadily, quietly adjusting itself to changing conditions — without the concentration camp or the quick-lime in the ditch. The world order which we seek is the cooperation of free countries, working together in a friendly, civilized society.

This Nation has placed its destiny in the hands and heads and hearts of its millions of free men and women; and its faith in freedom under the guidance of God. Freedom means the supremacy of human rights everywhere. Our support goes to those who struggle to gain those rights or keep them. Our strength is in our unity of purpose.

To that high concept there can be no end save victory.

75. Lend-Lease Act, 11 March 1941

BE IT enacted by the Senate and House of Representatives of the United States of America in Congress assembled, That this Act may be cited as "An Act to Promote the Defense of the United States."

Section 2. As used in this Act — (a) The term "defense article" means —

(1) Any weapon, munition, aircraft, vessel, or boat;

(2) Any machinery, facility, tool, material, or supply necessary for the manufacture, production, processing, repair, servicing, or operation of any article described in this subsection;

(3) Any component material or part of or equipment for any article described in this subsection;

(4) Any agricultural, industrial or other commodity or article for defense.

Such term "defense article" includes any article described in this subsection: Manufactured or procured pursuant to section 3, or to which the United States or any foreign government has or hereafter acquires title, possession, or control.

(b) The term "defense information" means any plan, specification, design, prototype, or information pertaining to any defense article.

Section 3. (a) Notwithstanding the provisions of any other law, the President may, from time to time, when he deems it in the interest of national defense, authorize the Secretary of War, the Secretary of the Navy, or the head of any other department or agency of the Government—

(1) To manufacture in arsenals, factories, and shipyards under their jurisdiction, or otherwise procure, to the extent to which funds are made available therefor, or contracts are authorized from time to time by the Congress, or both, any defense article for the government of any country whose defense the President deems vital to the defense of the United States.

(2) To sell, transfer title to, exchange, lease, lend, or otherwise dispose of, to any such government any defense article, but no defense article not manufactured or procured under paragraph (1) shall in any way be disposed of under this paragraph, except after consultation with the Chief of Staff of the Army or the Chief of Naval Operations of the Navy, or both. The value of defense articles disposed of in any way under authority of this paragraph, and procured from funds heretofore appropriated, shall not exceed $1,300,000,000. The value of such defense articles shall be determined by the head of the department or agency concerned or such other department, agency or officer as shall be designated in the manner provided in the rules and regulations issued hereunder. Defense articles procured from funds hereafter appropriated to any department or agency of the Government other than from funds authorized to be appropriated under this Act, shall not be disposed of in any way under authority of this paragraph except to the extent hereafter authorized by the Congress in the Acts appropriating such funds or otherwise.

(3) To test, inspect, prove, repair, outfit, recondition, or otherwise to place in good working order, to the extent to which funds are made available therefor, or contracts are authorized from time to time by the Congress, or both, any defense article for any such government, or to procure any or all such services by private contract.

(4) To communicate to any such government any defense information, pertaining to any defense article furnished to such government under paragraph (2) of this subsection.

(5) To release for export any defense article disposed of in any way under this subsection to any such government.

(b) The terms and conditions upon which any such foreign government receives any aid authorized under subsection (a) shall be those which the President deems satisfactory, and the benefit to the United States may be payment or repayment in kind or property, or any other direct or indirect benefit which the President deems satisfactory. . . .

(d) Nothing in this Act shall be construed to authorize or to permit the authorization of convoying vessels by naval vessels of the United States.

(e) Nothing in this Act shall be construed to authorize or to permit the authorization of the entry of any American vessel into a combat area in violation of section 3 of the Neutrality Act of 1939. . . .

Section 6. (a) There is hereby authorized to be appropriated from time to time, out of any money in the Treasury not otherwise appropriated, such amounts as may be necessary to carry out the provisions and accomplish the purposes of this Act. . . .

76. Lindbergh on Isolationism, 23 April 1941

Speech of Charles A. Lindbergh.

THERE ARE many viewpoints from which the issues of this war can be argued. Some are primarily idealistic. Some are primarily practical. One should, I believe, strive for a balance of both. But, since the subjects that can be covered in a single address are limited, tonight I shall discuss the war from a viewpoint which is primarily practical. It is not that I believe ideals are unimportant, even among the realities of war; but if a nation is to survive in a hostile world, its ideals must be backed by the hard logic of military practicability. If the outcome of war depended upon ideals alone, this would be a different world than it is today.

I know I will be severely criticized by the interventionists in America when I say we should not enter a war unless we have a reasonable chance of winning. That, they will claim, is far too materialistic a viewpoint. They will advance again the same arguments that were used to persuade France to declare war against Germany in 1939. But I do not believe that our American ideals, and our way of life, will gain through an unsuccessful war. And I know that the United States is not prepared to wage war in Europe successfully at this time. We are no better prepared today than France was when the interventionists in Europe persuaded her to attack the Siegfried Line.

I have said before, and I will say again, that I believe it will be a tragedy to the entire world if the British Empire collapses. That is one of the main reasons why I opposed this war before it was declared, and why I have constantly advocated a negotiated peace. I did not feel that England and France had a reasonable chance of winning. France has now been defeated; and, despite the propaganda and confusion of recent months, it is now obvious that England is losing the war. I believe this is realized even by the British Government. But they have one last desperate plan remaining. They hope that they may be able to persuade us to send another American Expeditionary Force to Europe, and to share with England militarily, as well as financially, the fiasco of this war.

I do not blame England for this hope, or for asking for our assistance.

But we now know that she declared a war under circumstances which led to the defeat of every nation that sided with her from Poland to Greece. We know that in the desperation of war England promised to all those nations armed assistance that she could not send. We know that she misinformed them, as she has misinformed us, concerning her state of preparation, her military strength, and the progress of the war.

In time of war, truth is always replaced by propaganda. I do not believe we should be too quick to criticize the actions of a belligerent nation. There is always the question whether we, ourselves, would do better under similar circumstances. But we in this country have a right to think of the welfare of America first, just as the people in England thought first of their own country when they encouraged the smaller nations of Europe to fight against hopeless odds. When England asks us to enter this war, she is considering her own future, and that of her empire. In making our reply, I believe we should consider the future of the United States and that of the Western Hemisphere.

It is not only our right, but is our obligation as American citizens to look at this war objectively and to weigh our chances for success if we should enter it. I have attempted to do this, especially from the standpoint of aviation; and I have been forced to the conclusion that we cannot win this war for England, regardless of how much assistance we extend.

I ask you to look at the map of Europe today and see if you can suggest any way in which we could win this war if we entered it. Suppose we had a large army in America, trained and equipped. Where would we send it to fight? The campaigns of the war show only too clearly how difficult it is to force a landing, or to maintain an army, on a hostile coast.

Suppose we took our Navy from the Pacific, and used it to convoy British shipping. That would not win the war for England. It would, at best, permit her to exist under the constant bombing of the German air fleet. Suppose we had an air force that we could send to Europe. Where could it operate? Some of our squadrons might be based in the British Isles; but it is physically impossible to base enough aircraft in the British Isles alone to equal in strength the aircraft that can be based on the Continent of Europe.

I have asked these questions on the supposition that we had in existence an Army and an air force large enough and well enough equipped to send to Europe; and that we would dare to remove our Navy from the Pacific. Even on this basis, I do not see how we could invade the Continent of Europe successfully as long as all of that Continent and most of Asia is under Axis domination. But the fact is that none of these suppositions are correct. We have only a one-ocean Navy. Our Army is still untrained and inadequately equipped for foreign war. Our air force is deplorably lacking in modern fighting planes.

When these facts are cited, the interventionists shout that we are defeatists, that we are undermining the principles of democracy, and that we are giving comfort to Germany by talking about our military weakness. But everything I mention here has been published in our newspapers, and in the reports of congressional hearings in Washington. Our military position is well known to the governments of Europe and Asia. Why, then, should it not be brought to the attention of our own people?

I say it is the interventionist in America, as it was in England and in France, who gives comfort to the enemy. I say it is they who are undermining the principles of democracy when they demand that we take a course to which more than 80 per cent of our citizens are opposed. I charge them with being the real defeatists, for their policy has led to the defeat of every country that followed their advice since this war began. There is no better way to give comfort to an enemy than to divide the people of a nation over the issue of foreign war. There is no shorter road to defeat than by entering a war with inadequate preparation. Every nation that has adopted the interventionist policy of depending on some one else for its own defense has met with nothing but defeat and failure.

When history is written, the responsibility for the downfall of the democracies of Europe will rest squarely upon the shoulders of the interventionists who led their nations into war uninformed and unprepared. With their shouts of defeatism, and their disdain of reality, they have already sent countless thousands of young men to death in Europe. From the campaign of Poland to that of Greece, their prophecies have been false and their policies have failed. Yet these are the people who are calling us defeatists in America today. And they have led this country, too, to the verge of war.

There are many such interventionists in America, but there are more people among us of a different type. That is why you and I are assembled here tonight. There is a policy open to this nation that will lead to success — a policy that leaves us free to follow our own way of life, and to develop our own civilization. It is not a new and untried idea. It was advocated by Washington. It was incorporated in the Monroe Doctrine. Under its guidance, the United States became the greatest nation in the world.

It is based upon the belief that the security of a nation lies in the strength and character of its own people. It recommends the maintenance of armed forces sufficient to defend this hemisphere from attack by any combination of foreign powers. It demands faith in an independent American destiny. This is the policy of the America First Committee today. It is a policy not of isolation, but of independence; not of defeat, but of courage. It is a policy that led this nation to success during the most trying years of our history, and it is a policy that will lead us to success again.

We have weakened ourselves for many months, and still worse, we have divided our own people by this dabbling in Europe's wars. While we should have been concentrating on American defense we have been forced to argue over foreign quarrels. We must turn our eyes and our faith back to our own country before it is too late. And when we do this, a different vista opens before us. Practically every difficulty we would face in invading Europe becomes an asset to us in defending America. Our enemy, and not we, would then have the problem of transporting millions of troops across the ocean and landing them on a hostile shore. They, and not we, would have to furnish the convoys to transport guns and trucks and munitions and fuel across three thousand miles of water. Our battleships and submarines would then be fighting close to their home bases. We would then do the bombing from the air and the torpedoing at sea. And if any part of an enemy convoy should ever pass our navy and our air force, they would still be faced with the guns of our coast artillery and behind them the divisions of our Army.

The United States is better situated from a military standpoint than any other nation in the world. Even in our present condition of unpreparedness no foreign power is in a position to invade us today. If we concentrate on our own defenses and build the strength that this nation should maintain, no foreign army will ever attempt to land on American shores.

War is not inevitable for this country. Such a claim is defeatism in the true sense. No one can make us fight abroad unless we ourselves are willing to do so. No one will attempt to fight us here if we arm ourselves as a great nation should be armed. Over a hundred million people in this nation are opposed to entering the war. If the principles of democracy mean anything at all, that is reason enough for us to stay out. If we are forced into a war against the wishes of an overwhelming majority of our people, we will have proved democracy such a failure at home that there will be little use fighting for it abroad.

The time has come when those of us who believe in an independent American destiny must band together and organize for strength. We have been led toward war by a minority of our people. This minority has power. It has influence. It has a loud voice. But it does not represent the American people. During the last several years I have traveled over this country from one end to the other. I have talked to many hundreds of men and women, and I have letters from tens of thousands more, who feel the same way as you and I.

Most of these people have no influence or power. Most of them have no means of expressing their convictions, except by their vote which has always been against this war. They are the citizens who have had to work too hard at their daily jobs to organize political meetings. Hitherto, they have relied upon their vote to express their feelings; but now they find that it is hardly remembered except in the oratory of a political campaign. These people — the majority of hardworking American citizens, are with us. They are the true strength of our country. And they are beginning to realize, as you and I, that there are times when we must sacrifice our normal interests in life in order to insure the safety and the welfare of our nation.

Such a time has come. Such a crisis is here. That is why the America First Committee has been formed — to give voice to the people who have no newspaper, or newsreel, or radio station at their command; to the people who must do the paying, and the fighting, and the dying if this country enters the war.

Whether or not we do enter the war rests upon the shoulders of you in this audience, upon us here on this platform, upon meetings of this kind that are being held by Americans in every section of the United States today. It depends upon the action we take, and the courage we show at this time. If you believe in an independent destiny for America, if you believe that this country should not enter the war in Europe, we ask you to join the America First Committee in its stand. We ask you to share our faith in the ability of this nation to defend itself, to develop its own civilization, and to contribute to the progress of mankind in a more constructive and intelligent way than has yet been found by the warring nations of Europe. We need your support, and we need it now. The time to act is here.

77. F.D. Roosevelt on the Atlantic Charter, 21 August 1941

OVER a week ago I held several important conferences at sea with the British Prime Minister. Because of the factor of safety to British, Canadian, and American ships, and their personnel, no prior announcement of these meetings could properly be made.

At the close, a public statement by the Prime Minister and the President was made. I quote it for the information of the Congress and for the record:

The President of the United States and the Prime Minister, Mr. Churchill, representing His Majesty's Government in the United Kingdom, have met at sea.

They have been accompanied by officials of their two Governments, including high-ranking officers of their military, naval, and air services.

The whole problem of the supply of munitions of war, as provided by the Lease-Lend Act, for the armed forces of the United States, and for those countries actively engaged in resisting aggression, has been further examined.

Lord Beaverbrook, the Minister of Supply of the British Government, has joined in these conferences. He is going to proceed to Washington to discuss further details with appropriate officials of the United States Government. These conferences will also cover the supply problems of the Soviet Union.

The President and the Prime Minister have had several conferences. They have considered the dangers to world civilization arising from the policies of military domination by conquest upon which the Hitlerite government of Germany and other governments associated therewith have embarked, and have made clear the steps which their countries are respectively taking for their safety in the face of these dangers.

They have agreed upon the following joint declaration:

Joint declaration of the President of the United States of America and the Prime Minister, Mr. Churchill, representing His Majesty's Government in the United Kingdom, being met together, deem it right to make known certain common principles in the national policies of their respective countries on which they base their hopes for a better future for the world.

First, their countries seek no aggrandizement, territorial or other;

Second, they desire to see no territorial changes that do not accord with the freely expressed wishes of the peoples concerned;

Third, they respect the right of all peoples to choose the form of government under which they will live; and they wish to see sovereign rights and self-government restored to those who have been forcibly deprived of them;

Fourth, they will endeavor, with due respect for their existing obligations, to further the enjoyment by all states, great or small, victor or vanquished, of access, on equal terms, to the trade and to the raw materials of the world which are needed for their economic prosperity;

Fifth, they desire to bring about the fullest collaboration between all nations in the economic field with the object of securing, for all, improved labor standards, economic advancement, and social security;

Sixth, after the final destruction of the Nazi tyranny, they hope to see established a peace which will afford to all nations the means of dwelling in safety within their own boundaries, and which will afford assurance that all the men in all the lands may live out their lives in freedom from fear and want;

Seventh, such a peace should enable all men to traverse the high seas and oceans without hindrance;

Eighth, they believe that all of the nations of the world, for realistic as well as spiritual reasons, must come to the abandonment of the use of force. Since no future peace can be maintained if land, sea, or air armaments continue to be employed by nations which threaten, or may threaten, aggression outside of their frontiers, they believe, pending the establishment of a wider and permanent system of general security, that the disarmament of such nations is essential. They will likewise aid and encourage all other practicable measures which will lighten for peace-loving peoples the crushing burden of armaments.

Franklin D. Roosevelt
Winston S. Churchill

The Congress and the President having heretofore determined, through the Lend-Lease Act, on the national policy of American aid to the democracies which East and West are waging war against dictatorships, the military and naval conversations at these meetings made clear gains in furthering the effectiveness of this aid.

Furthermore, the Prime Minister and I are arranging for conferences with the Soviet Union to aid it in its defense against the attack made by the principal aggressor of the modern world — Germany.

Finally, the declaration of principles at this time presents a goal which is worth while for our type of civilization to seek. It is so clearcut that it is difficult to oppose in any major particular without automatically admitting a willingness to accept compromise with nazi-ism; or to agree to a world peace which would give to nazi-ism domination over large numbers of conquered nations. Inevitably such a peace would be a gift to nazi-ism to take breath — armed breath — for a second war to extend the control over Europe and Asia, to the American Hemisphere itself.

It is perhaps unnecessary for me to call attention once more to the utter lack of validity of the spoken or written word of the Nazi government.

It is also unnecessary for me to point out that the declaration of principles includes, of necessity, the world need for freedom of religion and freedom of information. No society of the world organized under the announced principles could survive without these freedoms which are a part of the whole freedom for which we strive.

78. Axis Pact, 27 September 1940

Signed at Berlin by Germany, Italy, and Japan.

... *Article 1.* Japan recognizes and respects the leadership of Germany and Italy in the establishment of a new order in Europe.

Article 2. Germany and Italy recognize and respect the leadership of Japan in the establishment of a new order in Greater East Asia.

Article 3. Germany, Italy and Japan agree to cooperate in their efforts on aforesaid lines. They further undertake to assist one another with all political, economic and military means when one of the three Contracting Powers is attacked by a Power at present not involved in the European War or in the Chinese-Japanese conflict.

Article 4. With the view to implementing the present pact, joint technical commissions, the members of which are to be appointed by the respective Governments of Germany, Italy and Japan, will meet without delay.

Article 5. Germany, Italy and Japan affirm that the aforesaid terms do not in any way affect the political status which exists at present as between each of the three Contracting Parties and Soviet Russia. ...

79. Japanese Note to U.S., 20 November 1941

Japanese Ambassador in U.S. Kichisaburo Nomura to Hull.

1. BOTH the Governments of Japan and the United States undertake not to make any armed advancement into any of the regions in the Southeastern Asia and the Southern Pacific area excepting the part of French Indo-China where the Japanese troops are stationed at present.

2. The Japanese Government undertakes to withdraw its troops now stationed in French Indo-China upon either the restoration of peace between Japan and China or the establishment of an equitable peace in the Pacific area.

In the meantime the Government of Japan declares that it is prepared to remove its troops now stationed in the southern part of French Indo-China to the northern part of the said territory upon the conclusion of the present arrangement which shall later be embodied in the final agreement.

3. The Government of Japan and the United States shall cooperate with a view to securing the acquisition of those goods and commodities which the two countries need in Netherlands East Indies.

4. The Governments of Japan and the United States mutually undertake to restore their commercial relations to those prevailing prior to the freezing of the assets.

The Government of the United States shall supply Japan a required quantity of oil.

5. The Government of the United States undertakes to refrain from such measures and actions as will be prejudicial to the endeavors for the restoration of general peace between Japan and China.

80. U.S. Note to Japan, 26 November 1941

Hull to Nomura.

THE GOVERNMENT of the United States and the Government of Japan both being solicitous for the peace of the Pacific affirm that their national policies are directed toward lasting and extensive peace throughout the Pacific area, that they have no territorial designs in that area, that they have no intention of threatening other countries or of using military force aggressively against any neighboring nation, and that, accordingly, in their national policies they will actively support and give practical application to the following fundamental principles upon which their relations with each other and with all other governments are based:

(1) The principle of inviolability of territorial integrity and sovereignty of each and all nations.

(2) The principle of non-interference in the internal affairs of other countries.

(3) The principle of equality, including equality of commercial opportunity and treatment.

(4) The principle of reliance upon international cooperation and conciliation for the prevention and pacific settlement of controversies and for improvement of international conditions by peaceful methods and processes.

The Government of Japan and the Government of the United States have agreed that toward eliminating chronic political instability, preventing recurrent economic collapse, and providing a basis for peace, they will actively support and practically apply the following principles in their economic relations with each other and with other nations and peoples:

(1) The principle of non-discrimination in international commercial relations.

(2) The principle of international economic cooperation and abolition of extreme nationalism as expressed in excessive trade restrictions.

(3) The principle of non-discriminatory access by all nations to raw material supplies.

(4) The principle of full protection of the interests of consuming countries and populations as regards the operation of international commodity agreements.

(5) The principle of establishment of such institutions and arrangements of international finance as may lend aid to the essential enterprises and the continuous development of all countries and may permit payments through processes of trade consonant with the welfare of all countries.

SECTION II. *Steps to Be Taken by the Government of the United States and by the Government of Japan*

The Government of the United States and the Government of Japan propose to take steps as follows:

1. The Government of the United States and the Government of Japan will endeavor to conclude a multilateral non-aggression pact among the British Empire, China, Japan, the Netherlands, the Soviet Union, Thailand and the United States.

2. Both Governments will endeavor to conclude among the American, British, Chinese, Japanese, the Netherland and Thai Governments an agreement whereunder each of the Governments would pledge itself to respect the territorial integrity of French Indochina and, in the event that there should develop a threat to the territorial integrity of Indochina, to enter into immediate consultation with a view to taking such measures as may be deemed necessary and advisable to meet the threat in question. Such agreement would provide also that each of the Governments party to the agreement would not seek or accept preferential treatment in its trade or economic relations with Indochina and would use its influence to obtain for each of the signatories equality of treatment in trade and commerce with French Indochina.

3. The Government of Japan will withdraw all military, naval, air and police forces from China and from Indochina.

4. The Government of the United States and the Government of Japan will not support — militarily, politically, economically — any government or regime in China other than the National Government of the Republic of China with capital temporarily at Chungking.

5. Both Governments will give up all extraterritorial rights in China, including rights and interests in and with regard to international settlements and concessions, and rights under the Boxer Protocol of 1901.

Both Governments will endeavor to obtain the agreement of the British and other governments to give up extraterritorial rights in China, including rights in international settlements and in concessions and under the Boxer Protocol of 1901.

6. The Government of the United States and the Government of Japan will enter into negotiations for the conclusion between the United States and Japan of a trade agreement, based upon reciprocal most-favored-nation treatment and reduction of trade barriers by both countries, including an undertaking by the United States to bind raw silk on the free list.

7. The Government of the United States and the Government of Japan will, respectively, remove the freezing restrictions on Japanese funds in the United States and on American funds in Japan.

8. Both Governments will agree upon a plan for the stabilization of the dollar-yen rate, with the allocation of funds adequate for this purpose, half to be supplied by Japan and half by the United States . . . .

81. Cairo Conference, November 1943

Statement of F.D. Roosevelt, Prime Minister Winston Churchill, and Chiang Kai-shek, 26 November 1943.

... THE SEVERAL military missions have agreed upon future military operations against Japan. The Three Great Allies expressed their resolve to bring unrelenting pressure against their brutal enemies by sea, land, and air. This pressure is already rising.

The Three Great Allies are fighting this war to restrain and punish the aggression of Japan. They covet no gain for themselves and have no thought of territorial expansion. It is their purpose that Japan shall be stripped of all the islands in the Pacific which she has seized or occupied since the beginning of the first World War in 1914, and that all the territories Japan has stolen from the Chinese, such as Manchuria, Formosa, and the Pescadores, shall be restored to the Republic of China. Japan will also be expelled from all other territories which she has taken by violence and greed. The aforesaid three great powers, mindful of the enslavement of the people of Korea, are determined that in due course Korea shall become free and independent.

With these objects in view the three Allies, in harmony with those of the United Nations at war with Japan, will continue to persevere in the serious and prolonged operations necessary to procure the unconditional surrender of Japan.

82. Teheran Conference, November–December 1943

Statement of F.D. Roosevelt, Churchill, and Joseph Stalin, 1 December 1943.

WE — The President of the United States, the Prime Minister of Great Britain, and the Premier of the Soviet Union, have met these four days past, in this, the Capital of our Ally, Iran, and have shaped and confirmed our common policy.

We express our determination that our nations shall work together in war and in the peace that will follow.

As to war — our military staffs have joined in our round table discussions, and we have concerted our plans for the destruction of the German forces. We have reached complete agreement as to the scope and timing of the operations to be undertaken from the east, west and south.

The common understanding which we have here reached guarantees that victory will be ours.

And as to peace — we are sure that our concord will win an enduring Peace. We recognize fully the supreme responsibility resting upon us and all the United Nations to make a peace which will command the goodwill of the overwhelming mass of the peoples of the world and banish the scourge and terror of war for many generations.

With our Diplomatic advisors we have surveyed the problems of the future. We shall seek the cooperation and active participation of all nations, large and small, whose peoples in heart and mind are dedicated, as are our own peoples, to the elimination of tyranny and slavery, oppression and intolerance. We will welcome them, as they may choose to come, into a world family of Democratic Nations.

No power on earth can prevent our destroying the German armies by land, their U Boats by sea, and their war plants from the air.

Our attack will be relentless and increasing.

Emerging from these cordial conferences we look with confidence to the day when all peoples of the world may live free lives, untouched by tyranny, and according to their varying desires and their own consciences.

We came here with hope and determination. We leave here, friends in fact, in spirit and in purpose.

83. Yalta (Crimea) Conference, 4-11 February 1945

Statement of F.D. Roosevelt, Churchill, and Stalin, 11 February 1945; secret provisions published 24 March 1947.

...WE HAVE considered and determined the military plans of the three allied powers for the final defeat of the common enemy. The military staffs of the three allied nations have met in daily meetings throughout the Conference. These meetings have been most satisfactory from every point of view and have resulted in closer coordination of the military effort of the three allies than ever before. The fullest information has been interchanged. The timing, scope and coordination of new and even more powerful blows to be launched by our armies and airforces into the heart of Germany from the East, West, North and South have been fully agreed and planned in detail.

Our combined military plans will be made known only as we execute them, but we believe that the very close working partnership among the three staffs attained at this Conference will result in shortening the War. Meetings of the three staffs will be continued in the future whenever the need arises.

Nazi Germany is doomed. The German people will only make the cost of their defeat heavier to themselves by attempting to continue a hopeless resistance.

THE OCCUPATION AND CONTROL OF GERMANY

We have agreed on common policies and plans for enforcing the unconditional surrender terms which we shall impose together on Nazi Germany after German armed resistance has been finally crushed. These terms will not be made known until the final defeat of Germany has been accomplished. Under the agreed plan, the forces of the three powers will each occupy a separate zone of Germany. Coordinated administration and control has been provided for under the plan through a central control commission consisting of the Supreme Commanders of the three powers with headquarters in Berlin. It has been agreed that France should be invited by the three powers, if she should so desire, to take over a zone of occupation, and to participate as a fourth member of the control commission. The limits of the French zone will be agreed by the four governments concerned through their representatives on the European Advisory Commission.

It is our inflexible purpose to destroy German militarism and Nazism and to ensure that Germany will never again be able to disturb the peace of the world. We are determined to disarm and disband all German armed forces; break up for all time the German General Staff that has repeatedly contrived the resurgence of German militarism; remove or destroy all German military equipment; eliminate or control all German industry that could be used for military production; bring all war criminals to just and swift punishment and exact reparation in kind for the destruction wrought by the Germans; wipe out the Nazi Party, Nazi laws, organizations and institutions, remove all Nazi and militarist influences from public office and from cultural and economic life of the German people; and take in harmony such other measures in Germany as may be necessary to the future peace and safety of the world. It is not our purpose to destroy the people of Germany, but only when Nazism and militarism have been extirpated will there be hope for a decent life for Germans, and a place for them in the comity of nations.

REPARATION BY GERMANY

We have considered the question of the damage caused by Germany to the allied nations in this war and recognized it as just that Germany be obliged to make compensation for this damage in kind to the greatest extent possible. A commission for the compensation of damage will be established. The commission will be instructed to consider the question of the extent and methods for compensating damage caused by Germany to the allied countries. The commission will work in Moscow.

UNITED NATIONS CONFERENCE

We are resolved upon the earliest possible establishment with our allies of a general international organization to maintain peace and security. We believe that this is essential, both to prevent aggression and to remove the political, economic and social causes of war through the close and continuing collaboration of all peace-loving peoples.

The foundations were laid at Dumbarton Oaks. On the important question of voting procedure, however, agreement was not there reached. The present Conference has been able to resolve this difficulty.

We have agreed that a conference of United Nations should be called to meet at San Francisco in the United States on April 25, 1945, to prepare the charter of such an organization, along the lines proposed in the informal conversations at Dumbarton Oaks.

The Government of China and the Provisional Government of France will be immediately consulted and invited to sponsor invitations to the conference jointly with the Governments of the United States, Great Britain and the Union of Soviet Socialist Republics. As soon as the consultation with China and France has been completed, the text of the proposals on voting procedure will be made public.

Declaration on Liberated Europe

The Premier of the Union of Soviet Socialist Republics, the Prime Minister of the United Kingdom, and the President of the United States of America have consulted with each other in the common interests of the peoples of their countries and those of liberated Europe. They jointly declare their mutual agreement to concert during the temporary period of instability in liberated Europe the policies of their three governments in assisting the peoples liberated from the domination of Nazi Germany and the peoples of the former Axis satellite states of Europe to solve by democratic means their pressing political and economic problems.

The establishment of order in Europe and the rebuilding of national economic life must be achieved by processes which will enable the liberated peoples to destroy the last vestiges of Nazism and Fascism and to create democratic institutions of their own choice. This is a principle of the Atlantic Charter — the right of all peoples to choose the form of government under which they will live — the restoration of sovereign rights and self-government to those peoples who have been forcibly deprived of them by the aggressor nations.

To foster the conditions in which the liberated peoples may exercise these rights, the three governments will jointly assist the people in any European liberated state or former Axis satellite state in Europe where in their judgment conditions require (A) to establish conditions of internal peace; (B) to carry out emergency measures for the relief of distressed peoples; (C) to form interim governmental authorities broadly representative of all democratic elements in the population and pledged to the earliest possible establishment through free elections of governments responsive to the will of the people; and (D) to facilitate where necessary the holding of such elections.

The three governments will consult the other United Nations and provisional authorities or other governments in Europe when matters of direct interest to them are under consideration.

When, in the opinion of the three governments, conditions in any European liberated state or any former Axis satellite state in Europe make such action necessary, they will immediately consult together on the measures necessary to discharge the joint responsibilities set forth in this declaration.

By this declaration we reaffirm our faith in the principles of the Atlantic Charter, our pledge in the declaration by the United Nations, and our determination to build in cooperation with other peace-loving nations world order under law, dedicated to peace, security, freedom and general well-being of all mankind.

In issuing this declaration, the three powers express the hope that the Provisional Government of the French Republic may be associated with them in the procedure suggested.

Poland

A new situation has been created in Poland as a result of her complete liberation by the Red Army. This calls for the establishment of a Polish provisional government which can be more broadly based than was possible before the recent liberation of Western Poland. The provisional government which is now functioning in Poland should therefore be reorganized on a broader democratic basis with the inclusion of democratic leaders from Poland itself and from Poles abroad. This new government should then be called the Polish Provisional Government of National Unity.

M. Molotov, Mr. Harriman and Sir A. Clark Kerr are authorized as a commission to consult in the first instance in Moscow with members of the present provisional government and with other Polish democratic leaders from within Poland and from abroad, with a view to the reorganization of the present government along the above lines. This Polish Provisional Government of National Unity shall be pledged to the holding of free and unfettered elections as soon as possible on the basis of universal suffrage and secret ballot. In these elections all democratic and anti-Nazi parties shall have the right to take part and to put forward candidates.

When a Polish Provisional Government of National Unity has been properly formed in conformity with the above, the government of the U.S.S.R., which now maintains diplomatic relations with the present provisional government of Poland, and the government of the United Kingdom and the government of the U.S.A. will establish diplomatic relations with the new Polish Provisional Government of National Unity, and will exchange ambassadors by whose reports the respective governments will be kept informed about the situation in Poland.

The three heads of government consider that the Eastern frontier of Poland should follow the Curzon line with digressions from it in some regions of five to eight kilometres in favour of Poland. They recognize that Poland must receive substantial accessions of territory in the North and West. They feel that the opinion of the new Polish Provisional Government of National Unity should be sought in due course on the extent of these accessions and that the final delineation of the western frontier of Poland should thereafter await the peace conference.

Yugoslavia

We have agreed to recommend to Marshal Tito and Dr. Subasic that the agreement between them should be put into effect immediately, and that a new government should be formed on the basis of that agreement.

We also recommend that as soon as the new government has been formed it should declare that:

(1) The anti-Fascist assembly of National Liberation (Avnoj) should be extended to include members of the last Yugoslav Parliament (Skupschina) who have not compromised themselves by collaboration with

the enemy, thus forming a body to be known as a temporary Parliament; and,

(2) Legislative acts passed by the anti-Fascist Assembly of National Liberation will be subject to subsequent ratification by a constituent assembly.

There was also a general review of other Balkan questions . . . .

Secret Yalta Agreement on the Kuriles

The leaders of the three Great Powers — the Soviet Union, the United States of America and Great Britain — have agreed that in two or three months after Germany has surrendered and the war in Europe has terminated the Soviet Union shall enter into the war against Japan on the side of the Allies on condition that:

1. The status quo in Outer-Mongolia (The Mongolian People's Republic) shall be preserved;

2. The former rights of Russia violated by the treacherous attack of Japan in 1940 shall be restored, viz:

(a) the southern part of Sakhalin as well as all the islands adjacent to it shall be returned to the Soviet Union,

(b) the commercial port of Dairen shall be internationalized, the preeminent interests of the Soviet Union in this port being safeguarded and the lease of Port Arthur as a naval base of the USSR restored,

(c) the Chinese-Eastern Railroad and the South-Manchurian Railroad which provides an outlet to Dairen shall be jointly operated by the establishment of a joint Soviet-Chinese Company it being understood that the preeminent interests of the Soviet Union shall be safeguarded and that China shall retain full sovereignty in Manchuria;

3. The Kuril islands shall be handed over to the Soviet Union.

It is understood, that the agreement concerning Outer-Mongolia and the ports and railroads referred to above will require concurrence of Generalissimo Chiang Kai-shek. The President will take measures in order to obtain this concurrence on advice from Marshal Stalin.

The Heads of the three Great Powers have agreed that these claims of the Soviet Union shall be unquestionably fulfilled after Japan has been defeated.

For its part the Soviet Union expresses its readiness to conclude with the National Government of China a pact of friendship and alliance between the USSR and China in order to render assistance to China with its armed forces for the purpose of liberating China from the Japanese yoke.

Secret Yalta Agreement Concerning Germany [15]

Dismemberment of Germany

It was agreed that Article 12 (a) of the Surrender Terms for Germany should be amended to read as follows:

The United Kingdom, the United States of America and the Union of Soviet Socialist Republics shall possess supreme authority with respect to Germany. In the exercise of such authority they will take such steps, including the complete disarmament, demilitarization and dismemberment of Germany as they deem requisite for future peace and security.

The study of the procedure of the dismemberment of Germany was referred to a committee consisting of Mr. [Anthony] Eden [their Foreign Secretary] (chairman), Mr. [John] Winant [of the United States] and Mr. [Fedor T.] Gusev. This body would consider the desirability of associating with it a French representative.

Zone of Occupation for the French and Control Council for Germany

It was agreed that a zone in Germany, to be occupied by the French forces, should be allocated to France. This zone would be formed out of the British and American zones and its extent would be settled by the British and Americans in consultation with the French Provisional Government.

It was also agreed that the French Provisional Government should be invited to become a member of the Allied Control Council for Germany.

Reparation

The following protocol has been approved:

Protocol on the Talks between the Heads of Three Governments at the Crimean Conference on the German Reparations in Kind

1. Germany must pay in kind for the losses caused by her to the Allied nations in the course of the war. Reparations are to be received in the first instance by those countries which have borne the main burden of the war, have suffered the heaviest losses and have organized victory over the enemy.

2. Reparation in kind is to be exacted from Germany in three following forms:

(a) Removals within two years from the surrender of Germany or the cessation of organized resistance from the national wealth of Germany located on the territory of Germany herself as well as outside her territory (equipment, machine tools, ships, rolling stock, German investments abroad, shares of industrial, transport and other enterprises in Germany, etc.), these removals to be carried out chiefly for purpose of destroying the war potential of Germany.

(b) Annual deliveries of goods from current production for a period to be fixed.

(c) Use of German labor . . . .

84. Potsdam Declaration on Japan, July 1945

Signed by President Harry S. Truman and Churchill; concurred in by Chiang Kai-shek, 26 July 1945.

(1) WE — the President of the United States, the President of the National Government of the Republic of China, and the Prime Minister of Great Britain, representing the hundreds of millions of our countrymen, have conferred and agree that Japan shall be given an opportunity to end this war.

(2) The prodigious land, sea and air forces of the United States, the British Empire and of China, many times reinforced by their armies and air fleets from the west, are poised to strike the final blows upon Japan. This military power is sustained and inspired by the determination of all the Allied Nations to prosecute the war against Japan until she ceases to resist.

(3) The result of the futile and senseless German resistance to the might of the aroused free peoples of the world stands forth in awful clarity as an example to the people of Japan. The might that now converges on Japan is immeasurably greater than that which, when applied to the resisting Nazis, necessarily laid waste to the lands, the industry and the method of life of the whole German people. The full application of our military power, backed by our resolve, *will* mean the inevitable and complete destruction of the Japanese armed forces and just as inevitably the utter devastation of the Japanese homeland.

(4) The time has come for Japan to decide whether she will continue to be controlled by those self-willed militaristic advisers whose unintelligent calculations have brought the Empire of Japan to the threshold of annihilation, or whether she will follow the path of reason.

(5) Following are our terms. We will not deviate from them. There are no alternatives. We shall brook no delay.

(6) There must be eliminated for all time the authority and influence of those who have deceived and misled the people of Japan into embarking on world conquest, for we insist that a new order of peace, security and justice will be impossible until irresponsible militarism is driven from the world.

(7) Until such a new order is established *and* until there is convincing proof that Japan's war-making power is destroyed, points in Japanese territory to be designated by the Allies shall be occupied to secure the achievement of the basic objectives we are here setting forth.

(8) The terms of the Cairo Declaration shall be carried out and Japanese sovereignty shall be limited to the islands of Honshu, Hokkaido, Kyushu, Shikoku and such minor islands as we determine.

(9) The Japanese military forces, after being completely disarmed, shall be permitted to return to their homes with the opportunity to lead peaceful and productive lives.

(10) We do not intend that the Japanese shall be enslaved as a race or destroyed as a nation, but stern justice shall be meted out to all war criminals, including those who have visited cruelties upon our prisoners. The Japanese Government shall remove all obstacles to the revival and strengthening of democratic tendencies among the Japanese people. Freedom of speech, of religion, and of thought, as well as respect for the fundamental human rights shall be established.

(11) Japan shall be permitted to maintain such industries as will sustain her economy and permit the exaction of just reparations in kind, but not those which would enable her to re-arm for war. To this end, access to, as distinguished from control of, raw materials shall be permitted. Eventual Japanese participation in world trade relations shall be permitted.

(12) The occupying forces of the Allies shall be withdrawn from Japan as soon as these objectives have been accomplished and there has been established in accordance with the freely expressed will of the Japanese people a peacefully inclined and responsible government.

(13) We call upon the government of Japan to proclaim now the unconditional surrender of all Japanese armed forces, and to provide proper and adequate assurances of their good faith in such action. The alternative for Japan is prompt and utter destruction.

85. Potsdam (Berlin) Conference, 17 July–5 August 1945

Statement of Truman, Prime Minister Clement R. Attlee, and Stalin, majority of text published 5 August; full text published 24 March 1947.

I. *Establishment of a Council of Foreign Ministers.*

... 1. THERE SHALL BE established a Council composed of the foreign ministers of the United Kingdom, the Union of Soviet Socialist Republics, China, France and the United States. ...

3. (i) As its immediate important task, the Council shall be authorized to draw up, with a view to their submission to the United Nations, treaties of peace with Italy, Rumania, Bulgaria, Hungary and Finland, and to propose settlements of territorial questions outstanding on the termination of the war in Europe. The Council shall be utilized for the preparation of a peace settlement for Germany to be accepted by the government of Germany when a government adequate for the purpose is established.

(ii) For the discharge of each of these tasks the Council will be composed of the members representing those states which were signatory to the terms of surrender imposed upon the enemy state concerned. For the purpose of the peace settlement for Italy, France shall be regarded as a signatory to the terms of surrender for Italy. Other members will be invited to participate when matters directly concerning them are under discussion.

(iii) Other matters may from time to time be referred to the Council by agreement between the member governments.

4. (i) Whenever the Council is considering a question of direct interest to a state not represented thereon, such state should be invited to send representatives to participate in the discussion and study of that question.

(ii) The Council may adapt its procedure to the particular problem under consideration. In some cases it may hold its own preliminary discussions prior to the participation of other interested states. In other cases, the Council may convoke a formal conference of the state chiefly interested in seeking a solution of the particular problem. ...

II. *Germany*

... The Political and Economic Principles to Govern the Treatment of Germany in the Initial Control Period.

(A) POLITICAL PRINCIPLES

1. In accordance with the agreement on control machinery in Germany, supreme authority in Germany is exercised on instructions from their respective governments, by the Commanders-in-Chief of the armed forces of the United States of America, the United Kingdom, the Union of Soviet Socialist Republics, and the French Republic, each in his own zone of occupation, and also jointly, in matters affecting Germany as a whole, in their capacity as members of the Control Council.

2. So far as is practicable, there shall be uniformity of treatment of the German population throughout Germany.

3. The purposes of the occupation of Germany by which the Control Council shall be guided are:

(i) The complete disarmament and demilitarization of Germany and the elimination or control of all German industry that could be used for military production. To these ends:

(a) All German land, naval and air forces, the S.S., S.A., S.D., and Gestapo, with all their organizations, staffs and institutions, including the General Staff, the Officers' Corps, Reserve Corps, military schools, war veterans' organizations and all other military and quasi-military organizations, together with all clubs and associations which serve to keep alive the military tradition in Germany, shall be completely and finally abolished in such manner as permanently to prevent the revival or reorganization of German militarism and Nazism.

(b) All arms, ammunition and implements of war and all specialized facilities for their production shall be held at the disposal of the Allies or destroyed. The maintenance and production of all aircraft and all arms, ammunition and implements of war shall be prevented.

(ii) To convince the German people that they have suffered a total military defeat and that they cannot escape responsibility for what they have brought upon themselves, since their own ruthless warfare and the fanatical Nazi resistance have destroyed German economy and made chaos and suffering inevitable.

(iii) To destroy the National Socialist Party and its affiliated and supervised organizations, to dissolve all Nazi institutions, to ensure that they are not revived in any form, and to prevent all Nazi and militarist activity or propaganda.

(iv) To prepare for the eventual reconstruction of German political life on a democratic basis and for eventual peaceful cooperation in international life by Germany.

4. All Nazi laws which provided the basis of the Hitler regime or established discrimination on grounds of race, creed, or political opinion shall be abolished. No such discriminations, whether legal, administrative or otherwise, shall be tolerated

5. War criminals and those who have participated in planning or carrying out Nazi enterprises involving or resulting in atrocities or war crimes shall be arrested and brought to judgment. Nazi leaders, influential Nazi supporters and high officials of Nazi organizations and institutions and any other persons dangerous to the occupation or its objectives shall be arrested and interned.

6. All members of the Nazi party who have been more than nominal participants in its activities and all other persons hostile to allied purposes shall be removed from public and semi-public office, and from positions of responsibility in important private undertakings. Such persons shall be replaced by persons who, by their political and moral qualities, are deemed capable of assisting in developing genuine democratic institutions in Germany.

7. German education shall be so controlled as completely to eliminate Nazi and militarist doctrines and to make possible the successful development of democratic ideas.

8. The judicial system will be reorganized in accordance with the principles of democracy, of justice under law, and of equal rights for all citizens without distinction of race, nationality or religion.

9. The administration of affairs in Germany should be directed towards the decentralization of the political structure and the development of local responsibility. To this end:

(i) Local self-government shall be restored throughout Germany on democratic principles and in particular through elective councils as rapidly as is consistent with military security and the purposes of military occupation;

(ii) All democratic political parties with rights of assembly and of public discussion shall be allowed and encouraged throughout Germany;

(iii) Representative and elective principles shall be introduced into regional, provincial and state (land) administration as rapidly as may be justified by the successful application of these principles in local self-government;

(iv) For the time being no central German government shall be established. Notwithstanding this, however, certain essential central German administrative departments, headed by state secretaries, shall be established, particularly in the fields of finance, transport, communications, foreign trade and industry. Such departments will act under the direction of the Control Council.

10. Subject to the necessity for maintaining military security, freedom of speech, press and religion shall be permitted, and religious institutions shall be respected. Subject likewise to the maintenance of military security, the formation of free trade unions shall be permitted.

(B) ECONOMIC PRINCIPLES

11. In order to eliminate Germany's war potential, the production of arms, ammunition and implements of war as well as all types of aircraft and sea-going ships shall be prohibited and prevented. Production of metals, chemicals, machinery and other items that are directly necessary to a war economy shall be rigidly controlled and restricted to Germany's approved post-war peacetime needs to meet the objectives stated in paragraph 15. Productive capacity not needed for permitted production shall be removed in accordance with the reparations plan recommended by the Allied Commission on reparations and approved by the governments concerned or if not removed shall be destroyed.

12. At the earliest practicable date, the German economy shall be decentralized for the purpose of eliminating the present excessive concentration of economic power as exemplified in particular by cartels, syndicates, trusts and other monopolistic arrangements.

13. In organizing the German economy, primary emphasis shall be given to the development of agriculture and peaceful domestic industries.

. . . .

III. *Reparations from Germany*

1. Reparation claims of the U.S.S.R. shall be met by removals from the zone of Germany occupied by the U.S.S.R. and from appropriate German external assets.

2. The U.S.S.R. undertakes to settle the reparation claims of Poland from its own share of reparations.

3. The reparation claims of the United States, the United Kingdom and other countries entitled to reparations shall be met from the western zones and from appropriate German external assets.

4. In addition to the reparations to be taken by the U.S.S.R. from its own zone of occupation, the U.S.S.R. shall receive additionally from the western zones:

(A) 15 per cent of such usable and complete industrial capital equipment, in the first place from the metallurgical, chemical and machine manufacturing industries, as is unnecessary for the German peace economy and should be removed from the western zones of Germany, in exchange for an equivalent value of food, coal, potash, zinc, timber, clay products, petroleum products, and such other commodities as may be agreed upon.

(B) 10 per cent of such industrial capital equipment as is unnecessary for the German peace economy and should be removed from the western zones, to be transferred to the Soviet Government on reparations account without payment or exchange of any kind in return.

Removals of equipment as provided in (A) and (B) above shall be made simultaneously.

5. The amount of equipment to be removed from the western zones on account of reparations must be determined within six months from now at the latest. . . . .

VIII. *Poland*

We have taken note with pleasure of the agreement reached among representative Poles from Poland and abroad which has made possible the formation, in accordance with the decisions reached at the Crimea Conference, of a Polish Provisional Government of National Unity recognized by the three powers. The establishment by the British and United States Governments of diplomatic relations with the Polish Provisional Government has resulted in the withdrawal of their recognition from the former Polish Government in London, which no longer exists.

The British and United States Governments have taken measures to protect the interest of the Polish Provisional Government as the recognized government of the Polish State in the property belonging to the Polish State located in their territories and under their control, whatever the form of this property may be. They have further taken measures to prevent alienation to third parties of such property. All proper facilities will be given to the Polish Provisional Government for the exercise of the ordinary legal remedies for the recovery of any property belonging to the Polish State which may have been wrongfully alienated.

The three powers are anxious to assist the Polish Provisional Government in facilitating the return to Poland as soon as practicable of all Poles abroad who wish to go, including members of the Polish armed forces and the Merchant Marine. They expect that those Poles who return home shall be accorded personal and property rights on the same basis as all Polish citizens.

The three powers note that the Polish Provisional Government in accordance with the decisions of the Crimea Conference has agreed to the holding of free and unfettered elections as soon as possible on the basis of universal suffrage and secret ballot in which all democratic and anti-Nazi parties shall have the right to take part and to put forward candidates, and that representatives of the Allied press shall enjoy full freedom to report to the world upon developments in Poland before and during the elections.

In conformity with the agreement on Poland reached at the Crimea Conference the three heads of government have sought the opinion of the Polish Provisional Government of National Unity in regard to the accession of territory in the north and west which Poland should receive. The President of the National Council of Poland and members of the Polish Provisional Government of National Unity have been received at the conference and have fully presented their views. The three heads of government reaffirm their opinion that the final delimitation of the western frontier of Poland should await the peace settlement.

The three heads of government agree that, pending the final determination of Poland's western frontier, the former German territories east of a line running from the Baltic Sea immediately west of Swinemunde, and thence along the Oder River to the confluence of the western Neisse River and along the western Neisse to the Czechoslovak frontier, including that portion of East Prussia not placed under the administration of the Union of Soviet Socialist Republics in accordance with the understanding reached at this conference and including the area of the former free City of Danzig, shall be under the administration of the Polish State and for such purposes should not be considered as parts of the Soviet zone of occupation in Germany. . . . .

86. United Nations Charter, Preamble and Article 1-7, 26 June 1945

Signed at San Francisco.

WE THE PEOPLES of the United Nations, determined to save succeeding generations from the scourge of war, which twice in our life-time has brought untold sorrow to mankind, and to reaffirm faith in fundamental human rights, in the dignity and worth of the human person, in the equal rights of men and women and of nations large and small, and to establish conditions under which justice and respect for the obligations arising from treaties and other sources of international law can be maintained, and to promote social progress and better standards of life in larger freedom, and for these ends to practice tolerance and live together in peace with one another as good neighbors, and to unite our strength to maintain international peace and security, and to ensure, by the acceptance of principles and the institution of methods, that armed force shall not be used, save in the common interest, and to employ international machinery for the promotion of the economic and social advancement of all peoples, have resolved to combine our efforts to accomplish these aims.

Accordingly, our respective Governments, through representatives assembled in the city of San Francisco, who have exhibited their full powers found to be in good and due form, have agreed to the present Charter of the United Nations and do hereby establish an international organization to be known as the United Nations.

CHAPTER I. *Purposes and Principles*

ARTICLE 1. The Purposes of the United Nations are:

1. To maintain international peace and security, and to that end: to take effective collective measures for the prevention and removal of threats to the peace, and for the suppression of acts of aggression or other breaches of the peace, and to bring about by peaceful means, and in conformity with the principles of justice and international law, adjustment or settlement of international disputes or situations which might lead to a breach of the peace;

2. To develop friendly relations among nations based on respect for the principle of equal rights and self-determination of peoples, and to take other appropriate measures to strengthen universal peace;

3. To achieve international cooperation in solving international problems of an economic, social, cultural, or humanitarian character, and in promoting and encouraging respect for human rights and for fundamental freedoms for all without distinction as to race, sex, language, or religion; and

4. To be a center for harmonizing the actions of nations in the attainment of these common ends.

Article 2. The Organization and its Members, in pursuit of the Purposes stated in Article 1, shall act in accordance with the following Principles.

1. The Organization is based on the principle of the sovereign equality of all its Members.

2. All Members, in order to ensure to all of them the rights and benefits resulting from membership, shall fulfil in good faith the obligations assumed by them in accordance with the present Charter.

3. All Members shall settle their international disputes by peaceful means in such a manner that international peace and security, and justice, are not endangered.

4. All Members shall refrain in their international relations from the threat or use of force against the territorial integrity or political independence of any state, or in any other manner inconsistent with the Purposes of the United Nations.

5. All Members shall give the United Nations every assistance in any action it takes in accordance with the present Charter, and shall refrain from giving assistance to any state against which the United Nations is taking preventive or enforcement action.

6. The Organization shall ensure that states which are not Members of the United Nations act in accordance with these Principles so far as may be necessary for the maintenance of international peace and security.

7. Nothing contained in the present Charter shall authorize the United Nations to intervene in matters which are essentially within the domestic jurisdiction of any state or shall require the Members to submit such matters to settlement under the present Charter; but this principle shall not prejudice the application of enforcement measures under Chapter VII.

87. Baruch on Atomic Control, 14 June 1946

Speech of Bernard M. Baruch to the U.N. Atomic Energy Commission.

WE ARE HERE to make a choice between the quick and the dead.

That is our business.

Behind the black portent of the new atomic age lies a hope which, seized upon with faith, can work our salvation. If we fail, then we have damned every man to be the slave of Fear. Let us not deceive ourselves: We must elect World Peace or World Destruction.

Science has torn from nature a secret so vast in its potentialities that our minds cower from the terror it creates. Yet terror is not enough to inhibit the use of the atomic bomb. The terror created by weapons has never stopped man from employing them. For each new weapon a defense has been produced, in time. But now we face a condition in which adequate defense does not exist.

Science, which gave us this dread power, shows that it *can* be made a giant help to humanity, but science does *not* show us how to prevent its baleful use. So we have been appointed to obviate that peril by finding a meeting of the minds and the hearts of our peoples. Only in the will of mankind lies the answer. . . .

In this crisis, we represent not only our governments but, in a larger way, we represent the peoples of the world. We must remember that the peoples do not belong to the governments but that the governments belong to the peoples. We must answer their demands; we must answer the world's longing for peace and security.

In that desire the United States shares ardently and hopefully. The search of science for the absolute weapon has reached fruition in this country. But she stands ready to proscribe and destroy this instrument — to lift its use from death to life — if the world will join in a pact to that end. . . .

The United States proposes the creation of an International Atomic Development Authority, to which should be entrusted all phases of the development and use of atomic energy, starting with the raw material and including —

1. Managerial control or ownership of all atomic-energy activities potentially dangerous to world security.
2. Power to control, inspect, and license all other atomic activities.
3. The duty of fostering the beneficial uses of atomic energy.
4. Research and development responsibilities of an affirmative character intended to put the Authority in the forefront of atomic knowledge and thus to enable it to comprehend, and therefor to detect, misuse of atomic energy. To be effective, the Authority must itself be the world's leader in the field of atomic knowledge and development and thus supplement its legal authority with the great power inherent in possession of leadership in knowledge.

I offer this as a basis for beginning our discussion.

But I think the peoples we serve would not believe — and without faith nothing counts — that a treaty, merely outlawing possession or use of the atomic bomb, constitutes effective fulfilment of the instructions to this Commission. Previous failures have been recorded in trying the method of simple renunciation, unsupported by effective guaranties of security and armament limitation. No one would have faith in that approach alone.

Now, if ever, is the time to act for the common good. Public opinion supports a world movement toward security. If I read the signs aright, the peoples want a program not composed merely of pious thoughts but of enforceable sanctions — an international law with teeth in it.

We of this nation, desirous of helping to bring peace to the world and realizing the heavy obligations upon us arising from our possession of the means of producing the bomb and from the fact that it is part of our armament, are prepared to make our full contribution toward effective control of atomic energy.

When an adequate system for control of atomic energy, including the renunciation of the bomb as a weapon, has been agreed upon and put into effective operation and condign punishments set up for violations of the rules of control which are to be stigmatized as international crimes, we propose that —

1. Manufacture of atomic bombs shall stop;

2. Existing bombs shall be disposed of pursuant to the terms of the treaty; and

3. The Authority shall be in possession of full information as to the know-how for the production of atomic energy.

Let me repeat, so as to avoid misunderstanding: My country is ready to make its full contribution toward the end we seek, subject of course to our constitutional processes and to an adequate system of control becoming fully effective, as we finally work it out.

Now as to violations: In the agreement, penalties of as serious a nature as the nations may wish and as immediate and certain in their execution as possible should be fixed for —

1. Illegal possession or use of an atomic bomb;
2. Illegal possession, or separation, of atomic material suitable for use in an atomic bomb;
3. Seizure of any plant or other property belonging to or licensed by the Authority;
4. Willful interference with the activities of the Authority;
5. Creation or operation of dangerous projects in a manner contrary to, or in the absence of, a license granted by the international control body.

It would be a deception, to which I am unwilling to lend myself, were I not to say to you and to our peoples that the matter of punishment lies at the very heart of our present security system. It might as well be admitted, here and now, that the subject goes straight to the veto power contained in the Charter of the United Nations so far as it relates to the field of atomic energy. The Charter permits penalization only by concurrence of each of the five great powers — the Union of Soviet Socialist Republics, the United Kingdom, China, France, and the United States.

I want to make very plain that I am concerned here with the veto power only as it affects this particular problem. There must be no veto to protect those who violate their solemn agreements not to develop or use atomic energy for destructive purposes.

The bomb does not wait upon debate. To delay may be to die. The time between violation and preventive action or punishment would be all too short for extended discussion as to the course to be followed.

As matters now stand several years may be necessary for another country to produce a bomb, *de novo*. However, once the basic information is generally known, and the Authority has established producing plants for peaceful purposes in the several countries, an illegal seizure of such a plant might permit a malevolent nation to produce a bomb in 12 months, and if preceded by secret preparation and necessary facilities perhaps even in a much shorter time. The time required — the advance warning given of the possible use of a bomb — can only be generally estimated but obviously will depend upon many factors, including the success with which the Authority has been able to introduce elements of safety in the design of its plants and the degree to which illegal and secret preparation for the military use of atomic energy will have been eliminated. Presumably no nation would think of starting a war with only one bomb.

This shows how imperative speed is in detecting and penalizing violations.

The process of prevention and penalization — a problem of profound statecraft — is, as I read it, implicit in the Moscow statement, signed by the Union of Soviet Socialist Republics, the United States, and the United Kingdom a few months ago.

But before a country is ready to relinquish any winning weapons it must have more than words to reassure it. It must have a guarantee of safety, not only against the offenders in the atomic area but against the illegal users of other weapons — bacteriological, biological, gas — perhaps — why not? — against war itself.

In the elimination of war lies our solution, for only then will nations cease to compete with one another in the production and use of dread "secret" weapons which are evaluated solely by their capacity to kill. This devilish program takes us back not merely to the Dark Ages but from cosmos to chaos. If we succeed in finding a suitable way to control atomic weapons, it is reasonable to hope that we may also preclude the use of other weapons adaptable to mass destruction. When a man learns to say "A" he can, if he chooses, learn the rest of the alphabet too. . . .

I now submit the following measures as representing the fundamental features of a plan which would give effect to certain of the conclusions which I have epitomized.

1. *General*. The Authority should set up a thorough plan for control of the field of atomic energy, through various forms of ownership, dominion, licenses, operation, inspection, research, and management by competent personnel. After this is provided for, there should be as little interference as may be with the economic plans and the present private, corporate, and state relationships in the several countries involved.

2. *Raw Materials*. The Authority should have as one of its earliest purposes to obtain and maintain complete and accurate information on world supplies of uranium and thorium and to bring them under its dominion. The precise pattern of control for various types of deposits of such materials will have to depend upon the geological, mining, refining, and economic facts involved in different situations.

The Authority should conduct continuous surveys so that it will have the most complete knowledge of the world geology of uranium and thorium. Only after all current information on world sources of uranium and thorium is known to us all can equitable plans be made for their production, refining, and distribution.

3. *Primary Production Plants*. The Authority should exercise complete managerial control of the production of fissionable materials. This means that it should control and operate all plants producing fissionable materials in dangerous quantities and must own and control the product of these plants.

4. *Atomic Explosives*. The Authority should be given sole and exclusive

right to conduct research in the field of atomic explosives. Research activities in the field of atomic explosives are essential in order that the Authority may keep in the forefront of knowledge in the field of atomic energy and fulfill the objective of preventing illicit manufacture of bombs. Only by maintaining its position as the best-informed agency will the Authority be able to determine the line between intrinsically dangerous and non-dangerous activities.

5. *Strategic Distribution of Activities and Materials.* The activities entrusted exclusively to the Authority because they are intrinsically dangerous to security should be distributed throughout the world. Similarly, stockpiles of raw materials and fissionable materials should not be centralized.

6. *Non-Dangerous Activities.* A function of the Authority should be promotion of the peacetime benefits of atomic energy.

Atomic research (except in explosives), the use of research reactors, the production of radio-active tracers by means of non-dangerous reactors, the use of such tracers, and to some extent the production of power should be open to nations and their citizens under reasonable licensing arrangements from the Authority. Denatured materials, whose use we know also requires suitable safeguards, should be furnished for such purposes by the Authority under lease or other arrangement. Denaturing seems to have been overestimated by the public as a safety measure.

7. *Definition of Dangerous and Non-Dangerous Activities.* Although a reasonable dividing line can be drawn between dangerous and non-dangerous activities, it is not hard and fast. Provision should, therefore, be made to assure constant reexamination of the questions and to permit revision of the dividing line as changing conditions and new discoveries may require.

8. *Operations of Dangerous Activities.* Any plant dealing with uranium or thorium after it once reaches the potential of dangerous use must be not only subject to the most rigorous and competent inspection by the Authority, but its actual operation shall be under the management, supervision, and control of the Authority.

9. *Inspection.* By assigning intrinsically dangerous activities exclusively to the Authority, the difficulties of inspection are reduced. If the Authority is the only agency which may lawfully conduct dangerous activities, then visible operation by others than the Authority will constitute an unambiguous danger signal. Inspection will also occur in connection with the licensing functions of the Authority.

10. *Freedom of Access.* Adequate ingress and egress for all qualified representatives of the Authority must be assured. Many of the inspection activities of the Authority should grow out of, and be incidental to, its other functions. Important measures of inspection will be associated with the tight control of raw materials, for this is a keystone of the plan. The continuing activities of prospecting, survey, and research in relation to raw materials will be designed not only to serve the affirmative development functions of the Authority but also to assure that no surreptitious operations are conducted in the raw-materials field by nations or their citizens.

11. *Personnel.* The personnel of the Authority should be recruited on a basis of proven competence but also so far as possible on an international basis.

12. *Progress by Stages.* A primary step in the creation of the system of control is the setting forth, in comprehensive terms, of the functions, responsibilities, powers, and limitations of the Authority. Once a charter for the Authority has been adopted, the Authority and the system of control for which it will be responsible will require time to become fully organized and effective. The plan of control will, therefore, have to come into effect in successive stages. These should be specifically fixed in the Charter or means should be otherwise set forth in the Charter for transitions from one stage to another, as contemplated in the resolution of the United Nations Assembly which created this Commission.

13. *Disclosures.* In the deliberations of the United Nations Commission on Atomic Energy, the United States is prepared to make available the information essential to a reasonable understanding of the proposals which it advocates. Further disclosures must be dependent, in the interests of all, upon the effective ratification of the treaty. When the Authority is actually created, the United States will join the other nations in making available the further information essential to that organization for the performance of its functions. As the successive stages of international control are reached, the United States will be prepared to yield, to the extent required by each stage, national control of activities in this field to the Authority.

14. *International Control.* There will be questions about the extent of control to be allowed to national bodies, when the Authority is established. Purely national authorities for control and development of atomic energy should to the extent necessary for the effective operation of the Authority be subordinate to it. This is neither an endorsement nor a disapproval of the creation of national authorities. The Commission should evolve a clear demarcation of the scope of duties and responsibilities of such national authorities. . . .

88. Gromyko on Atomic Control, 5 March 1947

Speech of Soviet Representative Andrei A. Gromyko to the U.N. Security Council.

. . . IS IT possible to consider that the way outlined in the American proposals will lead us to a successful solution of the problem of atomic energy control to ensure its use only for peaceful purposes? No, this cannot be said. Without the conclusion of a convention on the prohibition of atomic weapons one cannot speak seriously about rigid international control for the establishment of which the Soviet Union stood and is standing now. Without the conclusion of such a convention it will be difficult, if not impossible, to solve the problem of the establishment of such a rigid control. . . .

In my statement of February 14th of this year I already drew the attention of the Security Council to the fact that the conclusion of a convention on the prohibition of atomic weapons would not mean that the working out of other questions, including that of inspection, should not be continued. However, the consideration of all the questions related to the establishments of atomic energy control, will inevitably require some time, and in view of this, the postponement of the conclusion of a convention on the prohibition of atomic weapons cannot be justified.

The conclusion of such a convention, besides the fact that it should represent a concrete and practical step towards the fulfilment of the General Assembly decision of 14 December 1946, would create more favourable conditions for the solution of other questions following from the General Assembly Resolution, to say nothing of the fact that the conclusion of such a convention would contribute to the strengthening of the mutual confidence among the Member States of the United Nations and to the strengthening of the authority of our Organization. . . .

The position of the Soviet Union on the questions of the control of atomic energy and inspection is clear. Strict international control and inspection of atomic energy should be established. At the same time this strict international control and strict inspection should not develop into interference with those branches of industry which are not connected with the production of atomic energy. The international control of atomic energy should not deal with those questions which are not connected with atomic energy.

Logic tells us that any thought may be reduced to an absurdity. This applies even to good thoughts and ideas. The transformation of atomic energy control into an unlimited control would mean to reduce to an absurdity the very idea of control of atomic energy in order to prevent its use for military purposes. Unlimited control would mean an unlimited interference of the control and controlling organ — or organs — in the economic life of the countries on whose territories this control would be carried out, and interference in their internal affairs. . . .

The United States proposals on control proceed from the erroneous premise that the interests of other States should be removed to the background during the exercise by the control organ of its control and inspectorial functions. Only by proceeding from such fundamentally vicious premises, was it possible to come to the conclusion contained in the proposals submitted to the Atomic Energy Commission by the United States representative on the necessity of transferring atomic enterprises to the possession and ownership of the international organ which is to be charged with responsibility for the realization of control. A proposal of this sort shows that the authors of the so-called Baruch plan completely ignore national interests of other countries and proceed from the necessity of subordinating the interests of these countries to the interests actually of one country; that is, the United States of America. . . .

I have already pointed out that the proposal on granting to an international control organ the right to possess establishments for the production of atomic energy and unlimited power to carry out other important functions connected with the ownership and management of the establishments and with the disposition of their production would lead to interference by the control organ in the internal affairs and internal life of States and eventually would lead to arbitrary action by the control organ in the solution of such problems as fall completely within the domestic jurisdiction of a State. I deem it necessary to emphasize that granting broad rights and powers of such a kind to the control organ is incompatible with the State sovereignty. Therefore, such proposals are unacceptable and must be rejected as unfounded. Not only do they not facilitate the solution of the problem of establishing strict and effective international control, but, on the contrary, they complicate the solution of this problem. . . .

How does the Soviet Union conceive the carrying out by the control organ of practical day-by-day activities, and how shall this organ take decisions relating to such day-by-day activities?

The position of the Soviet Union on this question has already been stated more than once. If it is necessary, I am prepared to repeat that such an organ must have the right to take in appropriate cases, decisions by majority vote. Does this mean, however, that it is possible by using references to international control, to agree in reality to granting the right of interference in the economic life of a country even through the decision of the majority in the control organ? The Soviet Union does not wish and cannot allow such a situation. The Soviet Union is aware that there will be a majority in the control organs which may take one-sided decisions, a majority of whose benevolent attitude toward the Soviet Union the Soviet people cannot count. Therefore the Soviet Union, and probably not only the Soviet Union, cannot allow that the fate of its national economy be handed over to this organ. The correctness of such a conclusion is confirmed by historical experience including the brief but very instructive experience of the activities of the United Nations organs. The Soviet delegation does not doubt that all those who objectively appraise the situation will correctly understand the position of the Soviet Union on this question. . . .

In reality, to grant to the control organ unlimited rights and possession and management of the atomic establishments, cannot be looked upon as anything but an attempt by the United States to secure for itself world monopoly in the field of atomic energy. This tendency has found its expression in the proposals submitted by the representative of the United States on the Atomic Energy Commission and later laid down as the basis of the report of the Atomic Energy Commission. . . .

I have already had an opportunity to state the point of view of the Soviet Delegation on the question of the principle of unanimity of the Five Powers-permanent Members of the Security Council, in connection with the discussion of the questions of the atomic energy control. The Soviet Delegation considers that it will be impossible to reach an agreement on this question as long as the unacceptable proposal on the question of the so-called "veto" is defended, since such a proposal is in contradiction with the principles of the United Nations. I have already pointed out that there seems to be no difference of opinion among us on the question of the necessity of punishing violators, and there was not any on this subject. All agree that certain sanctions should be applied against violators, if their guilt is proved. There is a divergence of opinion as to who should take decisions on sanctions and how they should be taken. Should such decisions be taken in accordance with the basic principles of the United Nations or in violation of these principles? The Soviet Delegation considers that such decisions should be taken in strict conformity with the basic principles of our Organization and should be taken by the organ which is charged with the primary responsibility for the maintenance of peace, that is, by the Security Council. The principle of unanimity of the Five Powers as such is not an obstacle to the effective control of atomic energy, no matter how someone tries to prove the opposite. . . .

89. Truman Doctrine, 12 March 1947
Message of President Harry S. Truman to Congress.

THE GRAVITY of the situation which confronts the world today necessitates my appearance before a joint session of the Congress. The foreign policy and the national security of this country are involved.

One aspect of the present situation, which I wish to present to you at this time for your consideration and decision, concerns Greece and Turkey.

The United States has received from the Greek Government an urgent appeal for financial and economic assistance. Preliminary reports from the American Economic Mission now in Greece and reports from the American Ambassador in Greece corroborate the statement of the Greek Government that assistance is imperative if Greece is to survive as a free nation.

I do not believe that the American people and the Congress wish to turn a deaf ear to the appeal of the Greek Government.

Greece is not a rich country. Lack of sufficient natural resources has always forced the Greek people to work hard to make both ends meet. Since 1940, this industrious, peace loving country has suffered invasion, four years of cruel enemy occupation, and bitter internal strife.

When forces of liberation entered Greece they found that the retreating Germans had destroyed virtually all the railways, roads, port facilities, communications, and merchant marine. More than a thousand villages had been burned. Eighty-five per cent of the children were tubercular. Livestock, poultry, and draft animals had almost disappeared. Inflation had wiped out practically all savings.

As a result of these tragic conditions, a militant minority, exploiting human want and misery, was able to create political chaos which, until now, has made economic recovery impossible.

Greece is today without funds to finance the importation of those goods which are essential to bare subsistence. Under these circumstances the people of Greece cannot make progress in solving their problems of reconstruction. Greece is in desperate need of financial and economic assistance to enable it to resume purchases of food, clothing, fuel and seeds. These are indispensable for the subsistence of its people and are obtainable only from abroad. Greece must have help to import the goods necessary to restore internal order and security so essential for economic and political recovery.

The Greek Government has also asked for the assistance of experienced American administrators, economists and technicians to insure that the financial and other aid given to Greece shall be used effectively in creating a stable and self-sustaining economy and in improving its public administration.

The very existence of the Greek state is today threatened by the terrorist activities of several thousand armed men, led by Communists, who defy the Government's authority at a number of points, particularly along the northern boundaries. A commission appointed by the United Nations Security Council is at present investigating disturbed conditions in Northern Greece and alleged border violations along the frontiers between Greece on the one hand and Albania, Bulgaria and Yugoslavia on the other.

Meanwhile, the Greek Government is unable to cope with the situation. The Greek Army is small and poorly equipped. It needs supplies and equipment if it is to restore the authority to the Government throughout Greek territory.

Greece must have assistance if it is to become a self-supporting and self-respecting democracy. The United States must supply that assistance. We have already extended to Greece certain types of relief and economic aid but these are inadequate. There is no other country to which democratic Greece can turn. No other nation is willing and able to provide the necessary support for a democratic Greek Government.

The British Government, which has been helping Greece, can give no further financial or economic aid after March 31. Great Britain finds itself under the necessity of reducing or liquidating its commitments in several parts of the world, including Greece.

We have considered how the United Nations might assist in this crisis. But the situation is an urgent one requiring immediate action, and the United Nations and its related organizations are not in a position to extend help of the kind that is required.

It is important to note that the Greek Government has asked for our aid in utilizing effectively the financial and other assistance we may give to Greece, and in improving its public administration. It is of the utmost importance that we supervise the use of any funds made available to Greece, in such a manner that each dollar spent will count toward making Greece self-supporting, and will help to build an economy in which a healthy democracy can flourish.

No government is perfect. One of the chief virtues of a democracy, however, is that its defects are always visible and under democratic processes can be pointed out and corrected. The Government of Greece is not perfect. Nevertheless, it represents 85 per cent of the members of the Greek Parliament who were chosen in an election last year. Foreign observers, including 692 Americans, considered this election to be a fair expression of the views of the Greek people.

The Greek Government has been operating in an atmosphere of chaos and extremism. It has made mistakes. The extension of aid by this country does not mean that the United States condones everything that the Greek Government has done or will do. We have condemned in the past, and we condemn now, extremist measures of the right or the left. We have in the past advised tolerance, and we advise tolerance now.

Greece's neighbor, Turkey, also deserves our attention. The future of Turkey as an independent and economically sound state is clearly no less important to the freedom-loving peoples of the world than the future of Greece. The circumstances in which Turkey finds itself today are considerably different from those of Greece. Turkey has been spared the disasters that have beset Greece. And during the war, the United States and Great Britain furnished Turkey with material aid. Nevertheless, Turkey now needs our support.

Since the war Turkey has sought financial assistance from Great Britain and the United States for the purpose of effecting that modernization necessary for the maintenance of its national integrity. That integrity is essential to the preservation of order in the Middle East.

The British Government has informed us that, owing to its own difficulties, it can no longer extend financial or economic aid to Turkey. As in the case of Greece, if Turkey is to have the assistance it needs, the United States must supply it. We are the only country able to provide that help.

I am fully aware of the broad implications involved if the United States extends assistance to Greece and Turkey, and I shall discuss these implications with you at this time.

One of the primary objectives of the foreign policy of the United States is the creation of conditions in which we and other nations will be able to work out a way of life free from coercion. This was a fundamental issue in the war with Germany and Japan. Our victory was won over countries which sought to impose their will, and their way of life, upon other nations.

To ensure the peaceful development of nations, free from coercion, the United States has taken a leading part in establishing the United Nations. The United Nations is designed to make possible lasting freedom and independence for all its members. We shall not realize our objectives, however, unless we are willing to help free people to maintain their free institutions and their national integrity against aggressive movements that seek to impose upon them totalitarian regimes. This is no more than a frank recognition that totalitarian regimes imposed on free peoples, by direct or indirect aggression, undermine the foundations of international peace and hence the security of the United States.

The peoples of a number of countries of the world have recently had totalitarian regimes forced upon them against their will. The Government of the United States has made frequent protests against coercion and intimidation, in violation of the Yalta Agreement, in Poland, Rumania and Bulgaria. I must also state that in a number of other countries there have been similar developments.

At the present moment in world history nearly every nation must choose between alternative ways of life. The choice is too often not a free one.

One way of life is based upon the will of the majority, and is distinguished by free institutions, representative government, free elections, guarantees of individual liberty, freedom of speech and religion, and freedom from political oppression.

The second way of life is based upon the will of a minority forcibly imposed upon the majority. It relies upon terror and oppression, a controlled press and radio, fixed elections, and the suppression of personal freedoms.

I believe that it must be the policy of the United States to support free peoples who are resisting attempted subjugation by armed minorities or by outside pressures.

I believe that we must assist free peoples to work out their own destinies in their own way.

I believe that our help should be primarily through economic and financial aid which is essential to economic stability and orderly political processes.

The world is not static, and the status quo is not sacred. But we cannot allow changes in the status quo in violation of the Charter of the United Nations by such methods as coercion, or by such subterfuges as political infiltration. In helping free and independent nations to maintain their freedom, the United States will be giving effect to the principles of the Charter of the United Nations.

It is necessary only to glance at a map to realize that the survival and integrity of the Greek nation are of grave importance in a much wider situation. If Greece should fall under the control of an armed minority, the effect upon its neighbor, Turkey, would be immediate and serious. Confusion and disorder might well spread throughout the entire Middle East.

Moreover, the disappearance of Greece as an independent state would have a profound effect upon those countries in Europe whose peoples are struggling against great difficulties to maintain their freedoms and their independence while they repair the damages of war.

It would be an unspeakable tragedy if these countries, which have struggled so long against overwhelming odds, should lose that victory for which they sacrificed so much. Collapse of free institutions and loss of independence would be disastrous not only for them but for the world. Discouragement and possibly failure would quickly be the lot of neighboring peoples striving to maintain their freedom and independence.

Should we fail to aid Greece and Turkey in this fateful hour, the effect will be far reaching to the West as well as to the East. We must take immediate and resolute action.

I therefore ask the Congress to provide authority for assistance to Greece and Turkey in the amount of $400,000,000 for the period ending June 30, 1948. In requesting these funds, I have taken into consideration the maximum amount of relief assistance which would be furnished to Greece out of the $350,000,000 which I recently requested that the Congress authorize for the prevention of starvation and suffering in countries devastated by the war.

In addition to funds, I ask the Congress to authorize the detail of American civilian and military personnel to Greece and Turkey, at the request of those countries, to assist in the tasks of reconstruction, and for the purpose of supervising the use of such financial and material assistance as may be furnished. I recommend that authority also be provided for the instruction and training of selected Greek and Turkish personnel.

Finally, I ask that the Congress provide authority which will permit the speediest and most effective use, in terms of needed commodities, supplies, and equipment, of such funds as may be authorized.

If further funds, or further authority, should be needed for purposes indicated in this message, I shall not hesitate to bring the situation before the Congress. On this subject the Executive and Legislative branches of the Government must work together.

This is a serious course upon which we embark. I would not recommend it except that the alternative is much more serious.

The United States contributed $341,000,000,000 toward winning World War II. This is an investment in world freedom and world peace.

The assistance that I am recommending for Greece and Turkey amounts to little more than 1 tenth of 1 per cent of this investment. It is only common sense that we should safeguard this investment and make sure that it was not in vain.

The seeds of totalitarian regimes are nurtured by misery and want. They spread and grow in the evil soil of poverty and strife. They reach their full growth when the hope of a people for a better life has died. We must keep that hope alive. The free peoples of the world look to us for support in maintaining their freedoms.

If we falter in our leadership, we may endanger the peace of the world — and we shall surely endanger the welfare of our own Nation.

Great responsibilities have been placed upon us by the swift movement of events. I am confident that the Congress will face these responsibilities squarely.

90. Economic Cooperative Act, 3 April 1948

Implementation of the Marshall Plan.

... SEC. 102. (a) Recognizing the intimate economic and other relationships between the United States and the nations of Europe, and recognizing that disruption following in the wake of war is not contained by national frontiers, the Congress finds that the existing situation in Europe endangers the establishment of a lasting peace, the general welfare and national interest of the United States, and the attainment of the objectives of the United Nations. The restoration or maintenance in European countries of principles of individual liberty, free institutions, and genuine independence rests largely upon the establishment of sound economic conditions, stable international economic relationships, and the achievement by the countries of Europe of a healthy economy independent of extraordinary outside assistance. The accomplishment of these objectives calls for a plan of European recovery, open to all such nations which cooperate in such plan, based upon a strong production effort, the expansion of foreign trade, the creation and maintenance of internal financial stability, and the development of economic cooperation, including all possible steps to establish and maintain equitable rates of exchange and to bring about the progressive elimination of trade barriers. Mindful of the advantages which the United States has enjoyed through the existence of a large domestic market with no internal trade barriers, and believing that similar advantages can accrue to the countries of Europe, it is declared to be the policy of the people of the United States to encourage these countries through a joint organization to exert sustained common efforts as set forth in the report of the Committee of European Economic Cooperation signed at Paris on September 22, 1947, which will speedily achieve that economic cooperation in Europe which is essential for lasting peace and prosperity. It is further declared to be the policy of the people of the United States to sustain and strengthen principles of individual liberty, free institutions, and genuine independence in Europe through assistance to those countries of Europe which participate in a joint recovery program based upon self-help and mutual cooperation: *Provided,* That no assistance to the participating countries herein contemplated shall seriously impair the economic stability of the United States. It is further declared to be the policy of the United States that continuity of assistance provided by the United States should, at all times, be dependent upon continuity of cooperation among countries participating in the program.

PURPOSES OF TITLE

(b) It is the purpose of this title to effectuate the policy set forth in subsection (a) of this section by furnishing material and financial assistance to the participating countries in such a manner as to aid them, through their own individual and concerted efforts, to become independent of extraordinary outside economic assistance within the period of operations under this title, by—

(1) promoting industrial and agricultural production in the participating countries;

(2) furthering the restoration or maintenance of the soundness of European currencies, budgets, and finances; and

(3) facilitating and stimulating the growth of international trade of participating countries with one another and with other countries by appropriate measures including reduction of barriers which may hamper such trade.

PARTICIPATING COUNTRIES

Sec. 103. (a) As used in this title, the term "participating country" means—

(1) any country, together with dependent areas under its administration, which signed the report of the Committee of European Economic Cooperation at Paris on September 22, 1947; and

(2) any other country (including any of the zones of occupation of Germany, any areas under international administration or control, and the Free Territory of Trieste or either of its zones) wholly or partly in Europe, together with dependent areas under its administration; provided such country adheres to, and for so long as it remains an adherent to, a joint program for European recovery designed to accomplish the purposes of this title. . . .

Sec. 114. (c) In order to carry out the provisions of this title . . . such funds shall be available as are hereafter authorized and appropriated to the President from time to time through June 30, 1952, . . . *Provided, however,* That for carrying out the provisions and accomplishing the purposes of this title for the period of one year following the date of enactment of this Act, there are hereby authorized to be so appropriated not to exceed $4,300,000,000. . . . Authorization in this title is limited to the period of twelve months in order that subsequent Congresses may pass on any subsequent authorizations. . . .

Sec. 115. (a) The secretary of State, after consultation with the Administrator, is authorized to conclude, with individual participating countries or any number of such countries or with an organization representing any such countries, agreements in furtherance of the purposes of this title. . . .

91. North Atlantic Treaty (NATO), 4 April 1949

Signed by U.S., Canada, Great Britain, France, Italy, Belgium, the Netherlands, Luxembourg, Norway, Denmark, Iceland, and Portugal; Greece and Turkey admitted, 1951; West Germany, 1955.

... ARTICLE 1. The Parties undertake, as set forth in the Charter of the United Nations, to settle any international disputes in which they may be involved by peaceful means in such a manner that international peace and security, and justice, are not endangered, and to refrain in their international relations from the threat or use of force in any manner inconsistent with the purposes of the United Nations.

Article 2. The Parties will contribute toward the further development of peaceful and friendly international relations by strengthening their free institutions, by bringing about a better understanding of the principles upon which these institutions are founded, and by promoting conditions of stability and well-being. They will seek to eliminate conflict in their international economic policies and will encourage economic collaboration between any or all of them.

Article 3. In order more effectively to achieve the objectives of this Treaty, the Parties, separately and jointly, by means of continuous and effective self-help and mutual aid, will maintain and develop their individual and collective capacity to resist armed attack.

Article 4. The Parties will consult together whenever, in the opinion of any of them, the territorial integrity, political independence or security of any of the Parties is threatened.

Article 5. The Parties agree that an armed attack against one or more of them in Europe or North America shall be considered an attack against them all; and consequently they agree that, if such an armed attack occurs, each of them, in exercise of the right of individual or collective self-defense recognized by Article 51 of the Charter of the United Nations, will assist the Party or Parties so attacked by taking forthwith, individually and in concert with the other Parties, such action as it deems necessary, including the use of armed force, to restore and maintain the security of the North Atlantic area.

Any such armed attack and all measures taken as a result thereof shall immediately be reported to the Security Council. Such measures shall be terminated when the Security Council has taken the measures necessary to restore and maintain international peace and security.

Article 6. For the purpose of Article 5 an armed attack on one or more of the Parties is deemed to include an armed attack on the territory of any of the Parties in Europe or North America, on the Algerian departments of France, on the occupation forces of any Party in Europe, on the islands under the jurisdiction of any Party in the North Atlantic area north of the Tropic of Cancer or on the vessels or aircraft in this area of any of the Parties.

Article 7. This Treaty does not affect, and shall not be interpreted as affecting, in any way the rights and obligations under the Charter of the Parties which are members of the United Nations, or the primary responsibility of the Security Council for the maintenance of international peace and security.

Article 8. Each Party declares that none of the international engagements now in force between it and any other of the Parties or any third state is in conflict with the provisions of this Treaty, and undertakes not to enter into any international engagement in conflict with this Treaty.

Article 9. The Parties hereby establish a council, on which each of them shall be represented, to consider matters concerning the implementation of this Treaty. The council shall be so organized as to be able to meet promptly at any time. The council shall set up such subsidiary bodies as may be necessary; in particular it shall establish immediately a defense committee which shall recommend measures for the implementation of Article 3 and 5.

Article 10. The Parties may, by unanimous agreement, invite any other European state in a position to further the principles of this Treaty and to contribute to the security of the North Atlantic area to accede to this Treaty. Any state so invited may become a party to the Treaty by depositing its instrument of accession with the Government of the United States of America. The Government of the United States of America will inform each of the Parties of the deposit of each such instrument of accession. ...

Article 12. After the Treaty has been in force for ten years, or at any time thereafter, the Parties shall, if any of them so requests, consult together for the purpose of reviewing the Treaty, having regard for the factors then affecting peace and security in the North Atlantic area, including the development of universal as well as regional arrangements under the Charter of the United Nations for the maintenance of international peace and security.

Article 13. After the Treaty has been in force for twenty years, any Party may cease to be a party one year after its notice of denunciation has been given to the Government of the United States of America, which will inform the Governments of the other Parties of the deposit of each notice of denunciation. ...

92. Truman's "Point Four" Program, 5 June 1950

SEC. 401. This title may be cited as the "Act for International Development."

Sec. 402. The Congress hereby finds as follows:

(a) The peoples of the United States and other nations have a common interest in the freedom and in the economic and social progress of all peoples. Such progress can further the secure growth of democratic ways of life, the expansion of mutually beneficial commerce, the development of international understanding and good will, and the maintenance of world peace.

(b) The efforts of the peoples living in economically underdeveloped areas of the world to realize their full capabilities and to develop the resources of the lands in which they live can be furthered through the cooperative endeavor of all nations to exchange technical knowledge and skills and to encourage the flow of investment capital.

(c) Technical assistance and capital investment can make maximum contribution to economic development only where there is understanding of the mutual advantages of such assistance and investment and where there is confidence of fair and reasonable treatment and due respect for the legitimate interests of the peoples of the countries to which the assistance is given and in which the investment is made and of the countries from which the assistance and investments are derived. In the case of investment this involves confidence on the part of the people of the underdeveloped areas that investors will conserve as well as develop local resources, will bear a fair share of local taxes and observe local laws, and will provide adequate wages and working conditions for local labor. It involves confidence on the part of investors, through intergovernmental agreements or otherwise, that they will not be deprived of their property without prompt, adequate, and effective compensation; that they will be given reasonable opportunity to remit their earnings and withdraw their capital; that they will have reasonable freedom to manage, operate, and control their enterprises; that they will enjoy security in the protection of their persons and property, including industrial and intellectual property, and nondiscriminatory treatment in taxation and in the conduct of their business affairs.

Sec. 403. (a) It is declared to be the policy of the United States to aid the efforts of the peoples of economically underdeveloped areas to develop their resources and improve their working and living conditions by encouraging the exchange of technical knowledge and skills and the flow of investment capital to countries which provide conditions under which such technical assistance and capital can effectively and constructively contribute to raising standards of living, creating new sources of wealth, increasing productivity and expanding purchasing power.

(b) It is further declared to be the policy of the United States that in order to achieve the most effective utilization of the resources of the United States, private and public, which are or may be available for aid in the development of economically underdeveloped areas, agencies of the United States Government, in reviewing requests of foreign governments for aid for such purposes, shall take into consideration (1) whether the assistance applied for is an appropriate part of a program reasonably designed to contribute to the balanced and integrated development of the country or area concerned; (2) whether any works or facilities which may be projected are actually needed in view of similar facilities existing in the area and are otherwise economically sound; and (3) with respect to projects for which capital is requested, whether private capital is available either in the country or elsewhere upon reasonable terms and in sufficient amounts to finance such projects. . . .

Sec. 405. The President is authorized to plan, undertake, administer, and execute bilateral technical cooperation programs carried on by any United States Government agency and, in so doing —

(a) To coordinate and direct existing and new technical cooperation programs.

(b) To assist other interested governments in the formulation of programs for the balanced and integrated development of the economic resources and productive capacities of economically underdeveloped areas. . . .

(e) To make and perform contracts or agreements in respect of technical cooperation programs on behalf of the United States Government with any person, corporation, or other body of persons however designated, whether within or without the United States, or with any foreign government or foreign government agency: *Provided,* That with respect to contracts or agreements which entail commitments for the expenditure of funds appropriated pursuant to the authority of this title, such contracts or agreements, within the limits of appropriations or contract authorizations hereafter made available may, subject to any future action of the Congress, run for not to exceed three years in any one case. . . .

(c) Assistance shall be made available only where the President determines that the country being assisted —

(1) Pays a fair share of the cost of the program.

(2) Provides all necessary information concerning such program and gives the program full publicity.

(3) Seeks to the maximum extent possible full coordination and integration of technical cooperation programs being carried on in that country.

(4) Endeavors to make effective use of the results of the program.

(5) Cooperates with other countries participating in the program in the mutual exchange of technical knowledge and skills. . . .

Sec. 416. (a) In order to carry out the provisions of this title, there shall be made available such funds as are hereafter authorized and appropriated from time to time for the purposes of this title: *Provided, however,* That for the purpose of carrying out the provisions of this title through June 30, 1951, there is hereby authorized to be appropriated a sum not to exceed $35,000,000, including any sums appropriated to carry on the activities of the Institute of Inter-American Affairs, and technical cooperation programs as defined in section 418 herein under the United States Information and Educational Exchange Act of 1948 (62 Stat. 6). . . .

Sec. 418. As used in this title —

(a) The term "technical cooperation programs" means programs for the international interchange of technical knowledge and skills designed to contribute to the balanced and integrated development of the economic resources and productive capacities of economically underdeveloped areas. Such activities may include, but need not be limited to, economic, engineering, medical, educational, agricultural, fishery, mineral, and fiscal surveys, demonstration, training, and similar projects that serve the purpose of promoting the development of economic resources and productive capacities of underdeveloped areas.

93. United Nations on the Soviet Invasion of Hungary, 4 November 1956

THE GENERAL ASSEMBLY,

Considering that the United Nations is based on the principle of the sovereign equality of all its Members,

Recalling that the enjoyment of human rights and of fundamental freedom in Hungary was specifically guaranteed by the Peace Treaty between Hungary and the Allied and Associated Powers signed at Paris on 10 February 1947, and that the general principle of these rights and this freedom is affirmed for all peoples in the Charter of the United Nations,

Convinced that recent events in Hungary manifest clearly the desire of the Hungarian people to exercise and to enjoy fully their fundamental rights, freedom and independence,

Condemning the use of Soviet military forces to suppress the efforts of the Hungarian people to reassert their rights,

Noting moreover the declaration of 30 October 1956 by the Government of the Union of Soviet Socialist Republics of its avowed policy of non-intervention in the internal affairs of other States,

Noting the communication of 1 November 1956 of the Government of Hungary to the Secretary-General regarding demands made by that Government to the Government of the Union of Soviet Socialist Republics for the instant and immediate withdrawal of Soviet forces,

Noting further the communication of 2 November 1956 from the Government of Hungary to the Secretary-General asking the Security Council to instruct the Government of the Union of Soviet Socialist Republics and the Government of Hungary to start negotiations immediately on the withrawal of Soviet forces.

Noting that the intervention of Soviet military forces in Hungary has resulted in grave loss of life and widespread bloodshed among the Hungarian people,

Taking note of the radio appeal of Prime Minister Imre Nagy of 4 November 1956,

1. *Calls upon* the Government on the Union of Soviet Socialist Republics to desist forthwith from all armed attack on the people of Hungary and from any form of intervention, in particular armed intervention, in the internal affairs of Hungary;

2. *Calls upon* the Union of Soviet Socialist Republics to cease the introduction of additional armed forces into Hungary and to withdraw all of its forces without delay from Hungarian territory;

3. *Affirms* the right of the Hungarian people to a government responsive to its national aspirations and dedicated to its independence and well-being;

4. *Requests* the Secretary-General to investigate the situation caused by foreign intervention in Hungary, to observe the situation directly through representatives named by him, and to report thereon to the General Assembly at the earliest moment, and as soon as possible to suggest methods to bring an end to the foreign intervention in Hungary in accordance with the principles of the Charter of the United Nations;

5. *Calls upon* the Government of Hungary and the Government of the Union of Soviet Socialist Republics to permit observers designated by the Secretary-General to enter the territory of Hungary, to travel freely therein, and to report their findings to the Secretary-General;

6. *Calls upon* all Members of the United Naions to co-operate with the Secretary-General and his representatives in the execution of his functions;

7. *Requests* the Secretary-General in consultation with the heads of appropriate specialized agencies to inquire, on an urgent basis, into the needs of the Hungarian people for food, medicine and other similar supplies, and to report to the General Assembly as soon as possible;

8. *Requests* all Members of the United Nations, and invites national and international humanitarian organizations to co-operate in making available such supplies as may be required by the Hungarian people.

94. U.S. Rights in Berlin, 31 December 1958

U.S. Note to the Soviet Union.

(A) A STATEMENT OF POLICY [3]

THE GOVERNMENT of the United States acknowledges the note which was addressed to it by the Government of the U.S.S.R. under date of November 27. . . .

The situation of Berlin of which the Soviet Government complains and which it considers abnormal is a result of the very nature of the German problem such as it has existed since 1945. When the empire of Hitler collapsed the Western Allies were in military possession of more than one-third of what subsequently was occupied by the Soviet authorities.

The Soviet Union was in possession of Berlin. On the basis of the agreements of September 12, 1944 and May 1, 1945, the Western Allies withdrew, thereby permitting a Soviet occupation of large parts of Mecklenburg, Saxony, Thuringia and Anhalt, and concurrently, the three Western Powers occupied the western sectors in Berlin, then an area of rubble.

The Soviet Union has directly and through its puppet regime — the so-called German Democratic Republic — consolidated its hold over the large areas which the Western Allies relinquished to it. It now demands that the Western Allies should relinquish the positions in Berlin which in effect were the *quid pro quo*.

The three Western Powers are there as occupying powers and they are not prepared to relinquish the rights which they acquired through victory just as they assume the Soviet Union is not willing now to restore to the occupancy of the Western Powers the position which they had won in Mecklenburg, Saxony, Thuringia and Anhalt and which, under the agreements of 1944 and 1945, they turned over for occupation by the Soviet Union.

The agreements made by the Four Powers cannot be considered obsolete because the Soviet Union has already obtained the full advantage therefrom and now wishes to deprive the other parties of their compensating advantages. These agreements are binding upon all of the signatories so long as they have not been replaced by others following free negotiations. . . .

The Soviet memorandum purports formally to repudiate the agreements of September 12, 1944 and May 1, 1945. This repudiation in fact involves other and more recent engagements. We refer in this connection to the Four Power agreement of June 20, 1949 whereby, among other things, the Soviet Union assumed "an obligation" to assure the normal functioning of transport and communication between Berlin and the Western Zones of Germany. This "obligation" the Soviet Union now purports to shed. The United States also refers to the "summit" agreement of July 23, 1955 whereby the Four Powers recognized "their common responsibility for the settlement of the German question," a phrase which necessarily includes the problem of Berlin. Apparently the Soviet Union now attempts to free itself from these agreed responsibilities and obligations.

The United States Government cannot prevent the Soviet Government from announcing the termination of its own authority in the quadripartite regime in the sector which it occupies in the city of Berlin. On the other hand, the Government of the United States will not and does not, in any way, accept a unilateral denunciation of the accords of 1944 and 1945; nor is it prepared to relieve the Soviet Union from the obligations which it assumed in June, 1949. Such action on the part of the Soviet Government would have no legal basis, since the agreements can only be terminated by mutual consent. The Government of the United States will continue to hold the Soviet Government directly responsible for the discharge of its obligations undertaken with respect to Berlin under existing agreements. As the Soviet Government knows, the French, British and United States Governments have the right to maintain garrisons in their sectors of Berlin and to have free access thereto. . . .

(B) CONGRESSIONAL AFFIRMATION CONCERNING UNITED STATES RIGHTS IN BERLIN: 1962 [4]

Whereas the primary purpose of the United States in its relations with all other nations is and has been to develop and sustain a just and enduring peace for all; and

Whereas it is the purpose of the United States to encourage and support the establishment of a free, unified, and democratic Germany; and

Whereas in connection with the termination of hostilities in World War II of [*sic*] the United States, the United Kingdom, France, and the Soviet Union freely entered into binding agreements under which the four powers have the right to remain in Berlin, with the right of ingress and egress, until the conclusion of a final settlement with the Government of Germany; and

Whereas no such final settlement has been concluded by the four powers and the aforementioned agreements continue in force: Now, therefore be it

Resolved by the House of Representatives (*the Senate concurring*), That it is the sense of the Congress —

(a) that the continued exercise of United States, British, and French rights in Berlin constitutes a fundamental political and moral determination;

(b) that the United States would regard as intolerable any violation by the Soviet Union directly or through others of those rights in Berlin, including the right of ingress and egress;

(c) that the United States is determined to prevent by whatever means may be necessary, including the use of arms, any violation of those rights by the Soviet Union directly or through others, and to fulfill our commitment to the people of Berlin with respect to their resolve for freedom.

(C) AMERICAN POLICY REGARDING THE CLOSING OF THE EAST BERLIN BORDER [5]

. . . On August 13, East German authorities put into effect several measures regulating movement at the boundary of the western sectors and the Soviet sector of the city of Berlin. These measures have the effect of limiting, to a degree approaching complete prohibition, passage from the Soviet sector to the western sectors of the city. These measures were accompanied by the closing of the sector boundary by a sizable deployment of police forces and by military detachments brought into Berlin for this purpose.

All this is a flagrant, and particularly serious, violation of the quadripartite status of Berlin. Freedom of movement with respect to Berlin was reaffirmed by the quadripartite agreement of New York of May 4, 1949, and by the decision taken at Paris on June 20, 1949, by the Council of the Ministers of Foreign Affairs of the Four Powers. The United States Government has never accepted that limitations can be imposed on freedom of movement within Berlin. The boundary between the Soviet sector and the western sectors of Berlin is not a state frontier. The United States Government considers that the measures which the East German authorities have taken are illegal. It reiterates that it does not accept the pretension that the Soviet sector of Berlin forms a part of the so-called "German Democratic Republic" and that Berlin is situated on its territory. Such a pretension is in itself a violation of the solemnly pledged word of the U.S.S.R. in the Agreement on the Zones of Occupation in Germany and the administration of Greater Berlin. Moreover, the United States Government cannot admit the right of the East German authorities to authorize their armed forces to enter the Soviet sector of Berlin.

By the very admission of the East German authorities, the measures which have just been taken are motivated by the fact that an ever increasing number of inhabitants of East Germany wish to leave this territory. The reasons for this exodus are known. They are simply the internal difficulties in East Germany.

To judge by the terms of a declaration of the Warsaw Pact powers published on August 13, the measures in question are supposed to have been recommended to the East German authorities by those powers. The United States Government notes that the powers which associated themselves with the U.S.S.R. by signing the Warsaw Pact are thus intervening in a domain in which they have no competence.

It is to be noted that this declaration states that the measures taken by the East German authorities are "in the interests of the German peoples themselves." It is difficult to see any basis for this statement, or to understand why it should be for the members of the Warsaw Pact to decide what are the interests of the German people. It is evident that no Germans, particularly those whose freedom of movement is being forcibly restrained, think this is so. This would become abundantly clear if all Germans were allowed a free choice, and the principle of self-determination were also applied in the Soviet sector of Berlin and in East Germany.

The United States Government solemnly protests against the measures referred to above, for which it holds the Soviet Government responsible. The United States Government expects the Soviet Government to put an end to these illegal measures. This unilateral infringement of the quadripartite status of Berlin can only increase existing tension and dangers.

95. Eisenhower on the Summit Conference and the U-2 Incident, 25 May 1960

Speech of President Dwight D. Eisenhower.

MY FELLOW AMERICANS: Tonight I want to talk with you about the remarkable events last week in Paris, and their meaning to our future. . . .

Last summer and fall I had many conversations with world leaders; some of these were with Chairman Khrushchev, here in America. Over those months a small improvement in relations between the Soviet Union and the West seemed discernible. A possibility developed that the Soviet leaders might at last be ready for serious talks about our most persistent problems — those of disarmament, mutual inspection, atomic control, and Germany, including Berlin.

To explore that possibility, our own and the British and French leaders met together, and later we agreed, with the Soviet leaders, to gather in Paris on May 16.

Of course we had no indication or thought that basic Soviet policies had turned about. But when there is even the slightest chance of strengthening peace, there can be no higher obligation than to pursue it. . . .

Our safety, and that of the free world, demand, of course, effective systems for gathering information about the military capabilities of other powerful nations, especially those that make a fetish of secrecy. This involves many techniques and methods. In these times of vast military machines and nuclear-tipped missiles, the ferreting out of this information is indispensable to free-world security. . . .

It was in the prosecution of one of these intelligence programs that the widely publicized U-2 incident occurred.

Aerial photography has been one of many methods we have used to keep ourselves and the free world abreast of major Soviet military developments. The usefulness of this work has been well established through four years of effort. The Soviets were well aware of it. Chairman Khrushchev has stated that he became aware of these flights several years ago. Only last week, in his Paris press conference, Chairman Khrushchev confirmed that he knew of these flights when he visited the United States last September.

Incidentally, this raises the natural question — why all the furor concerning one particular flight? He did not, when in America last September, charge that these flights were any threat to Soviet safety. He did not then see any reason to refuse to confer with American representatives.

This he did only about the flight that unfortunately failed, on May 1, far inside Russia.

Now, two questions have been raised about this particular flight; first, as to its timing, considering the imminence of the Summit meeting; second, our initial statements when we learned the flight had failed.

As to the timing, the question was really whether to halt the program and thus forgo the gathering of important information that was essential and that was likely to be unavailable at a later date. The decision was that the program should not be halted.

The plain truth is this: when a nation needs intelligence activity, there is no time when vigilance can be relaxed. Incidentally, from Pearl Harbor we learned that even negotiation itself can be used to conceal preparations for a surprise attack.

Next, as to our government's initial statement about the flight, this was issued to protect the pilot, his mission, and our intelligence processes, at a time when the true facts were still undetermined.

Our first information about the failure of this mission did not disclose whether the pilot was still alive, was trying to escape, was avoiding interrogation, or whether both plane and pilot had been destroyed. Protection of our intelligence system and the pilot, and concealment of the plane's mission, seemed imperative. It must be remembered that over a long period these flights had given us information of the greatest importance to the nation's security. In fact, their success has been nothing short of remarkable.

For these reasons, what is known in intelligence circles as a "covering statement" was issued. It was issued on assumptions that were later proved incorrect. Consequently, when later the status of the pilot was definitely established and there was no further possibility of avoiding exposure of the project, the factual details were set forth.

==I then made two facts clear to the public: first, our program of aerial reconnaissance had been undertaken with my approval; second, this government is compelled to keep abreast, by one means or another, of military activities of the Soviets, just as their government has for years engaged in espionage activities in our country and throughout the world.==
Our necessity to proceed with such activities was also asserted by our Secretary of State who, however, had been careful — as was I — not to say that these particular flights would be continued.

In fact, before leaving Washington I had directed that these U-2 flights be stopped. Clearly their usefulness was impaired. Moreover, continuing this particular activity in these new circumstances could not but complicate the relations of certain of our allies with the Soviets. And of course, new techniques, other than aircraft, are constantly being developed.

Now I wanted no public announcement of this decision until I could personally disclose it at the Summit meeting in conjunction with certain proposals I had prepared for the conference.

At my first Paris meeting with Mr. Khrushchev, and before his tirade was made public, I informed him of this discontinuance and the character of the constructive proposals I planned to make. These contemplated the establishment of a system of aerial surveillance operated by the United Nations.

The day before the first scheduled meeting, Mr. Khrushchev had advised President de Gaulle and Prime Minister Macmillan that he would make certain demands upon the United States as a precondition for beginning a Summit conference.

Although the United States was the only power against which he expressed his displeasure, he did not communicate this information to me. I was, of course, informed by our allies.

At the four-power meeting on Monday morning, he demanded of the United States four things: First, condemnation of U-2 flights as a method of espionage; second, assurance that they would not be continued; third, a public apology on behalf of the United States; and, fourth, punishment of all those who had any responsibility respecting this particular mission.

I replied by advising the Soviet leader that I had, during the previous week, stopped these flights and that they would not be resumed. I offered also to discuss the matter with him in personal meetings, while the regular business of the Summit might proceed. Obviously, I would not respond to his extreme demands. He knew, of course, by holding to those demands the Soviet Union was scuttling the Summit Conference.

In torpedoing the conference, Mr. Khrushchev claimed that he acted as the result of his own high moral indignation over alleged American acts of aggression. As I said earlier, he had known of these flights for a long time. It is apparent that the Soviets had decided even before the Soviet delegation left Moscow that my trip to the Soviet Union should be canceled and that nothing constructive from their viewpoint would come out of the Summit Conference. . . .

The conduct of our allies was magnificent. My colleagues and friends — President de Gaulle and Prime Minister Macmillan — stood sturdily with the American delegation in spite of persistent Soviet attempts to split the Western group. The NATO meeting after the Paris conference showed unprecedented unity and support for the alliance and for the position taken at the Summit meeting. I salute our allies for us all. . . .

A major American goal is a world of open societies.

Here in our country anyone can buy maps and aerial photographs showing our cities, our dams, our plants, our highways — indeed, our whole industrial and economic complex. We know that Soviet attachés regularly collect this information. Last fall Chairman Khrushchev's train passed no more than a few hundred feet from an operational ICBM, in plain view from his window. Our thousands of books and scientific journals, our magazines, newspapers and official publications, our radio and television, all openly describe to all the world every aspect of our society.

This is as it should be. We are proud of our freedom.

Soviet distrust, however, does still remain. To allay these misgivings I offered five years ago to open our skies to Soviet reconnaissance aircraft on a reciprocal basis. The Soviets refused. That offer is still open. At an appropriate time America will submit such a program to the United Nations, together with the recommendation that the United Nations itself conduct this reconnaissance. Should the United Nations accept this proposal, I am prepared to propose that America supply part of the aircraft and equipment required. . . .

96. Nuclear Test Ban Treaty, 5 August 1963

Signed at Moscow by U.S., Great Britain, and the Soviet Union.

. . . ARTICLE I. (1) Each of the Parties to this Treaty undertakes to prohibit, to prevent, and not to carry out any nuclear weapon test explosion, or any other nuclear explosion, at any place under its jurisdiction or control:

(a) in the atmosphere; beyond its limits, including outer space; or underwater, including territorial waters or high seas; or

(b) in any other environment if such explosion causes radioactive debris to be present outside the territorial limits of the State under whose jurisdiction or control such explosion is conducted. It is understood in this connection that the provisions of this subparagraph are without prejudice to the conclusion of a treaty resulting in the permanent banning of all nuclear test explosions, including all such explosions underground, the conclusion of which, as the Parties have stated in the Preamble to this Treaty, they seek to achieve.

(2) Each of the Parties to this Treaty undertakes furthermore to refrain from causing, encouraging, or in any way participating in, the carrying out of any nuclear weapon test explosion, or any other nuclear explosion, anywhere which would take place in any of the environments described, or have the effect referred to, in paragraph 1 of this Article.

Article II. (1) Any Party may propose amendments to this Treaty. The text of any proposed amendment shall be submitted to the Depositary Governments which shall circulate it to all Parties to this Treaty. Thereafter, if requested to do so by one-third or more of the Parties, the Depositary Governments shall convene a conference, to which they shall invite all the Parties, to consider such amendment.

(2) Any amendment to this Treaty must be approved by a majority of the votes of all the Parties to this Treaty, including the votes of all of the Original Parties. The amendment shall enter into force for all Parties upon the deposit of instruments of ratification by a majority of all the Parties, including the instruments of ratification of all of the Original Parties.

Article III. (1) This Treaty shall be open to all States for signature. Any State which does not sign this Treaty before its entry into force in accordance with paragraph 3 of this Article may accede to it at any time. . . .

Article IV. This Treaty shall be of unlimited duration. Each Party shall in exercising its national sovereignty have the right to withdraw from the Treaty if it decides that extraordinary events, related to the subject matter of this Treaty, have jeopardized the supreme interests of its country. It shall give notice of such withdrawal to all other Parties to the Treaty three months in advance. . . .

97. Fulbright on U.S. Foreign Policy, 25 March 1964

Speech of Arkansas Senator J. William Fulbright in the Senate.

FOREIGN POLICY—OLD MYTHS AND NEW REALITIES

Mr. FULBRIGHT. Mr. President, there is an inevitable divergence, attributable to the imperfections of the human mind, between the world as it is and the world as men perceive it. As long as our perceptions are reasonably close to objective reality, it is possible for us to act upon our problems in a rational and appropriate manner. But when our perceptions fail to keep pace with events, when we refuse to believe something because it displeases or frightens us, or because it is simply startlingly unfamiliar, then the gap between fact and perception becomes a chasm, and action becomes irrelevant and irrational.

There has always—and inevitably—been some divergence between the realities of foreign policy and our ideas about it. This divergence has in certain respects been growing, rather than narrowing; and we are handicapped, accordingly, by policies based on old myths, rather than current realities. This divergence is, in my opinion, dangerous and unnecessary—dangerous, because it can reduce foreign policy to a fraudulent game of imagery and appearances; unnecessary, because it can be overcome by the determination of men in high office to dispel prevailing misconceptions by the candid dissemination of unpleasant, but inescapable, facts.

Before commenting on some of the specific areas where I believe our policies are at least partially based on cherished myths, rather than objective facts, I should like to suggest two possible reasons for the growing divergence between the realities and our perceptions of current world politics. The first is the radical change in relations between and within the Communist and the free world; and the second is the tendency of too many of us to confuse means with ends and, accordingly, to adhere to prevailing practices with a fervor befitting immutable principles. . . . .

We are confronted with a complex and fluid world situation and we are not adapting ourselves to it. We are clinging to old myths in the face of new realities and we are seeking to escape the contradictions by narrowing the permissible bounds of public discussion, by relegating an increasing number of ideas and viewpoints to a growing category of "unthinkable thoughts." I believe that this tendency can and should be reversed, that it is within our ability, and unquestionably in our interests, to cut loose from established myths and to start thinking some "unthinkable thoughts"—about the cold war and East-West relations, about the underdeveloped countries and particularly those in Latin America, about the changing nature of the Chinese Communist threat in Asia and about the festering war in Vietnam . . . . If we persist in the view that all Communist regimes are equally hostile and equally threatening to the West, and that we can have no policy toward the captive nations except the eventual overthrow of their Communist regimes, then the West may enforce upon the Communist bloc a degree of unity which the Soviet Union has shown itself to be quite incapable of imposing—just as Stalin in the early postwar years frightened the West into a degree of unity that it almost certainly could not have attained by its own unaided efforts. If, on the other hand, we are willing to reexamine the view that all Communist regimes are alike in the threat which they pose for the West—a view which had a certain validity in Stalin's time—then we may be able to exert an important influence on the course of events within a divided Communist world.

. . . . Latin America is one of the areas of the world in which American policy is weakened by a growing divergency between old myths and new realities.

The crisis over the Panama Canal has been unnecessarily protracted for reasons of domestic politics and national pride and sensitivity on both sides—for reasons, that is, of only marginal relevance to the merits of the dispute. . . . .

I think the Panamanians have unquestionably been more emotional about the dispute than has the United States. I also think that there is less reason for emotionalism on the part of the United States than on the part of Panama. It is important for us to remember that the issue over the canal is only one of a great many in which the United States is involved, and by no means the most important. For Panama, on the other hand, a small nation with a weak economy and an unstable government, the canal is the preeminent factor in the nation's economy and in its foreign relations. Surely in a confrontation so unequal, it is not unreasonable to expect the United States to go a little farther than halfway in the search for a fair settlement.

We Americans would do well, for a start, to divest ourselves of the silly notion that the issue with Panama is a test of our courage and resolve. I believe that the Cuban missile crisis of 1962, involving a confrontation with nuclear weapons and intercontinental missiles, was indeed a test of our courage, and we acquitted ourselves extremely well in that instance. I am unable to understand how a controversy with a small and poor country, with virtually no military capacity, can possibly be regarded as a test of our bravery and will to defend our interests. It takes stubbornness but not courage to reject the entreaties of the weak. The real test in Panama is not of our valor but of our wisdom and judgment and commonsense.

We would also do well to disabuse ourselves of the myth that there is something morally sacred about the treaty of 1903. The fact of the matter is that the treaty was concluded under circumstances that reflect little credit on the United States . . . .

Under these circumstances, it seems to me entirely proper and necessary for the United States to take the initiative in proposing new arrangements that would redress some of Panama's grievances against the treaty as it now stands. I see no reason—certainly no reason of "weakness" or "dishonor"—why the United States cannot put an end to the semantic debate over whether treaty revisions are to be "negotiated" or "discussed" by stating positively and clearly that it is prepared to negotiate revisions in the canal treaty . . . .

The Far East is another area of the world in which American policy is handicapped by the divergence of old myths and new realities. Particularly with respect to China, an elaborate vocabulary of make-believe has become compulsory in both official and public discussion.

. . . .

We are committed, with respect to China and other areas in Asia, to inflexible policies of long standing from which we hesitate to depart because of the attribution to these policies of an aura of mystical sanctity. It may be that a thorough reevaluation of our Far Eastern policies would lead us to the conclusion that they are sound and wise, or at least that they represent the best available options. It may be, on the other hand, that a reevaluation would point up the need for greater or lesser changes in our policies. The point is that, whatever the outcome of a rethinking of policy might be, we have been unwilling to undertake it because of the fear of many Government officials, undoubtedly well founded, that even the suggestion of new policies toward China or Vietnam would provoke a vehement public outcry.

I do not think the United States can, or should, recognize Communist China, or acquiesce in its admission to the United Nations under present circumstances. It would be unwise to do so, because there is nothing to be gained by it so long as the Peiping regime maintains its attitude of implacable hostility toward the United States. I do not believe, however, that this state of affairs is necessarily permanent. As we have seen in our relations with Germany and Japan, hostility can give way in an astonishingly short time to close friendship; and, as we have seen in our relations with China, the reverse can occur with equal speed. It is not impossible that in time our relations with China will change again—if not to friendship, then perhaps to "competitive coexistence." It would therefore be extremely useful if we could introduce an element of flexibility, or, more precisely, of the capacity to be flexible, into our relations with Communist China . . . .

The situation in Vietnam poses a far more pressing need for a reevaluation of American policy. Other than withdrawal, which I do not think can be realistically considered under present circumstances, ...

It seems clear that only two realistic options are open to us in Vietnam in the immediate future: the expansion of the conflict in one way or another, or a renewed effort to bolster the capacity of the South Vietnamese to prosecute the war successfully on its present scale. The matter calls for thorough examination by responsible officials in the executive branch; and until they have had an opportunity to evaluate the contingencies and feasibilities of the options open to us, it seems to me that we have no choice but to support the South Vietnamese Government and Army by the most effective means available. Whatever specific policy decisions are made, it should be clear to all concerned that the United States will continue to meet its obligations and fulfill its commitments with respect to Vietnam . . . .

If Congress and public opinion are unduly susceptible to "shock," the executive branch, and particularly the Department of State, is subject to the malady of chronic and excessive caution. An effective foreign policy is one which concerns itself more with innovation abroad than with conciliation at home. A creative foreign policy—as President Truman, for one, knew—is not necessarily one which wins immediate general approval. It is sometimes necessary for leaders to do unpleasant and unpopular things, because, as Burke pointed out, the duty of the democratic politician to his constituents is not to comply with their every wish and preference but to give them the benefit of, and to be held responsible for, the exercise of his own best judgment.

We must dare to think about "unthinkable things," because when things become "unthinkable," thinking stops and action becomes mindless. If we are to disabuse ourselves of old myths and to act wisely and creatively upon the new realities of our time, we must think and talk about our problems with perfect freedom, remembering, as Woodrow Wilson said, that "The greatest freedom of speech is the greatest safety because, if a man is a fool, the best thing to do is to encourage him to advertise the fact by speaking."

98. Cooper on the Soviet Invasion of Czechoslovakia, 20-21 August 1968

Speech of U.S. Representative John Sherman Cooper to the U.N. General Assemble, 23 December 1968.

As we all know, the General Assembly, despite expressions of skepticism, went on to accept the Soviet proposal in substantial measure. It set up a special committee "to consider all aspects of the question (of defining aggression) so that an adequate definition of aggression may be prepared. . . ." That committee met in Geneva during the summer. All its members set about their task in good faith. It did not agree on a definition of aggression, but it received a number of proposed draft definitions; it heard the Soviet representative revive drafts previously proposed by the Soviet Union; it considered all proposals in some detail; and it submitted a report which is now before this committee.

One of the members of that special committee was Czechoslovakia. On the evening of August 21, some 6 weeks after the committee ended its meeting, the citizens of Czechoslovakia, an independent country, found themselves overnight the residents of an occupied territory.

We are all only too familiar with the story of what happened in Czechoslovakia on the night of August 21 and what has happened since, and we are all aware of the nobility and courage of the Czechoslovak people in the face of these events . . . .

we cannot escape three cardinal facts about the occupation of Czechoslovakia and international law:

First, so far as relations between the U.S.S.R. and Czechoslovakia are concerned, aggression had already been defined by treaty and, indeed, has been defined for over three decades.

Second, the Soviet invasion and occupation were so clear a violation of the existing law of aggression, laid down by the United Nations Charter, that the Soviet Union itself abandoned its early pretenses of explaining or justifying this action in any terms consistent with the charter.

Third, far from seeking to justify its action under the United Nations Charter, the Soviet Union has subsequently devised and announced to the world a new doctrine, unknown in international law, which on its face constitutes a rejection of the fundamental principles of the charter and the whole scheme of relations among states upon which the charter rests and which it seeks to establish. . . . .

What, then, is the meaning for the people of Czechoslovakia and other countries of the principle of equal rights and self-determination of peoples stated in the charter? The *Pravda* article answers:

The soldiers of the allied socialist countries now in Czechoslovakia . . . are fighting for the principle of self-determination of the peoples of Czechoslovakia not in words but in deeds, are fighting for their inalienable right to think out profoundly and decide their fate themselves. . . .

Finally, the article sums up the Soviet position in the following language:

Laws and legal norms are subjected to the laws of the class struggle, the laws of social development. These laws are clearly formulated in Marxist-Leninist teaching. . . .

Formal juridical reasoning must not overshadow a class approach . . . .

It is against this historical background, Mr. Chairman, that the official Soviet declarations endeavoring to justify the invasion of Czechoslovakia must be understood. For now the Soviet Union has put forward a new doctrine which breaches the principle of sovereign equality of states by denying the fundamental protections of the charter to a whole undetermined class of states denominated, in the words of Foreign Minister Gromyko, as the "Socialist commonwealth"—presumably reserving to itself the right to decide which states fall within this class and which do not.

Perhaps the core of the Soviet argument can be seen in the following paragraphs from the article printed in *Pravda* on September 25 of this year, entitled "Sovereignty and International Duties of Socialist Countries." That article undertook to refute

. . . the assertions, made in some places, that the actions of the five socialist countries run counter to the Marxist-Leninist principle of sovereignty and the rights of nations to self-determination.

The groundlessness of such reasoning (*Pravda* continued) consists primarily in that it is based on an abstract, non-class approach to the question of sovereignty and the rights of nations to self-determination. . . .

In short, the Soviet Union now claims the right to intervene by military force against independent countries whenever it deems the interests of the "class struggle" to require. In the history of the progressive development of international law under the charter, this new doctrine is a monstrous regression . . . .

99. U.S.-Soviet Strategic Arms Limitation Treaty (SALT I), 26 May 1972

DEPARTMENT OF STATE,
Washington, June 10, 1972.

THE PRESIDENT,
The White House.

THE PRESIDENT: I have the honor to submit to you the Treaty between the United States of America and the Union of Soviet Socialist Republics on the Limitation of Anti-Ballistic Missile Systems (ABM Treaty) and the Interim Agreement between the United States of America and the Union of Soviet Socialist Republics on Certain Measures with respect to the Limitation of Strategic Offensive Arms (Interim Agreement), including an associated Protocol. It is my recommendation that the ABM Treaty be transmitted to the Senate for its advice and consent to ratification.

The Interim Agreement, as its title indicates, is an agreement limited in scope and time. It is designed to limit the aggregate number of intercontinental ballistic missile (ICBM) launchers and submarine-launched ballistic missile (SLBM) launchers, and the number of modern ballistic missile submarines, pending the negotiation of a treaty covering more complete limitations of strategic offensive arms. In these circumstances, I am submitting to you the Interim Agreement and its Protocol (which is an integral part of the Agreement), with the recommendation that they be transmitted to both Houses of Congress for approval by a Joint Resolution.

The Interim Agreement can by its terms enter into force only upon the exchange of written notices of acceptance by both countries and only when and if the ABM Treaty is brought into force. Both signatories understand that, pending ratification and acceptance, neither will take any action that would be prohibited by the ABM Treaty or the Interim Agreement and Protocol, in the absence of notification by either signatory of its intention not to proceed with ratification or acceptance.

ABM Treaty

In broad outline, the ABM Treaty, signed on May 26, 1972, provides that:

—A nationwide ABM deployment, and a base for such deployment, are prohibited;

—An ABM deployment for defense of an individual region is prohibited, except as specifically permitted;

—Permitted ABM deployments will be limited to two widely separated deployment areas in each country—one for defense of the national capital, and the other for the defense of ICBMs;

—For these purposes no more than 100 ABM launchers and no more than 100 ABM interceptor missiles at launch sites may be deployed within each 150-kilometer radius ABM deployment area, for a total of 200 deployed ABM interceptors and 200 deployed ABM launchers for each Party;

—ABM radars will be strictly controlled; radars to support the ABM defense of the national capital may be deployed only in a specified number of small radar complexes within the ABM deployment area; radars to support the ICBM defense will be limited to a specified number within the ABM deployment area and will also be subject to qualitative constraint.

In order to assure the effectiveness of these basic provisions of the Treaty, a number of detailed corollary provisions were also agreed:

—Development, testing and deployment of ABM systems or ABM components that are sea-based, air-based, space-based or mobile land-based are prohibited;

—Deployment of ABM systems involving new types of basic components to perform the current functions of ABM launchers, interceptors or radars is prohibited;

—The conversion or testing of other systems, such as air defense systems, or components thereof to perform an ABM role is prohibited.

The Treaty also contains certain general provisions relating to the verification and implementation of the Treaty and to further negotiations:

—Each side will use national technical means for verification and the Parties agree not to interfere with such means and not to take deliberate concealment measures;

—A Standing Consultative Commission will be established to facilitate implementation of the Treaty and consider questions arising thereunder;

—The Parties will continue active negotiations for limitations on strategic offensive arms.

The ABM Treaty consists of a preamble and sixteen Articles. As indicated in Article I(1), it provides for limitations on anti-ballistic missile (ABM) systems as well as certain related measures. In the course of the negotiations, agreement was reached on a number of interpretive matters related to the Treaty. Enclosure 3 contains agreed interpretations and certain noteworthy unilateral statements.

Conclusion

I believe the Treaty limiting anti-ballistic missile systems, together with the accompanying Interim Agreement and its Protocol constraining strategic offensive arms, constitute the most important step in arms limitation ever taken by this country. In these agreements, the two most powerful nations on earth are adopting measures designed to curb the deployment of strategic arms.

The Parties have protected their vital interests during the careful negotiation and elaboration of these agreements. We did not agree to anything adversely affecting the national interests of our Allies, who were regularly consulted during the negotiations. The Congress has been kept closely informed throughout the negotiations. Ambassador Smith and other Delegation members conducted a total of thirty executive session briefings for Congressional Committees.

These Agreements should help to improve Soviet-American relations and preserve and strengthen international security and world order. The entry into force of these measures should significantly advance the cause of peace in the world, and I hope that they can be brought into force as soon as practicable.

Respectfully submitted,

WILLIAM P. ROGERS.

100. Truman on U.S. China Policy, 16 December 1945

... IT IS THE firm belief of this Government that a strong, united, and democratic China is of the utmost importance to the success of this United Nations Organization and for world peace. A China disorganized and divided either by foreign aggression, such as that undertaken by the Japanese, or by violent internal strife is an undermining influence to world stability and peace, now and in the future. The United States Government has long subscribed to the principle that the management of internal affairs is the responsibility of the peoples of the sovereign nations. Events of this century, however, would indicate that a breach of peace anywhere in the world threatens the peace of the entire world. It is thus in the most vital interest of the United States and all the United Nations that the people of China overlook no opportunity to adjust their internal differences promptly by methods of peaceful negotiation.

The Government of the United States believes it essential:

(1) That a cessation of hostilities be arranged between the armies of the National Government and the Chinese Communists and other dissident Chinese armed forces for the purpose of completing the return of all China to effective Chinese control, including the immediate evacuation of the Japanese forces.

(2) That a national conference of representatives of major political elements be arranged to develop an early solution to the present internal strife — a solution which will bring about the unification of China.

The United States and the other United Nations have recognized the present National Government of the Republic of China as the only legal government in China. It is the proper instrument to achieve the objective of a unified China.

The United States and the United Kingdom by the Cairo Declaration in 1943 and the Union of Soviet Socialist Republics by adhering to the Potsdam Declaration of last July and by the Sino-Soviet treaty and agreements of August 1945 are all committed to the liberation of China, including the return of Manchuria to Chinese control. These agreements were made with the National Government of the Republic of China. ...

The United States is cognizant that the present National Government of China is a "one-party government" and believes that peace, unity, and democratic reform in China will be furthered if the basis of this Government is broadened to include other political elements in the country. Hence, the United States strongly advocates that the national conference of representatives of major political elements in the country agree upon arrangements which would give those elements a fair and effective representation in the Chinese National Government. It is recognized that this would require modification of the one-party "political tutelage" established as an interim arrangement in the progress of the nation toward democracy by the father of the Chinese Republic, Dr. Sun Yat-sen.

The existence of autonomous armies such as that of the Communist army is inconsistent with, and actually makes impossible, political unity in China. With the institution of a broadly representative government, autonomous armies should be eliminated as such and all armed forces in China integrated effectively into the Chinese National Army.

In line with its often expressed views regarding self-determination, the United States Government considers that the detailed steps necessary to the achievement of political unity in China must be worked out by the Chinese themselves and that intervention by any foreign government in these matters would be inappropriate. The United States Government feels, however, that China has a clear responsibility to the other United Nations to eliminate armed conflict within its territory as constituting a threat to world stability and peace — a responsibility which is shared by the National Government and all Chinese political and military groups.

As China moves toward peace and unity along the lines described above, the United States would be prepared to assist the National Government in every reasonable way to rehabilitate the country, improve the agrarian and industrial economy, and establish a military organization capable of discharging China's national and international responsibilities for the maintenance of peace and order. In furtherance of such assistance, it would be prepared to give favorable consideration to Chinese requests for credits and loans under reasonable conditions for projects which would contribute toward the development of a healthy economy throughout China and healthy trade relations between China and the United States.

101. U.S. Trusteeship over the Japanese Mandated Islands, 2 April 1947

... ARTICLE 1. The Territory of the Pacific Islands, consisting of the islands formerly held by Japan under mandate in accordance with Article 22 of the Covenant of the League of Nations, is hereby designated as a strategic area and placed under the trusteeship system established in the Charter of the United Nations. The Territory of the Pacific Islands is hereinafter referred to as the trust territory.

Article 2. The United States of America is designated as the administering authority of the trust territory.

Article 3. The administering authority shall have full powers of administration, legislation, and jurisdiction over the territory subject to the provisions of this agreement, and may apply to the trust territory, subject to any modifications which the administering authority may consider desirable, such of the laws of the United States as it may deem appropriate to local conditions and requirements. ...

Article 5. ... The administering authority shall be entitled:

1. to establish naval, military and air bases and to erect fortifications in the trust territory;
2. to station and employ armed forces in the territory; and
3. to make use of volunteer forces, facilities and assistance from the trust territory in carrying out the obligations towards the Security Council undertaken in this regard by the administering authority, as well as for the local defense and the maintenance of law and order within the trust territory.

Article 6. ... The administering authority shall:

1. foster the development of such political institutions as are suited to the trust territory and shall promote the development of the inhabitants of the trust territory toward self-government or independence, as may be appropriate to the particular circumstances of the trust territory and its peoples and the freely expressed wishes of the peoples concerned; and to this end shall give to the inhabitants of the trust territory a progressively increasing share in the administrative services in the territory; shall develop their participation in government; shall give due recognition to the customs of the inhabitants in providing a system of law for the territory; and shall take other appropriate measures toward these ends;

2. promote the economic advancement and self-sufficiency of the inhabitants, and to this end shall regulate the use of natural resources; encourage the development of fisheries, agriculture, and industries; protect the inhabitants against the loss of their lands and resources; and improve the means of transportation and communication;

3. promote the social advancement of the inhabitants, and to this end shall protect the rights and fundamental freedoms of all elements of the population without discrimination; protect the health of the inhabitants; control the traffic in arms and ammunition, opium and other dangerous drugs, and alcohol and other spirituous beverages; and institute such other regulations as may be necessary to protect the inhabitants against social abuses; and

4. promote the educational advancement of the inhabitants, and to this end shall take steps toward the establishment of a general system of elementary education; facilitate the vocational and cultural advancement of the population; and shall encourage qualified students to pursue higher education, including training on the professional level.

Article 7. ... The administering authority shall guarantee to the inhabitants of the trust territory freedom of conscience, and, subject only to the requirements of public order and security, freedom of speech, of the press, and of assembly; freedom of worship and of religious teaching; and freedom of migration and movement. ...

Article 15. The terms of the present agreement shall not be altered, amended or terminated without the consent of the administering authority.

102. Acheson on U.S. Policies in Asia, 12 January 1950

Statement of Secretary of State Dean G. Acheson.

... I AM frequently asked: Has the State Department got an Asian policy? And it seems to me that that discloses such a depth of ignorance that it is very hard to begin to deal with it. The peoples of Asia are so incredibly diverse and their problems are so incredibly diverse that how could anyone, even the most utter charlatan believe that he had a uniform policy which would deal with all of them. On the other hand, there are very important similarities in ideas and in problems among the peoples of Asia and so what we come to . . . is the fact that there must be certain similarities of approach, and there must be very great dissimilarities in action. . . .

Let's come now to matters which Asia has in common. There is . . . a developing Asian consciousness . . . based upon two factors. . . .

One of these factors is a revulsion against the acceptance of misery and poverty as the normal condition of life. Throughout all of this vast area, you have that fundamental revolutionary aspect in mind and belief. The other common aspect that they have is the revulsion against foreign domination. Whether that foreign domination takes the form of colonialism or whether it takes the form of imperialism, they are through with it. . . .

Now let me come to another underlying and important factor which determines our relations and, in turn, our policy with the peoples of Asia. That is the attitude of the Soviet Union toward Asia, and particularly towards those parts of Asia which are contiguous to the Soviet Union. . . .

The attitude and interest of the Russians in North China, and in these other areas as well, long antedates communism. . . . But the Communist regime has added new methods, new skills, and new concepts to the thrust of Russian imperialism. This Communistic concept and techniques have armed Russian imperialism with a new and most insidious weapon of penetration. Armed with these new powers, what is happening in China is that the Soviet Union is detaching the northern provinces [areas] of China from China and is attaching them to the Soviet Union. This process is complete in outer Mongolia. It is nearly complete in Manchuria, and I am sure that in inner Mongolia and in Sinkiang there are very happy reports coming from Soviet agents to Moscow. This is what is going on. It is the detachment of these whole areas, vast areas — populated by Chinese — the detachment of these areas from China and their attachment to the Soviet Union.

I wish to state this and perhaps sin against my doctrine of nondogmatism, but I should like to suggest at any rate that this fact that the Soviet Union is taking the four northern provinces of China is the single most significant, most important fact, in the relation of any foreign power with Asia.

What does that mean for us? It means something very, very significant. It means that nothing that we do and nothing that we say must be allowed to obscure the reality of this fact. All the efforts of propaganda will not be able to obscure it. The only thing that can obscure it is the folly of ill-conceived adventures on our part which easily could do so, and I urge all who are thinking about these foolish adventures to remember that we must not seize the unenviable position which the Russians have carved out for themselves. We must not undertake to deflect from the Russians to ourselves the righteous anger, and the wrath, and the hatred of the Chinese people which must develop. It would be folly to deflect it to ourselves. We must take the position we have always taken — that anyone who violates the integrity of China is the enemy of China and is acting contrary to our own interest. That, I suggest to you this afternoon, is the first and the greatest rule in regard to the formulation of American policy toward Asia.

[margin note: excellent suggestions they have been followed. Will they be in the future?]

I suggest that the second rule is very like the first. That is to keep our own purposes perfectly straight, perfectly pure, and perfectly aboveboard and do not get them mixed-up with legal quibbles or the attempt to do one thing and really achieve another. . . .

What is the situation in regard to the military security of the Pacific area, and what is our policy in regard to it?

In the first place, the defeat and the disarmament of Japan has placed upon the United States the necessity of assuming the military defense of Japan so long as that is required, both in the interest of our security and in the interests of the security of the entire Pacific area and, in all honor, in the interest of Japanese security. We have American — and there are Australian — troops in Japan. I am not in a position to speak for the Australians, but I can assure you that there is no intention of any sort of abandoning or weakening the defenses of Japan and that whatever arrangements are to be made either through permanent settlement or otherwise, that defense must and shall be maintained.

This defensive perimeter runs along the Aleutians to Japan and then goes to the Ryukyus. We hold important defense positions in the Ryukyu Islands, and those we will continue to hold. In the interest of the population of the Ryukyu Islands, we will at an appropriate time offer to hold these islands under trusteeship of the United Nations. But they are essential parts of the defensive perimeter of the Pacific, and they must and will be held.

The defensive perimeter runs from the Ryukyus to the Philippine Islands. Our relations, our defensive relations with the Philippines are contained in agreements between us. Those agreements are being loyally carried out and will be loyally carried out. Both peoples have learned by bitter experience the vital connections between our mutual defense requirements. We are in no doubt about that, and it is hardly necessary for me to say an attack on the Philippines could not and would not be tolerated by the United States. But I hasten to add that no one perceives the imminence of any such attack.

So far as the military security of other areas in the Pacific is concerned, it must be clear that no person can guarantee these areas against military attack. But it must also be clear that such a guarantee is hardly sensible or necessary within the realm of practical relationship. . . .

Let's take the situation in Japan for a moment. There are three great factors to be faced. The security matter I have dealt with. Aside from that, there are the economic questions and the political questions. In the political field, General MacArthur has been very successful and the Japanese are hammering out with some effort, and with some backsliding, and regaining and backsliding again of progress, a political system which is based on nonmilitaristic institutions.

In the economic field, we have not been so successful. That is in very large part due to the inherent difficulty of the problem. The problem arises with the necessity of Japan being able to buy raw materials and sell goods. The former connections of Japan with the mainland and with some of the islands have been disrupted. That has produced difficulties. The willingness of other countries to receive Japanese goods has very much contracted since the war. . . .

In Korea, we have taken great steps which have ended our military occupation, and in cooperation with the United Nations, have established an independent and sovereign country recognized by nearly all the rest of the world. . . .

In the Philippines, we acted with vigor and speed to set up an independent sovereign nation which we have done. We have given the Philippines a billion dollars of direct economic aid since the war. We have spent another billion dollars in such matters as veterans' benefits and other payments in the Philippines. Much of that money has not been used as wisely as we wish it had been used, but here again, we come up against the matter of responsibility. It is the Philippine Government which is responsible. . . .

We are always ready to help and to advise. That is all we can and all we should do.

Elsewhere in southeast Asia, the limits of what we can do are to help where we are wanted. We are organizing the machinery through which we can make effective help possible. The western powers are all interested. We all know the techniques. We have all had expriences which can be useful to those governments which are newly starting out if they want it. It cannot be useful if they don't want it. . . .

So after this survey, what we conclude, I believe, is that there is a new day which has dawned in Asia. It is a day in which the Asian peoples are on their own, and know it, and intend to continue on their own. It is a day in which the old relationships between east and west are gone, relationships which at their worst were exploitation, and which at their best were paternalism. That relationship is over, and the relationship of east and west must now be in the Far East one of mutual respect and mutual helpfulness. We are their friends. Others are their friends. We and those others are willing to help, but we can help only where we are wanted and only where the conditions of help are really sensible and possible. So what we can see is that this new day in Asia, this new day which is dawning, may go on to a glorious noon or it may darken and it may drizzle out. But that decision lies within the countries of Asia and within the power of the Asian people. It is not a decision which a friend or even an enemy from the outside can decide for them.

103. Japan and U.S., Treaty of Peace, 8 September 1951

. . . THE ALLIED POWERS recognize the full sovereignty of the Japanese people over Japan and its territorial waters.

Article 2

(a) Japan, recognizing the independence of Korea, renounces all right, title and claim to Korea, including the islands of Quelpart, Port Hamilton and Dagelet.

(b) Japan renounces all right, title and claim to Formosa and the Pescadores.

(c) Japan renounces all right, title and claim to the Kurile Islands, and to that portion of Sakhalin and the islands adjacent to it over which Japan acquired sovereignty as a consequence of the Treaty of Portsmouth of September 5, 1905.

(d) Japan renounces all right, title and claim in connection with the League of Nations Mandate System, and accepts the action of the United Nations Security Council of April 2, 1947, extending the trusteeship system to the Pacific Islands formerly under mandate to Japan.

(e) Japan renounces all claim to any right or title to or interest in connection with any part of the Antarctic area, whether deriving from the activities of Japanese nationals or otherwise.

(f) Japan renounces all right, title and claim to the Spratly Islands and to the Paracel Islands.

Article 3

Japan will concur in any proposal of the United States to the United Nations to place under its trusteeship system, with the United States as the sole administering authority, Nansei Shoto south of 29° north latitude (including the Ryukyu Islands and the Daito Islands), Nanpo Shoto south of Sofu Gan (including the Bonin Islands, Rosario Island and the Volcano Islands) and Parece Vela and Marcus Island. Pending the making of such a proposal and affirmative action thereon, the United States will have the right to exercise all and any powers of administration, legislation and jurisdiction over the territory and inhabitants of these islands, including their territorial waters. . . .

Article 5

(a) Japan accepts the obligations set forth in Article 2 of the Charter of the United Nations. . . .

(c) The Allied Powers for their part recognize that Japan as a sovereign nation possesses the inherent right of individual or collective self-defense referred to in Article 51 of the Charter of the United Nations and that Japan may voluntarily enter into collective security arrangements.

Article 6

(a) All occupation forces of the Allied Powers shall be withdrawn from Japan as soon as possible after the coming into force of the present Treaty, and in any case not later than 90 days thereafter. Nothing in this provision shall, however, prevent the stationing or retention of foreign armed forces in Japanese territory under or in consequence of any bilateral or multilateral agreements which have been or may be made between one or more of the Allied Powers, on the one hand, and Japan on the other. . . .

Article 14

(a) It is recognized that Japan should pay reparations to the Allied Powers for the damage and suffering caused by it during the war. Nevertheless it is also recognized that the resources of Japan are not presently sufficient, if it is to maintain a viable economy, to make complete reparation for all such damage and suffering and at the same time meet its other obligations.

Therefore,

1. Japan will promptly enter into negotiations with Allied Powers so desiring, whose present territories were occupied by Japanese forces and damaged by Japan, with a view to assisting to compensate those countries for the cost of repairing the damage done, by making available the services of the Japanese people in production, salvaging and other work for the Allied Powers in question. Such arrangements shall avoid the imposition of additional liabilities on other Allied Powers, and, where the manufacturing of raw materials is called for, they shall be supplied by the Allied Powers in question, so as not to throw any foreign exchange burden upon Japan. . . .

104. Japan and U.S., Security Treaty, 8 September 1951

. . . ARTICLE I. Japan grants, and the United States of America accepts, the right, upon the coming into force of the Treaty of Peace and of this Treaty, to dispose United States land, air and sea forces in and about Japan. Such forces may be utilized to contribute to the maintenance of international peace and security in the Far East and to the security of Japan against armed attack from without, including assistance given at the express request of the Japanese Government to put down large-scale internal riots and disturbances in Japan, caused through instigation or intervention by an outside power or powers.

Article II. During the exercise of the right referred to in Article I, Japan will not grant, without the prior consent of the United States of America, any bases or any rights, powers or authority whatsoever, in or relating to bases or the right of garrison or of maneuver, or transit of ground, air or naval forces to any third power.

Article III. The conditions which shall govern the disposition of armed forces of the United States of America in and about Japan shall be determined by administrative agreements between the two Governments.

Article IV. This Treaty shall expire whenever in the opinion of the Governments of the United States of America and Japan there shall have come into force such United Nations arrangements or such alternative individual or collective security dispositions as will satisfactorily provide for the maintenance by the United Nations or otherwise of international peace and security in the Japan Area. . . .

105. U.N. Security Council on North Korea's Invasion of South Korea, 25 June 1950

THE SECURITY COUNCIL

Recalling the finding of the General Assembly in its resolution of 21 October 1949 that the Government of the Republic of Korea is a lawfully established government "having effective control and jurisdiction over that part of Korea where the United Nations Temporary Commission on Korea was able to observe and consult and in which the great majority of the people of Korea reside; and that this Government is based on elections which were a valid expression of the free will of the electorate of that part of Korea and which were observed by the Temporary Commission; and that this is the only such Government in Korea"; . . .

Noting with grave concern the armed attack upon the Republic of Korea by forces from North Korea,

Determines that this action constitutes a breach of the peace,

I. Calls for the immediate cessation of hostilities; and
Calls upon the authorities of North Korea to withdraw forthwith their armed forces to the thirty-eighth parallel;

II. Requests the United Nations Commission on Korea
   (a) To communicate its fully considered recommendations on the situation with the least possible delay;
   (b) To observe the withdrawal of the North Korean forces to the thirty-eighth parallel; and
   (c) To keep the Security Council informed on the execution of this resolution;

III. Calls upon all Members to render every assistance to the United Nations in the execution of this resolution and to refrain from giving assistance to the North Korean authorities.

106. U.N. Security Council on North Korea's Invasion of South Korea, 27 June 1950

THE SECURITY COUNCIL,

Having determined that the armed attack upon the Republic of Korea by forces from North Korea constitutes a breach of the peace,

Having called for an immediate cessation of hostilities, and

Having called upon the authorities of North Korea to withdraw forthwith their armed forces to the 38th parallel, and

Having noted from the report of the United Nations Commission for Korea that the authorities in North Korea have neither ceased hostilities nor withdrawn their armed forces to the 38th parallel and that urgent military measures are required to restore international peace and security, and

Having noted the appeal from the Republic of Korea to the United Nations for immediate and effective steps to secure peace and security,

Recommends that the Members of the United Nations furnish such assistance to the Republic of Korea as may be necessary to repel the armed attack and to restore international peace and security in the area.

107. Truman on Taiwan (Republic of China), 27 June 1950

IN KOREA the Government forces, which were armed to prevent border raids and to preserve internal security, were attacked by invading forces from North Korea. The Security Council of the United Nations called upon the invading troops to cease hostilities and to withdraw to the 38th parallel. This they have not done, but on the contrary have pressed the attack. The Security Council called upon all members of the United Nations to render every assistance to the United Nations in the execution of this resolution. In these circumstances I have ordered United States air and sea forces to give the Korean Government troops cover and support.

The attack upon Korea makes it plain beyond all doubt that Communism has passed beyond the use of subversion to conquer independent nations and will now use armed invasion and war. It has defied the orders of the Security Council of the United Nations issued to preserve international peace and security. In these circumstances the occupation of Formosa by Communist forces would be a direct threat to the security of the Pacific area and to United States forces performing their lawful and necessary functions in that area.

Accordingly I have ordered the Seventh Fleet to prevent any attack on Formosa. As a corollary of this action I am calling upon the Chinese Government on Formosa to cease all air and sea operations against the mainland. The Seventh Fleet will see that this is done. The determination of the future status of Formosa must await the restoration of security in the Pacific, a peace settlement with Japan, or consideration by the United Nations.

I have also directed that United States Forces in the Philippines be strengthened and that military assistance to the Philippine Government be accelerated.

I have similarly directed acceleration in the furnishing of military assistance to the forces of France and the Associated States in Indo-China and the dispatch of a military mission to provide close working relations with those forces. . . .

108. U.N. General Assembly on Communist China (People's Republic of China) 1 February 1951

THE GENERAL ASSEMBLY, . . .

1. Finds that the Central People's Government of the People's Republic of China, by giving direct aid and assistance to those who were already committing aggression in Korea and by engaging in hostilities against United Nations forces there, has itself engaged in aggression in Korea;
2. Calls upon the Central People's Government of the People's Republic of China to cause its forces and nationals in Korea to cease hostilities against the United Nations forces and to withdraw from Korea;
3. Affirms the determination of the United Nations to continue its action in Korea to meet the aggression;
4. Calls upon all States and authorities to continue to lend every assistance to the United Nations action in Korea;
5. Calls upon all States and authorities to refrain from giving any assistance to the aggressors in Korea;
6. Requests a Committee composed of the members of the Collective Measures Committee as a matter of urgency to consider additional measures to be employed to meet this aggression and to report thereon to the General Assembly, it being understood that the Committee is authorized to defer its report if the Good Offices Committee referred to in the following paragraph reports satisfactory progress in its efforts;
7. Affirms that it continues to be the policy of the United Nations to bring about a cessation of hostilities in Korea and the achievement of United Nations objectives in Korea by peaceful means, and requests the President of the General Assembly to designate forthwith two persons who would meet with him at any suitable opportunity to use their good offices to this end.

109. Republican Senators on U.S. Far Eastern Policy, 17 August 1951

. . . ONE of the most singular aspects of the administration's far-eastern policy is illustrated by its acknowledgment of the dynamic character of revolution. As Secretary Acheson has pointed out on so many occasions, international communism is a movement which plans to overthrow existing governments by force and violence if necessary. While holding this point of view our State Department has continually acted as though, if appeasement went far enough, the Russians and their satellites would consent to dwell peacefully side by side with the "free world."

It does not require prolonged reflection upon the disastrous results of the administration's far-eastern policy to draw some conclusions as to what the United States must do. Fear of Russia is no basis for a foreign policy; what we must have is a positive program based upon confidence in our abilities and resources. . . .

It has been extremely difficult to determine the full extent of the secret commitments which the administration has made. These commitments are the basis for a large part of our present foreign policy. The agreements made at Cairo, Teheran, Yalta, Quebec, Potsdam, and elsewhere were largely international executive arrangements drawn without consideration of the treaty-making power of the United States Senate.

In the past the confirmation and implementation of international commitments has required the advice and consent of the Senate. Treaties were public documents, open to the inspection of any citizen.

Ten years of secrecy changed all this. Negotiations were affected by the precarious health of some who represented us; decisions were made by irresponsible people. Practices of this character confused our people and left them in ignorance of what had been undertaken in their name. These hearings broke through this wall of secrecy. For the first time in years a congressional committee has been able to force out enough information to piece together a coherent picture of a foreign situation, discouraging though the picture was. . . .

Despite the legalistic administration arguments to the contrary, the fact remains that for the first time in the history of our Nation, the constitutional authority of Congress to declare war has been bypassed.

Recognizing the unique nature of the collective-security action of the United Nations, it is nevertheless our opinion that the Korean War should not be allowed to establish a precedent.

It is true that there was popular approval for the intervention of United States forces in Korea. It is also true, however, that this approval was, in measure, based upon the logical assumption that proper military plans and estimates were in existence. It was further assumed by most people that we were in a state of readiness to carry out whatever military objectives were assigned to our Armed Forces by our administration leaders.

Consultation after commitment, as was the case in the Korean intervention, is not in accordance with American constitutional procedures. . . .

If a truce is negotiated, based upon the restoration of the status quo at the thirty-eighth parallel, the Communists will remain in control of the northern half of the country, and the objectives of the United Nations will not have been fulfilled. We should be on our guard against any Munichlike respites which are only surrenders in disguise and make the ultimate reckoning infinitely more costly.

The aggressor, of course, has suffered grave losses, but for that matter, so has the victim of the attack. Indeed, all of Korea is the loser; the land and its people have suffered irreparable harm.

Any peace short of the liberation and unification of Korea is a delusion. Any settlement at the thirty-eighth parallel is a Chinese Communist victory.

General MacArthur had driven the North Koreans to the Yalu and had victory within his grasp when this new and formidable enemy entered the field. To make a settlement south of the Yalu therefore is to admit the success of the Chinese aggressors.

The United States will be confronted with a staggering bill for relief and rehabilitation in Korea; the taxpayer will be paying for generations for the cost of the conflict; and our troops will be pinned down in South Korea indefinitely.

On the other hand, the North Koreans will be able to resume their aggression on any flimsy pretext at any convenient opportunity, and the Russians having utilized the entire conflict as a proving ground similar to Finland and Spain can precipitate war somewhere else in the world.

STYLES BRIDGES.
ALEXANDER WILEY.
H. ALEXANDER SMITH.
BOURKE B. HICKENLOOPER.
WILLIAM F. KNOWLAND.
HARRY P. CAIN.
OWEN BREWSTER.
RALPH E. FLANDERS.

110. Korean Armistice Agreement, 27 June 1953

. . . ARTICLE I. A military demarcation line shall be fixed and both sides shall withdraw two (2) kilometers from this line so as to establish a demilitarized zone between the opposing forces. A demilitarized zone shall be established as a buffer zone to prevent the occurrence of incidents which might lead to a resumption of hostilities. . . .

4. The military demarcation line shall be plainly marked as directed by the Military Armistice Commission hereinafter established. The Commanders of the opposing sides shall have suitable markers erected along the boundary between the demilitarized zone and their respective areas. The Military Armistice Commission shall supervise the erection of all markers placed along the military demarcation line and along the boundaries of the demilitarized zone. . . .

Article II

. . . 13. In order to insure the stability of the military armistice . . . the Commanders of the opposing sides shall:

(a) Within seventy-two (72) hours after this armistice agreement becomes effective, withdraw all of their military forces, supplies, and equipment from the demilitarized zone except as otherwise provided herein. . . .

(b) Within ten (10) days after this armistice agreement becomes effective, withdraw all of their military forces, supplies, and equipment from the rear and the coastal islands and waters of Korea of the other side. . . .

(c) Cease the introduction into Korea of reinforcing military personnel; . . .

(d) Cease the introduction into Korea of reinforcing combat aircraft, armored vehicles, weapons, and ammunition; . . .

19. A military Armistice Commission is hereby established. . . .

24. The general mission of the Military Armistice Commission shall be to supervise the implementation of this armistice agreement and to settle through negotiations any violations of this armistice agreement. . . .

28. The Military Armistice Commission, or the senior member of either side thereof, is authorized to request the Neutral Nations Supervisory Commission to conduct special observations and inspections at places outside the demilitarized zone where violations of this armistice agreement have been reported to have occurred.

29. When the Military Armistice Commission determines that a violation of this armistice agreement has occurred, it shall immediately report such violation to the Commanders of the opposing sides. . . .

36. A Neutral Nations Supervisory Commission is hereby established.

37. The Neutral Nations Supervisory Commission shall be composed of four (4) senior officers, two (2) of whom shall be appointed by neutral nations nominated by the Commander-in-Chief, United Nations Command, namely, SWEDEN and SWITZERLAND, and two (2) of whom shall be appointed by neutral nations nominated jointly by the Supreme Commander of the Korean People's Army and the Commander of the Chinese People's Volunteers, namely, POLAND and CZECHOSLOVAKIA. . . .

41. The mission of the Neutral Nations Supervisory Commission shall be to carry out the functions of supervision, observation, inspection, and investigation, as stipulated in sub-paragraphs 13(c) and 13(d) and paragraph 28 hereof, and to report the results of such supervision, observation, inspection, and investigation to the Military Armistice Commission. . . .

Article III

51. . . . (a) Within sixty (60) days after this armistice agreement becomes effective each side shall, without offering any hindrance, directly repatriate and hand over in groups all those prisoners of war in its custody who insist on repatriation to the side to which they belonged at the time of capture. . . .

(b) Each side shall release all those remaining prisoners of war, who are not directly repatriated, from its military control and from its custody and hand them over to the Neutral Nations Repatriation Commission for disposition in accordance with the provisions in the annex hereto: "Terms of Reference for Neutral Nations Repatriation Commission." . . .

111. Wadsworth on China (People's Republic of China), 1 October 1960

(A) STATEMENT OF AMBASSADOR JAMES J. WADSWORTH TO THE GENERAL ASSEMBLY OF THE UNITED NATIONS, OCTOBER 1, 1960 [7]

MR. PRESIDENT,

The General Assembly has before it a draft resolution recommended by the General Committee which reads as follows:

"*The General Assembly*

"1. *Decides* to reject the request of the Union of Soviet Socialist Republics for the inclusion in the agenda of its fifteenth regular session of the item entitled 'Representation of China in the United Nations';

"2. *Decides* not to consider, at its fifteenth regular session, any proposals to exclude the representatives of the Government of the Republic of China or to seat representatives of the Central People's Government of the People's Republic of China."

The effect of the General Assembly's adoption of this recommendation will be that without further debate at this session the proposal to expel the Republic of China from this Organization and to seat in its place the People's Republic of China will once again be rejected, as it has been rejected every year since 1951. In the General Committee [129th meeting] I briefly stated the reasons for my delegation's strong opposition to the Soviet proposal. Now, before the entire membership of this great body, I should like to set forth our reasoning in more detail. . . .

In Korea, in the fall of 1950, when the United Nations forces had almost finished beating back the aggressor army of communist North Korea, one million Chinese communist troops poured into Korea to renew the aggression. For this, in February 1951, Communist China was condemned by a resolution of the General Assembly which remains valid to this day.

After two years of bitter war against the United Nations, an armistice was achieved in 1953. The Chinese Communists violated the armistice by callously refusing to account for thousands of prisoners of war in their hands, which they have never done to this day, and by illegally reinforcing their military forces in North Korea. They sabotaged the inspection system set up under the Armistice Agreement to prevent such violations, and to this day the only terms on which they have expressed willingness to see the Korean nation unified are such as to guarantee that the entire nation would be rendered helpless against their pressure and would fall into communist hands.

Throughout these years they have drummed into the minds of the helpless captive Chinese people the myth that the United States was the aggressor in Korea, and that the United Nations action here was part of a United States plot to strangle the new China in its cradle.

In the Taiwan Strait, Communist China has been using armed forces intermittently since 1950 as part of its violent campaign to seize Taiwan and the Pescadores, and thus to destroy the Republic of China. Twice, in 1955 and again in 1958, its acts of violence and threats against Taiwan reached such a pitch as to bring the spectre of general war to the Western Pacific; and to this day it continues its capricious and wanton bombardment of the off-shore islands, the only organized shooting that is going on in the world today.

Since 1955 the United States has sought, in over 100 ambassadorial meetings with representatives of Communist China, to work out an agreement by which neither side would use force in the Taiwan Strait. They have stubbornly refused to make any such agreement.

In South-East Asia also Communist China's record is one of aggressive pressure. They began in February 1950 by calling on all the peoples of South-East Asia to overthrow their Governments. For many years they gave material support and propaganda encouragement to communist guerrillas who were trying to overthrow the Governments of the Philippines and Malaya.

In North Viet-Nam, a communist State which owes its existence in great measure to the Chinese Communists, they have helped the regime to enlarge its army greatly both in troop strength and in weapons; all of this in violation of the armistice terms applying to that area.

The outrages of this regime in Tibet are well known. As early as February 1950, within months after their accession to power, they sent an army to subdue the traditional self-governing mountain kingdom of Tibet. In 1959 they tightened their control by summarily dissolving the Tibetan Government and establishing a so-called Tibetan autonomous region, which of course has no autonomy at all. This is colonial despotism. Thousands of Tibetans were massacred. The Dalai Lama, the spiritual and temporal leader of Tibet, was driven into asylum abroad, and the war against the Tibetans has continued through 1960, with frequent reports of heavy fighting. Communist troops from China have even violated international frontiers in their efforts to hunt down Tibetans trying to escape with their lives. This matter is so serious that the General Assembly will debate it this fall for the second year in succession.

In the past year the Chinese Communists have moved beyond Tibet and have made military incursions into the territory of the sovereign nations of South Asia. Prime Minister Nehru has described these incursions bluntly as aggression. Official maps issued by Communist China show as Chinese large areas long regarded by other States as their own territory. Characteristically, while conducting these aggressive moves, the Chinese Communists make loud charges of aggression against the very States which they offend. Thus, all along the borders between Communist China and non-Communist Asia there is trouble and discord. From Korea, South and West along the 6,000-mile arc that ends in the Himalayas, we find a history of Chinese Communist complicity, military aggression, subversion and outright seizure of territory....

Throughout the ten years of Communist China's violent career these actions have been accompanied by an official campaign of hate, hate propaganda against foreign Governments and against peoples which, in its massiveness and its viciousness must be unequalled in the history of the world.

The chief target of this abuse has been the United States....

Such then is the actual record of behaviour in the Chinese Communist régime which the Soviet Union proposes for admission to the United Nations....

Let it be remembered that what is proposed here is not only that the United Nations should seat the Chinese Communists, but that, in order to make room for them, the United Nations should, in effect, expel the Republic of China. That is a fate which the Charter, in Article 6, reserves exclusively for Members which have "persistently violated the Principles contained in the present Charter...." The Republic of China, through all the difficulties it has suffered, remains to this day the true repository of the ancient culture and genius of the Chinese people. It has never violated the United Nations Charter. It has fulfilled its obligations as a Member of the United Nations. It has never incurred the censure of this Organization. It has faithfully contributed its efforts and its vision to our work....

And, finally, it is sometimes argued that refusal to seat the Peiping régime in the United Nations denies representation in this world body to 600 million mainland Chinese. In view of the long record of aggressions and threats of war by the Peiping régime, this argument would have no validity under the Charter even if it were true. But the truth is that the rulers of Peiping do not represent the Chinese people. The Peiping régime was imposed by military force, and in ten years it has carried out political purges which have brought death to some 18 million Chinese people; and within the past two years, as all of you know, it has imposed the commune system, which is slave labour in all but name—and that system has been imposed upon 120 million families. Surely no government which represents its people has to resort to wholesale murder and mass slavery to keep itself in power.

I conclude. It is tragically true that the mainland of China today is, to a great extent, isolated from the rest of the world. But it is not we who have isolated it. The communist rulers of China have isolated themselves and some 600 million Chinese people into the bargain, from the standpoint of the world Organization, by a wall of fanatical hatred and violence against all those whom they cannot dominate. Their behaviour is the antithesis of everything for which the United Nations stands. To admit them here would be to stultify our Organization and to subject it to a stunning blow at the very moment when it faces new and historic tasks for the sake of freedom and peace....

(B) CONGRESSIONAL OPPOSITION TO THE SEATING OF COMMUNIST CHINA IN THE UNITED NATIONS [8]

SEC. 105. The Congress hereby reiterates its opposition to the seating in the United Nations of the Communist China regime as the representative of China, and it is hereby declared to be the continuing sense of the Congress that the Communist regime in China has not demonstrated its willingness to fulfill the obligations contained in the Charter of the United Nations and should not be recognized to represent China in the United Nations. In the event of the seating of representatives of the Chinese Communist regime in the Security Council or General Assembly of the United Nations, the President is requested to inform the Congress insofar as is compatible with the requirements of national security, of the implications of this action upon the foreign policy of the United States and our foreign relationships, including that created by membership in the United Nations, together with any recommendations which he may have with respect to the matter.

112. Katzenbach on China (People's Republic of China), 21 May 1968

Speech of Under Secretary of State Nicholas D. Katzenbach.

The evolution of our policy toward both mainland China and the Government of the Republic of China on Taiwan has been spelled out often. But misconceptions and misunderstandings persist. I shall attempt to sort out a few of them and perhaps dispel some of the gray areas around the periphery.

We have, of course, followed with great interest the developments going on on the mainland in recent years. Many of these, and especially the ones coming under the heading of Mao Tsetung's curiously misnamed "Cultural Revolution," have been fully reported by the press. We have, in general, refrained from commenting on these events, but I can summarize for you what we believe the situation there to be.

The Cultural Revolution, conceived by Mao as a means of eliminating individuals and viewpoints which deviated from the straight and true path he wanted China to follow, has now been raging for over 2 years. In that time hundreds of thousands, and perhaps even millions, of Communist Party and government officials and ordinary Chinese have come under criticism. Schools have been closed or disrupted. Key political, economic, and military officials have been dismissed. There has been intense political upheaval with major sectors of the economy and government thrown into confusion.

Since the major target of the Cultural Revolution was the organizational leadership of the Chinese Communist Party itself, the movement has had to rely primarily on *ad hoc* mass organizations of students or workers such as the famed Red Guards. At their worst these have spread terror and chaos. At a minimum they have created a vast disorganization throughout the country. By the middle of last year the leaders in Peking began to be alarmed by the degree to which the life of the country had been disrupted. They attempted to stem the violence and factionalism, which by this time had grown to enormous proportions, particularly in the cities.

· · · ·

We have followed Communist China's foreign policy closely ever since the Communist government came to power in 1949. Although right from the beginning we made efforts to maintain contacts and avoid hostile relations, the Communist authorities left little doubt that they wanted to eliminate any American representation from the Chinese mainland and to pursue a politically hostile policy toward this country.

Even after North Korea's invasion of the South in 1950 the United States avoided rigid restrictions on contact and trade with the Chinese mainland. Only after the massive Chinese intervention in Korea late in the fall of 1950 did we put such restrictions into effect.

For a brief period beginning in 1954 Peking attempted to improve its international image. It was during this period that it agreed to ambassadorial contacts with the United States. The original purpose of these meetings was to secure the release and exchange of Americans and Chinese who wanted to return home. An understanding was reached on the subject in September 1955; and we anticipated that it would, in the language of the public announcement,[2] be "expeditiously" implemented.

But the Chinese suddenly changed their posture. Developments on the question, they said, were contingent on U.S. action on a wide range of other issues. One demand was that we abandon our commitment to the defense of Taiwan, which was not then and is not now open to negotiation. Some of the issues they raised, such as the exchange of journalists and related questions of travel and exchange, I think we might have pursued more energetically. Further progress might possibly have been achieved at that time. Still, in view of Peking's failure to follow through on the earlier commitment, skepticism about their good faith was understandable

· · · ·

It is often argued that we are isolating Peking from the international community by opposing its participation in the United Nations and other international groups and by discouraging other states from establishing diplomatic relations or conducting trade with it.

But once again, it is not the attitude of the United States but that of the People's Republic of China which isolates it. The United States, influential though it may be, does not control and govern the organs of the United Nations or of other international bodies.

The Government of the United States cannot accept Peking's demand for participation in international organizations to the exclusion of the Republic of China. This view is shared by a majority of the members of the United Nations.

Under present circumstances, Communist China's participation in the Security Council, particularly, would weaken that body's ability to deal constructively with international problems.

The Chinese mistreatment of diplomats and diplomatic missions in Peking since 1967, including the entry or sacking of several embassies, and the highly undiplomatic activities of many of Peking's own officials abroad have hardly helped its cause in the international community.

Peking has declined to participate even in totally nonpolitical international activities, such as the International Geophysical Year. It rarely permits its scientists to attend even those international scientific meetings in which national membership is not a factor.

The Chinese have quarreled even with fellow Communist nations, with consequences for international Communist unity that are familiar to you. They have withdrawn from most of the organizations which formerly were known under the general label of the "world peace movement" and attempted either to set up rival organizations or disrupt already existing ones.

The United States would welcome a change in Peking's position which might indicate a shift in its attitude on the general conduct of international affairs. Few signs of any shift are discernible. Under these circumstances, any isolation which Peking senses is of its own choosing. · · · ·

113. U.N. Recognition of the People's Republic of China, 22 September 1971

The General Assembly,

Recalling the provisions of the Charter,

Decides that any proposal in the General Assembly which would result in depriving the Republic of China of representation in the United Nations is an Important Question under Article 18 of the Charter.

The General Assembly,

Having considered the item entitled "The Representation of China in the United Nations,"

Noting that since the founding of the United Nations, fundamental changes have occurred in China,

Having regard for the existing factual situation,

Noting that the Republic of China has been continuously represented as a member of the United Nations since 1945,

Believing that the People's Republic of China should be represented in the United Nations,

Recalling that Article 1, Paragraph 4, of the Charter of the United Nations establishes the United Nations as a center for harmonizing the actions of nations,

Believing that an equitable resolution of this problem should be sought in the light of the above-mentioned considerations and without prejudice to the eventual settlement of the conflicting claims involved,

1. *Hereby affirms* the right of representation of the People's Republic of China and recommends that it be seated as one of the five permanent members of the Security Council;

2. *Affirms* the continued right of representation of the Republic of China;

3. *Recommends* that all UN bodies and the Specialized Agencies take into account the provisions of this resolution in deciding the question of Chinese Representation.

114. Nixon's Visit to China, 21-28 February 1972

TEXT OF JOINT COMMUNIQUE, ISSUED AT SHANGHAI, FEBRUARY 27

President Richard Nixon of the United States of America visited the People's Republic of China at the invitation of Premier Chou En-lai of the People's Republic of China from February 21 to February 28, 1972. Accompanying the President were Mrs. Nixon, U.S. Secretary of State William Rogers, Assistant to the President Dr. Henry Kissinger, and other American officials.

. . . . the two sides stated that:

—progress toward the normalization of relations between China and the United States is in the interests of all countries;

—both wish to reduce the danger of international military conflict;

—neither should seek hegemony in the Asia-Pacific region and each is opposed to efforts by any other country or group of countries to establish such hegemony; and

—neither is prepared to negotiate on behalf of any third party or to enter into agreements or understandings with the other directed at other states.

Both sides are of the view that it would be against the interests of the peoples of the world for any major country to collude with another against other countries, or for major countries to divide up the world into spheres of interest.

The two sides reviewed the long-standing serious disputes between China and the United States. The Chinese side reaffirmed its position: The Taiwan question is the crucial question obstructing the normalization of relations between China and the United States; the Government of the People's Republic of China is the sole legal government of China; Taiwan is a province of China which has long been returned to the motherland; the liberation of Taiwan is China's internal affair in which no other country has the right to interfere; and all U.S. forces and military installations must be withdrawn from Taiwan. The Chinese Government firmly opposes any activities which aim at the creation of "one China, one Taiwan," "one China, two governments," "two Chinas," and "independent Taiwan" or advocate that "the status of Taiwan remains to be determined."

The U.S. side declared: The United States acknowledges that all Chinese on either side of the Taiwan Strait maintain there is but one China and that Taiwan is a part of China. The United States Government does not challenge that position. It reaffirms its interest in a peaceful settlement of the Taiwan question by the Chinese themselves. With this prospect in mind, it affirms the ultimate objective of the withdrawal of all U.S. forces and military installations from Taiwan. In the meantime, it will progressively reduce its forces and military installations on Taiwan as the tension in the area diminishes.

The two sides agreed that it is desirable to broaden the understanding between the two peoples. To this end, they discussed specific areas in such fields as science, technology, culture, sports and journalism, in which people-to-people contacts and exchanges would be mutually beneficial. Each side undertakes to facilitate the further development of such contacts and exchanges.

Both sides view bilateral trade as another area from which mutual benefit can be derived, and agreed that economic relations based on equality and mutual benefit are in the interest of the peoples of the two countries. They agree to facilitate the progressive development of trade between their two countries.

The two sides agreed that they will stay in contact through various channels, including the sending of a senior U.S. representative to Peking from time to time for concrete consultations to further the normalization of relations between the two countries and continue to exchange views on issues of common interest.

The two sides expressed the hope that the gains achieved during this visit would open up new prospects for the relations between the two countries. They believe that the normalization of relations between the two countries is not only in the interest of the Chinese and American peoples but also contributes to the relaxation of tension in Asia and the world. . . . .

115. U.S. Recognition of the People's Republic of China, 15 December 1978

JOINT COMMUNIQUE, DEC. 15

JOINT COMMUNIQUE ON THE ESTABLISHMENT OF DIPLOMATIC RELATIONS BETWEEN THE UNITED STATES OF AMERICA AND THE PEOPLE'S REPUBLIC OF CHINA JANUARY 1, 1979

The United States of America and the People's Republic of China have agreed to recognize each other and to establish diplomatic relations as of January 1, 1979.

The United States of America recognizes the Government of the People's Republic of China as the sole legal Government of China. Within this context, the people of the United States will maintain cultural, commercial, and other unofficial relations with the people of Taiwan.

The United States of America and the People's Republic of China reaffirm the principles agreed on by the two sides in the Shanghai Communique and emphasize once again that:

- Both wish to reduce the danger of international military conflict.
- Neither should seek hegemony in the Asia-Pacific region or in any other region of the world and each is opposed to efforts by any other country or group of countries to establish such hegemony.
- Neither is prepared to negotiate on behalf of any third party or to enter into agreements or understandings with the other directed at other states.
- The Government of the United States of America acknowledges the Chinese position that there is but one China and Taiwan is part of China.
- Both believe that normalization of Sino-American relations is not only in the interest of the Chinese and American peoples but also contributes to the cause of peace in Asia and the world.

The United States of America and the People's Republic of China will exchange Ambassadors and establish Embassies on March 1, 1979.

116. Eisenhower on U.S. Indochinese Policy, 21 July 1954

I AM GLAD, of course, that agreement has been reached at Geneva to stop the bloodshed in Indochina.

The United States has not been a belligerent in the war. The primary responsibility for the settlement in Indochina rested with those nations which participated in the fighting. Our role at Geneva has been at all times to try to be helpful where desired and to aid France and Cambodia, Laos, and Viet-Nam to obtain a just and honorable settlement which will take into account the needs of the interested people. Accordingly, the United States has not itself been party to or bound by the decisions taken by the Conference, but it is our hope that it will lead to the establishment of peace consistent with the rights and the needs of the countries concerned. The agreement contains features which we do not like, but a great deal depends on how they work in practice.

The United States is issuing at Geneva a statement to the effect that it is not prepared to join in the Conference declarations, but, as loyal members of the United Nations, we also say that, in compliance with the obligations and principles contained in Article 2 of the United Nations Charter, the United States will not use force to disturb the settlement. We also say that any renewal of Communist aggression would be viewed by us as a matter of grave concern.

As evidence of our resolve to assist Cambodia and Laos to play their part, in full independence and sovereignty, in the peaceful community of free nations, we are requesting agreement of the Governments of Cambodia and Laos to our appointment of an Ambassador or Minister to be resident at their respective capitals (Phnom Penh and Vientiane)....

117. Southeast Asia Collective Defense Treaty (SEATO), 8 September 1954

Signed at Manila by U.S., Great Britain, France, Australia, New Zealand, Pakistan, the Philippines, and Thailand.

... ARTICLE II. In order more effectively to achieve the objectives of this Treaty, the Parties, separately and jointly, by means of continuous and effective self-help and mutual aid will maintain and develop their individual and collective capacity to resist armed attack and to prevent and counter subversive activities directed from without against their territorial integrity and political stability.

Article III. The Parties undertake to strengthen their free institutions and to cooperate with one another in the further development of economic measures, including technical assistance, designed both to promote economic progress and social well-being and to further the individual and collective efforts of governments toward these ends.

Article IV. (1) Each Party recognizes that aggression by means of armed attack in the treaty area against any of the Parties or against any State or territory which the Parties by unanimous agreement may hereafter designate, would endanger its own peace and safety, and agrees that it will in that event act to meet the common danger in accordance with its constitutional processes. Measures taken under this paragraph shall be immediately reported to the Security Council of the United Nations.

(2) If, in the opinion of any of the Parties, the inviolability or the integrity of the territory or the sovereignty or political independence of any Party in the treaty area or of any other State or territory to which the provisions of paragraph 1 of this Article from time to time apply is threatened in any way other than by armed attack or is affected or threatened by any fact or situation which might endanger the peace of the area, the Parties shall consult immediately in order to agree on the measures which should be taken for the common defense.

(3) It is understood that no action on the territory of any State desig-

nated by unanimous agreement under paragraph 1 of this Article or on any territory so designated shall be taken except at the invitation or with the consent of the government concerned.

Article V. The Parties hereby establish a Council, on which each of them shall be represented, to consider matters concerning the implementation of this Treaty. The Council shall provide for consultation with regard to military and any other planning as the situation obtaining in the treaty area may from time to time require. The Council shall be so organized as to be able to meet at any time. . . .

Article VII. Any other State in a position to further the objectives of this Treaty and to contribute to the security of the area may, by unanimous agreement of the Parties, be invited to accede to this Treaty. . . .

Article VIII. As used in this Treaty, the "treaty area" is the general area of Southeast Asia, including also the entire territories of the Asian Parties, and the general area of the Southwest Pacific not including the Pacific area north of 21 degrees 30 minutes north latitude. The Parties may, by unanimous agreement, amend this Article to include within the treaty area the territory of any State acceding to this Treaty in accordance with Article VII or otherwise to change the treaty area. . . .

Article X. This Treaty shall remain in force indefinitely, but any Party may cease to be a Party one year after its notice of denunciation has been given to the Government of the Republic of the Philippines, which shall inform the Governments of the other Parties of the deposit of each notice of denunciation. . . .

Understanding of the United States of America

The United States of America in executing the present Treaty does so with the understanding that its recognition of the effect of aggression and armed attack and its agreement with reference thereto in Article IV, paragraph 1, apply only to communist aggression but affirms that in the event of other aggression or armed attack it will consult under the provisions of Article IV, paragraph 2.

Protocol to the Southeast Asia Collective Defense Treaty

Designation of States and territory as to which provisions of Article IV and Article III are to be applicable:

The Parties to the Southeast Asia Collective Defense Treaty unanimously designate for the purposes of Article IV of the Treaty the States of Cambodia and Laos and the free territory under the jurisdiction of the State of Vietnam.

The Parties further agree that the above mentioned states and territory shall be eligible in respect of the economic measures contemplated by Article III.

This Protocol shall enter into force simultaneously with the coming into force of the Treaty.

118. Taiwan (Republic of China) and U.S., Mutual Defense Treaty, 2 December 1954

(A) TEXT OF THE TREATY [3]

. . . ARTICLE II. In order more effectively to achieve the objective of this Treaty, the Parties separately and jointly by self-help and mutual aid will maintain and develop their individual and collective capacity to resist armed attack and communist subversive activities directed from without against their territorial integrity and political stability. . . .

Article V. Each Party recognizes that an armed attack in the West Pacific Area directed against the territories of either of the Parties would be dangerous to its own peace and safety and declares that it would act to meet the common danger in accordance with its constitutional processes.

Any such armed attack and all measures taken as a result thereof shall be immediately reported to the Security Council of the United Nations. Such measures shall be terminated when the Security Council has taken the measures necessary to restore and maintain international peace and security.

Article VI. For the purposes of Articles II and V, the terms "territorial" and "territories" shall mean in respect of the Republic of China, Taiwan and the Pescadores; and in respect of the United States of America the island territories in the West Pacific under its jurisdiction. The provisions of Articles II and V will be applicable to such other territories as may be determined by mutual agreement.

Article VII. The Government of the Republic of China grants, and the Government of the United States of America accepts, the right to dispose such United States land, air and sea forces in and about Taiwan and the Pescadores as may be required for their defense, as determined by mutual agreement. . . .

Article X. This Treaty shall remain in force indefinitely. Either Party may terminate it one year after notice has been given to the other Party. . . .

(B) INTERPRETATION OF THE TREATY BY THE COMMITTEE ON FOREIGN RELATIONS OF THE SENATE, FEBRUARY 8, 1955 [4]

(*With reference to Article V of the Treaty:*)

It is the understanding of the Senate that the obligations of the parties under Article V apply only in the event of external armed attacks; and that military operations by either party from the territories held by the Republic of China, shall not be undertaken except by joint agreement.

(*With reference to Article VI:*)

It is the understanding of the Senate that the "mutual agreement" referred to in Article VI, under which the provisions of Articles II and V may be made applicable to other territories, shall be construed as requiring the advice and consent of the Senate of the United States.

(*With reference to the status of Formosa and the Pescadores:*)

It is the understanding of the Senate that nothing in the treaty shall be construed as affecting or modifying the legal status or sovereignty of the territories to which it applies.

(C) JOINT [CONGRESSIONAL] RESOLUTION ON THE DEFENSE OF FORMOSA [5]

... Resolved by the Senate and House of Representatives of the United States of America in Congress assembled, That the President of the United States be and he hereby is authorized to employ the Armed Forces of the United States as he deems necessary for the specific purpose of securing and protecting Formosa and the Pescadores against armed attack, this authority to include the securing and protection of such related positions and territories of that area now in friendly hands and the taking of such other measures as he judges to be required or appropriate in assuring the defense of Formosa and the Pescadores.

This resolution shall expire when the President shall determine that the peace and security of the area is reasonably assured by international conditions created by action of the United Nations or otherwise, and shall so report to the Congress.

119. Johnson on Aid to Vietnam, 31 December 1963

Letter of President Lyndon B. Johnson.

DEAR GENERAL MINH: As we enter the New Year of 1964, I want to wish you, your Revolutionary Government, and your people full success in the long and arduous war which you are waging so tenaciously and bravely against the Viet Cong forces directed and supported by the Communist regime in Hanoi. . . .

This new year provides a fitting opportunity for me to pledge on behalf of the American Government and people a renewed partnership with your government and people in your brave struggle for freedom. The United States will continue to furnish you and your people with the fullest measure of support in this bitter fight. We shall maintain in Viet-Nam American personnel and material as needed to assist you in achieving victory.

Our aims are, I know, identical with yours: to enable your government to protect its people from the acts of terror perpetrated by Communist insurgents from the north. As the forces of your government become increasingly capable of dealing with this aggression, American military personnel in South Viet-Nam can be progressively withdrawn.

The United States Government shares the view of your government that "neutralization" of South Viet-Nam is unacceptable. As long as the Communist regime in North Viet-Nam persists in its aggressive policy, neutralization of South Viet-Nam would only be another name for a Communist takeover. Peace will return to your country just as soon as the authorities in Hanoi cease and desist from their terrorist aggression.

Thus, your government and mine are in complete agreement on the political aspects of your war against the forces of enslavement, brutality, and material misery. Within this framework of political agreement we can confidently continue and improve our cooperation. . . .

120. Tonkin Gulf Resolution, 7 August 1964

Joint Resolution of Congress.

To promote the maintenance of international peace and security in southeast Asia.

Whereas naval units of the Communist regime in Vietnam, in violation of the principles of the Charter of the United Nations and of international law, have deliberately and repeatedly attacked United States naval vessels lawfully present in international waters, and have thereby created a serious threat to international peace; and

Whereas these attacks are part of a deliberate and systematic campaign of aggression that the Communist regime in North Vietnam has been waging against its neighbors and the nations joined with them in the collective defense of their freedom; and

Whereas the United States is assisting the peoples of southeast Asia to protect their freedom and has no territorial, military or political ambitions in that area, but desires only that these peoples should be left in peace to work out their own destinies in their own way: Now, therefore, be it

Resolved by the Senate and House of Representatives of the United States of America in Congress assembled, That the Congress approves and supports the determination of the President, as Commander in Chief, to take all necessary measures to repel any armed attack against the forces of the United States and to prevent further aggression.

SEC. 2. The United States regards as vital to its national interest and to world peace the maintenance of international peace and security in southeast Asia. Consonant with the Constitution of the United States and the Charter of the United Nations and in accordance with its obligations under the Southeast Asia Collective Defense Treaty, the United States is, therefore, prepared, as the President determines, to take all necessary steps, including the use of armed force, to assist any member or protocol state of the Southeast Asia Collective Defense Treaty requesting assistance in defense of its freedom.

SEC. 3. This resolution shall expire when the President shall determine that the peace and security of the area is reasonably assured by international conditions created by action of the United Nations or otherwise, except that it may be terminated earlier by concurrent resolution of the Congress.

121. Johnson's Press Conference on the Tet Offensive in Vietnam, 2 February 1968

OPENING STATEMENT [1]

We have known for several months now that the Communists planned a massive winter-spring offensive. We have detailed information on Ho Chi Minh's order governing that offensive. Part of it is called a "general uprising."

We know the object was to overthrow the constitutional government in Saigon and to create a situation in which we and the Vietnamese would be willing to accept a Communist-dominated coalition government.

Another part of that offensive was planned as a massive attack across the frontiers of South Viet-Nam by North Vietnamese units. We have already seen the general uprising.

General Westmoreland's [Gen. William C. Westmoreland, Commander, U.S. Military Assistance Command, Viet-Nam] headquarters report the Communists appear to have lost over 10,000 men killed and some 2,300 detained. The United States has lost 249 men killed. The Vietnamese, who had to carry the brunt of the fighting in the cities, lost 553 killed, as of my most recent report from the Westmoreland headquarters.

There were also a number of attacks on United States airfields throughout the country. We have confirmed the loss of 15 fixed-wing aircraft, and 23 helicopters were destroyed. A good many more were damaged but will be returned to service. . . .

The biggest fact is that the stated purposes of the general uprising have failed. Communist leaders counted on popular support in the cities for their effort. They found little or none. On the other hand, there have been civilian casualties and disruption of public services. Just before I came into the room, I read a long cable from Ambassador Bunker [American Ambassador to the Republic of Viet-Nam Ellsworth Bunker] which described the vigor with which the Vietnamese Government and our own people are working together to deal with the problems of restoring civilian services and order in all of the cities. . . .

QUESTIONS AND ANSWERS

Q. Mr. President, in your state of the Union message, you said we were exploring certain so-called offers from Hanoi and as soon as you could you would report to the people on that. Is there anything you can tell us today about the status of possible peace negotiations with them?

The President: No. I would think that that statement is about as good as I could make on that general subject. That accurately describes what has been going on and what is going on. I do not have any success or results to report on it.

Q. Mr. President, does this present rampage in South Viet-Nam give you any reason to change any assessment that you have made previously about the situation in South Viet-Nam?

The President: I am sure that we will make adjustments to what we are doing there.

Insofar as changing our basic strategy, the answer would be "No." I think that there will be changes made here and there as a result of experience that comes from efforts such as they have made. Our best experts think that they had two purposes in mind.

First was a military success. That has been a complete failure. That is not to say that they have not disrupted services. It is just like when we have a riot in a town or when we have a very serious strike or bridges go out or lights—power failures and things. They have disrupted services. A few bandits can do that in any city in the land.

Obviously, they have in the Viet Cong hundreds and thousands; so it is nothing unexpected to anticipate that they will try in cooperation with their friends from the North to coordinate their activities.

The ferocity and the violence, the lack of—the deception and the lack of concern for the basic elements that appeal to human beings—they may have shocked a lot of people in that respect.

The ability to do what they have done has been anticipated, prepared for, and met. Now, so much for the military movements. This is not just a civilian judgment. This is the judgment of the military men in the field, for whatever

122. Nixon's Speech on U.S. Invasion of Cambodia, 30 April 1970

that judgment is worth to us back here as expert Monday morning quarterbacks.

That is the judgment of the best military advice I have here. I met with them yesterday at lunch at some length. I had General [Matthew B.] Ridgway come down and spend some time with me and talked to him.

I have spent a good deal of time talking to General [Maxwell D.] Taylor. I had all of the Joint Chiefs of Staff in yesterday. We explored and discussed what had happened, what was happening, what might happen, and so forth.

I have talked to the Pentagon this morning, very early, and have been in touch with Secretary McNamara before his testimony.

Their general conclusion is that as a military movement it has been a failure.

Their second objective, obviously, from the—what you can see from not only Viet-Nam but from other Communist capitals, even from some unknowing people here at home, is a psychological victory.

We have to realize that in moments of tenseness and trial, as we will have today and as we had in the past days, that there will be a great effort to exploit that and let that substitute for military victory they have not achieved.

I do not believe when the American people know the facts, when the world knows the facts, and when the results are laid out for them to examine, I do not believe that they will achieve a psychological victory . . . .

Good evening, my fellow Americans. Ten days ago, in my report to the Nation on Viet-Nam, I announced a decision to withdraw an additional 150,000 Americans from Viet-Nam over the next year.[2] I said then that I was making that decision despite our concern over increased enemy activity in Laos, in Cambodia, and in South Viet-Nam.

At that time, I warned that if I concluded that increased enemy activity in any of these areas endangered the lives of Americans remaining in Viet-Nam, I would not hesitate to take strong and effective measures to deal with that situation.

Despite that warning, North Viet-Nam has increased its military aggression in all these areas, and particularly in Cambodia . . . .

the enemy in the past 2 weeks has stepped up his guerrilla actions, and he is concentrating his main forces in these sanctuaries that you see on this map, where they are building up to launch massive attacks on our forces and those of South Viet-Nam.

North Viet-Nam in the last 2 weeks has stripped away all pretense of respecting the sovereignty or the neutrality of Cambodia. Thousands of their soldiers are invading the country from the sanctuaries; they are encircling the Capital of Phnom Penh. Coming from these sanctuaries, as you see here, they have moved into Cambodia and are encircling the Capital . . . .

In cooperation with the armed forces of South Viet-Nam, attacks are being launched this week to clean out major enemy sanctuaries on the Cambodian–Viet-Nam border.

A major responsibility for the ground operations is being assumed by South Vietnamese forces. For example, the attacks in several areas, including the Parrot's Beak that I referred to a moment ago, are exclusively South Vietnamese ground operations under South Vietnamese command, with the United States providing air and logistical support.

There is one area, however, immediately above Parrot's Beak, where I have concluded that a combined American and South Vietnamese operation is necessary.

Tonight American and South Vietnamese units will attack the headquarters for the entire Communist military operation in South Viet-Nam. This key control center has been occupied by the North Vietnamese and Viet Cong for 5 years in blatant violation of Cambodia's neutrality . . . .

If, when the chips are down, the world's most powerful nation, the United States of America, acts like a pitiful, helpless giant, the forces of totalitarianism and anarchy will threaten free nations and free institutions throughout the world.

It is not our power but our will and character that is being tested tonight. The question all Americans must ask and answer tonight is this: Does the richest and strongest nation in the history of the world have the character to meet a direct challenge by a group which rejects every effort to win a just peace, ignores our warning, tramples on solemn agreements, violates the neutrality of an unarmed people, and uses our prisoners as hostages?

If we fail to meet this challenge, all other nations will be on notice that despite its overwhelming power the United States, when a real crisis comes, will be found wanting . . . .

123. Cease-fire in Vietnam, 23 January 1973

AGREEMENT ON ENDING THE WAR AND RESTORING PEACE IN VIETNAM

The Parties participating in the Paris Conference on Vietnam,

With a view to ending the war and restoring peace in Vietnam on the basis of respect for the Vietnamese people's fundamental national rights and the South Vietnamese people's right to self-determination, and to contributing to the consolidation of peace in Asia and the world,

Have agreed on the following provisions and undertake to respect and to implement them:

Chapter I
THE VIETNAMESE PEOPLE'S FUNDAMENTAL NATIONAL RIGHTS

Article 1

The United States and all other countries respect the independence, sovereignty, unity, and territorial integrity of Vietnam as recognized by the 1954 Geneva Agreements on Vietnam.

Chapter II
CESSATION OF HOSTILITIES—WITHDRAWAL OF TROOPS

Article 2

A cease-fire shall be observed throughout South Vietnam as of 2400 hours G.M.T., on January 27, 1973.

At the same hour, the United States will stop all its military activities against the territory of the Democratic Republic of Vietnam ....

Article 3

The parties undertake to maintain the cease-fire and to ensure a lasting and stable peace.

As soon as the cease-fire goes into effect:

(a) The United States forces and those of the other foreign countries allied with the United States and the Republic of Vietnam shall remain in-place pending the implementation of the plan of troop withdrawal. The Four-Party Joint Military Commission described in Article 16 shall determine the modalities.

(b) The armed forces of the two South Vietnamese parties shall remain in-place. The Two-Party Joint Military Commission described in Article 17 shall determine the areas controlled by each party and the modalities of stationing.

(c) The regular forces of all services and arms and the irregular forces of the parties in South Vietnam shall stop all offensive activities against each other and shall strictly abide by the following stipulations:

—All acts of force on the ground, in the air, and on the sea shall be prohibited;

—All hostile acts, terrorism and reprisals by both sides will be banned.

Article 4

The United States will not continue its military involvement or intervene in the internal affairs of South Vietnam.

Article 5

Within sixty days of the signing of this Agreement, there will be a total withdrawal from South Vietnam of troops, military advisers, and military personnel, including technical military personnel and military personnel associated with the pacification program, armaments, munitions, and war material of the United States and those of the other foreign countries mentioned in Article 3 (a). Advisers from the above-mentioned countries to all paramilitary organizations and the police force will also be withdrawn within the same period of time.

THE EXERCISE OF THE SOUTH VIETNAMESE PEOPLE'S RIGHT TO SELF-DETERMINATION

Article 9

The Government of the United States of America and the Government of the Democratic Republic of Vietnam undertake to respect the following principles for the exercise of the South Vietnamese people's right to self-determination:

(a) The South Vietnamese people's right to self-determination is sacred, inalienable, and shall be respected by all countries.

(b) The South Vietnamese people shall decide themselves the political future of South Vietnam through genuinely free and democratic general elections under international supervision.

(c) Foreign countries shall not impose any political tendency or personality on the South Vietnamese people. ....

Article 13

The question of Vietnamese armed forces in South Vietnam shall be settled by the two South Vietnamese parties in a spirit of national reconciliation and concord, equality and mutual respect, without foreign interference, in accordance with the postwar situation. Among the questions to be discussed by the two South Vietnamese parties are steps to reduce their military effectives and to demobilize the troops being reduced. The two South Vietnamese parties will accomplish this as soon as possible ....

REGARDING CAMBODIA AND LAOS

Article 20

(a) The parties participating in the Paris Conference on Vietnam shall strictly respect the 1954 Geneva Agreements on Cambodia and the 1962 Geneva Agreements on Laos, which recognized the Cambodian and the Lao peoples' fundamental national rights, i.e., the independence, sovereignty, unity, and territorial integrity of these countries. The parties shall respect the neutrality of Cambodia and Laos.

The parties participating in the Paris Conference on Vietnam undertake to refrain from using the territory of Cambodia and the territory of Laos to encroach on the sovereignty and security of one another and of other countries.

(b) Foreign countries shall put an end to all military activities in Cambodia and Laos, totally withdraw from and refrain from reintroducing into these two countries troops, military advisers and military personnel, armaments, munitions and war material.

(c) The internal affairs of Cambodia and Laos shall be settled by the people of each of these countries without foreign interference. ....

124. Congress' "War Powers" Resolution, 4 October 1973

SHORT TITLE

SECTION 1. This joint resolution may be cited as the "War Powers Resolution".

PURPOSE AND POLICY

SEC. 2. (a) It is the purpose of this joint resolution to fulfill the intent of the framers of the Constitution of the United States and insure that the collective judgment of both the Congress and the President will apply to the introduction of United States Armed Forces into hostilities, or into situations where imminent involvement in hostilities is clearly indicated by the circumstances, and to the continued use of such forces in hostilities or in such situations.

(b) Under article I, section 8, of the Constitution, it is specifically provided that the Congress shall have the power to make all laws necessary and proper for carrying into execution, not only its own powers but also all other powers vested by the Constitution in the Government of the United States, or in any department or officer thereof.

(c) The constitutional powers of the President as Commander-in-Chief to introduce United States Armed Forces into hostilities, or into situations where imminent involvement in hostilities is clearly indicated by the circumstances, are exercised only pursuant to (1) a declaration of war, (2) specific statutory authorization, or (3) a national emergency created by attack upon the United States, its territories or possessions, or its armed forces.

CONSULTATION

SEC. 3. The President in every possible instance shall consult with Congress before introducing United States Armed Forces into hostilities or into situations where imminent involvement in hostilities is clearly indicated by the circumstances, and after every such introduction shall consult regularly with the Congress until United States Armed Forces are no longer engaged in hostilities or have been removed from such situations.

REPORTING

SEC. 4. (a) In the absence of a declaration of war, in any case in which United States Armed Forces are introduced—

(1) into hostilities or into situations where imminent involvement in hostilities is clearly indicated by the circumstances;

(2) into the territory, airspace or waters of a foreign nation, while equipped for combat, except for deployments which relate solely to supply, replacement, repair, or training of such forces; or

(3) in numbers which substantially enlarge United States Armed Forces equipped for combat already located in a foreign nation;

the President shall submit within 48 hours to the Speaker of the House of Representatives and to the President pro tempore of the Senate a report, in writing, setting forth—

(A) the circumstances necessitating the introduction of United States Armed Forces;

(B) the constitutional and legislative authority under which such introduction took place; and

(C) the estimated scope and duration of the hostilities or involvement.

(b) The President shall provide such other information as the Congress may request in the fulfillment of its constitutional responsibilities with respect to committing the Nation to war and to the use of United States Armed Forces abroad.

(c) Whenever United States Armed Forces are introduced into hostilities or into any situation described in subsection (a) of this section, the President shall, so long as such armed forces continue to be engaged in such hostilities or situation, report to the Congress periodically on the status of such hostilities or situation as well as on the scope and duration of such hostilities or situation, but in no event shall he report to the Congress less often than once every six months.

CONGRESSIONAL ACTION

SEC. 5. (a) Each report submitted pursuant to section 4(a)(1) shall be transmitted to the Speaker of the House of Representatives and to the President pro tempore of the Senate on the same calendar day. Each report so transmitted shall be referred to the Committee on Foreign Affairs of the House of Representatives and to the Committee on Foreign Relations of the Senate for appropriate action. If, when the report is transmitted, the Congress has adjourned sine die or has adjourned for any period in excess of three calendar days, the Speaker of the House of Representatives and the President pro tempore of the Senate, if they deem it advisable (or if petitioned by at least 30 percent of the membership of their respective Houses) shall jointly request the President to convene Congress in order that it may consider the report and take appropriate action pursuant to this section.

(b) Within sixty calendar days after a report is submitted or is required to be submitted pursuant to section 4(a)(1), whichever is earlier, the President shall terminate any use of United States Armed Forces with respect to which such report was submitted (or required to be submitted), unless the Congress (1) has declared war or has enacted a specific authorization for such use of United States Armed Forces, (2) has extended by law such sixty-day period, or (3) is physically unable to meet as a result of an armed attack upon the United States. Such sixty-day period shall be extended for not more than an additional thirty days if the President determines and certifies to the Congress in writing that unavoidable military necessity respecting the safety of United States Armed Forces requires the continued use of such armed forces in the course of bringing about a prompt removal of such forces.

(c) Notwithstanding subsection (b), at any time that United States Armed Forces are engaged in hostilities outside the territory of the United States, its possessions and territories without a declaration of war or specific statutory authorization, such forces shall be removed by the President if Congress so directs by concurrent resolution.

125. Kissinger on the Fall of Vietnam, 29 April 1975

Secretary of State Henry A. Kissinger's Press Conference.

Secretary Kissinger: Ladies and Gentlemen, when the President spoke before the Congress [April 10], he stated as our objective the stabilization of the situation in Viet-Nam.

We made clear at that time, as well as before many congressional hearings, that our purpose was to bring about the most controlled and the most humane solution that was possible and that these objectives required the course which the President had set.

Our priorities were as follows: We sought to save the American lives still in Viet-Nam. We tried to rescue as many South Vietnamese that had worked with the United States for 15 years in reliance on our commitments as we possibly could. And we sought to bring about as humane an outcome as was achievable under the conditions that existed.

Over the past two weeks, the American personnel in Viet-Nam have been progressively reduced. Our objective was to reduce at a rate that was significant enough so that we would finally be able to evacuate rapidly but which would not produce a panic which might prevent anybody from getting out.

Our objective was also to fulfill the human obligation which we felt to the tens of thousands of South Vietnamese who had worked with us for over a decade.

Finally, we sought, through various intermediaries, to bring about as humane a political evolution as we could . . . .

Q. Mr. Secretary, what caused the breakdown of the intent which was spoken of earlier on the Hill to try to achieve a measure of self-determination for the people of South Viet-Nam, and what is your total assessment now of the effectiveness or the noneffectiveness of the whole Paris accord operation, which you said at the outset was intended to achieve peace with honor for the United States?

Secretary Kissinger: Until Sunday night we thought there was some considerable hope that the North Vietnamese would not seek a solution by purely military means, and when the transfer of power to General Minh took place—a person who had been designated by the other side as a counterpart worth talking to, they would be prepared to talk with—we thought a negotiated solution in the next few days was highly probable.

Sometime Sunday night the North Vietnamese obviously changed signals. Why that is, we do not yet know, nor do I exclude that now that the American presence is totally removed and very little military structure is left in South Viet-Nam, that there may not be a sort of a negotiation, but what produced this sudden shift to a military option or what would seem to us to be a sudden shift to a military option, I have not had sufficient opportunity to analyze.

As to the effectiveness of the Paris accords, I think it is important to remember the mood in this country at the time that the Paris accords were being negotiated. I think it is worth remembering that the principal criticism that was then made was that the terms we insisted on were too tough, not that the terms were too generous.

We wanted what was considered peace with honor, was that the United States would not end a war by overthrowing a government with which it had been associated. That still seems an objective that was correct.

There were several other assumptions that were made at that time that were later falsified by events that were beyond the control of—that indeed were unforeseeable by—anybody who negotiated these agreements, including the disintegration of or the weakening of executive authority in the United States for reasons unconnected with foreign policy considerations.

So, the premises of the Paris accords, in terms of aid, of the possibility of aid, and in terms of other factors, tended to disintegrate. I see no purpose now in reviewing that particular history. Within the context of the time, it seemed the right thing to do. . . . .

126. State Department on the Monroe Doctrine, 14 July 1960

IN HIS remarks concerning [denouncing] the Monroe Doctrine at his press conference on July 12, Mr. Khrushchev again displayed his extraordinary ability to ignore facts.

In the first place, the principles of the Monroe Doctrine are as valid today as they were in 1823 when the Doctrine was proclaimed. Furthermore, the Monroe Doctrine's purpose of preventing any extension to this hemisphere of a despotic political system contrary to the independent status of the American states is supported by the inter-American security system through the Organization of American States. Specifically the Organization of American States Charter and the Rio Treaty provide the means for common action to protect the hemisphere against the interventionist and aggressive designs of international communism. Likewise, Mr. Khrushchev failed to mention that the Rio Treaty is the first of the regional treaties for which provision is made under article 51 of the United Nations Charter. . . .

One of the principal purposes of the Rio Treaty was to provide a method for dealing with threats of imperialistic powers seeking to establish their domination in the Western Hemisphere.

A further remarkable development was revealed in Mr. Khrushchev's meeting with the press. Speaking as the Head of the Soviet Government, he arrogated to himself the power to determine what international agreements should or should not be binding — even though the Soviet Union is not a party thereto. In this particular instance it was not only the Rio Treaty but also the treaty between the United States and Cuba covering Guantanamo which he has sought to abrogate. While disregard for treaties to which it is a party may be viewed by the U.S.S.R. as a convenient approach to international relations, such an effort can only be regarded by law-abiding states as another example of Soviet intervention in the affairs of other countries.

Mr. Khrushchev's latest references to U.S.-Cuban relations are of a piece with his threat of July 9.[3] As a pretext for his threat, he conjured up the straw man of a nonexistent menace of U.S. aggression against Cuba.

The threat of use of force, made so blatantly by the Soviet Chairman in relation to the affairs of nations of the Western Hemisphere, is contrary to the basic principle of the United Nations Charter which rejects the use of force in the settlement of international disputes. This naked menace to world peace, brandished so callously by the Soviet leader, reveals the hypocrisy of his protestations in behalf of peace.

Moreover, these statements of Mr. Khrushchev appear to be designed to establish a "Bolshevik Doctrine" providing for the use of Soviet military power in support of Communist movements anywhere in the world. Mr. Khrushchev speaks approvingly of the historically positive role of the Monroe Doctrine during the 19th century, when it was applied against the European imperialisms of that day, but declares that "everything has changed abruptly" now that it stands in the way of the new imperialism: international communism.

The principles which the United States Government enunciated in the face of the attempts of the old imperialism to intervene in the affairs of this hemisphere are as valid today for the attempts of the new imperialism. It consequently reaffirms with vigor the principles expressed by President Monroe:

We owe it . . . to candor . . . to declare that we should consider any attempt on their [European powers] part to extend their system to any portion of this hemisphere as dangerous to our peace and safety.

Today, nearly a century and a half later, the United States is gratified that these principles are not professed by itself alone but represent through solemn agreements the views of the American community as a whole.

127. Kennedy of the Latin American Alliance for Progress, 13 March 1961

Speech of President John F. Kennedy.

IT IS A great pleasure for Mrs. Kennedy and for me, for the Vice President and Mrs. Johnson, and for the Members of Congress, to welcome the ambassadorial corps of the hemisphere, our long-time friends, to the White House today. . . .

We meet together as firm and ancient friends, united by history and experience and by our determination to advance the values of American civilization. For this new world of ours is not merely an accident of geography. Our continents are bound together by a common history — the endless exploration of new frontiers. Our nations are the product of a common struggle — the revolt from colonial rule. And our people share a common heritage — the quest for the dignity and the freedom of man. . . .

First, I propose that the American Republics begin on a vast new 10-year plan for the Americas, a plan to transform the 1960's into an historic decade of democratic progress. These 10 years will be the years of maximum progress, maximum effort — the years when the greatest obstacles must be overcome, the years when the need for assistance will be the greatest. . . .

Let me stress that only the most determined efforts of the American nations themselves can bring success to this effort. They, and they alone, can mobilize their resources, enlist the energies of their people, and modify their social patterns so that all, and not just a privileged few, share in the fruits of growth. If this effort is made, then outside assistance will give a vital impetus to progress; without it, no amount of help will advance the welfare of the people.

Thus if the countries of Latin America are ready to do their part — and I am sure they are — then I believe the United States, for its part, should help provide resources of a scope and magnitude sufficient to make this bold development plan a success, just as we helped to provide, against nearly equal odds, the resources adequate to help rebuild the economies of Western Europe. For only an effort of towering dimensions can insure fulfillment of our plan for a decade of progress.

Secondly, I will shortly request a ministerial meeting of the Inter-American Economic and Social Council, a meeting at which we can begin the massive planning effort which will be at the heart of the Alliance for Progress. . . .

Third, I have this evening signed a request to the Congress for $500 million as a first step in fulfilling the Act of Bogotá. This is the first large-scale inter-American effort — instituted by my predecessor President Eisenhower — to attack the social barriers which block economic progress. The money will be used to combat illiteracy, improve the productivity and use of their land, wipe out disease, attack archaic tax and land-tenure structures, provide educational opportunities, and offer a broad range of projects designed to make the benefits of increasing abundance available to all. We will begin to commit these funds as soon as they are appropriated.

Fourth, we must support all economic integration which is a genuine step toward larger markets and greater competitive opportunity. The fragmentation of Latin American economies is a serious barrier to industrial growth. Projects such as the Central American common market and free-trade areas in South America can help to remove these obstacles.

Fifth, the United States is ready to cooperate in serious, case-by-case examinations of commodity market problems. Frequent violent changes in commodity prices seriously injure the economies of many Latin American countries, draining their resources and stultifying their growth. Together we must find practical methods of bringing an end to this pattern.

Sixth, we will immediately step up our food-for-peace emergency program, help to establish food reserves in areas of recurrent drought, and help provide school lunches for children and offer feed grains for use in rural development. . . .

Seventh, all the people of the hemisphere must be allowed to share in the expanding wonders of science, . . .

Eighth, we must rapidly expand the training of those needed to man the economies of rapidly developing countries. . . .

Ninth, we reaffirm our pledge to come to the defense of any American nation whose independence is endangered. As confidence in the collective security system of the OAS [Organization of American States] spreads, it will be possible to devote to constructive use a major share of those resources now spent on the instruments of war. . . .

Tenth, we invite our friends in Latin America to contribute to the enrichment of life and culture in the United States. . . .

With steps such as these we propose to complete the revolution of the Americas, to build a hemisphere where all men can hope for a suitable standard of living and all can live out their lives in dignity and in freedom. . . .

128. Bay of Pigs Invasion of Cuba, April–May 1961

(A) SUMMARY OF STATEMENT OF RAÚL ROA GARCIA, DELEGATE FROM CUBA, IN THE FIRST COMMITTEE OF THE UNITED NATIONS [11]

MR. ROA said he wished to state formally on behalf of his Government that the Republic of Cuba had been invaded that morning by a mercenary force organized, financed and armed by the Government of the United States and coming from Guatemala and Florida. . . .

In no case had Cuba obtained justice from the various international organizations whose support it had sought, but it had been given the backing of world public opinion and, particularly, of the under-developed countries, which were opposed to all forms of imperialism and colonialism. It had also had the support of men and women who were brave enough to defy the repressive Government of the United States. The evidence put forward by the Cuban Government had been confirmed by a report in *The New York Times* of 10 January 1961, which stated that the United States Government was helping to train an anti-Castro force at a secret base constructed in Guatemala with United States money. It was the Cuban people who were suffering the consequences of such policies, through the activities of murderers and saboteurs paid by and directed from the United States. . . .

The item under discussion had been referred to the First Committee because it related to international peace and security and the right to self-determination. The United Nations had no authority to intervene in matters within the domestic jurisdiction of States, and could deal with acts outside domestic jurisdiction only when they infringed the principles of the Charter, violated international treaties or endangered international peace and security. Cuba had never committed any such act. It had adhered strictly to the relevant articles of the Charter. By contrast, there was no treaty or other agreement which the United States had not broken in its policy towards Cuba. It had violated the fundamental principles of the inter-American system, and in particular had undermined the two pillars of that system, political sovereignty and economic security, the first being guaranteed by article 15 and the second by article 16 of the charter of the Organization of American States. It had disregarded the Protocol to the Convention on Duties and Rights of States in the Event of Civil Strife, under article 5 of which each Contracting State was pledged, in areas subject to its jurisdiction, to use all appropriate means to prevent any person, national or alien, from deliberately participating in the preparation, organization, or carrying out of a military enterprise having as its purpose the starting, promoting or supporting of civil strife in another Contracting State, whether or not the government of the latter had been recognized. Finally, it had violated title 18, sections 959 and 960, of the United States Code, under which it was a punishable offence for any person within the United States to enlist in the service of, or to assist any military expedition against, any foreign prince, state, colony, district, or people. . . .

Reports published in two United States newspapers, the *Miami Herald* and *The New York Times,* showed that the counter-revolutionary mercenaries being recruited in New York and Florida were being supplied with regulation United States Army uniforms bearing no insignia or labels, and that small craft were regularly leaving the Florida coast for Cuba with cargoes of explosives and other sabotage supplies and returning to their bases under the protection of the United States authorities. *The New York Times* had explained that the plan was to co-ordinate subversive activity inside Cuba with the arrival of guerrillas from Guatemala when sabotage activities had reached their peak. Mercenaries had been training in Guatemala since May 1960, and additional groups were continuing to arrive from the United States. The Guatemalan base, the same newspaper had reported, included a 4,500-foot airstrip and a concentration of transport aircraft and bombers, all of United States manufacture. Indeed, transports manned by United States crews [were] being used to deliver weapons in the Escambray Mountains of Cuba.

(B) STATEMENT OF ADLAI E. STEVENSON IN ANSWER TO THE CHARGES OF CUBA [12]

Dr. Roa, speaking for Cuba, has just charged the United States with aggression against Cuba and invasion coming from Florida. These charges are totally false, and I deny them categorically. The United States has committed no aggression against Cuba, and no offensive has been launched from Florida or from any other part of the United States.

We sympathize with the desire of the people of Cuba — including those in exile who do not stop being Cubans merely because they could no longer stand to live in today's Cuba — we sympathize with their desire to seek Cuban independence and freedom. We hope that the Cuban people will succeed in doing what Castro's revolution never really tried to do: that is, to bring democratic processes to Cuba.

But as President Kennedy has already said,

... there will not under any conditions be ... an intervention in Cuba by United States armed forces. This Government will do everything it possibly can — and I think it can meet its responsibilities — to make sure that there are no Americans involved in any action inside Cuba.

I wish to make clear also that we would be opposed to the use of our territory for mounting an offensive against any foreign government. ...

129. Rusk on Cuba, 2 February 1962

Statement of Secretary of State Dean Rusk.

... IN AUGUST 1960, 17 months ago, there was a meeting of foreign ministers which discussed the Cuban problem in San José, Costa Rica. At that time the foreign ministers agreed to condemn outside intervention in the affairs of this hemisphere, and they reaffirmed in broad terms their faith in democracy and their rejection of totalitarianism. But they were not then prepared to take concrete steps aimed at the Communist offensive in general and Cuba in particular. In fact Cuba was not even named in the declaration, and some delegations said that it should not be interpreted as applying specifically to Cuba.

But during these past 17 months there has been a far-reaching change in the attitudes of both governments and peoples.

The Communist nature of the Castro regime has become more apparent to all — and so have its aggressive designs.

The Castro regime voted consistently with the Communist bloc at the United Nations. It built up its military strength with the help of Communist arms. It used its embassies in Latin America as centers of espionage and subversion. Thirteen American governments broke off all diplomatic relations with Cuba. It sought to intimidate, subvert, and harass free governments and nations, as reported to our meeting by the Inter-American Peace Committee of the OAS. And Castro himself, in early December, publicly confessed what everyone had come to know: that he is a Marxist-Leninist and would be until he dies. ...

We met at Punta del Este against the background of these changes. What was accomplished?

First, in a strong resolution that named names and minced no words, we declared unanimously — except for Cuba, of course — that the Castro-Communist offensive in this hemisphere is a clear and present danger to the unity and freedom of the American Republics. Even as we met, reports came in from several countries of efforts by small Communist-led minorities to disrupt constitutional government and the will of the majority.

Second, the ministers agreed, again unanimously, that the hemisphere is bound together by two powerful ties: by its commitment to human rights, social justice, and political democracy and by its commitment to exclude from this hemisphere the intervention of outside powers. On these grounds we concluded, again unanimously, "That the present Government of Cuba, which has officially identified itself as a Marxist-Leninist government, is incompatible with the principles and objectives of the inter-American system."

Third, on the basis of this unanimous conclusion, a two-thirds majority decided "That this incompatibility excludes the present Government of Cuba from participation in the inter-American system." Seventeen had declared that "the present government of Cuba has voluntarily placed itself outside the inter-American system." Included in this majority were those who felt themselves to be, and are, under special attack by Castro communism.

Fourth, recognizing that the threat of Cuba is an active threat to the security of the hemisphere and not merely a matter of ideological incompatibility, the foreign ministers, once again unanimously, officially ejected the Cuban regime from the Inter-American Defense Board, where their representatives had already been excluded from confidential discussions. In addition we established special machinery within the OAS to recommend joint action that can block Communist subversive activities before they reach the level of insurrection or guerrilla war.

Fifth, this meeting decided, again unanimously, to prohibit trade and traffic in arms between Cuba and the other American countries. No American government is now selling arms to Cuba, but we are determined to do everything necessary to stop illicit trade or traffic to or from Cuba within this hemisphere.

Sixth, the Council of the Organization of American States was asked to explore further trade restrictions, applying to Cuba the same kind of machinery that was applied last year to the Dominican Republic, and giving special attention to items of strategic importance.

Seventh, and finally, the foreign ministers unanimously recognized that the struggle against communism in this hemisphere is not merely a question of a defense against subversion but of positive measures as well — economic, social, and political reforms and development, to meet the legitimate aspirations of our peoples. In this spirit the governments committed themselves anew to the great constructive tasks of the Alliance for Progress.

The rollcall of votes on these resolutions provided a dramatic demonstration of two important points.

First, that Cuba stands alone in the Americas. No other nation voted with its delegates in opposition to any of these resolutions. We listened to their long-playing records of invective and abuse and then got on with our business. They made no progress with their threats and pleas, they could find no comfort in any differences among the rest of us, and finally they withdrew altogether.

The other point is that honest debate was a sign of strength in the Organization. Unless we know that the votes which are cast represent the convictions of the governments, the votes themselves would fail to carry conviction. The fact that differences were registered is an insurance that the unanimity, when expressed, was genuine.

There was no disagreement over the incompatibility of the Cuban regime and the inter-American system. But some governments sincerely felt that additional legal and technical steps were necessary before the exclusion of Cuba from participation in the official agencies of the system could be finally settled. While they abstained on that vote, however, all joined in the condemnation of communism and the present Cuban regime. . . .

130. Cuban Missile Crisis, October–November 1962

(A) STATEMENT OF PRESIDENT JOHN F. KENNEDY, SEPTEMBER 13, 1962[15]

THERE has been a great deal of talk on the situation in Cuba in recent days both in the Communist camp and in our own, and I would like to take this opportunity to set the matter in perspective. . . .

Ever since communism moved into Cuba in 1958, Soviet technical and military personnel have moved steadily onto the island in increasing numbers at the invitation of the Cuban government. Now that movement has been increased. It is under our most careful surveillance. But I will repeat the conclusion that I reported last week, that these new shipments do not constitute a serious threat to any other part of this Hemisphere.

If the United States ever should find it necessary to take military action against communism in Cuba, all of Castro's Communist-supplied weapons and technicians would not change the result or significantly extend the time required to achieve that result.

However, unilateral military intervention on the part of the United States cannot currently be either required or justified, and it is regrettable that loose talk about such action in this country might serve to give a thin color of legitimacy to the Communist pretense that such a threat exists. But let me make this clear once again: If at any time the Communist buildup in Cuba were to endanger or interfere with our security in any way, including our base at Guantanamo, our passage to the Panama Canal, our missile and space activities at Cape Canaveral, or the lives of American citizens in this country, or if Cuba should ever attempt to export its aggressive purposes by force or the threat of force against any nation in this Hemisphere, or become an offensive military base of significant capacity for the Soviet Union, then this country will do whatever must be done to protect its own security and that of its allies.

We shall be alert to, and fully capable of dealing swiftly with, any such development. As President and Commander in Chief I have full authority now to take such action, and I have asked the Congress to authorize me to call up reserve forces should this or any other crisis make it necessary. ...

We shall continue to work with Cuban refugee leaders who are dedicated as we are to that nation's future return to freedom. We shall continue to keep the American people and the Congress fully informed. We shall increase our surveillance of the whole Caribbean area. We shall neither initiate nor permit aggression in this Hemisphere. ...

(B) JOINT RESOLUTION OF CONGRESS [16]

WHEREAS President James Monroe, announcing the Monroe Doctrine in 1823, declared that the United States would consider any attempt on the part of European powers "To extend their system to any portion of this Hemisphere as dangerous to our peace and safety"; and

WHEREAS in the Rio Treaty of 1947 the parties agreed that "an armed attack by any State against an American State shall be considered as an attack against all the American States, and, consequently, each one of the said contracting parties undertakes to assist in meeting the attack in the exercise of the inherent right of individual or collective self-defense recognized by article 51 of the Charter of the United Nations"; and

WHEREAS the Foreign Ministers of the Organization of American States at Punta del Este in January 1962 declared: "The present Government of Cuba has identified itself with the principles of Marxist-Leninist ideology, has established a political, economic, and social system based on that doctrine, and accepts military assistance from extracontinental Communist powers, including even the threat of military intervention in America on the part of the Soviet Union"; and Whereas the international Communist movement has increasingly extended into Cuba, its political, economic, and military sphere of influence; Now, therefore, be it

RESOLVED by the Senate and House of Representatives of the United States of America in Congress assembled, That the United States is determined

(a) to prevent by whatever means may be necessary, including the use of arms, the Marxist-Leninist regime in Cuba from extending, by force or the threat of force, its aggressive or subversive activities to any part of this hemisphere;

(b) to prevent in Cuba the creation or use of an externally supported military capability endangering the security of the United States; and

(c) to work with the Organization of American States and with freedom-loving Cubans to support the aspirations of the Cuban people for self-determination.

(C) ADDRESS TO THE NATION OF PRESIDENT JOHN F. KENNEDY, OCTOBER 22, 1962 [17]

Good evening, my fellow citizens. This Government, as promised, has maintained the closest surveillance of the Soviet military buildup on the island of Cuba. Within the past week unmistakable evidence has established the fact that a series of offensive missile sites is now in preparation on that imprisoned island. The purpose of these bases can be none other than to provide a nuclear strike capability against the Western Hemisphere. ...

The characteristics of these new missile sites indicate two distinct types of installations. Several of them include medium-range ballistic missiles capable of carrying a nuclear warhead for a distance of more than 1,000 nautical miles. Each of these missiles, in short, is capable of striking Washington, D.C., the Panama Canal, Cape Canaveral, Mexico City, or any other city in the southeastern part of the United States, in Central America, or in the Caribbean area.

Additional sites not yet completed appear to be designed for intermediate-range ballistic missiles capable of traveling more than twice as far — and thus capable of striking most of the major cities in the Western Hemisphere, ranging as far north as Hudson Bay, Canada, and as far south as Lima, Peru. In addition, jet bombers, capable of carrying nuclear weapons, are now being uncrated and assembled in Cuba, while the necessary air bases are being prepared.

This urgent transformation of Cuba into an important strategic base — by the presence of these large, long-range, and clearly offensive weapons of sudden mass destruction — constitutes an explicit threat to the peace and security of all the Americas, in flagrant and deliberate defiance of the Rio Pact of 1947, the traditions of this nation and Hemisphere, the Joint Resolution of the 87th Congress, the Charter of the United Nations, and my own public warnings to the Soviets on September 4 and 13.

This action also contradicts the repeated assurances of Soviet spokesmen, both publicly and privately delivered, that the arms buildup in Cuba would retain its original defensive character and that the Soviet Union had no need or desire to station strategic missiles on the territory of any other nation. ...

Neither the United States of America nor the world community of nations can tolerate deliberate deception and offensive threats on the part of any nation, large or small. ...

But this secret, swift, and extraordinary buildup of Communist missiles — in an area well known to have a special and historical relationship to the United States and the nations of the Western Hemisphere, in violation of Soviet assurances, and in defiance of American and hemispheric policy — this sudden, clandestine decision to station strategic weapons for the first time outside of Soviet soil — is a deliberately provocative and unjustified change in the *status quo* which cannot be accepted by this country if our courage and our commitments are ever to be trusted again by either friend or foe....

Acting, therefore, in the defense of our own security and of the entire Western Hemisphere, and under the authority entrusted to me by the Constitution as endorsed by the resolution of the Congress, I have directed that the following *initial* steps be taken immediately:

First: To halt this offensive buildup, a strict quarantine on all offensive military equipment under shipment to Cuba is being initiated. All ships of any kind bound for Cuba from whatever nation or port will, if found to contain cargoes of offensive weapons, be turned back. This quarantine will be extended, if needed, to other types of cargo and carriers. We are not at this time, however, denying the necessities of life as the Soviets attempted to do in their Berlin blockade of 1948.

Second: I have directed the continued and increased close surveillance of Cuba and its military buildup. The Foreign Ministers of the Organization of American States in their communique of October 3 rejected secrecy on such matters in this Hemisphere. Should these offensive military preparations continue, thus increasing the threat to the Hemisphere, further action will be justified. I have directed the Armed Forces to prepare for any eventualities; and I trust that, in the interests of both the Cuban people and the Soviet technicians at the sites, the hazards to all concerned of continuing this threat will be recognized.

Third: It shall be the policy of this nation to regard any nuclear missile launched from Cuba against any nation in the Western Hemisphere as an attack by the Soviet Union on the United States, requiring a full retaliatory response upon the Soviet Union.

Fourth: As a necessary military precaution I have reinforced our base at Guantanamo, evacuated today the dependents of our personnel there, and ordered additional military units to be on a standby alert basis.

Fifth: We are calling tonight for an immediate meeting of the Organ of Consultation, under the Organization of American States, to consider this threat to hemispheric security and to invoke articles six and eight of the Rio Treaty in support of all necessary action. The United Nations Charter allows for regional security arrangements — and the nations of this Hemisphere decided long ago against the military presence of outside powers. Our other allies around the world have also been alerted.

Sixth: Under the Charter of the United Nations, we are asking tonight that an emergency meeting of the Security Council be convoked without delay to take action against this latest Soviet threat to world peace. Our resolution will call for the prompt dismantling and withdrawal of all offensive weapons in Cuba, under the supervision of United Nations observers, before the quarantine can be lifted.

Seventh and finally: I call upon Chairman Khrushchev to halt and eliminate this clandestine, reckless, and provocative threat to world peace and to stable relations between our two nations....

The path we have chosen for the present is full of hazards, as all paths are; but it is the one most consistent with our character and courage as a nation and our commitments around the world. The cost of freedom is always high — but Americans have always paid it. And one path we shall never choose, and that is the path of surrender or submission....

(D) RESOLUTION OF THE COUNCIL OF THE ORGANIZATION OF AMERICAN STATES [18]

WHEREAS,

The Inter-American Treaty of Reciprocal Assistance of 1947 (Rio Treaty) recognizes the obligation of the American Republics to "provide for effective reciprocal assistance to meet armed attacks against any American State and in order to deal with threats of aggression against any of them"...

THE COUNCIL OF THE ORGANIZATION OF AMERICAN STATES, MEETING AS THE PROVISIONAL ORGAN OF CONSULTATION, RESOLVES:

1. To call for the immediate dismantling and withdrawal from Cuba of all missiles and other weapons with any offensive capability;

2. To recommend that the member states, in accordance with Articles 6 and 8 of the Inter-American Treaty of Reciprocal Assistance, take all measures, individually and collectively, including the use of armed force, which they may deem necessary to ensure that the Government of Cuba cannot continue to receive from the Sino-Soviet powers military material and related supplies which may threaten the peace and security of the Continent and to prevent the missiles in Cuba with offensive capability from ever becoming an active threat to the peace and security of the Continent;

3. To inform the Security Council of the United Nations of this resolution in accordance with Article 54 of the Charter of the United Nations and to express the hope that the Security Council will, in accordance with the draft resolution introduced by the United States, dispatch United Nations observers to Cuba at the earliest moment;

4. To continue to serve provisionally as Organ of Consultation and to request the Member States to keep the Organ of Consultation duly informed of measures taken by them in accordance with paragraph two of this resolution.

(E) INTERDICTION OF OFFENSIVE WEAPONS TO CUBA [19]

WHEREAS the peace of the world and the security of the United States and of all American States are endangered by reason of the establishment by the Sino-Soviet powers of an offensive military capability in Cuba, including bases for ballistic missiles with a potential range covering most of North and South America;

WHEREAS by a Joint Resolution passed by the Congress of the United States and approved on October 3, 1962, it was declared that the United States is determined to prevent by whatever means may be necessary, including the use of arms, the Marxist-Leninist regime in Cuba from extending, by force or the threat of force, its aggressive or subversive activities to any part of this hemisphere, and to prevent in Cuba the creation or use of an externally supported military capability endangering the security of the United States; and

WHEREAS the Organ of Consultation of the American Republics meeting in Washington on October 23, 1962, recommended that the Member States, in accordance with Articles six and eight of the Inter-American Treaty of Reciprocal Assistance, take all measures individually and collectively, including the use of armed force, which they may deem necessary to ensure that the Government of Cuba cannot continue to receive from the Sino-Soviet powers military material and related supplies which may threaten the peace and security of the Continent and to prevent the missiles in Cuba with offensive capability from ever becoming an active threat to the peace and security of the Continent:

NOW, THEREFORE, I, JOHN F. KENNEDY, President of the United States of America, acting under and by virtue of the authority conferred upon me by the Constitution and statutes of the United States, in accordance with the aforementioned resolutions of the United States Congress and of the Organ of Consultation of the American Republics, and to defend the security of the United States, do hereby proclaim that the forces under my command are ordered, beginning at 2:00 p.m. Greenwich time October 24, 1962, to interdict, subject to the instructions herein contained, the delivery of offensive weapons and associated materiel to Cuba.

For the purposes of this Proclamation, the following are declared to be prohibited materiel:

Surface-to-surface missiles; bomber aircraft; bombs, air-to-surface rockets and guided missiles; warheads for any of the above weapons; mechanical or electronic equipment to support or operate the above items; and any other classes of materiel hereafter designated by the Secretary of Defense for the purpose of effectuating this Proclamation.

To enforce this order, the Secretary of Defense shall take appropriate measures to prevent the delivery of prohibited materiel to Cuba, employing the land, sea and air forces of the United States in cooperation with any forces that may be made available by other American States.

The Secretary of Defense may make such regulations and issue such directives as he deems necessary to ensure the effectiveness of this order, including the designation, within a reasonable distance of Cuba, of prohibited or restricted zones and of prescribed routes.

Any vessel or craft which may be proceeding toward Cuba may be intercepted and may be directed to identify itself, its cargo, equipment and stores and its ports of call, to stop, to lie to, to submit to visit and search, or to proceed as directed. Any vessel or craft which fails or refuses to respond to or comply with directions shall be subject to being taken into custody. Any vessel or craft which it is believed is en route to Cuba and may be carrying prohibited materiel or may itself constitute such materiel shall, wherever possible, be directed to proceed to another destination of its own choice and shall be taken into custody if it fails or refuses to obey such directions. All vessels or craft taken into custody shall be sent into a port of the United States for appropriate disposition.

In carrying out this order, force shall not be used except in case of failure or refusal to comply with directions, or with regulations or directives of the Secretary of Defense issued hereunder, after reasonable efforts have been made to communicate them to the vessel or craft, or in case of self-defense. In any case, force shall be used only to the extent necessary.

(F) THE END OF THE CUBAN "CRISIS" [20]

I have today been informed by Chairman Khrushchev that all of the IL-28 bombers now in Cuba will be withdrawn in thirty days. He also agrees that these planes can be observed and counted as they leave. Inasmuch as this goes a long way toward reducing the danger which faced this Hemisphere four weeks ago, I have this afternoon instructed the Secretary of Defense to lift our naval quarantine.

In view of this action, I want to take this opportunity to bring the American people up to date on the Cuban crisis and to review the progress made thus far in fulfilling the understandings between Soviet Chairman Khrushchev and myself as set forth in our letters of October 27 and 28. Chairman Khrushchev, it will be recalled, agreed to remove from Cuba all weapons systems capable of offensive use, to halt the further introduction of such weapons into Cuba, and to permit appropriate United Nations observation and supervision to insure the carrying out and continuation of these commitments. We on our part agreed that, once these adequate arrangements for verification had been established, we would remove our naval quarantine and give assurances against invasion of Cuba.

The evidence to date indicates that all known offensive missile sites in Cuba have been dismantled. The missiles and their associated equipment have been loaded on Soviet ships. And our inspection at sea of these departing ships has confirmed that the number of missiles reported by the Soviet Union as having been brought into Cuba, which closely corresponded to our own information, has now been removed. In addition the Soviet Government has stated that all nuclear weapons have been withdrawn from Cuba and no offensive weapons will be reintroduced.

Nevertheless, important parts of the understanding of October 27th and 28th remain to be carried out. The Cuban Government has not yet permitted the United Nations to verify whether all offensive weapons have been removed, and no lasting safeguards have yet been established against the future introduction of offensive weapons back into Cuba.

Consequently, if the Western Hemisphere is to continue to be protected against offensive weapons, this Government has no choice but to pursue its own means of checking on military activities in Cuba. The importance of our continued vigilance is underlined by our identification in recent days of a number of Soviet ground combat units in Cuba, although we are informed that these and other Soviet units were associated with the protection of offensive weapons systems and will also be withdrawn in due course.

I repeat, we would like nothing better than adequate international arrangements for the task of inspection and verification in Cuba, and we are prepared to continue our efforts to achieve such arrangements. Until that is done, difficult problems remain. As for our part, if all offensive weapons are removed from Cuba and kept out of the Hemisphere in the future, under adequate verification and safeguards, and if Cuba is not used for the export of aggressive Communist purposes, there will be peace in the Caribbean. And as I said in September, we shall neither initiate nor permit aggression in this Hemisphere.

We will not, of course, abandon the political, economic, and other efforts of this Hemisphere to halt subversion from Cuba nor our purpose and hope that the Cuban people shall some day be truly free. But these policies are very different from any intent to launch a military invasion of the island.

In short, the record of recent weeks shows real progress, and we are hopeful that further progress can be made. The completion of the commitment on both sides and the achievement of a peaceful solution to the Cuban crisis might well open the door to the solution of other outstanding problems.

May I add this final thought. In this week of Thanksgiving there is much for which we can be grateful as we look back to where we stood only four weeks ago — the unity of this Hemisphere, the support of our allies, and the calm determination of the American people. These qualities may be tested many more times in this decade, but we have increased reason to be confident that those qualities will continue to serve the cause of freedom with distinction in the years to come.

131. Johnson's Speech on the U.S. Invasion of the Dominican Republic, 2 May 1965

Good evening, ladies and gentlemen: I have just come from a meeting with the leaders of both parties in the Congress, which was held in the Cabinet Room of the White House. I briefed them on the facts of the situation in the Dominican Republic. I want to make those same facts known to all the American people and to all the world.

There are times in the affairs of nations when great principles are tested in an ordeal of conflict and danger. This is such a time for the American nations.

At stake are the lives of thousands, the liberty of a nation, and the principles and the values of all the American Republics.

That is why the hopes and the concern of this entire hemisphere are on this Sabbath Sunday focused on the Dominican Republic.

In the dark mist of conflict and violence, revolution and confusion, it is not easy to find clear and unclouded truths.

But certain things are clear. And they require equally clear action. To understand, I think it is necessary to begin with the events of 8 or 9 days ago.

Last week our observers warned of an approaching political storm in the Dominican Republic. I immediately asked our Ambassador (W. Tapley Bennett, Jr.) to return to Washington at once so that we might discuss the situation and might plan a course of conduct. But events soon outran our hopes for peace.

Saturday, April 24—8 days ago—while Ambassador Bennett was conferring with the highest officials of your Government, revolution erupted in the Dominican Republic. Elements of the military forces of that country overthrew their government. However, the rebels themselves were divided. Some wanted to restore former President Juan Bosch. Others opposed his restoration. President Bosch, elected after the fall of Trujillo and his assassination, had been driven from office by an earlier revolution in the Dominican Republic.

Those who opposed Mr. Bosch's return formed a military committee in an effort to control that country. The others took to the street, and they began to lead a revolt on behalf of President Bosch. Control and effective government dissolved in conflict and confusion....

Meanwhile, all this time, from Saturday to Wednesday, the danger was mounting. Even though we were deeply saddened by bloodshed and violence in a close and friendly neighbor, we had no desire to interfere in the affairs of a sister Republic.

On Wednesday afternoon there was no longer any choice for the man who is your President. I was sitting in my little office reviewing the world situation with Secretary Rusk, Secretary McNamara, and Mr. McGeorge Bundy. Shortly after 3 o'clock I received a cable from our Ambassador, and he said that things were in danger; he had been informed the chief of police and governmental authorities could no longer protect us. We immediately started the necessary conference calls to be prepared.

At 5:14, almost 2 hours later, we received a cable that was labeled "critic," a word that is reserved for only the most urgent and immediate matters of national security.

The cable reported that Dominican law enforcement and military officials had informed our Embassy that the situation was completely out of control and that the police and the government could no longer give any guarantee concerning the safety of Americans or any foreign nationals.

Ambassador Bennett, who is one of our most experienced Foreign Service officers, went on in that cable to say that only an immediate landing of American forces could safeguard and protect the lives of thousands of Americans and thousands of other citizens of some 30 other countries. Ambassador Bennett urged your President to order an immediate landing.

In this situation hesitation and vacillation could mean death for many of our people, as well as many of the citizens of other lands.

I thought that we could not and we did not hesitate. Our forces, American forces, were ordered in immediately to protect American lives. They have done that. They have attacked no one, and although some of our servicemen gave their lives, not a single American civilian or the civilian of any other nation, as a result of this protection, lost their lives....

The American nations cannot, must not, and will not permit the establishment of another Communist government in the Western Hemisphere. This was the unanimous view of all the American nations when, in January 1962, they declared, and I quote: "The principles of communism are incompatible with the principles of the Inter-American system."

This is what our beloved President John F. Kennedy meant when, less than a week before his death, he told us: "We in this hemisphere must also use every resource at our command to prevent the establishment of another Cuba in this hemisphere...."

132. U.S.–Panama Treaties, 7 September 1977

1. Panama Canal Treaty

The United States of America and the Republic of Panama,

Acting in the spirit of the Joint Declaration of April 3, 1964, by the Representatives of the Governments of the United States of America and the Republic of Panama, and of the Joint Statement of Principles of February 7, 1974, initialed by the Secretary of State of the United States of America and the Foreign Minister of the Republic of Panama, and

Acknowledging the Republic of Panama's sovereignty over its territory,

Have decided to terminate the prior Treaties pertaining to the Panama Canal and to conclude a new Treaty to serve as the basis for a new relationship between them and, accordingly, have agreed upon the following:

Article I
Abrogation of Prior Treaties and Establishment of a New Relationship

1. Upon its entry into force, this Treaty terminates and supersedes:

(a) The Isthmian Canal Convention between the United States of America and the Republic of Panama, signed at Washington, November 18, 1903;

(b) The Treaty of Friendship and Cooperation signed at Washington, March 2, 1936, and the Treaty of Mutual Understanding and Cooperation and the related Memorandum of Understandings Reached, signed at Panama, January 25, 1955, between the United States of America and the Republic of Panama;

(c) All other treaties, conventions, agreements and exchanges of notes between the United States of America and the Republic of Panama concerning the Panama Canal which were in force prior to the entry into force of this Treaty; and

(d) Provisions concerning the Panama Canal which appear in other treaties, conventions, agreements and exchanges of notes between the United States of America and the Republic of Panama which were in force prior to the entry into force of this Treaty.

2. In accordance with the terms of this Treaty and related agreements, the Republic of Panama, as territorial sovereign, grants to the United States of America, for the duration of this Treaty, the rights necessary to regulate the transit of ships through the Panama Canal, and to manage, operate, maintain, improve, protect and defend the Canal. The Republic of Panama guarantees to the United States of America the peaceful use of the land and water areas which it has been granted the rights to use for such purposes pursuant to this Treaty and related agreements.

3. The Republic of Panama shall participate increasingly in the management and protection and defense of the Canal, as provided in this Treaty.

4. In view of the special relationship established by this Treaty, the United States of America and the Republic of Panama shall cooperate to assure the uninterrupted and efficient operation of the Panama Canal.

Article II
Ratification, Entry Into Force, and Termination

1. This Treaty shall be subject to ratification in accordance with the constitutional procedures of the two Parties. The instruments of ratification of this Treaty shall be exchanged at Panama at the same time as the instruments of ratification of the Treaty Concerning the Permanent Neutrality and Operation of the Panama Canal, signed this date, are exchanged. This Treaty shall enter into force, simultaneously with the Treaty Concerning the Permanent Neutrality and Operation of the Panama Canal, six calendar months from the date of the exchange of the instruments of ratification.

2. This Treaty shall terminate at noon, Panama time, December 31, 1999.

Article III
Canal Operation and Management

1. The Republic of Panama, as territorial sovereign, grants to the United States of America the rights to manage, operate, and maintain the Panama Canal, its complementary works, installations and equipment and to provide for the orderly transit of vessels through the Panama Canal. The United States of America accepts the grant of such rights and undertakes to exercise them in accordance with this Treaty and related agreements. . . .

3. Pursuant to the foregoing grant of rights, the United States of America shall, in accordance with the terms of this Treaty and the provisions of United States law, carry out its responsibilities by means of a United States Government agency called the Panama Canal Commission, which shall be constituted by and in conformity with the laws of the United States of America.

(a) The Panama Canal Commission shall be supervised by a Board composed of nine members, five of whom shall be nationals of the United States of America, and four of whom shall be Panamanian nationals proposed by the Republic of Panama for appointment to such positions by the United States of America in a timely manner. . . .

Article IV
Protection and Defense

1. The United States of America and the Republic of Panama commit themselves to protect and defend the Panama Canal. Each Party shall act, in accordance with its constitutional processes, to meet the danger resulting from an armed attack or other actions which threaten the security of the Panama Canal or of ships transiting it.

2. For the duration of this Treaty, the United States of America shall have primary responsibility to protect and defend the Canal. The rights of the United States of America to station, train, and move military forces within the Republic of Panama are described in the Agreement in Implementation of this Article, signed this date. The use of areas and installations and the legal status of the armed forces of the United States of America in the Republic of Panama shall be governed by the aforesaid Agreement. . . .

Done at Washington, this 7th day of September, 1977, in duplicate, in the English and Spanish languages, both texts being equally authentic.

For the Republic of Panama:	For the United States of America:
Omar Torrijos Herrera	Jimmy Carter
Head of Government of the Republic of Panama	*President of the United States of America*

2. Treaty Concerning the Permanent Neutrality and Operation of the Panama Canal

The United States of America and the Republic of Panama have agreed upon the following:

Article I

The Republic of Panama declares that the Canal, as an international transit waterway, shall be permanently neutral in accordance with the regime established in this Treaty. The same regime of neutrality shall apply to any other international waterway that may be built either partially or wholly in the territory of the Republic of Panama.

Article II

The Republic of Panama declares the neutrality of the Canal in order that both in time of peace and in time of war it shall remain secure and open to peaceful transit by the vessels of all nations on terms of entire equality, so that there will be no discrimination against any nation, or its citizens or subjects, concerning the conditions or charges of transit, or for any other reason, and so that the Canal, and therefore the Isthmus of Panama, shall not be the target of reprisals in any armed conflict between other nations of the world. The foregoing shall be subject to the following requirements:

(a) Payment of tolls and other charges for transit and ancillary services, provided they have been fixed in conformity with the provisions of Article III (c);

(b) Compliance with applicable rules and regulations, provided such rules and regulations are applied in conformity with the provisions of Article III (c);

(c) The requirement that transiting vessels commit no acts of hostility while in the Canal; and

(d) Such other conditions and restrictions as are established by this Treaty. . . .

Article IV

The United States of America and the Republic of Panama agree to maintain the regime of neutrality established in this Treaty, which shall be maintained in order that the Canal shall remain permanently neutral, notwithstanding the termination of any other treaties entered into by the two Contracting Parties.

Article V

After the termination of the Panama Canal Treaty, only the Republic of Panama shall operate the Canal and maintain military forces, defense sites and military installations within its national territory.

Article VI

1. In recognition of the important contributions of the United States of America and of the Republic of Panama to the construction, operation, maintenance, and protection and defense of the Canal, vessels of war and auxiliary vessels of those nations shall, notwithstanding any other provisions of this Treaty, be entitled to transit the Canal irrespective of their internal operation, means of propulsion, origin, destination, armament or cargo carried. Such vessels of war and auxiliary vessels will be entitled to transit the Canal expeditiously. . . .

Article VIII

This Treaty shall be subject to ratification in accordance with the constitutional procedures of the two Parties. The instruments of ratification of this Treaty shall be exchanged at Panama at the same time as the instruments of ratification of the Panama Canal Treaty, signed this date, are exchanged. This Treaty shall enter into force, simultaneously with the Panama Canal Treaty, six calendar months from the date of the exchange of the instruments of ratification.

Done at Washington, this 7th day of September, 1977, in the English and Spanish languages, both texts being equally authentic.

For the Republic of Panama:	For the United States of America:
Omar Torrijos Herrera	Jimmy Carter
Head of Government of the Republic of Panama	*President of the United States of America*

133. U.S., Great Britain, and France on Arab-Israeli Borders, 25 May 1950

THE GOVERNMENTS of the United Kingdom, France, and the United States, having had occasion during the recent Foreign Ministers meeting in London to review certain questions affecting the peace and stability of the Arab states and of Israel, and particularly that of the supply of arms and war material to these states, have resolved to make the following statements:

1. The three Governments recognize that the Arab states and Israel all need to maintain a certain level of armed forces for the purposes of assuring their internal security and their legitimate self-defense and to permit them to play their part in the defense of the area as a whole. All applications for arms or war material for these countries will be considered in the light of these principles. In this connection the three Governments wish to recall and reaffirm the terms of the statements made by their representatives on the Security Council on August 4, 1949, in which they declared their opposition to the development of an arms race between the Arab states and Israel.

2. The three Governments declare that assurances have been received from all the states in question, to which they permit arms to be supplied from their countries, that the purchasing state does not intend to undertake any act of aggression against any other state. Similar assurances will be requested from any other state in the area to which they permit arms to be supplied in the future.

3. The three Governments take this opportunity of declaring their deep interest in and their desire to promote the establishment and maintenance of peace and stability in the area and their unalterable opposition to the use of force or threat of force between any of the states in that area. The three Governments, should they find that any of these states was preparing to violate frontiers or armistice lines, would, consistently with their obligations as members of the United Nations, immediately take action, both within and outside the United Nations, to prevent such violation.

134. Dulles on the Egyptian Aswan Dam Project, 2 April 1957

Statement of Secretary of State John Foster Dulles.

THERE WERE, of course, a number of reasons which dictated our declining to go ahead with the Aswan Proposal.

There was, perhaps first of all and most imperative, the fact that the Appropriations Committee of the Senate had unanimously passed a resolution providing that none of the 1957 funds could be used for the Aswan Dam.

There was the fact that we had come to the feeling in our own mind that it was very dubious whether a project of this magnitude could be carried through with mutual advantage. It is a tremendous project, involving an estimated billion and a half dollars — probably it would cost more than that. And the Egyptian component of that, in terms of domestic currency and effort, would involve a gigantic effort and call for an austerity program over a period of 12 to 15 years. Undoubtedly, that would be a burden and cause of complaint on the part of the Egyptian people, and probably the responsibility for that would be placed upon the foreign lenders and they would end up by being disliked instead of liked.

Then there was the further fact that the Egyptians had during the immediately preceding period been developing ever closer relations with the Soviet-bloc countries. Only a few days before I was asked for a definitive answer by the Egyptians, they had recognized Communist China — being the first Arab nation to do so. And, indeed, it became I think, the first nation in the world to do so since the attack on Korea.

And in that way the Egyptians, in a sense, forced upon us an issue to which I think there was only one proper response. That issue was, do nations which play both sides get better treatment than nations which are stalwart and work with us? That question was posed by the manner in which the Egyptians presented their final request to us, and stalwart allies were watching very carefully to see what the answer would be — stalwart allies which included some in the same area.

Under all the circumstances I think there was no doubt whatsoever as to the propriety of the answer given. It was given in a courteous manner, as you will find if you will go back and reread the statement which was given out at the time, which reaffirmed our friendship for the Egyptian people and indicated our willingness in other ways to try to assist the Egyptian economy. . . .

We did not expect . . . [Colonel Nasser to react to U.S. withdrawal from the Aswan Dam project by seizing the Suez Canal], although we now know that the seizure of the Canal Company had been planned by President Nasser for some time. I don't recall that I recently mentioned it, but President Tito in a speech of his last November said that President Nasser had told him at their first meeting [February 1955] that it was his intention to seize the Suez Canal Company because Egypt as an independent nation could not tolerate this exercise of authority on Egyptian soil by foreigners. That was while the Aswan Dam matter was, I think, being discussed by the World Bank. But it was a year or more before our decision not to go ahead with the dam.

135. Dulles on the British-French-Israeli Invasion of Egypt, October-November 1956

Speech to the U.N. General Assembly, 1 November 1956.

MR. DULLES (United States of America): I doubt that any representative ever spoke from this rostrum with as heavy a heart as I have brought here tonight. We speak on a matter of vital importance, where the United States finds itself unable to agree with three nations with which it has ties of deep friendship, of admiration and of respect, and two of which constitute our oldest and most trusted and reliable allies.

The fact that we differ with such friends has led us to reconsider and reevaluate our position with the utmost care, and that has been done at the highest levels of our Government, but even after that reevaluation we still find ourselves in disagreement. And, because it seems to us that that disagreement involves principles which far transcend the immediate issue, we feel impelled to make our point of view known to you and, through you, to the world.

This is the first time that this Assembly has met pursuant to the "Uniting for peace" resolution which the General Assembly adopted in 1950 [*Resolution 377(V)*]. I was a member of the United States delegation and had the primary responsibility for handling that proposal in committee and on the floor of this Assembly. It was then the period of the communist attack upon the Republic of Korea, and at that time surely we little thought that the resolution would be invoked for the first time under the conditions which now prevail.

What are the facts that bring us here? There is, first of all, the fact that there occurred, beginning last Monday, 29 October 1956, a deep penetration of Egypt by Israel forces. Then, quickly following upon that action, there came action by France and the United Kingdom in subjecting Egypt first to a twelve-hour ultimatum, and then to an armed attack, which is now going on from the air with the declared purpose of gaining temporary control of the Suez Canal, presumably to make it more secure. Then there is the third fact that after the matter had been brought to the Security Council, it was sought to deal with it by a draft resolution which was vetoed by the United Kingdom and France, which cast the only dissenting votes against the draft resolution. . . .

This problem of the Suez Canal, which perhaps lies at the basis of a considerable part of the forcible action now being taken, has been dealt with over the past three months in many ways and on many occasions. I doubt whether, in all history, so sincere and so sustained an effort has been made to find a just and peaceful solution. . . .

In the Security Council, six principles were unanimously adopted [S/3675]. Egypt, which participated in the proceedings, although it is not a member of the Council, concurred. Those principles were, in essence, the ones which had been adopted by the eighteen nations which met in London [S/3665]. A second part of the draft resolution which was presented to the Security Council looked forward to the implementation of the principles. That part was not adopted — owing, in that case, to a veto by the Soviet Union.

Despite that fact, there occurred under the auspices of the Secretary-General — to whom I should like to pay a tribute for his great contribution to the efforts at a just and peaceful solution of this problem — exchanges of views on how the six principles could be implemented. I do not think it is an exaggeration to say something which I am quite sure the Secretary-General would confirm — that is, that very considerable progress was made and that it seemed that a just and peaceful solution, acceptable to all, was near at hand. It was hoped that those negotiations would continue. . . .

Thus, peaceful processes seemed to be at work. As I have said, it appeared — at least to us — that those peaceful processes had not run their course. While I should be the last to say that there can never be circumstances where force may not be resorted to, and certainly there can be resort to force for defensive purposes under Article 51 of the Charter, it seems to us that, in the circumstances which I have described, the violent armed attack by three Members of the United Nations upon a fourth cannot be treated as anything but a grave error inconsistent with the principles and purposes of the Charter; an error which, if persisted in, would gravely undermine this Organization and its Charter. . . .

At the moment, we are the constituted authority, and while, under the Charter, we do not have the power of action, we do have a power of recommendation, a power which, if it reflects the moral judgment of the world community, world opinion, will be influential upon the present situation.

It is animated by such considerations that the United States has introduced a draft resolution [A/3256] which I should like to read out:

"*The General Assembly,*

"*Noting* the disregard on many occasions by parties to the Israel-Arab armistice agreements of 1949 of the terms of such agreements, and that the armed forces of Israel have penetrated deeply into Egyptian territory in violation of the General Armistice Agreement between Egypt and Israel of 24 February 1949,

"*Noting* that armed forces of France and the United Kingdom of Great Britain and Northern Ireland are conducting military operations against Egyptian territory,

"*Noting* that traffic through the Suez Canal is now interrupted to the serious prejudice of many nations,

"*Expressing* its grave concern over these developments,

"1. *Urges* as a matter of priority that all parties now involved in hostilities in the area agree to an immediate cease-fire and, as part thereof, halt the movement of military forces and arms into the area;

"2. *Urges* the parties to the armistice agreements promptly to withdraw all forces behind the armistice lines, to desist from raids across the armistice lines into neighbouring territory, and to observe scrupulously the provisions of the armistice agreements;

"3. *Recommends* that all Member States refrain from introducing military goods in the area of hostilities and in general refrain from any acts which would delay or prevent the implementation of the present resolution;

"4. *Urges* that, upon the cease-fire being effective, steps be taken to reopen the Suez Canal and restore secure freedom of navigation;

"5. *Requests* the Secretary-General to observe and promptly report on the compliance with the present resolution to the Security Council and to the General Assembly, for such further action as they may deem appropriate in accordance with the Charter;

"6. *Decides* to remain in emergency session pending compliance with the present resolution." . . .

When we wrote the Charter at San Francisco in 1945, we thought that we had perhaps seen the worst in war and that our task was to prevent a recurrence of what had been. Indeed, what then had been was tragic enough. But now we know that what can be will be infinitely more tragic than what we saw in the Second World War. I believe that at this critical juncture we owe the highest duty to ourselves, to our peoples, and to posterity to take action which will ensure that this fire which has started shall not spread but shall be promptly extinguished; and then to turn with renewed vigour to curing the injustices out of which this trouble has risen.

136. Eisenhower Doctrine for the Middle East, 5 January 1957

(A) PRESIDENT EISENHOWER'S REQUEST FOR CONGRESSIONAL AUTHORIZATION TO USE THE ARMED FORCES OF THE UNITED STATES IN THE MIDDLE EAST [17]

FIRST may I express to you my deep appreciation of your courtesy in giving me, at some inconvenience to yourselves, this early opportunity of addressing you on a matter I deem to be of grave importance to our country. . . .

I

The Middle East has abruptly reached a new and critical stage in its long and important history. In past decades many of the countries in that area were not fully self-governing. Other nations exercised considerable authority in the area and the security of the region was largely built around their power. But since the First World War there has been a steady evolution toward self-government and independence. This development the United States has welcomed and has encouraged. Our country supports without reservation the full sovereignty and independence of each and every nation in the Middle East.

The evolution to independence has in the main been a peaceful process. But the area has been often troubled. Persistent cross-currents of distrust and fear with raids back and forth across national boundaries have brought about a high degree of instability in much of the Mid East. Just recently there have been hostilities involving Western European nations that once exercised much influence in the area. Also the relatively large attack by Israel in October has intensified the basic differences between that nation and its Arab neighbors. All this instability has been heightened and, at times, manipulated by International Communism.

II

. . . The reason for Russia's interest in the Middle East is solely that of power politics. Considering her announced purpose of communizing the world, it is easy to understand her hope of dominating the Middle East.

This region has always been the crossroads of the continents of the Eastern Hemisphere. The Suez Canal enables the nations of Asia and

Europe to carry on the commerce that is essential if these countries are to maintain well-rounded and prosperous economies. The Middle East provides a gateway between Eurasia and Africa.

It contains about two thirds of the presently known oil deposits of the world and it normally supplies the petroleum needs of many nations of Europe, Asia and Africa. The nations of Europe are peculiarly dependent upon this supply, and this dependency relates to transportation as well as to production. This has been vividly demonstrated since the closing of the Suez Canal and some of the pipelines. Alternate ways of transportation and, indeed, alternate sources of power can, if necessary, be developed. But these cannot be considered as early prospects.

These things stress the immense importance of the Middle East. If the nations of that area should lose their independence, if they were dominated by alien forces hostile to freedom, that would be both a tragedy for the area and for many other free nations whose economic life would be subject to near strangulation. Western Europe would be endangered just as though there had been no Marshall Plan, no North Atlantic Treaty Organization. The free nations of Asia and Africa, too, would be placed in serious jeopardy. And the countries of the Middle East would lose the markets upon which their economies depend. All this would have the most adverse, if not disastrous, effect upon our own nation's economic life and political prospects. . . .

V

Under these circumstances I deem it necessary to seek the cooperation of the Congress. Only with that cooperation can we give the reassurance needed to deter aggression, to give courage and confidence to those who are dedicated to freedom and thus prevent a chain of events which would gravely endanger all of the free world. . . .

VI

. . . The action which I propose would have the following features.

It would, first of all, authorize the United States to cooperate with and assist any nation or group of nations in the general area of the Middle East in the development of economic strength dedicated to the maintenance of national independence.

It would, in the second place, authorize the Executive to undertake in the same region programs of military assistance and cooperation with any nation or group of nations which desire such aid.

It would, in the third place, authorize such assistance and cooperation to include the employment of the armed forces of the United States to secure and protect the territorial integrity and political independence of such nations, requesting such aid, against overt armed aggression from any nation controlled by International Communism. . . .

The present proposal would, in the fourth place, authorize the President to employ, for economic and defensive military purposes, sums available under the Mutual Security Act of 1954, as amended, without regard to existing limitations. . . .

VII

. . . The proposed legislation is primarily designed to deal with the possibility of Communist aggression, direct and indirect. There is imperative need that any lack of power in the area should be made good, not by external or alien force, but by the increased vigor and security of the independent nations of the area.

Experience shows that indirect aggression rarely if ever succeeds where there is reasonable security against direct aggression; where the government possesses loyal security forces, and where economic conditions are such as not to make Communism seem an attractive alternative. The program I suggest deals with all three aspects of this matter and thus with the problem of indirect aggression. . . .

VIII

Let me refer again to the requested authority to employ the armed forces of the United States to assist to defend the territorial integrity and the political independenc of any nation in the area against Communist armed aggression. Such authority would not be exercised except at the desire of the nation attacked. Beyond this it is my profound hope that this authority would never have to be exercised at all.

Nothing is more necessary to assure this than that our policy with respect to the defense of the area be promptly and clearly determined and declared. Thus the United Nations and all friendly governments, and indeed governments which are not friendly, will know where we stand. . . .

IX

The occasion has come for us to manifest again our national unity in support of freedom and to show our deep respect for the rights and independence of every nation — however great, however small. We seek not violence, but peace. To this purpose we must now devote our energies, our determination, ourselves.

(B) TEXT OF CONGRESSIONAL JOINT RESOLUTION AS REQUESTED BY PRESIDENT EISENHOWER, JANUARY 5, 1957 [18]

Resolved by the Senate and House of Representatives of the United States of America in Congress assembled, . . .

SEC. 2. The President is authorized to undertake, in the general area of the Middle East, military assistance programs with any nation or group of nations of that area desiring such assistance. Furthermore, he is authorized to employ the Armed Forces of the United States as he deems necessary to secure and protect the territorial integrity and political independence of any such nation or group of nations requesting such aid against overt armed aggression from any nation controlled by international communism: *Provided,* That such employment shall be consonant with the treaty obligations of the United States and with the Charter of the United Nations and actions and recommendations of the United Nations; and, as specified in article 51 of the United Nations Charter, measures pursuant thereto shall be immediately reported to the Security Council and shall not in any way affect the authority and responsibility of the Security Council to take at any time such action as it deems necessary in order to maintain or restore international peace and security.

SEC. 3. The President is hereby authorized, when he determines that such use is important to the security of the United States, to use for the purposes of this joint resolution, without regard to the provisions of any other law or regulation, not to exceed $200,000,000 from any appropriations now available for carrying out the provisions of the Mutual Security Act of 1954, as amended. This authorization is in addition to other existing authorizations with respect to the use of such appropriations.

SEC. 4. The President shall within the month of January of each year report to the Congress his action hereunder.

SEC. 5. This joint resolution shall expire when the President shall determine that the peace and security of the nations in the general area of the Middle East are reasonably assured by international conditions created by action of the United Nations or otherwise.

(C) JOINT RESOLUTION ON THE MIDDLE EAST ENACTED BY CONGRESS AND APPROVED BY PRESIDENT EISENHOWER, MARCH 9, 1957 [19]

Resolved by the Senate and House of Representatives of the United States of America in Congress assembled,

That the President be and hereby is authorized to cooperate with and assist any nation or group of nations in the general area of the Middle East desiring such assistance in the development of economic strength dedicated to the maintenance of national independence.

SEC. 2. The President is authorized to undertake, in the general area of the Middle East, military assistance programs with any nation or group of nations of that area desiring such assistance. Furthermore, the United States regards as vital to the national interest and world peace the preservation of the independence and integrity of the nations of the Middle East. To this end, if the President determines the necessity thereof, the United States is prepared to use armed forces to assist any such nation or group of such nations requesting assistance against armed aggression from any country controlled by international communism: *Provided,* That such employment shall be consonant with the treaty obligations of the United States and with the Constitution of the United States.

SEC. 3. The President is hereby authorized to use during the balance of fiscal year 1957 for economic and military assistance under this joint resolution not to exceed $200,000,000 from any appropriation now available for carrying out the provisions of the Mutual Security Act of 1954, as amended, in accord with the provisions of such Act: . . . Nothing contained in this joint resolution shall be construed as itself authorizing the appropriation of additional funds for the purpose of carrying out the provisions of the first section or of the first sentence of section 2 of this joint resolution. . . .

SEC. 6. This joint resolution shall expire when the President shall determine that the peace and security of the nations in the general area of the Middle East are reasonably assured by international conditions created by action of the United Nations or otherwise except that it may be terminated earlier by a concurrent resolution of the two Houses of Congress.

137. Eisenhower on U.S. Intervention in Lebanon, 15 July 1958

TO THE CONGRESS OF THE UNITED STATES:

On July 14, 1958, I received an urgent request from the President of the Republic of Lebanon that some United States forces be stationed in Lebanon. President Chamoun stated that without an immediate showing of United States support, the Government of Lebanon would be unable to survive. This request by President Chamoun was made with the concurrence of all the members of the Lebanese Cabinet. I have replied that we would do this and a contingent of United States Marines has now arrived in Lebanon. This initial dispatch of troops will be augmented as required. United States forces will be withdrawn as rapidly as circumstances permit.

Simultaneously, I requested that an urgent meeting of the United Nations Security Council be held on July 15, 1958. At that meeting, the permanent representative of the United States reported to the Council the action which this Government has taken. He also expressed the hope that the United Nations could soon take further effective measures to meet more fully the situation in Lebanon. We will continue to support the United Nations to this end.

United States forces are being sent to Lebanon to protect American lives and by their presence to assist the Government of Lebanon in the preservation of Lebanon's territorial integrity and independence, which have been deemed vital to United States national interests and world peace.

About 2 months ago a violent insurrection broke out in Lebanon, particularly along the border with Syria which, with Egypt, forms the United Arab Republic. This revolt was encouraged and strongly backed by the official Cairo, Damascus, and Soviet radios which broadcast to Lebanon in the Arabic language. The insurrection was further supported by sizable amounts of arms, ammunition, and money and by personnel infiltrated from Syria to fight against the lawful authorities. The avowed purpose of these activities was to overthrow the legally constituted Government of Lebanon and to install by violence a government which would subordinate the independence of Lebanon to the policies of the United Arab Republic.

Lebanon referred this situation to the United Nations Security Council. In view of the international implications of what was occurring in Lebanon, the Security Council on June 11, 1958, decided to send observers into Lebanon for the purpose of insuring that further outside assistance to the insurrection would cease. The Secretary-General of the United Nations subsequently undertook a mission to the area to reinforce the work of the observers.

It was our belief that the efforts of the Secretary-General and of the United Nations observers were helpful in reducing further aid in terms of personnel and military equipment from across the frontiers of Lebanon. There was a basis for hope that the situation might be moving toward a peaceful solution, consonant with the continuing integrity of Lebanon, and that the aspect of indirect aggression from without was being brought under control.

The situation was radically changed, however, on July 14, when there was a violent outbreak in Baghdad, in nearby Iraq. Elements in Iraq strongly sympathetic to the United Arab Republic seem to have murdered or driven from office individuals comprising the lawful Government of that country. We do not yet know in detail to what extent they have succeeded. We do have reliable information that important Iraqi leaders have been murdered.

We share with the Government of Lebanon the view that these events in Iraq demonstrate a ruthlessness of aggressive purpose which tiny Lebanon cannot combat without further evidence of support from other friendly nations.

After the most detailed consideration, I have concluded that, given the developments in Iraq, the measures thus far taken by the United Nations Security Council are not sufficient to preserve the independence and integrity of Lebanon. I have considered, furthermore, the question of our responsiblity to protect and safeguard American citizens in Lebanon of whom there are about 2,500. Pending the taking of adequate measures by the United Nations, the United States will be acting pursuant to what the United Nations Charter recognizes is an inherent right — the right of all nations to work together and to seek help when necessary to preserve their independence. I repeat that we wish to withdraw our forces as soon as the United Nations has taken further effective steps designed to safeguard Lebanese independence.

It is clear that events which have been occurring in Lebanon represent indirect aggression from without, and that such aggression endangers the independence and integrity of Lebanon.

It is recognized that the step now being taken may have serious consequences. I have, however, come to the considered and sober conclusion that despite the risks involved this action is required to support the principles of justice and international law upon which peace and a stable international order depend.

Our Government has acted in response to an appeal for help from a small and peaceful nation which has long had ties of closest friendship with the United States. Readiness to help a friend in need is an admirable characteristic of the American people, and I am, in this message, informing the Congress of the reasons why I believe that the United States could not in honor stand idly by in this hour of Lebanon's grave peril. As we act at the request of a friendly government to help it to preserve its independence and to preserve law and order which will protect American lives, we are acting to reaffirm and strengthen principles upon which the safety and security of the United States depend.

138. U.N. Security Council Resolution 242 on the Middle East, 22 November 1967

U.N. SECURITY COUNCIL RESOLUTION 242*

The Security Council,

Expressing its continuing concern with the grave situation in the Middle East,

Emphasizing the inadmissibility of the acquisition of territory by war and the need to work for a just and lasting peace in which every State in the area can live in security,

Emphasizing further that all Member States in their acceptance of the Charter of the United Nations have undertaken a commitment to act in accordance with Article 2 of the Charter,

1. *Affirms* that the fulfillment of Charter principles requires the establishment of a just and lasting peace in the Middle East which should include the application of both the following principles:

(i) Withdrawal of Israeli armed forces from territories occupied in the recent conflict;

(ii) Termination of all claims or states of belligerency and respect for and acknowledgement of the sovereignty, territorial integrity and political independence of every State in the area and their right to live in peace within secure and recognized boundaries free from threats or acts of force;

2. *Affirms further* the necessity

(a) For guaranteeing freedom of navigation through international waterways in the area;

(b) For achieving a just settlement of the refugee problem;

(c) For guaranteeing the territorial inviolability and political independence of every State in the area, through measures including the establishment of demilitarized zones,

3. *Requests* the Secretary-General to designate a Special Representative to proceed to the Middle East to establish and maintain contacts with the States concerned in order to promote agreement and assist efforts to achieve a peaceful and accepted settlement in accordance with the provisions and principles in this resolution;

4. *Requests* the Secretary-General to report to the Security Council on the progress of the efforts of the Special Representative as soon as possible.

---

*Adopted unanimously on Nov. 22, 1967.

139. Scali on the Middle Eastern Yom Kippur (Ramadan) War, 6-25 October 1973

Speech of U.S. Representative John A. Scali to U.N. Security Council, 13 November 1973.

The Middle East

The last example of United Nations activity which I want to discuss with you is the Middle East. I raise this not only because it represents an accomplishment, fragile and tender to be sure, but one to which we can point with some pride. It also, I believe, provides an example of how the United Nations operates at its best.

Let me first briefly run through the events at the United Nations of the past month:

—On October 6 in the early hours of the morning, Secretary Kissinger, in New York for a series of meetings with other United Nations members, learned of the imminent possibility of hostilities in the Middle East. Unfortunately, his efforts to avert the fighting were frustrated due to lack of time.

—On October 7, the United States called for Security Council consideration of the Middle East situation. In the absence of any agreement within the Council on the Middle East, we refrained from proposing specific action, the rejection of which might have frozen diplomatic positions and hindered future action.

—On October 21, the United States and the U.S.S.R. proposed a joint resolution calling for a cease-fire-in-place and negotiations on a permanent settlement. The Security Council passed the resolution at 1:00 a.m. the following day.

—On October 23, the United States and the U.S.S.R. proposed, and the Security Council passed, a second resolution, reaffirming the Security Council's call for a cease-fire.

—On October 24, the eight nonaligned members of the Security Council proposed the establishment of a United Nations Emergency Force and its dispatch to the Middle East. The Security Council accepted this proposal, with an American-inspired amendment that the permanent members of the Security Council be barred from serving on the Force.

—On November 2, the Security Council agreed on the composition of the Emergency Force. The majority of national components of this Force are, for the first time in United Nations history, to be non-European, non-Western; in other words, nonaligned.

—On November 9, I handed Secretary General Waldheim a note informing him of an agreement reached, with Secretary Kissinger's assistance, between the Governments of Egypt and Israel. This agreement, in implementation of the United Nations cease-fire, established a U.N.-supervised corridor to the Egyptian 3d Army on the east bank of the Suez Canal, provided for the exchange of all prisoners of war, and for the regular provision of food, water, and medical supplies to the town of Suez.

—On November 11, Egyptian and Israeli representatives, meeting under U.N. auspices, signed this agreement . . . .

Reflecting on what has happened, I would note that:

—There was virtually no possibility of the United Nations taking any meaningful action in this instance until the United States and the U.S.S.R. had reached at least a minimal agreement on steps to be taken.

—The rest of the United Nations membership were prepared to take advantage of U.S.-Soviet agreement but insisted on doing more than merely rubberstamping a series of superpower accords.

—The nonaligned, in putting forward their own proposals, showed themselves capable of acting effectively and responsibly.

—Once agreement had been arrived at, the United Nations was capable of expeditious, decisive, and effective action.

—In sum, East-West cooperation is a prerequisite for a more effective United Nations, but it is not enough. The rest of the United Nations membership must be willing to take advantage of this new situation. The United States, for its part, must be prepared to allow the rest of the United Nations membership to play an important role in determining that organization's and the world's future . . . .

140. Israeli-Egyptian Camp David Agreement, 17 September 1978

Muhammad Anwar al-Sadat, President of the Arab Republic of Egypt, and Menachem Begin, Prime Minister of Israel, met with Jimmy Carter, President of the United States of America, at Camp David from September 5 to September 17, 1978, and have agreed on the following framework for peace in the Middle East. They invite other parties to the Arab-Israeli conflict to adhere to it.

Preamble

The search for peace in the Middle East must be guided by the following:

- The agreed basis for a peaceful settlement of the conflict between Israel and its neighbors is United Nations Security Council Resolution 242, in all its parts.
- After four wars during thirty years, despite intensive human efforts, the Middle East, which is the cradle of civilization and the birthplace of three great religions, does not yet enjoy the blessings of peace. The people of the Middle East yearn for peace so that the vast human and natural resources of the region can be turned to the pursuits of peace and so that this area can become a model for coexistence and cooperation among nations.
- The historic initiative of President Sadat in visiting Jerusalem and the reception accorded to him by the Parliament, government and people of Israel, and the reciprocal visit of Prime Minister Begin to Ismailia, the peace proposals made by both leaders, as well as the warm reception of these missions by the peoples of both countries, have created an unprecedented opportunity for peace which must not be lost if this generation and future generations are to be spared the tragedies of war.
- The provisions of the Charter of the United Nations and the other accepted norms of international law and legitimacy now provide accepted standards for the conduct of relations among all states.
- To achieve a relationship of peace, in the spirit of Article 2 of the United Nations Charter, future negotiations between Israel and any neighbor prepared to negotiate peace and security with it, are necessary for the purpose of carrying out all the provisions and principles of Resolutions 242 and 338. ● ● ● ●

A. West Bank and Gaza

1. Egypt, Israel, Jordan and the representatives of the Palestinian people should participate in negotiations on the resolution of the Palestinian problem in all its aspects. To achieve that objective, negotiations relating to the West Bank and Gaza should proceed in three stages:

(a) Egypt and Israel agree that, in order to ensure a peaceful and orderly transfer of authority, and taking into account the security concerns of all the parties, there should be transitional arrangements for the West Bank and Gaza for a period not exceeding five years. In order to provide full autonomy to the inhabitants, under these arrangements the Israeli military government and its civilian administration will be withdrawn as soon as a self-governing authority has been freely elected by the inhabitants of these areas to replace the existing military government. To negotiate the details of a transitional arrangement, the Government of Jordan will be invited to join the negotiations on the basis of this framework. These new arrangements should give due consideration both to the principle of self-government by the inhabitants of these territories and to the legitimate security concerns of the parties involved.

(b) Egypt, Israel, and Jordan will agree on the modalities for establishing the elected self-governing authority in the West Bank and Gaza. The delegations of Egypt and Jordan may include Palestinians from the West Bank and Gaza or other Palestinians as mutually agreed. The parties will negotiate an agreement which will define the powers and responsibilities of the self-governing authority to be exercised in the West Bank and Gaza. A withdrawal of Israeli armed forces will take place and there will be a redeployment of the remaining Israeli forces into specified security locations. The agreement will also include arrangements for assuring internal and external security and public order. A strong local police force will be established, which may include Jordanian citizens. In addition, Israeli and Jordanian forces will participate in joint patrols and in the manning of control posts to assure the security of the borders.

(c) When the self-governing authority (administrative council) in the West Bank and Gaza is established and inaugurated, the transitional period of five years will begin. As soon as possible, but not later than the third year after the beginning of the transitional period, negotiations will take place to determine the final status of the West Bank and Gaza and its relationship with its neighbors, and to conclude a peace treaty between Israel and Jordan by the end of the transitional period. These negotiations will be conducted among Egypt, Israel, Jordan, and the elected representatives of the inhabitants of the West Bank and Gaza. Two separate but related committees will be convened, one committee, consisting of representatives of the four parties which will negotiate and agree on the final status of the West Bank and Gaza, and its relationship with its neighbors, and the second committee, consisting of representatives of Israel and representatives of Jordan to be joined by the elected representatives of the inhabitants of the West Bank and Gaza, to negotiate the peace treaty between Israel and Jordan, taking into account the agreement reached on the final status of the West Bank and Gaza. The negotiations shall be based on all the provisions and principles of UN Security Council Resolution 242. The negotiations will resolve, among other matters, the location of the boundaries and the nature of the security arrangements. The solution from the negotiations must also recognize the legitimate rights of the Palestinian people and their just requirements. In this way, the Palestinians will participate in the determination of their own future ● ● ● ●

FRAMEWORK FOR THE CONCLUSION OF A PEACE TREATY BETWEEN EGYPT AND ISRAEL

In order to achieve peace between them, Israel and Egypt agree to negotiate in good faith with a goal of concluding within three months of the signing of this framework a peace treaty between them.

It is agreed that:

The site of the negotiations will be under a United Nations flag at a location or locations to be mutually agreed.

All of the principles of U.N. Resolution 242 will apply in this resolution of the dispute between Israel and Egypt.

Unless otherwise mutually agreed, terms of the peace treaty will be implemented between two and three years after the peace treaty is signed.

The following matters are agreed between the parties:

(a) the full exercise of Egyptian sovereignty up to the internationally recognized border between Egypt and mandated Palestine;

(b) the withdrawal of Israeli armed forces from the Sinai;

(c) the use of airfields left by the Israelis near El Arish, Rafah, Ras en Naqb, and Sharm el Sheikh for civilian purposes only, including possible commercial use by all nations;

(d) the right of free passage by ships of Israel through the Gulf of Suez and the Suez Canal on the basis of the Constantinople Convention of 1888 applying to all nations; the Strait of Tiran and the Gulf of Aqaba are international waterways to be open to all nations for unimpeded and nonsuspendable freedom of navigation and overflight;

(e) the construction of a highway between the Sinai and Jordan near Elat with guaranteed free and peaceful passage by Egypt and Jordan; and

(f) the stationing of military forces listed below . . . .

141. Israeli-Egyptian Peace Treaty, 26 March 1979

The Government of the Arab Republic of Egypt and the Government of the State of Israel;

PREAMBLE

Convinced of the urgent necessity of the establishment of a just, comprehensive and lasting peace in the Middle East in accordance with Security Council Resolutions 242 and 338;

Reaffirming their adherence to the "Framework for Peace in the Middle East Agreed at Camp David," dated September 17, 1978;

Noting that the aforementioned Framework as appropriate is intended to constitute a basis for peace not only between Egypt and Israel but also between Israel and each of its other Arab neighbors which is prepared to negotiate peace with it on this basis;

Desiring to bring to an end the state of war between them and to establish a peace in which every state in the area can live in security;

Convinced that the conclusion of a Treaty of Peace between Egypt and Israel is an important step in the search for comprehensive peace in the area and for the attainment of the settlement of the Arab-Israeli conflict in all its aspects;

Inviting the other Arab parties to this dispute to join the peace process with Israel guided by and based on the principles of the aforementioned Framework;

Desiring as well to develop friendly relations and cooperation between themselves in accordance with the United Nations Charter and the principles of international law governing international relations in times of peace;

Agree to the following provisions in the free exercise of their sovereignty, in order to implement the "Framework for the Conclusion of a Peace Treaty Between Egypt and Israel":

ARTICLE I

1. The state of war between the Parties will be terminated and peace will be established between them upon the exchange of instruments of ratification of this Treaty.

2. Israel will withdraw all its armed forces and civilians from the Sinai behind the international boundary between Egypt and mandated Palestine, as provided in the annexed protocol (Annex I), and Egypt will resume the exercise of its full sovereignty over the Sinai.

3. Upon completion of the interim withdrawal provided for in Annex I, the Parties will establish normal and friendly relations, in accordance with Article III (3).

ARTICLE II

The permanent boundary between Egypt and Israel is the recognized international boundary between Egypt and the former mandated territory of Palestine, as shown on the map at Annex II, without prejudice to the issue of the status of the Gaza Strip. The parties recognize this boundary as inviolable. Each will respect the territorial integrity of the other, including their territorial waters and airspace.

ARTICLE III

1. The Parties will apply between them the provisions of the Charter of the United Nations and the principles of international law governing relations among states in times of peace. In particular:

a. They recognize and will respect each other's sovereignty, territorial integrity and political independence;

b. They recognize and will respect each other's right to live in peace within their secure and recognized boundaries;

c. They will refrain from the threat or use of force, directly or indirectly, against each other and will settle all disputes between them by peaceful means.

2. Each Party undertakes to ensure that acts or threats of belligerency, hostility, or violence do not originate from and are not committed from within its territory, or by any forces subject to its control or by any other forces stationed on its territory, against the population, citizens or property of the other Party. Each Party also undertakes to refrain from organizing, instigating, inciting, assisting or participating in acts or threats of belligerency, hostility, subversion or violence against the other Party, anywhere, and undertakes to ensure that perpetrators of such acts are brought to justice.

3. The Parties agree that the normal relationship established between them will include full recognition, diplomatic, economic and cultural relations, termination of economic boycotts and discriminatory barriers to the free movement of people and goods, and will guarantee the mutual enjoyment of citizens of the due process of law. The process by which they undertake to achieve such a relationship parallel to the implementation of other provisions of this treaty is set out in the annexed protocol • • • •

Done at Washington, D.C. this 26th day of March, 1979, in triplicate in the English, Arabic, and Hebrew languages, each text being equally authentic. In case of any divergence of interpretation, the English text shall prevail.

For the Government of the
Arab Republic of Egypt:

A. Sadat

For the Government
of Israel:

M. Begin

Witnessed By:

Jimmy Carter

Jimmy Carter, President
of the United States of America

LETTERS

March 26, 1979

Dear Mr. President:

This letter confirms that Egypt and Israel have agreed as follows:

The Governments of Egypt and Israel recall that they concluded at Camp David and signed at the White House on September 17, 1978, the annexed documents entitled "A Framework for Peace in the Middle East Agreed at Camp David" and "Framework for the conclusion of a Peace Treaty between Egypt and Israel."

For the purpose of achieving a comprehensive peace settlement in accordance with the abovementioned Frameworks, Egypt and Israel will proceed with the implementation of those provisions relating to the West Bank and the Gaza Strip. They have agreed to start negotiations within a month after the exchange of the instruments of ratification of the Peace Treaty. In accordance with the "Framework for Peace in the Middle East," the Hashemite Kingdom of Jordan is invited to join the negotiations. The Delegations of Egypt and Jordan may include Palestinians from the West Bank and Gaza Strip or other Palestinians as mutually agreed. The purpose of the negotiation shall be to agree, prior to the elections, on the modalities for establishing the elected self-governing authority (administrative council), define its powers and responsibilities, and agree upon other related issues. In the event Jordan decides not to take part in the negotiations, the negotiations will be held by Egypt and Israel • • • •

For the Government of
Israel:

M. Begin
Menachem Begin

For the Government of the
Arab Republic of Egypt:

A. Sadat
Mohamed Anwar El-Sadat

The President,
  The White House.

142. Ford-Shah Exchange of Toasts, 15 May 1975

President Gerald R. Ford and the Shah of Iran at a White House Dinner.

President Ford

Your Imperial Majesties the Shahanshah and Shahbanou: I warmly welcome the Imperial Majesties to the White House this evening, and I am sure by the reception that has been indicated here, everybody joins me on this wonderful occasion.

Your visit here is, of course, a tribute to the long legacy of a very close and very cooperative tie between Iran and the United States, and I hope, on the other hand, that you will think upon this as a visit between old friends.

I am the seventh President, Your Imperial Majesty, to have met with you on such an occasion. The facts speak volumes for the continuity and the duration of our bilateral relations and the importance that we attach to the broadening and the deepening of those ties and those interests of peace and progress throughout the world. These are objectives to which the United States remains deeply committed. These objectives Iran shares with us.

Our nations have thus brought together a very unique relationship, working together cooperatively for the past several decades on the basis of a mutual respect, and I am looking forward to continuing this great tradition with yourself, and this country and your country. And it is, as I see it, a living and a growing tradition.

Recently, our common bonds have acquired a new scope as Iran, under Your Imperial Majesty's wise leadership, has made extraordinary strides in its economic development and its relationships with other countries of its region and the world.

The progress that you have made serves as a superb model to nations everywhere. Iran has moved from a country once in need of aid to one which last year committed a substantial part of its gross national product to aiding less fortunate nations.

Iran is also playing a very leading role in what we hope will be a very successful effort to establish a more effective economic relationship between the oil producers, the industrialized nations, and the developing nations. . . .

Just as Iran's role and potential goes far beyond its own border, so, too, His Imperial Majesty is one of the world's great statesmen. His experience of over 30 years as Iran's leader has been marked by dedication to progress and prosperity at home and significant contributions to the cause of peace and cooperation abroad . . . .

His Imperial Majesty

Mr. President, Mrs. Ford, distinguished guests: It is difficult to find words to express our sentiments of gratitude for the warm welcome that you, Mr. President and Mrs. Ford, have reserved for us today . . . .

I wanted to come to this country that I knew before to meet the President of this country for whom we have developed, since he assumed this high office, a sentiment of respect for a man who is not shrinking in front of events. And may I congratulate you for the great leadership and the right decisions that you took for your country and, may I add, for all the peoples who want to live in freedom.

This is precisely what this world needs—courage, dignity, and love of the other human being. We are proud of being a good and, I believe, a trusted friend of the United States of America, and this will continue because this friendship is based on permanent and durable reasons—these reasons being that we share the same philosophy of life, the same ideals. And I could not imagine another kind of living which would be worth living.

Your country has been of great help to us during our time of needs. This is something that we do not forget as what Iran can do in this changing world and this world of interdependency. In addition to our continuous friendship with you, we will try to be of any utility and help to other nations which would eventually need that help . . . .

143. Lodge on U.S. and South Africa, 1 April 1960

Statement of Ambassador Henry Cabot Lodge to U.N. Security Council.

(A) STATEMENT OF AMBASSADOR HENRY CABOT LODGE TO THE UNITED NATIONS SECURITY COUNCIL, APRIL 1, 1960 [21]

ON MONDAY, March 21, in various parts of the Union of South Africa, people of African origin carried out mass demonstrations against laws which require them to carry passes. These demonstrations led to clashes with the police. According to figures made public by the South African mission to the United Nations, at least 68 Africans were killed and over 220 were injured.

The tragic events that day and subsequently have caused shock and distress beyond the borders of South Africa. Within the Union of South Africa a state of acute tension prevails. All these facts together constitute the immediate and compelling cause of this meeting of the Security Council.

The situation before the Council is of deep concern to the United States. We say this because our primary desire is to help promote within the framework of the charter the objectives of the United Nations. . . .

United States representatives have often stated in General Assembly discussions our belief that the Assembly can properly consider questions of racial discrimination where they are matters of governmental policy. The United States believes that in this case also the charter provides a definite basis for Security Council consideration.

When governmental policies within one country evoke the deep concern of a great part of mankind, they inevitably contribute to tension among nations. This is especially true of racial tensions and the violence which sometimes results. They are more subtle and more complex than some of the political disputes between states which the Council has considered, but in the long run they may be even more destructive to the peace of mankind. . . .

It is clear that the source of the conflict from which the recent tragic events have flowed is the policy of *apartheid* followed by the Government of the Union of South Africa. The United Nations is no stranger to this question. The General Assembly has pronounced itself repeatedly in opposition to the policy of *apartheid* and similar practices. Last year once again the Assembly, by an overwhelming vote, including that of the United States, noted the continuance of the *apartheid* policy in the Union of South Africa and made a solemn appeal for the observance of the human rights provisions of the charter. . . .

Now [Mr. President], we confront a draft resolution submitted by the representative of Ecuador which points a constructive way for the Council to proceed. This draft represents a serious and responsible reflection of the views which have been expressed in the Council. It deplores the loss of lives in the recent disturbances in South Africa, and it extends to the many families of the victims the deepest sympathies of the Council. It calls upon the Government of South Africa to initiate measures aimed at bringing about racial harmony based on equality. It also provides that the Secretary-General through his great skill and resourcefulness should make arrangements which will help in upholding the purposes and principles of the Charter. This I think is a constructive step. It seeks to build a bridge and not a wall. That is what we should try to do.

The United States will vote for this resolution. We hope the actions of the Council will be taken by those concerned in the spirit in which it is intended — to encourage the peaceful evolution of a society in South Africa in which men of all races can live together in harmony, with mutual respect for the different cultures and ways of life which now exist there.

(B) RESOLUTION OF THE UNITED NATIONS SECURITY COUNCIL OF APRIL 1, 1960 [22]

The Security Council, Having considered the complaint of 29 Member States contained in document S/4279 and Add. 1 concerning "the situation arising out of the large-scale killings of unarmed and peaceful demonstra-

144. Herter on the U.N. in the Congo (Zaire), 21 July 1960

Statement of Secretary of State Christian A. Herter.

tors against racial discrimination and segregation in the Union of South Africa,"

Recognizing that such a situation has been brought about by the racial policies of the Government of the Union of South Africa and the continued disregard by that Government of the resolutions of the General Assembly calling upon it to revise its policies and bring them into conformity with its obligations and responsibilities under the Charter,

Taking into account the strong feelings and grave concern aroused among Governments and peoples of the world by happenings in the Union of South Africa,

1. *Recognizes* that the situation in the Union of South Africa is one that has led to international friction and if continued might endanger international peace and security;

2. *Deplores* that the recent disturbances in the Union of South Africa should have led to the loss of life of so many Africans and extends to the families of the victims its deepest sympathies;

3. *Deplores* the policies and actions of the Government of the Union of South Africa which have given rise to the present situation;

4. *Calls upon* the Government of the Union of South Africa to initiate measures aimed at bringing about racial harmony based on equality in order to ensure that the present situation does not continue or recur and to abandon its policies of apartheid and racial discrimination;

5. *Requests* the Secretary-General, in consultation with the Government of the Union of South Africa, to make such arrangements as would adequately help in upholding the purposes and principles of the Charter and to report to the Security Council whenever necessary and appropriate.

I WANT to report briefly on the situation in the Congo as it affects our interests.

Our first concern was for the welfare and safety of the some 2,000 Americans living in this widespread area. A number of them are members of our official family connected with the Embassy at Léopoldville and the consulate at Elisabethville. The vast majority, however, were missionaries of many denominations who have been carrying on their work for many years in remote areas. I am glad to say that our records indicate that over 1,500 American citizens have now been safely evacuated. Almost all of those who remain are doing so on their own decision.

The breakdown of public order in the Congo shortly after independence and the appeal of that young country to the United Nations for help drew immediate response from that body. On July 13 the Security Council adopted a resolution authorizing the Secretary-General "to take the necessary steps . . . to provide . . . military assistance" in the Congo, until the Congolese Government can maintain order.

The United States not only voted in support of this resolution but put its logistic and communications resources at the disposal of the United Nations. At the request of the Secretary-General we have, I think, set a remarkable record in bringing aid and assistance to the Congo. Starting from scratch on July 14, the United States had as of today transported approximately 3,500 troops with 300 tons of equipment from three African countries and one European country. We have flown in 400 tons of desperately needed flour and airlifted from the United States and Europe communications and transport equipment essential to the proper functioning of the U.N. Command in the Congo. In this brief time a total of over 125 flights of transport planes provided by the United States have been made to the Congo. This support operation is continuing day and night. By the end of this week we shall have transported an additional 2,000 troops and approximately 100 tons of equipment to the U.N. Command in Léopoldville.

The United States effort, of course, is conducted entirely in response to a request of the United Nations. Our own troops are not involved in the United Nations action. You will recall that it was mutually understood that the major powers should not supply troops. The United States has abided by the letter and spirit of this understanding. . . .

145. U.N. General Assembly on Colonial Independence, 14 December 1960

(A) THE DECLARATION OF DECEMBER 14, 1960 [26]

THE GENERAL ASSEMBLY,

Mindful of the determination proclaimed by the peoples of the world in the Charter of the United Nations to reaffirm faith in fundamental human rights, in the dignity and worth of the human person, in the equal rights of men and women and of nations large and small and to promote social progress and better standards of life in larger freedom,

Conscious of the need for the creation of conditions of stability and well-being and peaceful and friendly relations based on respect for the principles of equal rights and self-determination of all peoples, and of universal respect for, and observance of, human rights and fundamental freedoms for all without distinction as to race, sex, language or religion,

Recognizing the passionate yearning for freedom in all dependent peoples and the decisive role of such peoples in the attainment of their independence,

Aware of the increasing conflicts resulting from the denial of or impediments in the way of freedom of such peoples, which constitute a serious threat to world peace,

Considering the important role of the United Nations in assisting the movement for independence in Trust and Non-Self-Governing Territories,

Recognizing that the peoples of the world ardently desire the end of colonialism in all its manifestations,

Convinced that the continued existence of colonialism prevents the development of international economic co-operation, impedes the social, cultural and economic development of dependent peoples and militates against the United Nations ideal of universal peace,

Affirming that peoples may, for their own ends, freely dispose of their natural wealth and resources without prejudice to any obligations arising out of international economic co-operation, based upon the principle of mutual benefit, and international law,

Believing that the process of liberation is irresistible and irreversible and that, in order to avoid serious crises, an end must be put to colonialism and all practices of segregation and discrimination associated therewith,

Welcoming the emergence in recent years of a large number of dependent territories into freedom and independence, and recognizing the increasingly powerful trends towards freedom in such territories which have not yet attained independence,

Convinced that all peoples have an inalienable right to complete freedom, the exercise of their sovereignty and the integrity of their national territory,

Solemnly proclaims the necessity of bringing to a speedy and unconditional end colonialism in all its forms and manifestations;

And to this end

Declares that:

1. The subjection of peoples to alien subjugation, domination and exploitation constitutes a denial of fundamental human rights, is contrary to the Charter of the United Nations and is an impediment to the promotion of world peace and co-operation.

2. All peoples have the right to self-determination; by virtue of that right they freely determine their political status and freely pursue their economic, social and cultural development.

3. Inadequacy of political, economic, social or educational preparedness should never serve as a pretext for delaying independence.

4. All armed action or repressive measures of all kinds directed against dependent peoples shall cease in order to enable them to exercise peacefully and freely their right to complete independence, and the integrity of their national territory shall be respected.

5. Immediate steps shall be taken, in Trust and Non-Self-Governing Territories of all other territories which have not yet attained independence, to transfer all powers to the peoples of those territories, without any conditions or reservations, in accordance with their freely expressed will and desire, without any distinction as to race, creed or colour, in order to enable them to enjoy complete independence and freedom.

6. Any attempt aimed at the partial or total disruption of the national unity and the territorial integrity of a country is incompatible with the purposes and principles of the Charter of the United Nations.

7. All States shall observe faithfully and strictly the provisions of the Charter of the United Nations, the Universal Declaration of Human Rights and the present Declaration on the basis of equality, non-interference in the internal affairs of all States, and respect for the sovereign rights of all peoples and their territorial integrity.

(B) REASONS FOR UNITED STATES ABSTENTION [27]

I wish to explain the attitude of the United States toward the 43-power resolution just adopted without opposition and the reasons for our abstention in the vote.

The United States, as I said in my previous intervention in this debate, warmly supports and endorses the interest and concern of the United Nations in promoting larger freedom for peoples everywhere. The support of freedom is a concept springing from deeply held beliefs of the American people. . . .

There are difficulties in the language and thought of this resolution, which I shall comment on more specifically in a moment, which made it impossible for us to support it, because they seemed to negate certain clear provisions of the United Nations Charter. . . .

In examining with care, as we have done, the major aspects of this resolution we have reached the conclusion that operative paragraphs 3, 4, and 5 are susceptible to serious misinterpretations which could cause basic misunderstanding of the attitude of the various governments here on the need for orderly and effective preparations for self-government or independence in accordance with the Charter provisions. Although we are sure that this was not the intent of the sponsors of the resolution, paragraph 3 permits the interpretation that the question of preparation for independence is wholly irrelevant. Adequate preparation for self-government or independence is a matter of elementary prudence and is a responsibility which must be accepted by those administering dependent peoples. It is clearly essential that emerging peoples be reasonably able to undertake the responsibilities they will have to face. On the other hand, we would never agree that false allegations in respect of political, economic, social, or educational preparation should be used to retard political development.

Paragraph 4, written in unqualified language, seems to preclude even legitimate measures for the maintenance of law and order, and this is, of course, incompatible with the obligations of administering authorities toward the peoples under their administration.

As for paragraph 5, here again is a very strong statement that only complete independence and freedom is the acceptable political goal for dependent peoples. This paragraph also calls for immediate steps to transfer all powers to the peoples of trust and non-self-governing territories without any conditions or reservations. . . .

Like many other members of the United Nations, we regard the provisions of chapters XI and XII of the Charter, which deal specifically with non-self-governing and trust territories, as controlling so far as the territories for which we are responsible are concerned. The United States Government will continue to advance these territories and their peoples toward self-government or independence in accordance with the provisions of the charter and the obligations we have assumed in the trusteeship agreement.

I would call attention, Mr. President, to a very wise statement which was made not long ago from this rostrum by the distinguished representative of India [V. K. Krishna Menon] in which he said, while discussing his country's or his delegation's position on another matter, "We did not feel that we could fully support it unless we could support every word of it.". . .

146. Vance on U.S. Relations with Africa, 12 May 1978

Statement of Secretary of State Cyrus R. Vance.

I am pleased to have this opportunity to appear before the African Affairs Subcommittee. I look forward to discussing with you the many critical issues which we now face in Africa.

Over the past 2 years, under the previous Administration as well as this, we have made significant strides in our relations with Africa. . . .

Horn of Africa

Recent developments in the Horn are an example of the complexity and difficulties we face.

As you know, we have wanted to improve our relations with **Somalia.** However, we were unwilling to do so as long as Somali forces were invading Ethiopia.

Following the withdrawal of the Somali army from the Ogaden, President Carter sent Assistant Secretary [for African Affairs Richard] Moose to Mogadiscio for discussions with President Siad Barre. During this trip we began our discussions to obtain assurances from Siad that he would respect the internationally recognized borders of his neighbors as a precondition for any U.S. military assistance. Mr. Moose also informed the Somali leader that any U.S. aid would be limited in scope and confined to defensive items only. This matter is under active and continuing review. We will, of course, keep the committee informed of our deliberations. . . .

Our relations with **Ethiopia**, though not good, have not deteriorated completely, and we would not like to see them broken off. Continued dialogue with that government is in our interest and in the interest of peace and stability in the region. We expect to announce the naming of a new Ambassador to Ethiopia in the near future.[1]

The Cuban presence in Ethiopia which now is at the 16-17,000 level is of serious concern to us. I will discuss the Soviet and Cuban role in Africa later. But let me say now that it is still not clear whether the Cubans will play a major combat role in Eritrea similar to their operations in the Ogaden.

We will continue to urge all of the parties concerned to make every effort toward a peaceful resolution of the dispute and withdrawal of Cuban forces. We face no less a challenge in dealing with issues of transition to majority rule and racial equality in South Africa, Namibia, and Rhodesia.

South Africa

In South Africa the basic problem we face is simply stated, yet terribly complex: How best can we encourage peaceful change?

We cannot ignore apartheid and the growing crisis within South Africa. We have to make it clear that a deterioration in our bilateral relations is inevitable if progress is not made. Recent actions by the Congress clearly indicate that it shares this concern.

At the same time, we have to maintain our ability to work with the South African Government for peaceful change in Rhodesia, Namibia, and South Africa itself. We have made it clear to South Africa that progress on each of the three will be recognized and have done so with regard to Namibia.

We understand the difficulties involved in change within South Africa. We are not seeking to impose a simplistic formula for South Africa's future. Rather, we have urged the South African Government to begin to take truly significant steps—such as talking with acknowledged representative black leaders—away from apartheid and toward a system in which the full range of rights would be accorded to all inhabitants of South Africa, black and white alike.

South Africa's potential for nuclear weapons development is another reason why it is important that we try to maintain an effective working relationship with that government. South Africa has the technical capability to produce a nuclear weapon. In recent months we have actively sought South Africa's agreement to sign the Nonproliferation Treaty (NPT). We have held talks with them on this question and will again.

Some have urged that we cease all nuclear cooperation with South Africa because of apartheid. We believe that this question must be addressed in the context of the strong desirability of South Africa's adherence to the NPT and the application of safeguards with respect to the operation of all nuclear facilities in South Africa.

Namibia

Substantial progress has been made toward resolution of the Namibia problem as a result of a year-long effort by ourselves and the other four Western Security Council members, operating as the so-called contact group. Recent South African acceptance of the contact group proposal for a Namibian settlement was a significant breakthrough.[2] We are now making approaches to the front-line states [Angola, Botswana, Mozambique, Tanzania, Zambia], Nigeria, and the South West Africa People's Organization (SWAPO), urging SWAPO's prompt acceptance of the settlement proposal.

Time is critical. If we do not obtain SWAPO's acceptance of the proposal in the near future, South Africa may go ahead with Namibian independence on its own terms • • •

Rhodesia

This is also a crucial time in the effort to achieve a peaceful resolution of the Rhodesia problem. • • •

The major question remaining is whether the internal and external nationalist parties can agree either to some formula for power-sharing during the transition, or to a neutral transition administration. The nub of the problem is that each side now seeks to dominate the transition government in a way that is unacceptable to the other and would make fair elections impossible.

But it is also clear that it is in the interest of both sides to keep the door open to a negotiated settlement including all the parties. The patriotic front had said it would attend a meeting with all parties and is willing to discuss all issues further; the Salisbury parties have not totally rejected a meeting of all parties but say they are skeptical of its success.

We believe the Anglo-American proposals provide the best elements for a settlement that will be acceptable to both sides: a cease-fire; a U.N. peacekeeping force; U.N. observers to monitor elections and activities of the police; a neutral transition administration with powers over defense, law and order, and electoral arrangements in the hands of an impartial administrator; integration of existing forces into one army that would be loyal to the elected government; and a democratic constitution with guarantees of individual rights for all, white as well as black. • • •

Soviets and Cubans

A discussion of the issues and problems we face in Africa would not be complete without mention of Soviet and Cuban activities. Their increasing intervention raises serious problems. It escalates the level of conflict. It jeopardizes the independence of African states. It creates concern among moderates that Soviet weapons and Cuban troops can be used to determine the outcome of any dispute on the continent.

We are making a strenuous effort to counter Cuban and Soviet intervention in the disputes of African nations • • •

Conclusion

Major challenges lie ahead, in implementing our policy and in countering Soviet and Cuban intervention.

It will be necessary for us to work closely with the Congress if we are to achieve our goals. We will need your support in a variety of ways:

• In providing long-term development assistance and humanitarian relief;

• In giving sympathetic consideration to military assistance for countries threatened by Soviet arms and Cuban troops; and

• In achieving and implementing negotiated settlements in southern Africa.

The involvement of the Foreign Relations Committee and the Congress as a whole in our Africa policy is key to the greater public understanding we seek. We need your counsel and your advice. We also need your help in explaining to the American people the great stakes our country has in a positive approach to Africa. □